THE COMPLETE POEMS
AND PLAYS OF
T. S. ELIOT

Also by T. S. Eliot

COLLECTED POEMS 1909–1962
FOUR QUARTETS
THE WASTE LAND *and* OTHER POEMS
THE WASTE LAND
A facsimile and transcript of the original drafts
Edited by Valerie Eliot
SELECTED POEMS
INVENTIONS OF THE MARCH HARE
Poems 1909–1917
Edited by Christopher Ricks
OLD POSSUM'S BOOK OF PRACTICAL CATS

correspondence
THE LETTERS OF T. S. ELIOT
Volume I – 1898–1922
Edited by Valerie Eliot

plays
MURDER IN THE CATHEDRAL
THE FAMILY REUNION
THE COCKTAIL PARTY
THE CONFIDENTIAL CLERK
THE ELDER STATESMAN

literary criticism
SELECTED ESSAYS
THE USE OF POETRY *and* THE USE OF CRITICISM
THE VARIETIES OF METAPHYSICAL POETRY
Edited by Ronald Schuchard
TO CRITICIZE THE CRITIC
ON POETRY AND POETS
FOR LANCELOT ANDREWES
SELECTED PROSE OF T. S. ELIOT

social criticism
THE IDEA OF CHRISTIAN SOCIETY
Edited by David Edwards
NOTES TOWARDS THE DEFINITION OF CULTURE

for students
A CONCORDANCE TO THE COMPLETE
POEMS AND PLAYS OF T. S. ELIOT
Edited by John Dawson, Peter Holland and David McKitterick
A STUDENT'S GUIDE TO THE SELECTED POEMS
OF T. S. ELIOT
By B. C. Southam

T. S. ELIOT

The Complete Poems and Plays

faber and faber

First published in 1969
by Faber and Faber Limited
Bloomsbury House,
74–77 Great Russell Street, London
WC1B 3DA

This paperback edition first published in 2004
Printed and bound by CPI Group (UK) Ltd, Croydon, CR0 4YY

ISBN 978-0-571-22516-3

CONTENTS

COLLECTED POEMS 1909–1962

CONTENTS

CONTENTS

CONTENTS

PLAYS

APPENDIX

POEMS WRITTEN IN EARLY YOUTH

PRUFROCK
and Other Observations
1917

For Jean Verdenal, 1889–1915
mort aux Dardanelles

Or puoi la quantitate
comprender dell'amor ch'a te mi scalda,
quando dismento nostra vanitate,
trattando l'ombre come cosa salda.

The Love Song of J. Alfred Prufrock

S'i' credesse che mia risposta fosse
a persona che mai tornasse al mondo,
questa fiamma staria sanza più scosse;
ma però che già mai di questo fondo
non tornò vivo alcun, s'i' odo il vero,
sanza tema d'infamia ti rispondo.

Let us go then, you and I,
When the evening is spread out against the sky
Like a patient etherised upon a table;
Let us go, through certain half-deserted streets,
The muttering retreats
Of restless nights in one-night cheap hotels
And sawdust restaurants with oyster-shells:
Streets that follow like a tedious argument
Of insidious intent
To lead you to an overwhelming question . . .
Oh, do not ask, 'What is it?'
Let us go and make our visit.

In the room the women come and go
Talking of Michelangelo.

The yellow fog that rubs its back upon the window-panes,
The yellow smoke that rubs its muzzle on the window-panes,
Licked its tongue into the corners of the evening,
Lingered upon the pools that stand in drains,
Let fall upon its back the soot that falls from chimneys,
Slipped by the terrace, made a sudden leap,
And seeing that it was a soft October night,
Curled once about the house, and fell asleep.

And indeed there will be time
For the yellow smoke that slides along the street

Rubbing its back upon the window-panes;
There will be time, there will be time
To prepare a face to meet the faces that you meet;
There will be time to murder and create,
And time for all the works and days of hands
That lift and drop a question on your plate;
Time for you and time for me,
And time yet for a hundred indecisions,
And for a hundred visions and revisions,
Before the taking of a toast and tea.

   In the room the women come and go
Talking of Michelangelo.

   And indeed there will be time
To wonder, 'Do I dare?' and, 'Do I dare?'
Time to turn back and descend the stair,
With a bald spot in the middle of my hair —
(They will say: 'How his hair is growing thin!')
My morning coat, my collar mounting firmly to the chin,
My necktie rich and modest, but asserted by a simple pin —
(They will say: 'But how his arms and legs are thin!')
Do I dare
Disturb the universe?
In a minute there is time
For decisions and revisions which a minute will reverse.

   For I have known them all already, known them all —
Have known the evenings, mornings, afternoons,
I have measured out my life with coffee spoons;
I know the voices dying with a dying fall
Beneath the music from a farther room.
   So how should I presume?

   And I have known the eyes already, known them all —
The eyes that fix you in a formulated phrase,
And when I am formulated, sprawling on a pin,
When I am pinned and wriggling on the wall,
Then how should I begin

To spit out all the butt-ends of my days and ways?
   And how should I presume?

   And I have known the arms already, known them all —
Arms that are braceleted and white and bare
(But in the lamplight, downed with light brown hair!)
Is it perfume from a dress
That makes me so digress?
Arms that lie along a table, or wrap about a shawl.
   And should I then presume?
   And how should I begin?

      .   .   .   .   .

   Shall I say, I have gone at dusk through narrow streets
And watched the smoke that rises from the pipes
Of lonely men in shirt-sleeves, leaning out of windows? . . .

   I should have been a pair of ragged claws
Scuttling across the floors of silent seas.

      .   .   .   .   .

   And the afternoon, the evening, sleeps so peacefully!
Smoothed by long fingers,
Asleep . . . tired . . . or it malingers,
Stretched on the floor, here beside you and me.
Should I, after tea and cakes and ices,
Have the strength to force the moment to its crisis?
But though I have wept and fasted, wept and prayed,
Though I have seen my head (grown slightly bald)
     brought in upon a platter,
I am no prophet — and here's no great matter;
I have seen the moment of my greatness flicker,
And I have seen the eternal Footman hold my coat, and snicker,
And in short, I was afraid.

   And would it have been worth it, after all,
After the cups, the marmalade, the tea,
Among the porcelain, among some talk of you and me,
Would it have been worth while,
To have bitten off the matter with a smile,
To have squeezed the universe into a ball
To roll it towards some overwhelming question,

To say: 'I am Lazarus, come from the dead,
Come back to tell you all, I shall tell you all'—
If one, settling a pillow by her head,
    Should say: 'That is not what I meant at all.
    That is not it, at all.'

    And would it have been worth it, after all,
Would it have been worth while,
After the sunsets and the dooryards and the sprinkled streets,
After the novels, after the teacups, after the skirts that trail along
        the floor —
And this, and so much more? —
It is impossible to say just what I mean!
But as if a magic lantern threw the nerves in patterns on a screen:
Would it have been worth while
If one, settling a pillow or throwing off a shawl,
And turning toward the window, should say:
    'That is not it at all,
    That is not what I meant, at all.'

.   .   .   .   .

    No! I am not Prince Hamlet, nor was meant to be;
Am an attendant lord, one that will do
To swell a progress, start a scene or two,
Advise the prince; no doubt, an easy tool,
Deferential, glad to be of use,
Politic, cautious, and meticulous;
Full of high sentence, but a bit obtuse;
At times, indeed, almost ridiculous —
Almost, at times, the Fool.

    I grow old . . . I grow old . . .
I shall wear the bottoms of my trousers rolled.

    Shall I part my hair behind? Do I dare to eat a peach?
I shall wear white flannel trousers, and walk upon the beach.
I have heard the mermaids singing, each to each.

I do not think that they will sing to me.

I have seen them riding seaward on the waves
Combing the white hair of the waves blown back
When the wind blows the water white and black.

We have lingered in the chambers of the sea
By sea-girls wreathed with seaweed red and brown
Till human voices wake us, and we drown.

Portrait of a Lady

Thou hast committed—
Fornication: but that was in another country,
And besides, the wench is dead.
                                        The Jew of Malta

I

Among the smoke and fog of a December afternoon
You have the scene arrange itself — as it will seem to do —
With 'I have saved this afternoon for you';
And four wax candles in the darkened room,
Four rings of light upon the ceiling overhead,
An atmosphere of Juliet's tomb
Prepared for all the things to be said, or left unsaid.
We have been, let us say, to hear the latest Pole
Transmit the Preludes, through his hair and finger-tips.
'So intimate, this Chopin, that I think his soul
Should be resurrected only among friends
Some two or three, who will not touch the bloom
That is rubbed and questioned in the concert room.'
— And so the conversation slips
Among velleities and carefully caught regrets
Through attenuated tones of violins
Mingled with remote cornets
And begins.
'You do not know how much they mean to me, my friends,
And how, how rare and strange it is, to find
In a life composed so much, so much of odds and ends,
(For indeed I do not love it ... you knew? you are not blind!
How keen you are!)
To find a friend who has these qualities,
Who has, and gives
Those qualities upon which friendship lives.
How much it means that I say this to you —
Without these friendships — life, what *cauchemar!*'

18

Among the windings of the violins
And the ariettes
Of cracked cornets
Inside my brain a dull tom-tom begins
Absurdly hammering a prelude of its own,
Capricious monotone
That is at least one definite 'false note.'
— Let us take the air, in a tobacco trance,
Admire the monuments,
Discuss the late events,
Correct our watches by the public clocks.
Then sit for half an hour and drink our bocks.

II

Now that lilacs are in bloom
She has a bowl of lilacs in her room
And twists one in her fingers while she talks.
'Ah, my friend, you do not know, you do not know
What life is, you who hold it in your hands';
(Slowly twisting the lilac stalks)
'You let it flow from you, you let it flow,
And youth is cruel, and has no more remorse
And smiles at situations which it cannot see.'
I smile, of course,
And go on drinking tea.

'Yet with these April sunsets, that somehow recall
My buried life, and Paris in the Spring,
I feel immeasurably at peace, and find the world
To be wonderful and youthful, after all.'

The voice returns like the insistent out-of-tune
Of a broken violin on an August afternoon:
'I am always sure that you understand
My feelings, always sure that you feel,
Sure that across the gulf you reach your hand.

You are invulnerable, you have no Achilles' heel.
You will go on, and when you have prevailed

You can say: at this point many a one has failed.
But what have I, but what have I, my friend,
To give you, what can you receive from me?
Only the friendship and the sympathy
Of one about to reach her journey's end.

I shall sit here, serving tea to friends. . . .'

I take my hat: how can I make a cowardly amends
For what she has said to me?
You will see me any morning in the park
Reading the comics and the sporting page.
Particularly I remark
An English countess goes upon the stage.
A Greek was murdered at a Polish dance,
Another bank defaulter has confessed.
I keep my countenance,
I remain self-possessed
Except when a street-piano, mechanical and tired
Reiterates some worn-out common song
With the smell of hyacinths across the garden
Recalling things that other people have desired.
Are these ideas right or wrong?

III

The October night comes down; returning as before
Except for a slight sensation of being ill at ease
I mount the stairs and turn the handle of the door
And feel as if I had mounted on my hands and knees.
'And so you are going abroad; and when do you return?
But that's a useless question.
You hardly know when you are coming back,
You will find so much to learn.'
My smile falls heavily among the bric-à-brac.

'Perhaps you can write to me.'
My self-possession flares up for a second;
This is as I had reckoned.
'I have been wondering frequently of late

(But our beginnings never know our ends!)
Why we have not developed into friends.'
I feel like one who smiles, and turning shall remark
Suddenly, his expression in a glass.
My self-possession gutters; we are really in the dark.

'For everybody said so, all our friends,
They all were sure our feelings would relate
So closely! I myself can hardly understand.
We must leave it now to fate.
You will write, at any rate.
Perhaps it is not too late.
I shall sit here, serving tea to friends.'

And I must borrow every changing shape
To find expression . . . dance, dance
Like a dancing bear,
Cry like a parrot, chatter like an ape.
Let us take the air, in a tobacco trance —

Well! and what if she should die some afternoon,
Afternoon grey and smoky, evening yellow and rose;
Should die and leave me sitting pen in hand
With the smoke coming down above the housetops;
Doubtful, for a while
Not knowing what to feel or if I understand
Or whether wise or foolish, tardy or too soon . . .
Would she not have the advantage, after all?
This music is successful with a 'dying fall'
Now that we talk of dying —
And should I have the right to smile?

Preludes

I

The winter evening settles down
With smell of steaks in passageways.
Six o'clock.
The burnt-out ends of smoky days.
And now a gusty shower wraps
The grimy scraps
Of withered leaves about your feet
And newspapers from vacant lots;
The showers beat
On broken blinds and chimney-pots,
And at the corner of the street
A lonely cab-horse steams and stamps.

And then the lighting of the lamps.

II

The morning comes to consciousness
Of faint stale smells of beer
From the sawdust-trampled street
With all its muddy feet that press
To early coffee-stands.

With the other masquerades
That time resumes,
One thinks of all the hands
That are raising dingy shades
In a thousand furnished rooms.

III

You tossed a blanket from the bed,
You lay upon your back, and waited;

You dozed, and watched the night revealing
The thousand sordid images
Of which your soul was constituted;
They flickered against the ceiling.
And when all the world came back
And the light crept up between the shutters
And you heard the sparrows in the gutters,
You had such a vision of the street
As the street hardly understands;
Sitting along the bed's edge, where
You curled the papers from your hair,
Or clasped the yellow soles of feet
In the palms of both soiled hands.

IV

His soul stretched tight across the skies
That fade behind a city block,
Or trampled by insistent feet
At four and five and six o'clock;
And short square fingers stuffing pipes,
And evening newspapers, and eyes
Assured of certain certainties,
The conscience of a blackened street
Impatient to assume the world.

I am moved by fancies that are curled
Around these images, and cling:
The notion of some infinitely gentle
Infinitely suffering thing.

Wipe your hand across your mouth, and laugh;
The worlds revolve like ancient women
Gathering fuel in vacant lots.

Rhapsody on a Windy Night

Twelve o'clock.
Along the reaches of the street
Held in a lunar synthesis,
Whispering lunar incantations
Dissolve the floors of memory
And all its clear relations,
Its divisions and precisions.
Every street lamp that I pass
Beats like a fatalistic drum,
And through the spaces of the dark
Midnight shakes the memory
As a madman shakes a dead geranium.

Half-past one,
The street-lamp sputtered,
The street-lamp muttered,
The street-lamp said, 'Regard that woman
Who hesitates towards you in the light of the door
Which opens on her like a grin.
You see the border of her dress
Is torn and stained with sand,
And you see the corner of her eye
Twists like a crooked pin.'

The memory throws up high and dry
A crowd of twisted things;
A twisted branch upon the beach
Eaten smooth, and polished
As if the world gave up
The secret of its skeleton,
Stiff and white.
A broken spring in a factory yard,

24

Rust that clings to the form that the strength has left
Hard and curled and ready to snap.

Half-past two,
The street-lamp said,
'Remark the cat which flattens itself in the gutter,
Slips out its tongue
And devours a morsel of rancid butter.'
So the hand of the child, automatic,
Slipped out and pocketed a toy that was running along the quay,
I could see nothing behind that child's eye.
I have seen eyes in the street
Trying to peer through lighted shutters,
And a crab one afternoon in a pool,
An old crab with barnacles on his back,
Gripped the end of a stick which I held him.

Half-past three,
The lamp sputtered,
The lamp muttered in the dark.
The lamp hummed:
'Regard the moon,
La lune ne garde aucune rancune,
She winks a feeble eye,
She smiles into corners.
She smooths the hair of the grass.
The moon has lost her memory.
A washed-out smallpox cracks her face,
Her hand twists a paper rose,
That smells of dust and eau de Cologne,
She is alone
With all the old nocturnal smells
That cross and cross across her brain.'
The reminiscence comes
Of sunless dry geraniums
And dust in crevices,
Smells of chestnuts in the streets,
And female smells in shuttered rooms,
And cigarettes in corridors
And cocktail smells in bars.

The lamp said,
'Four o'clock,
Here is the number on the door.
Memory!
You have the key,
The little lamp spreads a ring on the stair.
Mount.
The bed is open; the tooth-brush hangs on the wall,
Put your shoes at the door, sleep, prepare for life.'

The last twist of the knife.

Morning at the Window

They are rattling breakfast plates in basement kitchens,
And along the trampled edges of the street
I am aware of the damp souls of housemaids
Sprouting despondently at area gates.

The brown waves of fog toss up to me
Twisted faces from the bottom of the street,
And tear from a passer-by with muddy skirts
An aimless smile that hovers in the air
And vanishes along the level of the roofs.

The Boston Evening Transcript

The readers of the *Boston Evening Transcript*
Sway in the wind like a field of ripe corn.

When evening quickens faintly in the street,
Wakening the appetites of life in some
And to others bringing the *Boston Evening Transcript*,
I mount the steps and ring the bell, turning
Wearily, as one would turn to nod good-bye to La Rochefoucauld,
If the street were time and he at the end of the street,
And I say, 'Cousin Harriet, here is the *Boston Evening Transcript*.'

Aunt Helen

Miss Helen Slingsby was my maiden aunt,
And lived in a small house near a fashionable square
Cared for by servants to the number of four.
Now when she died there was silence in heaven
And silence at her end of the street.
The shutters were drawn and the undertaker wiped his feet —
He was aware that this sort of thing had occurred before.
The dogs were handsomely provided for,
But shortly afterwards the parrot died too.
The Dresden clock continued ticking on the mantelpiece,
And the footman sat upon the dining-table
Holding the second housemaid on his knees —
Who had always been so careful while her mistress lived.

Cousin Nancy

Miss Nancy Ellicott
Strode across the hills and broke them,
Rode across the hills and broke them —
The barren New England hills —
Riding to hounds
Over the cow-pasture.

Miss Nancy Ellicott smoked
And danced all the modern dances;
And her aunts were not quite sure how they felt about it,
But they knew that it was modern.

Upon the glazen shelves kept watch
Matthew and Waldo, guardians of the faith,
The army of unalterable law.

Mr. Apollinax

Ω τῆς καινότητος. Ἡράκλεις, τῆς παραδοξολογίας.
εὐμήχανος ἄνθρωπος.

LUCIAN

When Mr. Apollinax visited the United States
His laughter tinkled among the teacups.
I thought of Fragilion, that shy figure among the birch-trees,
And of Priapus in the shrubbery
Gaping at the lady in the swing.
In the palace of Mrs. Phlaccus, at Professor Channing-Cheetah's
He laughed like an irresponsible fœtus.
His laughter was submarine and profound
Like the old man of the sea's
Hidden under coral islands
Where worried bodies of drowned men drift down in the green silence,
Dropping from fingers of surf.

I looked for the head of Mr. Apollinax rolling under a chair
Or grinning over a screen
With seaweed in its hair.
I heard the beat of centaur's hoofs over the hard turf
As his dry and passionate talk devoured the afternoon.
'He is a charming man' — 'But after all what did he mean?' —
'His pointed ears. . . . He must be unbalanced.' —
'There was something he said that I might have challenged.'
Of dowager Mrs. Phlaccus, and Professor and Mrs. Cheetah
I remember a slice of lemon, and a bitten macaroon.

Hysteria

As she laughed I was aware of becoming involved in her laughter and being part of it, until her teeth were only accidental stars with a talent for squad-drill. I was drawn in by short gasps, inhaled at each momentary recovery, lost finally in the dark caverns of her throat, bruised by the ripple of unseen muscles. An elderly waiter with trembling hands was hurriedly spreading a pink and white checked cloth over the rusty green iron table, saying: 'If the lady and gentleman wish to take their tea in the garden, if the lady and gentleman wish to take their tea in the garden . . .' I decided that if the shaking of her breasts could be stopped, some of the fragments of the afternoon might be collected, and I concentrated my attention with careful subtlety to this end.

Conversation Galante

I observe: 'Our sentimental friend the moon!
Or possibly (fantastic, I confess)
It may be Prester John's balloon
Or an old battered lantern hung aloft
To light poor travellers to their distress.'
   She then: 'How you digress!'

And I then: 'Someone frames upon the keys
That exquisite nocturne, with which we explain
The night and moonshine; music which we seize
To body forth our own vacuity.'
   She then: 'Does this refer to me?'
   'Oh no, it is I who am inane.

'You, madam, are the eternal humorist,
The eternal enemy of the absolute,
Giving our vagrant moods the slightest twist!
With your air indifferent and imperious
At a stroke our mad poetics to confute —'
   And — 'Are we then so serious?'

La Figlia Che Piange

O quam te memorem virgo . . .

Stand on the highest pavement of the stair —
Lean on a garden urn —
Weave, weave the sunlight in your hair —
Clasp your flowers to you with a pained surprise —
Fling them to the ground and turn
With a fugitive resentment in your eyes:
But weave, weave the sunlight in your hair.

So I would have had him leave,
So I would have had her stand and grieve,
So he would have left
As the soul leaves the body torn and bruised,
As the mind deserts the body it has used.
I should find
Some way incomparably light and deft,
Some way we both should understand,
Simple and faithless as a smile and shake of the hand.

She turned away, but with the autumn weather
Compelled my imagination many days,
Many days and many hours:
Her hair over her arms and her arms full of flowers.
And I wonder how they should have been together!
I should have lost a gesture and a pose.
Sometimes these cogitations still amaze
The troubled midnight and the noon's repose.

POEMS
1920

Gerontion

Thou hast nor youth nor age
But as it were an after dinner sleep
Dreaming of both.

Here I am, an old man in a dry month,
Being read to by a boy, waiting for rain.
I was neither at the hot gates
Nor fought in the warm rain
Nor knee deep in the salt marsh, heaving a cutlass,
Bitten by flies, fought.
My house is a decayed house,
And the Jew squats on the window-sill, the owner,
Spawned in some estaminet of Antwerp,
Blistered in Brussels, patched and peeled in London.
The goat coughs at night in the field overhead;
Rocks, moss, stonecrop, iron, merds.
The woman keeps the kitchen, makes tea,
Sneezes at evening, poking the peevish gutter.
                              I an old man,
A dull head among windy spaces.

Signs are taken for wonders. 'We would see a sign!'
The word within a word, unable to speak a word,
Swaddled with darkness. In the juvescence of the year
Came Christ the tiger

In depraved May, dogwood and chestnut, flowering judas,
To be eaten, to be divided, to be drunk
Among whispers; by Mr. Silvero
With caressing hands, at Limoges
Who walked all night in the next room;
By Hakagawa, bowing among the Titians;
By Madame de Tornquist, in the dark room
Shifting the candles; Fräulein von Kulp

Who turned in the hall, one hand on the door. Vacant shuttles
Weave the wind. I have no ghosts,
An old man in a draughty house
Under a windy knob.

After such knowledge, what forgiveness? Think now
History has many cunning passages, contrived corridors
And issues, deceives with whispering ambitions,
Guides us by vanities. Think now
She gives when our attention is distracted
And what she gives, gives with such supple confusions
That the giving famishes the craving. Gives too late
What's not believed in, or if still believed,
In memory only, reconsidered passion. Gives too soon
Into weak hands, what's thought can be dispensed with
Till the refusal propagates a fear. Think
Neither fear nor courage saves us. Unnatural vices
Are fathered by our heroism. Virtues
Are forced upon us by our impudent crimes.
These tears are shaken from the wrath-bearing tree.

The tiger springs in the new year. Us he devours. Think at last
We have not reached conclusion, when I
Stiffen in a rented house. Think at last
I have not made this show purposelessly
And it is not by any concitation
Of the backward devils.
I would meet you upon this honestly.
I that was near your heart was removed therefrom
To lose beauty in terror, terror in inquisition.
I have lost my passion: why should I need to keep it
Since what is kept must be adulterated?
I have lost my sight, smell, hearing, taste and touch:
How should I use them for your closer contact?

These with a thousand small deliberations
Protract the profit of their chilled delirium,
Excite the membrane, when the sense has cooled,
With pungent sauces, multiply variety
In a wilderness of mirrors. What will the spider do,

Suspend its operations, will the weevil
Delay? De Bailhache, Fresca, Mrs. Cammel, whirled
Beyond the circuit of the shuddering Bear
In fractured atoms. Gull against the wind, in the windy straits
Of Belle Isle, or running on the Horn.
White feathers in the snow, the Gulf claims,
And an old man driven by the Trades
To a sleepy corner.

                                        Tenants of the house,
Thoughts of a dry brain in a dry season.

Burbank with a Baedeker:
Bleistein with a Cigar

Tra-la-la-la-la-la-laire — nil nisi divinum stabile est; caetera fumus — the gondola stopped, the old palace was there, how charming its grey and pink — goats and monkeys, with such hair too! — so the countess passed on until she came through the little park, where Niobe presented her with a cabinet, and so departed.

Burbank crossed a little bridge
    Descending at a small hotel;
Princess Volupine arrived,
    They were together, and he fell.

Defunctive music under sea
    Passed seaward with the passing bell
Slowly: the God Hercules
    Had left him, that had loved him well.

The horses, under the axletree
    Beat up the dawn from Istria
With even feet. Her shuttered barge
    Burned on the water all the day.

But this or such was Bleistein's way:
    A saggy bending of the knees
And elbows, with the palms turned out,
    Chicago Semite Viennese.

A lustreless protrusive eye
    Stares from the protozoic slime
At a perspective of Canaletto.
    The smoky candle end of time

Declines. On the Rialto once.
    The rats are underneath the piles.
The Jew is underneath the lot.
    Money in furs. The boatman smiles,

Princess Volupine extends
    A meagre, blue-nailed, phthisic hand
To climb the waterstair. Lights, lights,
    She entertains Sir Ferdinand

Klein. Who clipped the lion's wings
    And flea'd his rump and pared his claws?
Thought Burbank, meditating on
    Time's ruins, and the seven laws.

Sweeney Erect

And the trees about me,
Let them be dry and leafless; let the rocks
Groan with continual surges; and behind me
Make all a desolation. Look, look, wenches!

Paint me a cavernous waste shore
   Cast in the unstilled Cyclades,
Paint me the bold anfractuous rocks
   Faced by the snarled and yelping seas.

Display me Aeolus above
   Reviewing the insurgent gales
Which tangle Ariadne's hair
   And swell with haste the perjured sails.

Morning stirs the feet and hands
   (Nausicaa and Polypheme).
Gesture of orang-outang
   Rises from the sheets in steam.

This withered root of knots of hair
   Slitted below and gashed with eyes,
This oval O cropped out with teeth:
   The sickle motion from the thighs

Jackknifes upward at the knees
   Then straightens out from heel to hip
Pushing the framework of the bed
   And clawing at the pillow slip.

Sweeney addressed full length to shave
   Broadbottomed, pink from nape to base,
Knows the female temperament
   And wipes the suds around his face.

(The lengthened shadow of a man
  Is history, said Emerson
Who had not seen the silhouette
  Of Sweeney straddled in the sun.)

Tests the razor on his leg
  Waiting until the shriek subsides.
The epileptic on the bed
  Curves backward, clutching at her sides.

The ladies of the corridor
  Find themselves involved, disgraced,
Call witness to their principles
  And deprecate the lack of taste

Observing that hysteria
  Might easily be misunderstood;
Mrs. Turner intimates
  It does the house no sort of good.

But Doris, towelled from the bath,
  Enters padding on broad feet,
Bringing sal volatile
  And a glass of brandy neat.

A Cooking Egg

En l'an trentiesme de mon aage
Que toutes mes hontes j'ay beues . . .

Pipit sate upright in her chair
  Some distance from where I was sitting;
Views of Oxford Colleges
  Lay on the table, with the knitting.

Daguerreotypes and silhouettes,
  Her grandfather and great great aunts,
Supported on the mantelpiece
  An *Invitation to the Dance*.

     . . . . .

I shall not want Honour in Heaven
  . For I shall meet Sir Philip Sidney
And have talk with Coriolanus
  And other heroes of that kidney.

I shall not want Capital in Heaven
  For I shall meet Sir Alfred Mond.
We two shall lie together, lapt
  In a five per cent. Exchequer Bond.

I shall not want Society in Heaven,
  Lucretia Borgia shall be my Bride;
Her anecdotes will be more amusing
  Than Pipit's experience could provide.

I shall not want Pipit in Heaven:
  Madame Blavatsky will instruct me
In the Seven Sacred Trances;
  Piccarda de Donati will conduct me.

     . . . . .

But where is the penny world I bought
  To eat with Pipit behind the screen?
The red-eyed scavengers are creeping
  From Kentish Town and Golder's Green;

Where are the eagles and the trumpets?

  Buried beneath some snow-deep Alps.
Over buttered scones and crumpets
  Weeping, weeping multitudes
Droop in a hundred A.B.C.'s.

Le Directeur

Malheur à la malheureuse Tamise
Qui coule si près du Spectateur.
Le directeur
Conservateur
Du Spectateur
Empeste la brise.
Les actionnaires
Réactionnaires
Du Spectateur
Conservateur
Bras dessus bras dessous
Font des tours
A pas de loup.
Dans un égout
Une petite fille
En guenilles
Camarde
Regarde
Le directeur
Du Spectateur
Conservateur
Et crève d'amour.

Mélange Adultère de Tout

En Amérique, professeur;
En Angleterre, journaliste;
C'est à grands pas et en sueur
Que vous suivrez à peine ma piste.
En Yorkshire, conférencier;
A Londres, un peu banquier,
Vous me paierez bien la tête.
C'est à Paris que je me coiffe
Casque noir de jemenfoutiste.
En Allemagne, philosophe
Surexcité par Emporheben
Au grand air de Bergsteigleben;
J'erre toujours de-ci de-là
A divers coups de tra là là
De Damas jusqu' à Omaha.
Je célébrai mon jour de fête
Dans une oasis d'Afrique
Vêtu d'une peau de girafe.

On montrera mon cénotaphe
Aux côtes brûlantes de Mozambique.

Lune de Miel

Ils ont vu les Pays-Bas, ils rentrent à Terre Haute;
Mais une nuit d'été, les voici à Ravenne,
A l'aise entre deux draps, chez deux centaines de punaises;
La sueur aestivale, et une forte odeur de chienne.
Ils restent sur le dos écartant les genoux
De quatre jambes molles tout gonflées de morsures.
On relève le drap pour mieux égratigner.
Moins d'une lieue d'ici est Saint Apollinaire
En Classe, basilique connue des amateurs
De chapiteaux d'acanthe que tournoie le vent.

Ils vont prendre le train de huit heures
Prolonger leurs misères de Padoue à Milan
Où se trouve la Cène, et un restaurant pas cher.
Lui pense aux pourboires, et rédige son bilan.
Ils auront vu la Suisse et traversé la France.
Et Saint Apollinaire, raide et ascétique,
Vieille usine désaffectée de Dieu, tient encore
Dans ses pierres écroulantes la forme précise de Byzance.

The Hippopotamus

And when this epistle is read among you, cause that
it be read also in the church of the Laodiceans.

The broad-backed hippopotamus
Rests on his belly in the mud;
Although he seems so firm to us
He is merely flesh and blood.

Flesh and blood is weak and frail,
Susceptible to nervous shock;
While the True Church can never fail
For it is based upon a rock.

The hippo's feeble steps may err
In compassing material ends,
While the True Church need never stir
To gather in its dividends.

The 'potamus can never reach
The mango on the mango-tree;
But fruits of pomegranate and peach
Refresh the Church from over sea.

At mating time the hippo's voice
Betrays inflexions hoarse and odd,
But every week we hear rejoice
The Church, at being one with God.

The hippopotamus's day
Is passed in sleep; at night he hunts;
God works in a mysterious way —
The Church can sleep and feed at once.

49

I saw the 'potamus take wing
Ascending from the damp savannas,
And quiring angels round him sing
The praise of God, in loud hosannas.

Blood of the Lamb shall wash him clean
And him shall heavenly arms enfold,
Among the saints he shall be seen
Performing on a harp of gold.

He shall be washed as white as snow,
By all the martyr'd virgins kist,
While the True Church remains below
Wrapt in the old miasmal mist.

Dans le Restaurant

Le garçon délabré qui n'a rien à faire
Que de se gratter les doigts et se pencher sur mon épaule:
   'Dans mon pays il fera temps pluvieux,
   Du vent, du grand soleil, et de la pluie;
   C'est ce qu'on appelle le jour de lessive des gueux.'
(Bavard, baveux, à la croupe arrondie,
Je te prie, au moins, ne bave pas dans la soupe).
   'Les saules trempés, et des bourgeons sur les ronces —
   C'est là, dans une averse, qu'on s'abrite.
J'avais sept ans, elle était plus petite.
   Ellé était toute mouillée, je lui ai donné des primevères.'
Les taches de son gilet montent au chiffre de trente-huit.
   'Je la chatouillais, pour la faire rire.
   J'éprouvais un instant de puissance et de délire.'

   Mais alors, vieux lubrique, à cet âge . . .
'Monsieur, le fait est dur.
   Il est venu, nous peloter, un gros chien;
   Moi j'avais peur, je l'ai quittée à mi-chemin.
   C'est dommage.'
     Mais alors, tu as ton vautour!
Va t'en te décrotter les rides du visage;
Tiens, ma fourchette, décrasse-toi le crâne.
De quel droit payes-tu des expériences comme moi?
Tiens, voilà dix sous, pour la salle-de-bains.

Phlébas, le Phénicien, pendant quinze jours noyé,
Oubliait les cris des mouettes et la houle de Cornouaille,
Et les profits et les pertes, et la cargaison d'étain:
Un courant de sous-mer l'emporta très loin,
Le repassant aux étapes de sa vie antérieure.
Figurez-vous donc, c'était un sort pénible;
Cependant, ce fut jadis un bel homme, de haute taille.

Whispers of Immortality

Webster was much possessed by death
And saw the skull beneath the skin;
And breastless creatures under ground
Leaned backward with a lipless grin.

Daffodil bulbs instead of balls
Stared from the sockets of the eyes!
He knew that thought clings round dead limbs
Tightening its lusts and luxuries.

Donne, I suppose, was such another
Who found no substitute for sense,
To seize and clutch and penetrate;
Expert beyond experience,

He knew the anguish of the marrow
The ague of the skeleton;
No contact possible to flesh
Allayed the fever of the bone.

.   .   .   .   .

Grishkin is nice: her Russian eye
Is underlined for emphasis;
Uncorseted, her friendly bust
Gives promise of pneumatic bliss.

The couched Brazilian jaguar
Compels the scampering marmoset
With subtle effluence of cat;
Grishkin has a maisonnette;

The sleek Brazilian jaguar
Does not in its arboreal gloom

Distil so rank a feline smell
As Grishkin in a drawing-room.

And even the Abstract Entities
Circumambulate her charm;
But our lot crawls between dry ribs
To keep our metaphysics warm.

Mr. Eliot's Sunday Morning Service

Look, look, master, here comes two religious caterpillars.
The Jew of Malta.

Polyphiloprogenitive
The sapient sutlers of the Lord
Drift across the window-panes.
· In the beginning was the Word.

In the beginning was the Word.
Superfetation of τὸ ἕν,
And at the mensual turn of time
Produced enervate Origen.

A painter of the Umbrian school
Designed upon a gesso ground
The nimbus of the Baptized God.
The wilderness is cracked and browned

But through the water pale and thin
Still shine the unoffending feet
And there above the painter set
The Father and the Paraclete.

.   .   .   .   .

The sable presbyters approach
The avenue of penitence;
The young are red and pustular
Clutching piaculative pence.

Under the penitential gates
Sustained by staring Seraphim
Where the souls of the devout
Burn invisible and dim.

Along the garden-wall the bees
With hairy bellies pass between

The staminate and pistillate,
Blest office of the epicene.

Sweeney shifts from ham to ham
Stirring the water in his bath.
The masters of the subtle schools
Are controversial, polymath.

Sweeney Among the Nightingales

ὤμοι, πέπληγμαι καιρίαν πληγὴν ἔσω.

Apeneck Sweeney spreads his knees
Letting his arms hang down to laugh,
The zebra stripes along his jaw
Swelling to maculate giraffe.

The circles of the stormy moon
Slide westward toward the River Plate,
Death and the Raven drift above
And Sweeney guards the hornèd gate.

Gloomy Orion and the Dog
Are veiled; and hushed the shrunken seas;
The person in the Spanish cape
Tries to sit on Sweeney's knees

Slips and pulls the table cloth
Overturns a coffee-cup,
Reorganised upon the floor
She yawns and draws a stocking up;

The silent man in mocha brown
Sprawls at the window-sill and gapes;
The waiter brings in oranges
Bananas figs and hothouse grapes;

The silent vertebrate in brown
Contracts and concentrates, withdraws;
Rachel *née* Rabinovitch
Tears at the grapes with murderous paws;

She and the lady in the cape
Are suspect, thought to be in league;

Therefore the man with heavy eyes
Declines the gambit, shows fatigue,

Leaves the room and reappears
Outside the window, leaning in,
Branches of wistaria
Circumscribe a golden grin;

The host with someone indistinct
Converses at the door apart,
The nightingales are singing near
The Convent of the Sacred Heart,

And sang within the bloody wood
When Agamemnon cried aloud
And let their liquid siftings fall
To stain the stiff dishonoured shroud.

THE WASTE LAND
1922

'Nam Sibyllam quidem Cumis ego ipse oculis meis vidi in ampulla pendere, et cum illi pueri dicerent: Σίβυλλα τί θέλεις; respondebat illa: ἀποθανεῖν θέλω.'

For Ezra Pound
il miglior fabbro.

I. The Burial of the Dead

April is the cruellest month, breeding
Lilacs out of the dead land, mixing
Memory and desire, stirring
Dull roots with spring rain.
Winter kept us warm, covering
Earth in forgetful snow, feeding
A little life with dried tubers.
Summer surprised us, coming over the Starnbergersee
With a shower of rain; we stopped in the colonnade,
And went on in sunlight, into the Hofgarten,   10
And drank coffee, and talked for an hour.
Bin gar keine Russin, stamm' aus Litauen, echt deutsch.
And when we were children, staying at the archduke's,
My cousin's, he took me out on a sled,
And I was frightened. He said, Marie,
Marie, hold on tight. And down we went.
In the mountains, there you feel free.
I read, much of the night, and go south in the winter.

What are the roots that clutch, what branches grow
Out of this stony rubbish? Son of man,   20
You cannot say, or guess, for you know only
A heap of broken images, where the sun beats,
And the dead tree gives no shelter, the cricket no relief,
And the dry stone no sound of water. Only
There is shadow under this red rock,
(Come in under the shadow of this red rock),
And I will show you something different from either
Your shadow at morning striding behind you
Or your shadow at evening rising to meet you;
I will show you fear in a handful of dust.   30
                    Frisch weht der Wind
                    Der Heimat zu

THE WASTE LAND, 1922

Mein Irisch Kind
Wo weilest du?

'You gave me hyacinths first a year ago;
'They called me the hyacinth girl.'
— Yet when we came back, late, from the hyacinth garden,
Your arms full, and your hair wet, I could not
Speak, and my eyes failed, I was neither
Living nor dead, and I knew nothing,   40
Looking into the heart of light, the silence.
Oed' und leer das Meer.

   Madame Sosostris, famous clairvoyante,
Had a bad cold, nevertheless
Is known to be the wisest woman in Europe,
With a wicked pack of cards. Here, said she,
Is your card, the drowned Phoenician Sailor,
(Those are pearls that were his eyes. Look!)
Here is Belladonna, the Lady of the Rocks,
The lady of situations.   50
Here is the man with three staves, and here the Wheel,
And here is the one-eyed merchant, and this card,
Which is blank, is something he carries on his back,
Which I am forbidden to see. I do not find
The Hanged Man. Fear death by water.
I see crowds of people, walking round in a ring.
Thank you. If you see dear Mrs. Equitone,
Tell her I bring the horoscope myself:
One must be so careful these days.

   Unreal City,   60
Under the brown fog of a winter dawn,
A crowd flowed over London Bridge, so many,
I had not thought death had undone so many.
Sighs, short and infrequent, were exhaled,
And each man fixed his eyes before his feet.
Flowed up the hill and down King William Street,
To where Saint Mary Woolnoth kept the hours
With a dead sound on the final stroke of nine.
There I saw one I knew, and stopped him, crying: 'Stetson!
'You who were with me in the ships at Mylae!   70

'That corpse you planted last year in your garden,
'Has it begun to sprout? Will it bloom this year?
'Or has the sudden frost disturbed its bed?
'O keep the Dog far hence, that's friend to men,
'Or with his nails he'll dig it up again!
'You! hypocrite lecteur! — mon semblable, — mon frère!'

II. A Game of Chess

The Chair she sat in, like a burnished throne,
Glowed on the marble, where the glass
Held up by standards wrought with fruited vines
From which a golden Cupidon peeped out   80
(Another hid his eyes behind his wing)
Doubled the flames of sevenbranched candelabra
Reflecting light upon the table as
The glitter of her jewels rose to meet it,
From satin cases poured in rich profusion.
In vials of ivory and coloured glass
Unstoppered, lurked her strange synthetic perfumes,
Unguent, powdered, or liquid — troubled, confused
And drowned the sense in odours; stirred by the air
That freshened from the window, these ascended   90
In fattening the prolonged candle-flames,
Flung their smoke into the laquearia,
Stirring the pattern on the coffered ceiling.
Huge sea-wood fed with copper
Burned green and orange, framed by the coloured stone,
In which sad light a carvèd dolphin swam.
Above the antique mantel was displayed
As though a window gave upon the sylvan scene
The change of Philomel, by the barbarous king
So rudely forced; yet there the nightingale   100
Filled all the desert with inviolable voice
And still she cried, and still the world pursues,
'Jug Jug' to dirty ears.
And other withered stumps of time
Were told upon the walls; staring forms
Leaned out, leaning, hushing the room enclosed.
Footsteps shuffled on the stair.
Under the firelight, under the brush, her hair

Spread out in fiery points
Glowed into words, then would be savagely still. 110

   'My nerves are bad tonight. Yes, bad. Stay with me.
   Speak to me. Why do you never speak? Speak.
     What are you thinking of? What thinking? What?
   I never know what you are thinking. Think.'

   I think we are in rats' alley
Where the dead men lost their bones.

   'What is that noise?'
              The wind under the door.
'What is that noise now? What is the wind doing?'
              Nothing again nothing. 120
                         'Do
'You know nothing? Do you see nothing? Do you remember
Nothing?'

    I remember
Those are pearls that were his eyes.
'Are you alive, or not? Is there nothing in your head?'
                       But
O O O O that Shakespeherian Rag —
It's so elegant
So intelligent 130
'What shall I do now? What shall I do?
I shall rush out as I am, and walk the street
With my hair down, so. What shall we do tomorrow?
What shall we ever do?'
               The hot water at ten.
And if it rains, a closed car at four.
And we shall play a game of chess,
Pressing lidless eyes and waiting for a knock upon the door.

   When Lil's husband got demobbed, I said —
I didn't mince my words, I said to her myself, 140
HURRY UP PLEASE ITS TIME
Now Albert's coming back, make yourself a bit smart.
He'll want to know what you done with that money he gave you

To get yourself some teeth. He did, I was there.
You have them all out, Lil, and get a nice set,
He said, I swear, I can't bear to look at you.
And no more can't I, I said, and think of poor Albert,
He's been in the army four years, he wants a good time,
And if you don't give it him, there's others will, I said.
Oh is there, she said. Something o' that, I said.   150
Then I'll know who to thank, she said, and give me a straight look.
HURRY UP PLEASE ITS TIME
If you don't like it you can get on with it, I said.
Others can pick and choose if you can't.
But if Albert makes off, it won't be for lack of telling.
You ought to be ashamed, I said, to look so antique.
(And her only thirty-one.)
I can't help it, she said, pulling a long face,
It's them pills I took, to bring it off, she said.
(She's had five already, and nearly died of young George.)   160
The chemist said it would be all right, but I've never been the same.
You *are* a proper fool, I said.
Well, if Albert won't leave you alone, there it is, I said,
What you get married for if you don't want children?
HURRY UP PLEASE ITS TIME
Well, that Sunday Albert was home, they had a hot gammon,
And they asked me in to dinner, to get the beauty of it hot —
HURRY UP PLEASE ITS TIME
HURRY UP PLEASE ITS TIME
Goonight Bill. Goonight Lou. Goonight May. Goonight.   170
Ta ta. Goonight. Goonight.
Good night, ladies, good night, sweet ladies, good night, good night.

III. The Fire Sermon

The river's tent is broken; the last fingers of leaf
Clutch and sink into the wet bank. The wind
Crosses the brown land, unheard. The nymphs are departed.
Sweet Thames, run softly, till I end my song.
The river bears no empty bottles, sandwich papers,
Silk handkerchiefs, cardboard boxes, cigarette ends
Or other testimony of summer nights. The nymphs are departed.
And their friends, the loitering heirs of City directors;   180
Departed, have left no addresses.
By the waters of Leman I sat down and wept . . .
Sweet Thames, run softly till I end my song,
Sweet Thames, run softly, for I speak not loud or long.
But at my back in a cold blast I hear
The rattle of the bones, and chuckle spread from ear to ear.

A rat crept softly through the vegetation
Dragging its slimy belly on the bank
While I was fishing in the dull canal
On a winter evening round behind the gashouse   190
Musing upon the king my brother's wreck
And on the king my father's death before him.
White bodies naked on the low damp ground
And bones cast in a little low dry garret,
Rattled by the rat's foot only, year to year.
But at my back from time to time I hear
The sound of horns and motors, which shall bring
Sweeney to Mrs. Porter in the spring.
O the moon shone bright on Mrs. Porter
And on her daughter   200
They wash their feet in soda water
Et O ces voix d'enfants, chantant dans la coupole!

Twit twit twit
Jug jug jug jug jug jug

67

So rudely forc'd.
Tereu

  Unreal City
Under the brown fog of a winter noon
Mr. Eugenides, the Smyrna merchant
Unshaven, with a pocket full of currants   210
C.i.f. London: documents at sight,
Asked me in demotic French
To luncheon at the Cannon Street Hotel
Followed by a weekend at the Metropole.

  At the violet hour, when the eyes and back
Turn upward from the desk, when the human engine waits
Like a taxi throbbing waiting,
I Tiresias, though blind, throbbing between two lives,
Old man with wrinkled female breasts, can see
At the violet hour, the evening hour that strives   220
Homeward, and brings the sailor home from sea,
The typist home at teatime, clears her breakfast, lights
Her stove, and lays out food in tins.
Out of the window perilously spread
Her drying combinations touched by the sun's last rays,
On the divan are piled (at night her bed)
Stockings, slippers, camisoles, and stays.
I Tiresias, old man with wrinkled dugs
Perceived the scene, and foretold the rest —
I too awaited the expected guest.   230
He, the young man carbuncular, arrives,
A small house agent's clerk, with one bold stare,
One of the low on whom assurance sits
As a silk hat on a Bradford millionaire.
The time is now propitious, as he guesses,
The meal is ended, she is bored and tired,
Endeavours to engage her in caresses
Which still are unreproved, if undesired.
Flushed and decided, he assaults at once;
Exploring hands encounter no defence;   240
His vanity requires no response,
And makes a welcome of indifference.

THE WASTE LAND, 1922

(And I Tiresias have foresuffered all
Enacted on this same divan or bed;
I who have sat by Thebes below the wall
And walked among the lowest of the dead.)
Bestows one final patronising kiss,
And gropes his way, finding the stairs unlit . . .

    She turns and looks a moment in the glass,
Hardly aware of her departed lover;   250
Her brain allows one half-formed thought to pass:
'Well now that's done: and I'm glad it's over.'
When lovely woman stoops to folly and
Paces about her room again, alone,
She smooths her hair with automatic hand,
And puts a record on the gramophone.

    'This music crept by me upon the waters'
And along the Strand, up Queen Victoria Street.
O City city, I can sometimes hear
Beside a public bar in Lower Thames Street,   260
The pleasant whining of a mandoline
And a clatter and a chatter from within
Where fishmen lounge at noon: where the walls
Of Magnus Martyr hold
Inexplicable splendour of Ionian white and gold.

           The river sweats
           Oil and tar
           The barges drift
           With the turning tide
           Red sails   270
           Wide
           To leeward, swing on the heavy spar.
           The barges wash
           Drifting logs
           Down Greenwich reach
           Past the Isle of Dogs.
                   Weialala leia
                   Wallala leialala

Elizabeth and Leicester
Beating oars   280
The stern was formed
A gilded shell
Red and gold
The brisk swell
Rippled both shores
Southwest wind
Carried down stream
The peal of bells
White towers
        Weialala leia   290
        Wallala leialala

'Trams and dusty trees.
Highbury bore me. Richmond and Kew
Undid me. By Richmond I raised my knees
Supine on the floor of a narrow canoe.'

'My feet are at Moorgate, and my heart
Under my feet. After the event
He wept. He promised "a new start."
I made no comment. What should I resent?'

'On Margate Sands.   300
I can connect
Nothing with nothing.
The broken fingernails of dirty hands.
My people humble people who expect
Nothing.'
      la la

To Carthage then I came

Burning burning burning burning
O Lord Thou pluckest me out
O Lord Thou pluckest   310

burning

IV. Death by Water

Phlebas the Phoenician, a fortnight dead,
Forgot the cry of gulls, and the deep sea swell
And the profit and loss.
                              A current under sea
Picked his bones in whispers. As he rose and fell
He passed the stages of his age and youth
Entering the whirlpool.
                              Gentile or Jew
O you who turn the wheel and look to windward,   320
Consider Phlebas, who was once handsome and tall as you.

V. What the Thunder said

After the torchlight red on sweaty faces
After the frosty silence in the gardens
After the agony in stony places
The shouting and the crying
Prison and palace and reverberation
Of thunder of spring over distant mountains
He who was living is now dead
We who were living are now dying
With a little patience   330

Here is no water but only rock
Rock and no water and the sandy road
The road winding above among the mountains
Which are mountains of rock without water
If there were water we should stop and drink
Amongst the rock one cannot stop or think
Sweat is dry and feet are in the sand
If there were only water amongst the rock
Dead mountain mouth of carious teeth that cannot spit
Here one can neither stand nor lie nor sit   340
There is not even silence in the mountains
But dry sterile thunder without rain
There is not even solitude in the mountains
But red sullen faces sneer and snarl
From doors of mudcracked houses
                            If there were water

    And no rock
    If there were rock
    And also water
    And water   350
    A spring
    A pool among the rock
    If there were the sound of water only

THE WASTE LAND, 1922

Not the cicada
And dry grass singing
But sound of water over a rock
Where the hermit-thrush sings in the pine trees
Drip drop drip drop drop drop drop
But there is no water

Who is the third who walks always beside you?   360
When I count, there are only you and I together
But when I look ahead up the white road
There is always another one walking beside you
Gliding wrapt in a brown mantle, hooded
I do not know whether a man or a woman
— But who is that on the other side of you?

What is that sound high in the air
Murmur of maternal lamentation
Who are those hooded hordes swarming
Over endless plains, stumbling in cracked earth   370
Ringed by the flat horizon only
What is the city over the mountains
Cracks and reforms and bursts in the violet air
Falling towers
Jerusalem Athens Alexandria
Vienna London
Unreal

A woman drew her long black hair out tight
And fiddled whisper music on those strings
And bats with baby faces in the violet light   380
Whistled, and beat their wings
And crawled head downward down a blackened wall
And upside down in air were towers
Tolling reminiscent bells, that kept the hours
And voices singing out of empty cisterns and exhausted wells.

In this decayed hole among the mountains
In the faint moonlight, the grass is singing
Over the tumbled graves, about the chapel
There is the empty chapel, only the wind's home.

It has no windows, and the door swings,   390
Dry bones can harm no one.
Only a cock stood on the rooftree
Co co rico co co rico
In a flash of lightning. Then a damp gust
Bringing rain

  Ganga was sunken, and the limp leaves
Waited for rain, while the black clouds
Gathered far distant, over Himavant.
The jungle crouched, humped in silence.
Then spoke the thunder   400
DA
Datta: what have we given?
My friend, blood shaking my heart
The awful daring of a moment's surrender
Which an age of prudence can never retract
By this, and this only, we have existed
Which is not to be found in our obituaries
Or in memories draped by the beneficent spider
Or under seals broken by the lean solicitor
In our empty rooms   410
DA
Dayadhvam: I have heard the key
Turn in the door once and turn once only
We think of the key, each in his prison
Thinking of the key, each confirms a prison
Only at nightfall, aethereal rumours
Revive for a moment a broken Coriolanus
DA
Damyata: The boat responded
Gaily, to the hand expert with sail and oar   420
The sea was calm, your heart would have responded
Gaily, when invited, beating obedient
To controlling hands

                           I sat upon the shore
Fishing, with the arid plain behind me
Shall I at least set my lands in order?
London Bridge is falling down falling down falling down

Poi s'ascose nel foco che gli affina
Quando fiam uti chelidon — O swallow swallow
Le Prince d'Aquitaine à la tour abolie   430
These fragments I have shored against my ruins
Why then Ile fit you. Hieronymo's mad againe.
Datta. Dayadhvam. Damyata.
                    Shantih shantih shantih

Notes on the Waste Land

Not only the title, but the plan and a good deal of the incidental symbolism of the poem were suggested by Miss Jessie L. Weston's book on the Grail legend: *From Ritual to Romance* (Cambridge). Indeed, so deeply am I indebted, Miss Weston's book will elucidate the difficulties of the poem much better than my notes can do; and I recommend it (apart from the great interest of the book itself) to any who think such elucidation of the poem worth the trouble. To another work of anthropology I am indebted in general, one which has influenced our generation profoundly; I mean *The Golden Bough;* I have used especially the two volumes *Adonis, Attis, Osiris.* Anyone who is acquainted with these works will immediately recognise in the poem certain references to vegetation ceremonies.

I. THE BURIAL OF THE DEAD

Line 20. Cf. Ezekiel II, i.

23. Cf. Ecclesiastes XII, v.

31. V. Tristan und Isolde, I, verses 5–8.

42. Id. III, verse 24.

46. I am not familiar with the exact constitution of the Tarot pack of cards, from which I have obviously departed to suit my own convenience. The Hanged Man, a member of the traditional pack, fits my purpose in two ways: because he is associated in my mind with the Hanged God of Frazer, and because I associate him with the hooded figure in the passage of the disciples of Emmaus in Part V. The Phoenician Sailor and the Merchant appear later; also the 'crowds of people', and Death by Water is executed in Part IV. The Man with Three Staves (an authentic member of the Tarot pack) I associate, quite arbitrarily, with the Fisher King himself.

60. Cf. Baudelaire:

'Fourmillante cité, cité pleine de rêves,

'Où le spectre en plein jour raccroche le passant.'

63. Cf. Inferno III, 55–57:

> si lunga tratta
> di gente, ch'io non avrei mai creduto
> che morte tanta n'avesse disfatta.

64. Cf. Inferno IV, 25–27:

> Quivi, secondo che per ascoltare,
> non avea pianto ma' che di sospiri
> che l'aura eterna facevan tremare.

68. A phenomenon which I have often noticed.

74. Cf. the Dirge in Wesbster's *White Devil*.

76. V. Baudelaire, Preface to *Fleurs du Mal*.

II. A GAME OF CHESS

77. Cf. *Antony and Cleopatra*, II, ii, l. 190.

92. Laquearia. V. *Aeneid*, I, 726:

> dependent lychni laquearibus aureis
> incensi, et noctem flammis funalia vincunt.

98. Sylvan scene. V. Milton, *Paradise Lost*, IV, 140.

99. V. Ovid, *Metamorphoses*, VI, Philomela.

100. Cf. Part III, l. 204.

115. Cf. Part III, l. 195.

118. Cf. Webster: 'Is the wind in that door still?'

126. Cf. Part I, l. 37, 48.

138. Cf. the game of chess in Middleton's *Women beware Women*.

III. THE FIRE SERMON

176. V. Spenser, *Prothalamion*.

192. Cf. *The Tempest*, I, ii.

196. Cf. Marvell, *To His Coy Mistress*.

197. Cf. Day, *Parliament of Bees*:

> 'When of the sudden, listening, you shall hear,
> 'A noise of horns and hunting, which shall bring
> 'Actaeon to Diana in the spring,
> 'Where all shall see her naked skin . . .'

199. I do not know the origin of the ballad from which these lines are taken: it was reported to me from Sydney, Australia.

202. V. Verlaine, *Parsifal*.

210. The currants were quoted at a price 'cost insurance and freight to London'; and the Bill of Lading, etc., were to be handed to the buyer upon payment of the sight draft.

THE WASTE LAND, 1922

218. Tiresias, although a mere spectator and not indeed a 'character', is yet the most important personage in the poem, uniting all the rest. Just as the one-eyed merchant, seller of currants, melts into the Phoenician Sailor, and the latter is not wholly distinct from Ferdinand Prince of Naples, so all the women are one woman, and the two sexes meet in Tiresias. What Tiresias *sees*, in fact, is the substance of the poem. The whole passage from Ovid is of great anthropological interest:

. . . Cum Iunone iocos et 'maior vestra profecto est
Quam quae contingit maribus', dixisse, 'voluptas.'
Illa negat; placuit quae sit sententia docti
Quaerere Tiresiae : Venus huic erat utraque nota.
Nam duo magnorum viridi coeuntia silva
Corpora serpentum baculi violaverat ictu
Deque viro factus, mirabile, femina septem
Egerat autumnos; octavo rursus eosdem
Vidit et 'est vestrae si tanta potentia plagae',
Dixit 'ut auctoris sortem in contraria mutet,
Nunc quoque vos feriam!' percussis anguibus isdem
Forma prior rediit genetivaque venit imago.
Arbiter hic igitur sumptus de lite iocosa
Dicta Iovis firmat; gravius Saturnia iusto
Nec pro materia fertur doluisse suique
Iudicis aeterna damnavit lumina nocte,
At pater omnipotens (neque enim licet inrita cuiquam
Facta dei fecisse deo) pro lumine adempto
Scire futura dedit poenamque levavit honore.

221. This may not appear as exact as Sappho's lines, but I had in mind the 'longshore' or 'dory' fisherman, who returns at nightfall.

253. V. Goldsmith, the song in *The Vicar of Wakefield*.

257. V. *The Tempest*, as above.

264. The interior of St. Magnus Martyr is to my mind one of the finest among Wren's interiors. See *The Proposed Demolition of Nineteen City Churches:* (P. S. King & Son, Ltd.).

266. The Song of the (three) Thames-daughters begins here. From line 292 to 306 inclusive they speak in turn. V. *Götterdämmerung*, III, i: the Rhine-daughters.

279. V. Froude, *Elizabeth*, Vol. I, ch. iv, letter of De Quadra to Philip of Spain:

'In the afternoon we were in a barge, watching the games on the river. (The Queen) was alone with Lord Robert and myself on the poop, when they began to talk nonsense, and went so far that Lord Robert at last said, as I was on the spot there was no reason why they should not be married if the queen pleased.'

293. Cf. *Purgatorio*, V. 133:

'Ricorditi di me, che son la Pia;
'Siena mi fé, disfecemi Maremma.'

307. V. St. Augustine's *Confessions:* 'to Carthage then I came, where a cauldron of unholy loves sang all about mine ears.'

308. The complete text of the Buddha's Fire Sermon (which corresponds in importance to the Sermon on the Mount) from which these words are taken, will be found translated in the late Henry Clarke Warren's *Buddhism in Translation* (Harvard Oriental Series). Mr. Warren was one of the great pioneers of Buddhist studies in the Occident.

309. From St. Augustine's *Confessions* again. The collocation of these two representatives of eastern and western asceticism, as the culmination of this part of the poem, is not an accident.

V. WHAT THE THUNDER SAID

In the first part of Part V three themes are employed: the journey to Emmaus, the approach to the Chapel Perilous (see Miss Weston's book) and the present decay of eastern Europe.

357. This is *Turdus aonalaschkae pallasii*, the hermit-thrush which I have heard in Quebec Province. Chapman says (*Handbook of Birds of Eastern North America*) 'it is most at home in secluded woodland and thickety retreats. . . . Its notes are not remarkable for variety or volume, but in purity and sweetness of tone and exquisite modulation they are unequalled.' Its 'water-dripping song' is justly celebrated.

360. The following lines were stimulated by the account of one of the Antarctic expeditions (I forget which, but I think one of Shackleton's): it was related that the party of explorers, at the extremity of their strength, had the constant delusion that there was *one more member* than could actually be counted.

366-76. Cf. Hermann Hesse, *Blick ins Chaos:* 'Schon ist halb Europa, schon ist zumindest der halbe Osten Europas auf dem Wege zum Chaos, fährt betrunken im heiligen Wahn am Abgrund entlang und singt dazu, singt betrunken und hymnisch wie Dmitri Karamasoff sang. Ueber diese Lieder lacht der Bürger beleidigt, der Heilige und Seher hört sie mit Tränen.'

401. 'Datta, dayadhvam, damyata' (Give, sympathise, control). The fable of the meaning of the Thunder is found in the *Brihadaranyaka* — *Upanishad*, 5, 1. A translation is found in Deussen's *Sechzig Upanishads des Veda*, p. 489.

407. Cf. Webster, *The White Devil*, V, vi:

'. . . they'll remarry

Ere the worm pierce your winding-sheet, ere the spider
Make a thin curtain for your epitaphs.'

411. Cf. *Inferno*, XXXIII, 46:

'ed io senti chiavar l'uscio di sotto
all' orribile torre.'

Also F. H. Bradley, *Appearance and Reality*, p. 306.

'My external sensations are no less private to my self than are my thoughts or my feelings. In either case my experience falls within my own circle, a circle closed on the outside; and, with all its elements alike, every sphere is opaque to the others which surround it. . . . In brief, regarded as an existence which appears in a soul, the whole world for each is peculiar and private to that soul.'

424. V. Weston: *From Ritual to Romance;* chapter on the Fisher King.

427. V. *Purgatorio*, XXVI, 148.

' "Ara vos prec per aquella valor
"que vos guida al som de l'escalina,
"sovenha vos a temps de ma dolor."

Poi s'ascose nel foco che li affina.'

428. V. *Pervigilium Veneris*. Cf. Philomela in Parts II and III.

429. V. Gerard de Nerval, Sonnet *El Desdichado*.

431. V. Kyd's *Spanish Tragedy*.

433. Shantih. Repeated as here, a formal ending to an Upanishad. 'The Peace which passeth understanding' is our equivalent to this word.

THE HOLLOW MEN
1925

Mistah Kurtz — he dead.

The Hollow Men

A penny for the Old Guy

I

We are the hollow men
We are the stuffed men
Leaning together
Headpiece filled with straw. Alas!
Our dried voices, when
We whisper together
Are quiet and meaningless
As wind in dry grass
Or rats' feet over broken glass
In our dry cellar

Shape without form, shade without colour,
Paralysed force, gesture without motion;

Those who have crossed
With direct eyes, to death's other Kingdom
Remember us — if at all — not as lost
Violent souls, but only
As the hollow men
The stuffed men.

II

Eyes I dare not meet in dreams
In death's dream kingdom
These do not appear:
There, the eyes are
Sunlight on a broken column
There, is a tree swinging

And voices are
In the wind's singing
More distant and more solemn
Than a fading star.

Let me be no nearer
In death's dream kingdom
Let me also wear
Such deliberate disguises
Rat's coat, crowskin, crossed staves
In a field
Behaving as the wind behaves
No nearer —

Not that final meeting
In the twilight kingdom

III

This is the dead land
This is cactus land
Here the stone images
Are raised, here they receive
The supplication of a dead man's hand
Under the twinkle of a fading star.

Is it like this
In death's other kingdom
Waking alone
At the hour when we are
Trembling with tenderness
Lips that would kiss
Form prayers to broken stone.

IV

The eyes are not here
There are no eyes here
In this valley of dying stars
In this hollow valley
This broken jaw of our lost kingdoms

THE HOLLOW MEN, 1925

In this last of meeting places
We grope together
And avoid speech
Gathered on this beach of the tumid river

Sightless, unless
The eyes reappear
As the perpetual star
Multifoliate rose
Of death's twilight kingdom
The hope only
Of empty men.

V

Here we go round the prickly pear
Prickly pear prickly pear
Here we go round the prickly pear
At five o'clock in the morning.

Between the idea
And the reality
Between the motion
And the act
Falls the Shadow

       For Thine is the Kingdom

Between the conception
And the creation
Between the emotion
And the response
Falls the Shadow

       Life is very long

Between the desire
And the spasm
Between the potency
And the existence
Between the essence
And the descent
Falls the Shadow

       For Thine is the Kingdom

85

THE HOLLOW MEN, 1925

For Thine is
Life is
For Thine is the

This is the way the world ends
This is the way the world ends
This is the way the world ends
Not with a bang but a whimper.

ASH-WEDNESDAY
1930

ASH-WEDNESDAY, 1930

I

Because I do not hope to turn again
Because I do not hope
Because I do not hope to turn
Desiring this man's gift and that man's scope
I no longer strive to strive towards such things
(Why should the agèd eagle stretch its wings?)
Why should I mourn
The vanished power of the usual reign?

Because I do not hope to know again
The infirm glory of the positive hour
Because I do not think
Because I know I shall not know
The one veritable transitory power
Because I cannot drink
There, where trees flower, and springs flow, for there is nothing
    again

Because I know that time is always time
And place is always and only place
And what is actual is actual only for one time
And only for one place
I rejoice that things are as they are and
I renounce the blessèd face
And renounce the voice
Because I cannot hope to turn again
Consequently I rejoice, having to construct something
Upon which to rejoice
And pray to God to have mercy upon us
And I pray that I may forget
These matters that with myself I too much discuss
Too much explain

ASH-WEDNESDAY, 1930

Because I do not hope to turn again
Let these words answer
For what is done, not to be done again
May the judgement not be too heavy upon us

Because these wings are no longer wings to fly
But merely vans to beat the air
The air which is now thoroughly small and dry
Smaller and dryer than the will
Teach us to care and not to care
Teach us to sit still.

Pray for us sinners now and at the hour of our death
Pray for us now and at the hour of our death.

II

Lady, three white leopards sat under a juniper-tree
In the cool of the day, having fed to satiety
On my legs my heart my liver and that which had been contained
In the hollow round of my skull. And God said
Shall these bones live? shall these
Bones live? And that which had been contained
In the bones (which were already dry) said chirping:
Because of the goodness of this Lady
And because of her loveliness, and because
She honours the Virgin in meditation,
We shine with brightness. And I who am here dissembled
Proffer my deeds to oblivion, and my love
To the posterity of the desert and the fruit of the gourd.
It is this which recovers
My guts the strings of my eyes and the indigestible portions
Which the leopards reject. The Lady is withdrawn
In a white gown, to contemplation, in a white gown.
Let the whiteness of bones atone to forgetfulness.
There is no life in them. As I am forgotten
And would be forgotten, so I would forget
Thus devoted, concentrated in purpose. And God said
Prophesy to the wind, to the wind only for only
The wind will listen. And the bones sang chirping
With the burden of the grasshopper, saying

Lady of silences
Calm and distressed
Torn and most whole
Rose of memory
Rose of forgetfulness
Exhausted and life-giving
Worried reposeful
The single Rose

Is now the Garden
Where all loves end
Terminate torment
Of love unsatisfied
The greater torment
Of love satisfied
End of the endless
Journey to no end
Conclusion of all that
Is inconclusible
Speech without word and
Word of no speech
Grace to the Mother
For the Garden
Where all love ends.

Under a juniper-tree the bones sang, scattered and shining
We are glad to be scattered, we did little good to each other,
Under a tree in the cool of the day, with the blessing of sand,
Forgetting themselves and each other, united
In the quiet of the desert. This is the land which ye
Shall divide by lot. And neither division nor unity
Matters. This is the land. We have our inheritance.

III

At the first turning of the second stair
I turned and saw below
The same shape twisted on the banister
Under the vapour in the fetid air
Struggling with the devil of the stairs who wears
The deceitful face of hope and of despair.

At the second turning of the second stair
I left them twisting, turning below;
There were no more faces and the stair was dark,
Damp, jaggèd, like an old man's mouth drivelling, beyond repair,
Or the toothed gullet of an agèd shark.

At the first turning of the third stair
Was a slotted window bellied like the fig's fruit
And beyond the hawthorn blossom and a pasture scene
The broadbacked figure drest in blue and green
Enchanted the maytime with an antique flute.
Blown hair is sweet, brown hair over the mouth blown,
Lilac and brown hair;
Distraction, music of the flute, stops and steps of the mind over the
    third stair,
Fading, fading; strength beyond hope and despair
Climbing the third stair.

Lord, I am not worthy
Lord, I am not worthy
        but speak the word only.

IV

Who walked between the violet and the violet
Who walked between
The various ranks of varied green
Going in white and blue, in Mary's colour,
Talking of trivial things
In ignorance and in knowledge of eternal dolour
Who moved among the others as they walked,
Who then made strong the fountains and made fresh the
    springs

Made cool the dry rock and made firm the sand
In blue of larkspur, blue of Mary's colour,
Sovegna vos

Here are the years that walk between, bearing
Away the fiddles and the flutes, restoring
One who moves in the time between sleep and waking,
    wearing

White light folded, sheathed about her, folded.
The new years walk, restoring
Through a bright cloud of tears, the years, restoring
With a new verse the ancient rhyme. Redeem
The time. Redeem
The unread vision in the higher dream
While jewelled unicorns draw by the gilded hearse.

The silent sister veiled in white and blue
Between the yews, behind the garden god,
Whose flute is breathless, bent her head and signed but spoke no
    word

94

ASH-WEDNESDAY, 1930

But the fountain sprang up and the bird sang down
Redeem the time, redeem the dream
The token of the word unheard, unspoken

Till the wind shake a thousand whispers from the yew

And after this our exile

V

If the lost word is lost, if the spent word is spent
If the unheard, unspoken
Word is unspoken, unheard;
Still is the unspoken word, the Word unheard,
The Word without a word, the Word within
The world and for the world;
And the light shone in darkness and
Against the Word the unstilled world still whirled
About the centre of the silent Word.

O my people, what have I done unto thee.

Where shall the word be found, where will the word
Resound? Not here, there is not enough silence
Not on the sea or on the islands, not
On the mainland, in the desert or the rain land,
For those who walk in darkness
Both in the day time and in the night time
The right time and the right place are not here
No place of grace for those who avoid the face
No time to rejoice for those who walk among noise and deny the voice

Will the veiled sister pray for
Those who walk in darkness, who chose thee and oppose thee,
Those who are torn on the horn between season and season, time and
    time, between
Hour and hour, word and word, power and power, those who wait
In darkness? Will the veiled sister pray
For children at the gate
Who will not go away and cannot pray:
Pray for those who chose and oppose

O my people, what have I done unto thee.

Will the veiled sister between the slender
Yew trees pray for those who offend her
And are terrified and cannot surrender
And affirm before the world and deny between the rocks
In the last desert between the last blue rocks
The desert in the garden the garden in the desert
Of drouth, spitting from the mouth the withered apple-seed.

O my people.

VI

Although I do not hope to turn again
Although I do not hope
Although I do not hope to turn

Wavering between the profit and the loss
In this brief transit where the dreams cross
The dreamcrossed twilight between birth and dying
(Bless me father) though I do not wish to wish these things
From the wide window towards the granite shore
The white sails still fly seaward, seaward flying
Unbroken wings

And the lost heart stiffens and rejoices
In the lost lilac and the lost sea voices
And the weak spirit quickens to rebel
For the bent golden-rod and the lost sea smell
Quickens to recover
The cry of quail and the whirling plover
And the blind eye creates
The empty forms between the ivory gates
And smell renews the salt savour of the sandy earth

This is the time of tension between dying and birth
The place of solitude where three dreams cross
Between blue rocks
But when the voices shaken from the yew-tree drift away
Let the other yew be shaken and reply.
Blessèd sister, holy mother, spirit of the fountain, spirit of the garden,
Suffer us not to mock ourselves with falsehood
Teach us to care and not to care
Teach us to sit still
Even among these rocks,
Our peace in His will

ASH-WEDNESDAY, 1930

And even among these rocks
Sister, mother
And spirit of the river, spirit of the sea,
Suffer me not to be separated

And let my cry come unto Thee.

ARIEL POEMS

Journey of the Magi

'A cold coming we had of it,
Just the worst time of the year
For a journey, and such a long journey:
The ways deep and the weather sharp,
The very dead of winter.'
And the camels galled, sore-footed, refractory,
Lying down in the melting snow.
There were times we regretted
The summer palaces on slopes, the terraces,
And the silken girls bringing sherbet.
Then the camel men cursing and grumbling
And running away, and wanting their liquor and women,
And the night-fires going out, and the lack of shelters,
And the cities hostile and the towns unfriendly
And the villages dirty and charging high prices:
A hard time we had of it.
At the end we preferred to travel all night,
Sleeping in snatches,
With the voices singing in our ears, saying
That this was all folly.

Then at dawn we came down to a temperate valley,
Wet, below the snow line, smelling of vegetation,
With a running stream and a water-mill beating the
        darkness,
And three trees on the low sky.
And an old white horse galloped away in the meadow.
Then we came to a tavern with vine-leaves over the lintel,
Six hands at an open door dicing for pieces of silver,
And feet kicking the empty wine-skins.
But there was no information, so we continued
And arrived at evening, not a moment too soon
Finding the place; it was (you may say) satisfactory.

All this was a long time ago, I remember,
And I would do it again, but set down
This set down
This: were we led all that way for
Birth or Death? There was a Birth, certainly,
We had evidence and no doubt. I had seen birth and death,
But had thought they were different; this Birth was
Hard and bitter agony for us, like Death, our death.
We returned to our places, these Kingdoms,
But no longer at ease here, in the old dispensation,
With an alien people clutching their gods.
I should be glad of another death.

A Song for Simeon

Lord, the Roman hyacinths are blooming in bowls and
The winter sun creeps by the snow hills;
The stubborn season has made stand.
My life is light, waiting for the death wind,
Like a feather on the back of my hand.
Dust in sunlight and memory in corners
Wait for the wind that chills towards the dead land.

   Grant us thy peace.
I have walked many years in this city,
Kept faith and fast, provided for the poor,
Have given and taken honour and ease.
There went never any rejected from my door.
Who shall remember my house, where shall live my children's children
When the time of sorrow is come?
They will take to the goat's path, and the fox's home,
Fleeing from the foreign faces and the foreign swords.

   Before the time of cords and scourges and lamentation
Grant us thy peace.
Before the stations of the mountain of desolation,
Before the certain hour of maternal sorrow,
Now at this birth season of decease,
Let the Infant, the still unspeaking and unspoken Word,
Grant Israel's consolation
To one who has eighty years and no to-morrow.

   According to thy word.
They shall praise Thee and suffer in every generation
With glory and derision,
Light upon light, mounting the saints' stair.
Not for me the martyrdom, the ecstasy of thought and prayer,
Not for me the ultimate vision.

Grant me thy peace.
(And a sword shall pierce thy heart,
Thine also).
I am tired with my own life and the lives of those after me,
I am dying in my own death and the deaths of those after me.
Let thy servant depart,
Having seen thy salvation.

Animula

'Issues from the hand of God, the simple soul'
To a flat world of changing lights and noise,
To light, dark, dry or damp, chilly or warm;
Moving between the legs of tables and of chairs,
Rising or falling, grasping at kisses and toys,
Advancing boldly, sudden to take alarm,
Retreating to the corner of arm and knee,
Eager to be reassured, taking pleasure
In the fragrant brilliance of the Christmas tree,
Pleasure in the wind, the sunlight and the sea;
Studies the sunlit pattern on the floor
And running stags around a silver tray;
Confounds the actual and the fanciful,
Content with playing-cards and kings and queens,
What the fairies do and what the servants say.
The heavy burden of the growing soul
Perplexes and offends more, day by day;
Week by week, offends and perplexes more
With the imperatives of 'is and seems'
And may and may not, desire and control.
The pain of living and the drug of dreams
Curl up the small soul in the window seat
Behind the *Encyclopaedia Britannica.*
Issues from the hand of time the simple soul
Irresolute and selfish, misshapen, lame,
Unable to fare forward or retreat,
Fearing the warm reality, the offered good,
Denying the importunity of the blood,
Shadow of its own shadows, spectre in its own gloom,
Leaving disordered papers in a dusty room;
Living first in the silence after the viaticum.

Pray for Guiterriez, avid of speed and power,
For Boudin, blown to pieces,
For this one who made a great fortune,
And that one who went his own way.
Pray for Floret, by the boarhound slain between the yew trees,
Pray for us now and at the hour of our birth.

Marina

*Quis hic locus, quae
regio, quae mundi plaga?*

What seas what shores what grey rocks and what islands
What water lapping the bow
And scent of pine and the woodthrush singing through the fog
What images return
O my daughter.

Those who sharpen the tooth of the dog, meaning
Death
Those who glitter with the glory of the hummingbird, meaning
Death
Those who sit in the sty of contentment, meaning
Death
Those who suffer the ecstasy of the animals, meaning
Death

Are become unsubstantial, reduced by a wind,
A breath of pine, and the woodsong fog
By this grace dissolved in place

What is this face, less clear and clearer
The pulse in the arm, less strong and stronger —
Given or lent? more distant than stars and nearer than the eye

Whispers and small laughter between leaves and hurrying feet
Under sleep, where all the waters meet.

Bowsprit cracked with ice and paint cracked with heat.
I made this, I have forgotten
And remember.
The rigging weak and the canvas rotten
Between one June and another September.

Made this unknowing, half conscious, unknown, my own.
The garboard strake leaks, the seams need caulking.
This form, this face, this life
Living to live in a world of time beyond me; let me
Resign my life for this life, my speech for that unspoken,
The awakened, lips parted, the hope, the new ships.

What seas what shores what granite islands towards my timbers
And woodthrush calling through the fog
My daughter.

The Cultivation of Christmas Trees

There are several attitudes towards Christmas,
Some of which we may disregard:
The social, the torpid, the patently commercial,
The rowdy (the pubs being open till midnight),
And the childish — which is not that of the child
For whom the candle is a star, and the gilded angel
Spreading its wings at the summit of the tree
Is not only a decoration, but an angel.
The child wonders at the Christmas Tree:
Let him continue in the spirit of wonder
At the Feast as an event not accepted as a pretext;
So that the glittering rapture, the amazement
Of the first-remembered Christmas Tree,
So that the surprises, delight in new possessions
(Each one with its peculiar and exciting smell),
The expectation of the goose or turkey
And the expected awe on its appearance,
So that the reverence and the gaiety
May not be forgotten in later experience,
In the bored habituation, the fatigue, the tedium,
The awareness of death, the consciousness of failure,
Or in the piety of the convert
Which may be tainted with a self-conceit
Displeasing to God and disrespectful to the children
(And here I remember also with gratitude
St. Lucy, her carol, and her crown of fire):
So that before the end, the eightieth Christmas
(By 'eightieth' meaning whichever is the last)
The accumulated memories of annual emotion
May be concentrated into a great joy
Which shall be also a great fear, as on the occasion
When fear came upon every soul:
Because the beginning shall remind us of the end
And the first coming of the second coming.

UNFINISHED POEMS

Sweeney Agonistes

Fragments of an Aristophanic Melodrama

Orestes: *You don't see them, you don't — but* I *see them: they are hunting me down, I must move on.*

Choephoroi.

Hence the soul cannot be possessed of the divine union, until it has divested itself of the love of created beings.

St. John of the Cross.

Fragment of a Prologue

DUSTY.　　DORIS.

DUSTY: How about Pereira?

DORIS:　　　　　　　What about Pereira?
I don't care.

DUSTY:　　　　　　　You don't care!
Who pays the rent?

DORIS:　　　　　　　Yes he pays the rent

DUSTY: Well some men don't and some men do
Some men don't and you know who

DORIS: You can have Pereira

DUSTY:　　　　　　　What about Pereira?

DORIS: He's no gentleman, Pereira:
You can't trust him!

DUSTY:　　　　　　　Well that's true.
He's no gentleman if you can't trust him
And *if* you can't trust him —
Then you never know what he's going to do.

DORIS: No it wouldn't do to be too nice to Pereira.

DUSTY: Now Sam's a gentleman through and through.

DORIS: I like Sam

DUSTY:　　　　　　　*I* like Sam
Yes and Sam's a nice boy too.
He's a funny fellow

DORIS:　　　　　　　He *is* a funny fellow
He's like a fellow once I knew.
He could make you laugh.

DUSTY: Sam can make you laugh:
   Sam's all right
DORIS: But Pereira won't do.
   We can't have Pereira
DUSTY: Well what you going to do?
TELEPHONE: Ting a ling ling
     Ting a ling ling
DUSTY: That's Pereira
DORIS: Yes that's Pereira
DUSTY: Well what you going to do?
TELEPHONE: Ting a ling ling
     Ting a ling ling
DUSTY: That's Pereira
DORIS: Well can't you stop that horrible noise?
   Pick up the receiver
DUSTY: What'll I say?
DORIS: Say what you like: say I'm ill,
   Say I broke my leg on the stairs
   Say we've had a fire
DUSTY: Hello Hello are you there?
   Yes this is Miss Dorrance's *flat* —
   Oh Mr. Pereira is that you? how do you do!
   Oh I'm *so* sorry. I *am* so sorry
   But Doris came home with a terrible chill
   No, just a chill
   Oh I *think* it's only a chill
   Yes indeed I hope so too —
   Well I *hope* we shan't have to call a doctor
   Doris just hates having a doctor
   She says will you ring up on Monday
   She hopes to be all right on Monday
   I say do you mind if I ring off now
   She's got her feet in mustard and water
   I said I'm giving her mustard and water
   All right, Monday you'll phone through.
   Yes I'll tell her. Good bye. Goooood bye.
   I'm sure, that's very kind of *you*.
      Ah-h-h
DORIS: Now I'm going to cut the cards for to-night.
   Oh guess what the first is

UNFINISHED POEMS

DUSTY: First is. What is?

DORIS: The King of Clubs

DUSTY: That's Pereira

DORIS: It might be Sweeney

DUSTY: It's Pereira

DORIS: It might *just* as well be Sweeney

DUSTY: Well anyway it's very queer.

DORIS: Here's the four of diamonds, what's that mean?

DUSTY: (*reading*) 'A small sum of money, or a present
                    Of wearing apparel, or a party'.
                    That's queer too.

DORIS: Here's the three. What's that mean?

DUSTY: 'News of an absent friend'. — Pereira!

DORIS: The Queen of Hearts! — Mrs. Porter!

DUSTY: Or it might be you

DORIS: Or it might be you
        We're all hearts. You can't be sure.
        It just depends on what comes next.
        You've got to *think* when you read the cards,
        It's not a thing that anyone can do.

DUSTY: Yes I know you've a touch with the cards
        What comes next?

DORIS: What comes next. It's the six.

DUSTY: 'A quarrel. An estrangement. Separation of friends'.

DORIS: Here's the two of spades.

DUSTY: The *two* of *spades*!
        THAT'S THE COFFIN!!

DORIS: THAT'S THE COFFIN?
        Oh good heavens what'll I do?
        Just before a party too!

DUSTY: Well it needn't be yours, it may mean a friend.

DORIS: No it's mine. I'm sure it's mine.
        I dreamt of weddings all last night.
        Yes it's mine. I know it's mine.
        Oh good heavens what'll I do.
        Well I'm not going to draw any more,
        You cut for luck. You cut for luck.
        It might break the spell. You cut for luck.

DUSTY: The Knave of Spades.

DORIS: That'll be Snow

DUSTY: Or it might be Swarts
DORIS: Or it might be Snow
DUSTY: It's a funny thing how I draw court cards —
DORIS: There's a lot in the way you pick them up
DUSTY: There's an awful lot in the way you feel
DORIS: Sometimes they'll tell you nothing at all
DUSTY: You've got to know what you want to ask them
DORIS: You've got to know what you want to know
DUSTY: It's no use asking them too much
DORIS: It's no use asking more than once
DUSTY: Sometimes they're no use at all.
DORIS: I'd like to know about that coffin.
DUSTY: Well I never! What did I tell you?
        Wasn't I saying I always draw court cards?
        The Knave of Hearts!
                    (*Whistle outside of the window.*)
                    Well I *never*
        What a co*in*cidence! Cards are queer!
                    (*Whistle again.*)
DORIS: Is that Sam?
DUSTY: Of course it's Sam!
DORIS: Of course, the Knave of Hearts *is* Sam!
DUSTY (*leaning out of the window*): Hello Sam!
WAUCHOPE: Hello dear
        How many's up there?
DUSTY: Nobody's up here
        How many's down there?
WAUCHOPE: Four of us here.
        Wait till I put the car round the corner
        We'll be right up
DUSTY: All right, come up.
DUSTY (*to* DORIS): Cards are queer.
DORIS: I'd like to know about that coffin.
        KNOCK KNOCK KNOCK
        KNOCK KNOCK KNOCK
        KNOCK
        KNOCK
        KNOCK

UNFINISHED POEMS

DORIS. DUSTY. WAUCHOPE. HORSFALL. KLIPSTEIN.
KRUMPACKER.

WAUCHOPE: Hello Doris! Hello Dusty! How do you do!
How come? how come? will you permit me —
I think you girls both know Captain Horsfall —
We want you to meet two friends of ours,
American gentlemen here on business.
Meet Mr. Klipstein. Meet Mr. Krumpacker.

KLIPSTEIN: How do you do

KRUMPACKER: How do you do

KLIPSTEIN: I'm very pleased to make your acquaintance

KRUMPACKER: Extremely pleased to become acquainted

KLIPSTEIN: Sam — I should say Loot Sam Wauchope

KRUMPACKER: Of the Canadian Expeditionary Force —

KLIPSTEIN: The Loot has told us a lot about you.

KRUMPACKER: We were all in the war together
Klip and me and the Cap and Sam.

KLIPSTEIN: Yes we did our bit, as you folks say,
I'll tell the world we got the Hun on the run

KRUMPACKER: What about that poker game? eh what Sam?
What about that poker game in Bordeaux?
Yes Miss Dorrance you get Sam
To tell about that poker game in Bordeaux.

DUSTY: Do you know London well, Mr. Krumpacker?

KLIPSTEIN: No we never been here before

KRUMPACKER: We hit this town last night for the first time

KLIPSTEIN: And I certainly hope it won't be the last time.

DORIS: You like London, Mr. Klipstein?

KRUMPACKER: Do we like London? do we like London!
Do we like London!! Eh what Klip?

KLIPSTEIN: Say, Miss — er — uh — London's swell.
We like London fine.

KRUMPACKER: Perfectly slick.

DUSTY: Why don't you come and live here then?

KLIPSTEIN: Well, no, Miss — er — you haven't quite got it
(I'm afraid I didn't quite catch your name —
But I'm very pleased to meet you all the same) —
London's a little too gay for us
Yes I'll say a little too gay.

KRUMPACKER: Yes London's a little too gay for us

119

Don't think I mean anything *coarse* —
But I'm afraid we couldn't stand the pace.
What about it Klip?

KLIPSTEIN: You said it, Krum.

London's a slick place, London's a swell place,
London's a fine place to come on a visit —

KRUMPACKER: Specially when you got a real live Britisher
A guy like Sam to show you around.
Sam of course is at *home* in London,
And he's promised to show us around.

Fragment of an Agon

SWEENEY. WAUCHOPE. HORSFALL. KLIPSTEIN.
KRUMPACKER. SWARTS. SNOW. DORIS. DUSTY.

SWEENEY: I'll carry you off
    To a cannibal isle.
DORIS: You'll be the cannibal!
SWEENEY: You'll be the missionary!
    You'll be my little seven stone missionary!
    I'll gobble you up. I'll be the cannibal.
DORIS: You'll carry me off? To a cannibal isle?
SWEENEY: I'll be the cannibal.
DORIS: I'll be the missionary.
    I'll convert you!
SWEENEY: I'll convert *you*!
    Into a stew.
    A nice little, white little, missionary stew.
DORIS: You wouldn't eat me!
SWEENEY: Yes I'd eat you!
    In a nice little, white little, soft little, tender little,
    Juicy little, right little, missionary stew.
    You see this egg
    You see this egg
    Well that's life on a crocodile isle.
    There's no telephones
    There's no gramophones
    There's no motor cars
    No two-seaters, no six-seaters,
    No Citroën, no Rolls-Royce.
    Nothing to eat but the fruit as it grows.
    Nothing to see but the palmtrees one way
    And the sea the other way,
    Nothing to hear but the sound of the surf.
    Nothing at all but three things
DORIS: What things?

SWEENEY: Birth, and copulation and death.
        That's all, that's all, that's all, that's all,
        Birth, and copulation, and death.
DORIS: I'd be bored.
SWEENEY: You'd be bored.
        Birth, and copulation, and death.
DORIS: I'd be bored.
SWEENEY: You'd be bored.
        Birth, and copulation, and death.
        That's all the facts when you come to brass tacks:
        Birth, and copulation, and death.
        I've been born, and once is enough.
        You don't remember, but I remember,
        Once is enough.

SONG BY WAUCHOPE AND HORSFALL
SWARTS AS TAMBO. SNOW AS BONES

Under the bamboo
Bamboo bamboo
Under the bamboo tree
Two live as one
One live as two
Two live as three
Under the bam
Under the boo
Under the bamboo tree.

Where the breadfruit fall
And the penguin call
And the sound is the sound of the sea
Under the bam
Under the boo
Under the bamboo tree

Where the Gauguin maids
In the banyan shades
Wear palmleaf drapery
Under the bam
Under the boo
Under the bamboo tree.

Tell me in what part of the wood
Do you want to flirt with me?
Under the breadfruit, banyan, palmleaf
Or under the bamboo tree?
Any old tree will do for me
Any old wood is just as good
Any old isle is just my style
Any fresh egg
Any fresh egg
And the sound of the coral sea.

DORIS: I don't like eggs; I never liked eggs;
And I don't like life on your crocodile isle.

SONG BY KLIPSTEIN AND KRUMPACKER

SNOW AND SWARTS AS BEFORE

My little island girl
My little island girl
I'm going to stay with you
And we wont worry what to do
We won't have to catch any trains
And we won't go home when it rains
We'll gather hibiscus flowers
For it won't be minutes but hours
For it won't be hours but years

diminuendo ⎰ *And the morning*
And the evening
And noontide
And night
Morning
Evening
Noontime
Night

DORIS: That's not life, that's no life
Why I'd just as soon be dead.
SWEENEY: That's what life is. Just is
DORIS: What is?
What's that life is?

SWEENEY: Life is death.
          I knew a man once did a girl in —
DORIS: Oh Mr. Sweeney, please don't talk,
          I cut the cards before you came
          And I drew the coffin
SWARTS: *You* drew the coffin?
DORIS: I drew the COFFIN very last card.
          I don't care for such conversation
          A woman runs a terrible risk.
SNOW: Let Mr. Sweeney continue his story.
          I assure you, Sir, we are very interested.
SWEENEY: I knew a man once did a girl in.
          Any man might do a girl in
          Any man has to, needs to, wants to
          Once in a lifetime, do a girl in
          Well he kept her there in a bath
          With a gallon of lysol in a bath
SWARTS: These fellows always get pinched in the end.
SNOW: Excuse me, they don't all get pinched in the end.
          What about them bones on Epsom Heath?
          I seen that in the papers
          You seen it in the papers
          They *don't* all get pinched in the end.
DORIS: A woman runs a terrible risk.
SNOW: Let Mr. Sweeney continue his story.
SWEENEY: This one didn't get pinched in the end
          But that's another story too.
          This went on for a couple of months
          Nobody came
          And nobody went
          But he took in the milk and he paid the rent.
SWARTS: What did he do?
          All that time, what did he do?
SWEENEY: What did he do! what did he do?
          That don't apply.
          Talk to live men about what they do.
          He used to come and see me sometimes
          I'd give him a drink and cheer him up.
DORIS: Cheer him up?
DUSTY: Cheer him up?

UNFINISHED POEMS

SWEENEY: Well here again that don't apply
            But I've gotta use words when I talk to you.
            But here's what I was going to say.
            He didn't know if he was alive
                        and the girl was dead
            He didn't know if the girl was alive
                        and he was dead
            He didn't know if they were both alive
                        or both were dead
            If he was alive then the milkman wasn't
                        and the rent-collector wasn't
            And if they were alive then he was dead.
            There wasn't any joint
            There wasn't any joint
            For when you're alone
            When you're alone like he was alone
            You're either or neither
            I tell you again it don't apply
            Death or life or life or death
            Death is life and life is death
            I gotta use words when I talk to you
            But if you understand or if you don't
            That's nothing to me and nothing to you
            We all gotta do what we gotta do
            We're gona sit here and drink this booze
            We're gona sit here and have a tune
            We're gona stay and we're gona go
            And somebody's gotta pay the rent
DORIS: I know who
SWEENEY: But that's nothing to me and nothing to you.

            FULL CHORUS: WAUCHOPE, HORSFALL, KLIPSTEIN,
                        KRUMPACKER
            When you're alone in the middle of the night and
                        you wake in a sweat and a hell of a fright
            When you're alone in the middle of the bed and
                        you wake like someone hit you in the head
            You've had a cream of a nightmare dream and
                        you've got the hoo-ha's coming to you.

Hoo hoo hoo

You dreamt you waked up at seven o'clock and it's
    foggy and it's damp and it's dawn and it's dark

And you wait for a knock and the turning of a lock
    for you know the hangman's waiting for you.

And perhaps you're alive

And perhaps you're dead

Hoo ha ha

Hoo ha ha

Hoo

Hoo

Hoo

KNOCK   KNOCK   KNOCK

KNOCK   KNOCK   KNOCK

KNOCK

KNOCK

KNOCK

Coriolan

I. Triumphal March

Stone, bronze, stone, steel, stone, oakleaves, horses' heels
Over the paving.
And the flags. And the trumpets. And so many eagles.
How many? Count them. And such a press of people.
We hardly knew ourselves that day, or knew the City.
This is the way to the temple, and we so many crowding the way.
So many waiting, how many waiting? what did it matter, on such a day?
Are they coming? No, not yet. You can see some eagles. And hear the
    trumpets.
Here they come. Is he coming?
The natural wakeful life of our Ego is a perceiving.
We can wait with our stools and our sausages.
What comes first? Can you see? Tell us. It is

    5,800,000 rifles and carbines,
      102,000 machine guns,
       28,000 trench mortars,
       53,000 field and heavy guns,
I cannot tell how many projectiles, mines and fuses,
       13,000 aeroplanes,
       24,000 aeroplane engines,
       50,000 ammunition waggons,
now   55,000 army waggons,
       11,000 field kitchens,
        1,150 field bakeries.

What a time that took. Will it be he now? No,
Those are the golf club Captains, these the Scouts,
And now the *société gymnastique de Poissy*
And now come the Mayor and the Liverymen. Look
There he is now, look:
There is no interrogation in his eyes
Or in the hands, quiet over the horse's neck,
And the eyes watchful, waiting, perceiving, indifferent.
O hidden under the dove's wing, hidden in the turtle's breast,

UNFINISHED POEMS

Under the palmtree at noon, under the running water
At the still point of the turning world. O hidden.

Now they go up to the temple. Then the sacrifice.
Now come the virgins bearing urns, urns containing
Dust
Dust
Dust of dust, and now
Stone, bronze, stone, steel, stone, oakleaves, horses' heels
Over the paving.

This is all we could see. But how many eagles! and how many trumpets!
(And Easter Day, we didn't get to the country,
So we took young Cyril to church. And they rang a bell
And he said right out loud, *crumpets*.)
                         Don't throw away that sausage,
It'll come in handy. He's artful. Please, will you
Give us a light?
Light
Light
Et les soldats faisaient la haie? ILS LA FAISAIENT.

II. Difficulties of a Statesman

CRY what shall I cry?
All flesh is grass: comprehending
The Companions of the Bath, the Knights of the British Empire, the
     Cavaliers,
O Cavaliers! of the Legion of Honour,
The Order of the Black Eagle (1st and 2nd class),
And the Order of the Rising Sun.
Cry cry what shall I cry?
The first thing to do is to form the committees:
The consultative councils, the standing committees, select committees
     and sub-committees.
One secretary will do for several committees.
What shall I cry?
Arthur Edward Cyril Parker is appointed telephone operator
At a salary of one pound ten a week rising by annual increments of five
     shillings
To two pounds ten a week; with a bonus of thirty shillings at Christmas
And one week's leave a year.
A committee has been appointed to nominate a commission of
     engineers
To consider the Water Supply.
A commission is appointed
For Public Works, chiefly the question of rebuilding the fortifications.
A commission is appointed
To confer with a Volscian commission
About perpetual peace: the fletchers and javelin-makers and smiths
Have appointed a joint committee to protest against the reduction of
     orders.
Meanwhile the guards shake dice on the marches
And the frogs (O Mantuan) croak in the marshes.
Fireflies flare against the faint sheet lightning
What shall I cry?
Mother mother

Here is the row of family portraits, dingy busts, all looking remarkably
    Roman,
Remarkably like each other, lit up successively by the flare
Of a sweaty torchbearer, yawning.
O hidden under the. . . Hidden under the. . . Where the dove's foot
    rested and locked for a moment,
A still moment, repose of noon, set under the upper branches of noon's
    widest tree
Under the breast feather stirred by the small wind after noon
There the cyclamen spreads its wings, there the clematis droops over
    the lintel
O mother (not among these busts, all correctly inscribed)
I a tired head among these heads
Necks strong to bear them
Noses strong to break the wind
Mother
May we not be some time, almost now, together,
If the mactations, immolations, oblations, impetrations,
Are now observed
May we not be
O hidden
Hidden in the stillness of noon, in the silent croaking night.
Come with the sweep of the little bat's wing, with the small flare of the
    firefly or lightning bug,
'Rising and falling, crowned with dust', the small creatures,
The small creatures chirp thinly through the dust, through the night.
O mother
What shall I cry?
We demand a committee, a representative committee, a committee of
    investigation
RESIGN RESIGN RESIGN

MINOR POEMS

Eyes that last I saw in tears

Eyes that last I saw in tears
Through division
Here in death's dream kingdom
The golden vision reappears
I see the eyes but not the tears
This is my affliction.

This is my affliction
Eyes I shall not see again
Eyes of decision
Eyes I shall not see unless
At the door of death's other kingdom
Where, as in this,
The eyes outlast a little while
A little while outlast the tears
And hold us in derision.

The wind sprang up at four o'clock

The wind sprang up at four o'clock
The wind sprang up and broke the bells
Swinging between life and death
Here, in death's dream kingdom
The waking echo of confusing strife
Is it a dream or something else
When the surface of the blackened river
Is a face that sweats with tears?
I saw across the blackened river
The camp fire shake with alien spears.
Here, across death's other river
The Tartar horsemen shake their spears.

Five-Finger Exercises

I. *Lines to a Persian Cat*

The songsters of the air repair
To the green fields of Russell Square.
Beneath the trees there is no ease
For the dull brain, the sharp desires
And the quick eyes of Woolly Bear.
There is no relief but in grief.
O when will the creaking heart cease?
When will the broken chair give ease?
Why will the summer day delay?
When will Time flow away?

II. *Lines to a Yorkshire Terrier*

In a brown field stood a tree
And the tree was crookt and dry.
In a black sky, from a green cloud
Natural forces shriek'd aloud,
Screamed, rattled, muttered endlessly.
Little dog was safe and warm
Under a cretonne eiderdown,
Yet the field was cracked and brown
And the tree was cramped and dry.
Pollicle dogs and cats all must
Jellicle cats and dogs all must
Like undertakers, come to dust.
Here a little dog I pause
Heaving up my prior paws,
Pause, and sleep endlessly.

III. *Lines to a Duck in the Park*

The long light shakes across the lake,
The forces of the morning quake,

The dawn is slant across the lawn,
Here is no eft or mortal snake
But only sluggish duck and drake.
I have seen the morning shine,
I have had the Bread and Wine,
Let the feathered mortals take
That which is their mortal due,
Pinching bread and finger too,
Easier had than squirming worm;
For I know, and so should you
That soon the enquiring worm shall try
Our well-preserved complacency.

IV. *Lines to Ralph Hodgson Esqre.*

How delightful to meet Mr. Hodgson!
(Everyone wants to know *him*)
With his musical sound
And his Baskerville Hound
Which, just at a word from his master
Will follow you faster and faster
And tear you limb from limb.
How delightful to meet Mr. Hodgson!
Who is worshipped by all waitresses
(They regard him as something apart)
While on his palate fine he presses
The juice of the gooseberry tart.
How delightful to meet Mr. Hodgson!
 (Everyone wants to know *him*).
He has 999 canaries
And round his head finches and fairies
In jubilant rapture skim.
How delightful to meet Mr. Hodgson!
 (Everyone wants to meet *him*).

V. *Lines for Cuscuscaraway and Mirza Murad Ali Beg*

How unpleasant to meet Mr. Eliot!
With his features of clerical cut,
And his brow so grim

And his mouth so prim
And his conversation, so nicely
Restricted to What Precisely
And If and Perhaps and But.
How unpleasant to meet Mr. Eliot!
With a bobtail cur
In a coat of fur
And a porpentine cat
And a wopsical hat:
How unpleasant to meet Mr. Eliot!
    (Whether his mouth be open or shut).

Landscapes

★

I. New Hampshire

Children's voices in the orchard
Between the blossom- and the fruit-time:
Golden head, crimson head,
Between the green tip and the root.
Black wing, brown wing, hover over;
Twenty years and the spring is over;
To-day grieves, to-morrow grieves,
Cover me over, light-in-leaves;
Golden head, black wing,
Cling, swing,
Spring, sing,
Swing up into the apple-tree.

II. Virginia

Red river, red river,
Slow flow heat is silence
No will is still as a river
Still. Will heat move
Only through the mocking-bird
Heard once? Still hills
Wait. Gates wait. Purple trees,
White trees, wait, wait,
Delay, decay. Living, living,
Never moving. Ever moving
Iron thoughts came with me
And go with me:
Red river, river, river.

III. Usk

Do not suddenly break the branch, or
Hope to find
The white hart behind the white well.
Glance aside, not for lance, do not spell
Old enchantments. Let them sleep.
'Gently dip, but not too deep',
Lift your eyes
Where the roads dip and where the roads rise
Seek only there
Where the grey light meets the green air
The hermit's chapel, the pilgrim's prayer.

IV. Rannoch, by Glencoe

Here the crow starves, here the patient stag
Breeds for the rifle. Between the soft moor
And the soft sky, scarcely room
To leap or soar. Substance crumbles, in the thin air
Moon cold or moon hot. The road winds in
Listlessness of ancient war,
Languor of broken steel,
Clamour of confused wrong, apt
In silence. Memory is strong
Beyond the bone. Pride snapped,
Shadow of pride is long, in the long pass
No concurrence of bone.

V. Cape Ann

O quick quick quick, quick hear the song-sparrow,
Swamp-sparrow, fox-sparrow, vesper-sparrow
At dawn and dusk. Follow the dance
Of the goldfinch at noon. Leave to chance
The Blackburnian warbler, the shy one. Hail
With shrill whistle the note of the quail, the bob-white
Dodging by bay-bush. Follow the feet
Of the walker, the water-thrush. Follow the flight
Of the dancing arrow, the purple martin. Greet
In silence the bullbat. All are delectable. Sweet sweet sweet
But resign this land at the end, resign it
To its true owner, the tough one, the sea-gull.

The palaver is finished.

Lines for an Old Man

The tiger in the tiger-pit
Is not more irritable than I.
The whipping tail is not more still
Than when I smell the enemy
Writhing in the essential blood
Or dangling from the friendly tree.
When I lay bare the tooth of wit
The hissing over the archèd tongue
Is more affectionate than hate,
More bitter than the love of youth,
And inaccessible by the young.
Reflected from my golden eye
The dullard knows that he is mad.

Tell me if I am not glad!

CHORUSES FROM 'THE ROCK' 1934

CHORUSES FROM 'THE ROCK', 1934

I

The Eagle soars in the summit of Heaven,
The Hunter with his dogs pursues his circuit.
O perpetual revolution of configured stars,
O perpetual recurrence of determined seasons,
O world of spring and autumn, birth and dying!
The endless cycle of idea and action,
Endless invention, endless experiment,
Brings knowledge of motion, but not of stillness;
Knowledge of speech, but not of silence;
Knowledge of words, and ignorance of the Word.
All our knowledge brings us nearer to our ignorance,
All our ignorance brings us nearer to death,
But nearness to death no nearer to GOD.
Where is the Life we have lost in living?
Where is the wisdom we have lost in knowledge?
Where is the knowledge we have lost in information?
The cycles of Heaven in twenty centuries
Bring us farther from GOD and nearer to the Dust.

I journeyed to London, to the timekept City,
Where the River flows, with foreign flotations.
There I was told: we have too many churches,
And too few chop-houses. There I was told:
Let the vicars retire. Men do not need the Church
In the place where they work, but where they spend their Sundays.
In the City, we need no bells:
Let them waken the suburbs.
I journeyed to the suburbs, and there I was told:
We toil for six days, on the seventh we must motor
To Hindhead, or Maidenhead.
If the weather is foul we stay at home and read the papers.
In industrial districts, there I was told
Of economic laws.

In the pleasant countryside, there it seemed
That the country now is only fit for picnics.
And the Church does not seem to be wanted
In country or in suburb; and in the town
Only for important weddings.

CHORUS LEADER:

Silence! and preserve respectful distance.
For I perceive approaching
The Rock. Who will perhaps answer our doubtings.
The Rock. The Watcher. The Stranger.
He who has seen what has happened
And who sees what is to happen.
The Witness. The Critic. The Stranger.
The God-shaken, in whom is the truth inborn.

Enter the ROCK, *led by a* BOY:

THE ROCK:

The lot of man is ceaseless labour,
Or ceaseless idleness, which is still harder,
Or irregular labour, which is not pleasant.
I have trodden the winepress alone, and I know
That it is hard to be really useful, resigning
The things that men count for happiness, seeking
The good deeds that lead to obscurity, accepting
With equal face those that bring ignominy,
The applause of all or the love of none.
All men are ready to invest their money
But most expect dividends.
I say to you: *Make perfect your will.*
I say: take no thought of the harvest,
But only of proper sowing.

The world turns and the world changes,
But one thing does not change.
In all of my years, one thing does not change.
However you disguise it, this thing does not change:
The perpetual struggle of Good and Evil.
Forgetful, you neglect your shrines and churches;
The men you are in these times deride

CHORUSES FROM 'THE ROCK', 1934

What has been done of good, you find explanations
To satisfy the rational and enlightened mind.
Second, you neglect and belittle the desert.
The desert is not remote in southern tropics,
The desert is not only around the corner,
The desert is squeezed in the tube-train next to you,
The desert is in the heart of your brother.
The good man is the builder, if he build what is good.
I will show you the things that are now being done,
And some of the things that were long ago done,
That you may take heart. Make perfect your will.
Let me show you the work of the humble. Listen.

The lights fade; in the semi-darkness the voices of WORKMEN *are heard
chanting.*

   In the vacant places
   We will build with new bricks
   There are hands and machines
   And clay for new brick
   And lime for new mortar
   Where the bricks are fallen
   We will build with new stone
   Where the beams are rotten
   We will build with new timbers
   Where the word is unspoken
   We will build with new speech
   There is work together
   A Church for all
   And a job for each
   Every man to his work.

Now a group of WORKMEN *is silhouetted against the dim sky. From farther
away, they are answered by voices of the* UNEMPLOYED.

   No man has hired us
   With pocketed hands
   And lowered faces
   We stand about in open places
   And shiver in unlit rooms.
   Only the wind moves
   Over empty fields, untilled

Where the plough rests, at an angle
To the furrow. In this land
There shall be one cigarette to two men,
To two women one half pint of bitter
Ale. In this land
No man has hired us.
Our life is unwelcome, our death
Unmentioned in 'The Times'.

Chant of WORKMEN *again.*
The river flows, the seasons turn
The sparrow and starling have no time to waste.
If men do not build
How shall they live?
When the field is tilled
And the wheat is bread
They shall not die in a shortened bed
And a narrow sheet. In this street
There is no beginning, no movement, no peace and no end
But noise without speech, food without taste.
Without delay, without haste
We would build the beginning and the end of this street.
We build the meaning:
A Church for all
And a job for each
Each man to his work.

II

Thus your fathers were made
Fellow citizens of the saints, of the household of GOD, being built upon
   the foundation
Of apostles and prophets, Christ Jesus Himself the chief cornerstone.
But you, have you built well, that you now sit helpless in a ruined
   house?
Where many are born to idleness, to frittered lives and squalid deaths,
   embittered scorn in honeyless hives,
And those who would build and restore turn out the palms of their
   hands, or look in vain towards foreign lands for alms to be more or
   the urn to be filled.
Your building not fitly framed together, you sit ashamed and wonder
   whether and how you may be builded together for a habitation of
   GOD in the Spirit, the Spirit which moved on the face of the waters
   like a lantern set on the back of a tortoise.
And some say: 'How can we love our neighbour? For love must be
   made real in act, as desire unites with desired; we have only our
   labour to give and our labour is not required.
We wait on corners, with nothing to bring but the songs we can sing
   which nobody wants to hear sung;
Waiting to be flung in the end, on a heap less useful than dung'.
You, have you built well, have you forgotten the cornerstone?
Talking of right relations of men, but not of relations of men to GOD.
'Our citizenship is in Heaven'; yes, but that is the model and type for
   your citizenship upon earth.

When your fathers fixed the place of GOD,
And settled all the inconvenient saints,
Apostles, martyrs, in a kind of Whipsnade,
Then they could set about imperial expansion
Accompanied by industrial development.
Exporting iron, coal and cotton goods
And intellectual enlightenment

And everything, including capital
And several versions of the Word of GOD:
The British race assured of a mission
Performed it, but left much at home unsure.

Of all that was done in the past, you eat the fruit, either rotten or
    ripe.
And the Church must be forever building, and always decaying, and
    always being restored.
For every ill deed in the past we suffer the consequence:
For sloth, for avarice, gluttony, neglect of the Word of GOD,
For pride, for lechery, treachery, for every act of sin.
And of all that was done that was good, you have the inheritance.
For good and ill deeds belong to a man alone, when he stands alone on
    the other side of death,
But here upon earth you have the reward of the good and ill that was
    done by those who have gone before you.
And all that is ill you may repair if you walk together in humble
    repentance, expiating the sins of your fathers;
And all that was good you must fight to keep with hearts as devoted as
    those of your fathers who fought to gain it.
The Church must be forever building, for it is forever decaying within
    and attacked from without;
For this is the law of life; and you must remember that while there is
    time of prosperity
The people will neglect the Temple, and in time of adversity they will
    decry it.

What life have you if you have not life together?
There is no life that is not in community,
And no community not lived in praise of GOD.
Even the anchorite who meditates alone,
For whom the days and nights repeat the praise of GOD,
Prays for the Church, the Body of Christ incarnate.
And now you live dispersed on ribbon roads,
And no man knows or cares who is his neighbour
Unless his neighbour makes too much disturbance,
But all dash to and fro in motor cars,
Familiar with the roads and settled nowhere.
Nor does the family even move about together,

But every son would have his motor cycle,
And daughters ride away on casual pillions.

Much to cast down, much to build, much to restore;
Let the work not delay, time and the arm not waste;
Let the clay be dug from the pit, let the saw cut the stone,
Let the fire not be quenched in the forge.

III

The Word of the LORD came unto me, saying:
O miserable cities of designing men,
O wretched generation of enlightened men,
Betrayed in the mazes of your ingenuities,
Sold by the proceeds of your proper inventions:
I have given you hands which you turn from worship,
I have given you speech, for endless palaver,
I have given you my Law, and you set up commissions,
I have given you lips, to express friendly sentiments,
I have given you hearts, for reciprocal distrust.
I have given you power of choice, and you only alternate
Between futile speculation and unconsidered action.
Many are engaged in writing books and printing them,
Many desire to see their names in print,
Many read nothing but the race reports.
Much is your reading, but not the Word of GOD,
Much is your building, but not the House of GOD.
Will you build me a house of plaster, with corrugated roofing,
To be filled with a litter of Sunday newspapers?

IST MALE VOICE:
A Cry from the East:
What shall be done to the shore of smoky ships?
Will you leave my people forgetful and forgotten
To idleness, labour, and delirious stupor?
There shall be left the broken chimney,
The peeled hull, a pile of rusty iron,
In a street of scattered brick where the goat climbs,
Where My Word is unspoken.

2ND MALE VOICE:
A Cry from the North, from the West and from the South
Whence thousands travel daily to the timekept City;

Where My Word is unspoken,
In the land of lobelias and tennis flannels
The rabbit shall burrow and the thorn revisit,
The nettle shall flourish on the gravel court,
And the wind shall say: 'Here were decent godless people:
Their only monument the asphalt road
And a thousand lost golf balls'.

CHORUS:

We build in vain unless the LORD build with us.
Can you keep the City that the LORD keeps not with you?
A thousand policemen directing the traffic
Cannot tell you why you come or where you go.
A colony of cavies or a horde of active marmots
Build better than they that build without the LORD.
Shall we lift up our feet among perpetual ruins?
I have loved the beauty of Thy House, the peace of Thy sanctuary,
I have swept the floors and garnished the altars.
Where there is no temple there shall be no homes,
Though you have shelters and institutions,
Precarious lodgings while the rent is paid,
Subsiding basements where the rat breeds
Or sanitary dwellings with numbered doors
Or a house a little better than your neighbour's;
When the Stranger says: 'What is the meaning of this city?
Do you huddle close together because you love each other?'
What will you answer? 'We all dwell together
To make money from each other'? or 'This is a community'?
And the Stranger will depart and return to the desert.
O my soul, be prepared for the coming of the Stranger,
Be prepared for him who knows how to ask questions.

O weariness of men who turn from GOD
To the grandeur of your mind and the glory of your action,
To arts and inventions and daring enterprises,
To schemes of human greatness thoroughly discredited,
Binding the earth and the water to your service,
Exploiting the seas and developing the mountains,
Dividing the stars into common and preferred,
Engaged in devising the perfect refrigerator,

CHORUSES FROM 'THE ROCK', 1934

Engaged in working out a rational morality,
Engaged in printing as many books as possible,
Plotting of happiness and flinging empty bottles,
Turning from your vacancy to fevered enthusiasm
For nation or race or what you call humanity;
Though you forget the way to the Temple,
There is one who remembers the way to your door:
Life you may evade, but Death you shall not.
You shall not deny the Stranger.

IV

There are those who would build the Temple,
And those who prefer that the Temple should not be built.
In the days of Nehemiah the Prophet
There was no exception to the general rule.
In Shushan the palace, in the month Nisan,
He served the wine to the king Artaxerxes,
And he grieved for the broken city, Jerusalem;
And the King gave him leave to depart
That he might rebuild the city.
So he went, with a few, to Jerusalem,
And there, by the dragon's well, by the dung gate,
By the fountain gate, by the king's pool,
Jerusalem lay waste, consumed with fire;
No place for a beast to pass.
There were enemies without to destroy him,
And spies and self-seekers within,
When he and his men laid their hands to rebuilding the wall.
So they built as men must build
With the sword in one hand and the trowel in the other.

V

O Lord, deliver me from the man of excellent intention and impure
heart: for the heart is deceitful above all things, and desperately
wicked.

Sanballat the Horonite and Tobiah the Ammonite and Geshem the
Arabian: were doubtless men of public spirit and zeal.

Preserve me from the enemy who has something to gain: and from the
friend who has something to lose.

Remembering the words of Nehemiah the Prophet: 'The trowel in hand,
and the gun rather loose in the holster.'

Those who sit in a house of which the use is forgotten: are like snakes
that lie on mouldering stairs, content in the sunlight.

And the others run about like dogs, full of enterprise, sniffing and
barking: they say, 'This house is a nest of serpents, let us destroy it,

And have done with these abominations, the turpitudes of the Christians.'
And these are not justified, nor the others.

And they write innumerable books; being too vain and distracted for
silence: seeking every one after his own elevation, and dodging his
emptiness.

If humility and purity be not in the heart, they are not in the home: and
if they are not in the home, they are not in the City.

The man who has builded during the day would return to his hearth at
nightfall: to be blessed with the gift of silence, and doze before he
sleeps.

But we are encompassed with snakes and dogs: therefore some must
labour, and others must hold the spears.

VI

It is hard for those who have never known persecution,
And who have never known a Christian,
To believe these tales of Christian persecution.
It is hard for those who live near a Bank
To doubt the security of their money.
It is hard for those who live near a Police Station
To believe in the triumph of violence.
Do you think that the Faith has conquered the World
And that lions no longer need keepers?
Do you need to be told that whatever has been, can still be?
Do you need to be told that even such modest attainments
As you can boast in the way of polite society
Will hardly survive the Faith to which they owe their significance?
Men! polish your teeth on rising and retiring;
Women! polish your fingernails:
You polish the tooth of the dog and the talon of the cat.
Why should men love the Church? Why should they love her laws?
She tells them of Life and Death, and of all that they would forget.
She is tender where they would be hard, and hard where they like to be
    soft.
She tells them of Evil and Sin, and other unpleasant facts.
They constantly try to escape
From the darkness outside and within
By dreaming of systems so perfect that no one will need to be good.
But the man that is will shadow
The man that pretends to be.
And the Son of Man was not crucified once for all,
The blood of the martyrs not shed once for all,
The lives of the Saints not given once for all:
But the Son of Man is crucified always
And there shall be Martyrs and Saints.
And if blood of Martyrs is to flow on the steps
We must first build the steps;
And if the Temple is to be cast down
We must first build the Temple.

VII

In the beginning GOD created the world. Waste and void. Waste and
void. And darkness was upon the face of the deep.

And when there were men, in their various ways, they struggled in
torment towards GOD

Blindly and vainly, for man is a vain thing, and man without GOD is a
seed upon the wind: driven this way and that, and finding no place
of lodgement and germination.

They followed the light and the shadow, and the light led them forward
to light and the shadow led them to darkness,

Worshipping snakes or trees, worshipping devils rather than nothing:
crying for life beyond life, for ecstasy not of the flesh.

Waste and void. Waste and void. And darkness on the face of the deep.

And the Spirit moved upon the face of the water.

And men who turned towards the light and were known of the light

Invented the Higher Religions; and the Higher Religions were good

And led men from light to light, to knowledge of Good and Evil.

But their light was ever surrounded and shot with darkness

As the air of temperate seas is pierced by the still dead breath of the
Arctic Current;

And they came to an end, a dead end stirred with a flicker of life,

And they came to the withered ancient look of a child that has died of
starvation.

Prayer wheels, worship of the dead, denial of this world, affirmation of
rites with forgotten meanings

In the restless wind-whipped sand, or the hills where the wind will not
let the snow rest.

Waste and void. Waste and void. And darkness on the face of the deep.

Then came, at a predetermined moment, a moment in time and of time,

A moment not out of time, but in time, in what we call history: transect-
ing, bisecting the world of time, a moment in time but not like a
moment of time,

A moment in time but time was made through that moment: for without
the meaning there is no time, and that moment of time gave the
meaning.

Then it seemed as if men must proceed from light to light, in the light
of the Word,
Through the Passion and Sacrifice saved in spite of their negative being;
Bestial as always before, carnal, self-seeking as always before, selfish and
purblind as ever before,
Yet always struggling, always reaffirming, always resuming their march
on the way that was lit by the light;
Often halting, loitering, straying, delaying, returning, yet following no
other way.

But it seems that something has happened that has never happened
before: though we know not just when, or why, or how, or where.
Men have left GOD not for other gods, they say, but for no god; and this
has never happened before
That men both deny gods and worship gods, professing first Reason,
And then Money, and Power, and what they call Life, or Race, or
Dialectic.
The Church disowned, the tower overthrown, the bells upturned, what
have we to do
But stand with empty hands and palms turned upwards
In an age which advances progressively backwards?

VOICE OF THE UNEMPLOYED (*afar off*):
In this land
There shall be one cigarette to two men,
To two women one half pint of bitter
Ale. . . .
CHORUS:
What does the world say, does the whole world stray in high-powered
cars on a by-pass way?
VOICE OF THE UNEMPLOYED (*more faintly*):
In this land
No man has hired us. . . .

CHORUS:
Waste and void. Waste and void. And darkness on the face of the deep.
Has the Church failed mankind, or has mankind failed the Church?
When the Church is no longer regarded, not even opposed, and men
have forgotten
All gods except Usury, Lust and Power.

VIII

O Father we welcome your words,
And we will take heart for the future,
Remembering the past.

The heathen are come into thine inheritance,
And thy temple have they defiled.

Who is this that cometh from Edom?

He has trodden the wine-press alone.

There came one who spoke of the shame of Jerusalem
And the holy places defiled;
Peter the Hermit, scourging with words.
And among his hearers were a few good men,
Many who were evil,
And most who were neither.
Like all men in all places,

Some went from love of glory,
Some went who were restless and curious,
Some were rapacious and lustful.
Many left their bodies to the kites of Syria
Or sea-strewn along the routes;
Many left their souls in Syria,
Living on, sunken in moral corruption;
Many came back well broken,
Diseased and beggared, finding
A stranger at the door in possession:
Came home cracked by the sun of the East
And the seven deadly sins in Syria.
But our King did well at Acre.
And in spite of all the dishonour,

CHORUSES FROM 'THE ROCK', 1934

The broken standards, the broken lives,
The broken faith in one place or another,
There was something left that was more than the tales
Of old men on winter evenings.
Only the faith could have done what was good of it;
Whole faith of a few,
Part faith of many.
Not avarice, lechery, treachery,
Envy, sloth, gluttony, jealousy, pride:
It was not these that made the Crusades,
But these that unmade them.

Remember the faith that took men from home
At the call of a wandering preacher.
Our age is an age of moderate virtue
And of moderate vice
When men will not lay down the Cross
Because they will never assume it.
Yet nothing is impossible, nothing,
To men of faith and conviction.
Let us therefore make perfect our will.
O GOD, help us.

IX

Son of Man, behold with thine eyes, and hear with thine ears
And set thine heart upon all that I show thee.
Who is this that has said: the House of GOD is a House of Sorrow;
We must walk in black and go sadly, with longdrawn faces,
We must go between empty walls, quavering lowly, whispering faintly,
Among a few flickering scattered lights?
They would put upon GOD their own sorrow, the grief they should feel
For their sins and faults as they go about their daily occasions.
Yet they walk in the street proudnecked, like thoroughbreds ready for
    races,
Adorning themselves, and busy in the market, the forum,
And all other secular meetings.
Thinking good of themselves, ready for any festivity,
Doing themselves very well.
Let us mourn in a private chamber, learning the way of penitence,
And then let us learn the joyful communion of saints.
The soul of Man must quicken to creation.
Out of the formless stone, when the artist unites himself with stone,
Spring always new forms of life, from the soul of man that is joined to
    the soul of stone;
Out of the meaningless practical shapes of all that is living or lifeless
Joined with the artist's eye, new life, new form, new colour.
Out of the sea of sound the life of music,
Out of the slimy mud of words, out of the sleet and hail of verbal
    imprecisions,
Approximate thoughts and feelings, words that have taken the place of
    thoughts and feelings,
There spring the perfect order of speech, and the beauty of incantation.

LORD, shall we not bring these gifts to Your service?
Shall we not bring to Your service all our powers
For life, for dignity, grace and order,
And intellectual pleasures of the senses?

CHORUSES FROM 'THE ROCK', 1934

The LORD who created must wish us to create
And employ our creation again in His service
Which is already His service in creating.
For Man is joined spirit and body,
And therefore must serve as spirit and body.
Visible and invisible, two worlds meet in Man;
Visible and invisible must meet in His Temple;
You must not deny the body.

Now you shall see the Temple completed:
After much striving, after many obstacles;
For the work of creation is never without travail;
The formed stone, the visible crucifix,
The dressed altar, the lifting light,

Light

Light

The visible reminder of Invisible Light.

X

You have seen the house built, you have seen it adorned
By one who came in the night, it is now dedicated to GOD.
It is now a visible church, one more light set on a hill
In a world confused and dark and disturbed by portents of fear.
And what shall we say of the future? Is one church all we can build?
Or shall the Visible Church go on to conquer the World?

The great snake lies ever half awake, at the bottom of the pit of the world, curled
In folds of himself until he awakens in hunger and moving his head to right and to left prepares for his hour to devour.
But the Mystery of Iniquity is a pit too deep for mortal eyes to plumb. Come
Ye out from among those who prize the serpent's golden eyes,
The worshippers, self-given sacrifice of the snake. Take
Your way and be ye separate.
Be not too curious of Good and Evil;
Seek not to count the future waves of Time;
But be ye satisfied that you have light
Enough to take your step and find your foothold.

O Light Invisible, we praise Thee!
Too bright for mortal vision.
O Greater Light, we praise Thee for the less;
The eastern light our spires touch at morning,
The light that slants upon our western doors at evening,
The twilight over stagnant pools at batflight,
Moon light and star light, owl and moth light,
Glow-worm glowlight on a grassblade.
O Light Invisible, we worship Thee!

We thank Thee for the lights that we have kindled,
The light of altar and of sanctuary;

166

CHORUSES FROM 'THE ROCK', 1934

Small lights of those who meditate at midnight
And lights directed through the coloured panes of windows
And light reflected from the polished stone,
The gilded carven wood, the coloured fresco.
Our gaze is submarine, our eyes look upward
And see the light that fractures through unquiet water.
We see the light but see not whence it comes.
O Light Invisible, we glorify Thee!

In our rhythm of earthly life we tire of light. We are glad when the day
ends, when the play ends; and ecstasy is too much pain.
We are children quickly tired: children who are up in the night and fall
asleep as the rocket is fired; and the day is long for work or play.
We tire of distraction or concentration, we sleep and are glad to sleep,
Controlled by the rhythm of blood and the day and the night and the
seasons.
And we must extinguish the candle, put out the light and relight it;
Forever must quench, forever relight the flame.
Therefore we thank Thee for our little light, this is dappled with shadow.
We thank Thee who hast moved us to building, to finding, to forming
at the ends of our fingers and beams of our eyes.
And when we have built an altar to the Invisible Light, we may set
thereon the little lights for which our bodily vision is made.
And we thank Thee that darkness reminds us of light.
O Light Invisible, we give Thee thanks for Thy great glory!

FOUR QUARTETS

Burnt Norton

τοῦ λόγου δ'ἐόντος ξυνοῦ ζώουσιν οἱ πολλοί
ὡς ἰδίαν ἔχοντες φρόνησιν.
l. p. 77. Fr. 2.
ὁδὸς ἄνω κάτω μία καὶ ὡυτή.
·*l. p. 89. Fr. 60.*
Diels: *Die Fragmente der Vorsokratiker* Herakleitos).

I

Time present and time past
Are both perhaps present in time future
And time future contained in time past.
If all time is eternally present
All time is unredeemable.
What might have been is an abstraction
Remaining a perpetual possibility
Only in a world of speculation.
What might have been and what has been
Point to one end, which is always present.
Footfalls echo in the memory
Down the passage which we did not take
Towards the door we never opened
Into the rose-garden. My words echo
Thus, in your mind.
                    But to what purpose
Disturbing the dust on a bowl of rose-leaves
I do not know.
                    Other echoes
Inhabit the garden. Shall we follow?
Quick, said the bird, find them, find them,
Round the corner. Through the first gate,
Into our first world, shall we follow
The deception of the thrush? Into our first world.
There they were, dignified, invisible,
Moving without pressure, over the dead leaves,

In the autumn heat, through the vibrant air,
And the bird called, in response to
The unheard music hidden in the shrubbery,
And the unseen eyebeam crossed, for the roses
Had the look of flowers that are looked at.
There they were as our guests, accepted and accepting.
So we moved, and they, in a formal pattern,
Along the empty alley, into the box circle,
To look down into the drained pool.
Dry the pool, dry concrete, brown edged,
And the pool was filled with water out of sunlight,
And the lotos rose, quietly, quietly,
The surface glittered out of heart of light,
And they were behind us, reflected in the pool.
Then a cloud passed, and the pool was empty.
Go, said the bird, for the leaves were full of children,
Hidden excitedly, containing laughter.
Go, go, go, said the bird: human kind
Cannot bear very much reality.
Time past and time future
What might have been and what has been
Point to one end, which is always present.

II

Garlic and sapphires in the mud
Clot the bedded axle-tree.
The trilling wire in the blood
Sings below inveterate scars
Appeasing long forgotten wars.
The dance along the artery
The circulation of the lymph
Are figured in the drift of stars
Ascend to summer in the tree
We move above the moving tree
In light upon the figured leaf
And hear upon the sodden floor
Below, the boarhound and the boar
Pursue their pattern as before
But reconciled among the stars.

FOUR QUARTETS

At the still point of the turning world. Neither flesh nor fleshless;
Neither from nor towards; at the still point, there the dance is,
But neither arrest nor movement. And do not call it fixity,
Where past and future are gathered. Neither movement from nor
     towards,
Neither ascent nor decline. Except for the point, the still point,
There would be no dance, and there is only the dance.
I can only say, *there* we have been: but I cannot say where.
And I cannot say, how long, for that is to place it in time.
The inner freedom from the practical desire,
The release from action and suffering, release from the inner
And the outer compulsion, yet surrounded
By a grace of sense, a white light still and moving,
Erhebung without motion, concentration
Without elimination, both a new world
And the old made explicit, understood
In the completion of its partial ecstasy,
The resolution of its partial horror.
Yet the enchainment of past and future
Woven in the weakness of the changing body,
Protects mankind from heaven and damnation
Which flesh cannot endure.
                         Time past and time future
Allow but a little consciousness.
To be conscious is not to be in time
But only in time can the moment in the rose-garden,
The moment in the arbour where the rain beat,
The moment in the draughty church at smokefall
Be remembered; involved with past and future.
Only through time time is conquered.

III

Here is a place of disaffection
Time before and time after
In a dim light: neither daylight
Investing form with lucid stillness
Turning shadow into transient beauty
With slow rotation suggesting permanence
Nor darkness to purify the soul

Emptying the sensual with deprivation
Cleansing affection from the temporal.
Neither plenitude nor vacancy. Only a flicker
Over the strained time-ridden faces
Distracted from distraction by distraction
Filled with fancies and empty of meaning
Tumid apathy with no concentration
Men and bits of paper, whirled by the cold wind
That blows before and after time,
Wind in and out of unwholesome lungs
Time before and time after.
Eructation of unhealthy souls
Into the faded air, the torpid
Driven on the wind that sweeps the gloomy hills of London.
Hampstead and Clerkenwell, Campden and Putney,
Highgate, Primrose and Ludgate. Not here
Not here the darkness, in this twittering world.

   Descend lower, descend only
Into the world of perpetual solitude,
World not world, but that which is not world,
Internal darkness, deprivation
And destitution of all property,
Desiccation of the world of sense,
Evacuation of the world of fancy,
Inoperancy of the world of spirit;
This is the one way, and the other
Is the same, not in movement
But abstention from movement; while the world moves
   appetency, on its metalled ways
     e past and time future.

IV

    ve buried the day,
     the sun away.
      will the clematis
      dril and spray

FOUR QUARTETS

Fingers of yew be curled
Down on us? After the kingfisher's wing
Has answered light to light, and is silent, the light is still
At the still point of the turning world.

V

Words move, music moves
Only in time; but that which is only living
Can only die. Words, after speech, reach
Into the silence. Only by the form, the pattern,
Can words or music reach
The stillness, as a Chinese jar still
Moves perpetually in its stillness.
Not the stillness of the violin, while the note lasts,
Not that only, but the co-existence,
Or say that the end precedes the beginning,
And the end and the beginning were always there
Before the beginning and after the end.
And all is always now. Words strain,
Crack and sometimes break, under the burden,
Under the tension, slip, slide, perish,
Decay with imprecision, will not stay in place,
Will not stay still. Shrieking voices
Scolding, mocking, or merely chattering,
Always assail them. The Word in the desert
Is most attacked by voices of temptation,
The crying shadow in the funeral dance,
The loud lament of the disconsolate chimera.

The detail of the pattern is movement,
As in the figure of the ten stairs.
Desire itself is movement
Not in itself desirable;
Love is itself unmoving,
Only the cause and end of movement,
Timeless, and undesiring
Except in the aspect of time
Caught in the form of limitation
Between un-being and being.

Sudden in a shaft of sunlight
Even while the dust moves
There rises the hidden laughter
Of children in the foliage
Quick now, here, now, always —
Ridiculous the waste sad time
Stretching before and after.

East Coker

I

In my beginning is my end. In succession
Houses rise and fall, crumble, are extended,
Are removed, destroyed, restored, or in their place
Is an open field, or a factory, or a by-pass.
Old stone to new building, old timber to new fires,
Old fires to ashes, and ashes to the earth
Which is already flesh, fur and faeces,
Bone of man and beast, cornstalk and leaf.
Houses live and die: there is a time for building
And a time for living and for generation
And a time for the wind to break the loosened pane
And to shake the wainscot where the field-mouse trots
And to shake the tattered arras woven with a silent motto.

In my beginning is my end. Now the light falls
Across the open field, leaving the deep lane
Shuttered with branches, dark in the afternoon,
Where you lean against a bank while a van passes,
And the deep lane insists on the direction
Into the village, in the electric heat
Hypnotised. In a warm haze the sultry light
Is absorbed, not refracted, by grey stone.
The dahlias sleep in the empty silence.
Wait for the early owl.

In that open field
If you do not come too close, if you do not come too close,
On a summer midnight, you can hear the music
Of the weak pipe and the little drum
And see them dancing around the bonfire
The association of man and woman

177

In daunsinge, signifying matrimonie —
A dignified and commodious sacrament.
Two and two, necessarye coniunction,
Holding eche other by the hand or the arm
Whiche betokeneth concorde. Round and round the fire
Leaping through the flames, or joined in circles,
Rustically solemn or in rustic laughter
Lifting heavy feet in clumsy shoes,
Earth feet, loam feet, lifted in country mirth
Mirth of those long since under earth
Nourishing the corn. Keeping time,
Keeping the rhythm in their dancing
As in their living in the living seasons
The time of the seasons and the constellations
The time of milking and the time of harvest
The time of the coupling of man and woman
And that of beasts. Feet rising and falling.
Eating and drinking. Dung and death.

    Dawn points, and another day
Prepares for heat and silence. Out at sea the dawn wind
Wrinkles and slides. I am here
Or there, or elsewhere. In my beginning.

II

What is the late November doing
With the disturbance of the spring
And creatures of the summer heat,
And snowdrops writhing under feet
And hollyhocks that aim too high
Red into grey and tumble down
Late roses filled with early snow?
Thunder rolled by the rolling stars
Simulates triumphal cars
Deployed in constellated wars
Scorpion fights against the Sun
Until the Sun and Moon go down
Comets weep and Leonids fly
Hunt the heavens and the plains

Whirled in a vortex that shall bring
The world to that destructive fire
Which burns before the ice-cap reigns.

 That was a way of putting it — not very satisfactory:
A periphrastic study in a worn-out poetical fashion,
Leaving one still with the intolerable wrestle
With words and meanings. The poetry does not matter.
It was not (to start again) what one had expected.
What was to be the value of the long looked forward to,
Long hoped for calm, the autumnal serenity
And the wisdom of age? Had they deceived us,
Or deceived themselves, the quiet-voiced elders,
Bequeathing us merely a receipt for deceit?
The serenity only a deliberate hebetude,
The wisdom only the knowledge of dead secrets
Useless in the darkness into which they peered
Or from which they turned their eyes. There is, it seems to us,
At best, only a limited value
In the knowledge derived from experience.
The knowledge imposes a pattern, and falsifies,
For the pattern is new in every moment
And every moment is a new and shocking
Valuation of all we have been. We are only undeceived
Of that which, deceiving, could no longer harm.
In the middle, not only in the middle of the way
But all the way, in a dark wood, in a bramble,
On the edge of a grimpen, where is no secure foothold,
And menaced by monsters, fancy lights,
Risking enchantment. Do not let me hear
Of the wisdom of old men, but rather of their folly,
Their fear of fear and frenzy, their fear of possession,
Of belonging to another, or to others, or to God.
The only wisdom we can hope to acquire
Is the wisdom of humility: humility is endless.

The houses are all gone under the sea.

The dancers are all gone under the hill.

III

O dark dark dark. They all go into the dark,
The vacant interstellar spaces, the vacant into the vacant,
The captains, merchant bankers, eminent men of letters.
The generous patrons of art, the statesmen and the rulers,
Distinguished civil servants, chairmen of many committees,
Industrial lords and petty contractors, all go into the dark,
And dark the Sun and Moon, and the Almanach de Gotha
And the Stock Exchange Gazette, the Directory of Directors,
And cold the sense and lost the motive of action.
And we all go with them, into the silent funeral,
Nobody's funeral, for there is no one to bury.
I said to my soul, be still, and let the dark come upon you
Which shall be the darkness of God. As, in a theatre,
The lights are extinguished, for the scene to be changed
With a hollow rumble of wings, with a movement of darkness on
　　　darkness,
And we know that the hills and the trees, the distant panorama
And the bold imposing façade are all being rolled away —
Or as, when an underground train, in the tube, stops too long between
　　　stations
And the conversation rises and slowly fades into silence
And you see behind every face the mental emptiness deepen
Leaving only the growing terror of nothing to think about;
Or when, under ether, the mind is conscious but conscious of
　　　nothing—
I said to my soul, be still, and wait without hope
For hope would be hope for the wrong thing; wait without love
For love would be love of the wrong thing; there is yet faith
But the faith and the love and the hope are all in the waiting.
Wait without thought, for you are not ready for thought:
So the darkness shall be the light, and the stillness the dancing.
Whisper of running streams, and winter lightning.
The wild thyme unseen and the wild strawberry,
The laughter in the garden, echoed ecstasy
Not lost, but requiring, pointing to the agony
Of death and birth.

FOUR QUARTETS

You say I am repeating
Something I have said before. I shall say it again.
Shall I say it again? In order to arrive there,
To arrive where you are, to get from where you are not,
    You must go by a way wherein there is no ecstasy.
In order to arrive at what you do not know
    You must go by a way which is the way of ignorance.
In order to possess what you do not possess
    You must go by the way of dispossession.
In order to arrive at what you are not
    You must go through the way in which you are not.
And what you do not know is the only thing you know
And what you own is what you do not own
And where you are is where you are not.

IV

The wounded surgeon plies the steel
That questions the distempered part;
Beneath the bleeding hands we feel
The sharp compassion of the healer's art
Resolving the enigma of the fever chart.

Our only health is the disease
If we obey the dying nurse
Whose constant care is not to please
But to remind of our, and Adam's curse,
And that, to be restored, our sickness must grow worse.

The whole earth is our hospital
Endowed by the ruined millionaire,
Wherein, if we do well, we shall
Die of the absolute paternal care
That will not leave us, but prevents us everywhere.

The chill ascends from feet to knees,
The fever sings in mental wires.
If to be warmed, then I must freeze
And quake in frigid purgatorial fires
Of which the flame is roses, and the smoke is briars.

FOUR QUARTETS

The dripping blood our only drink,
The bloody flesh our only food:
In spite of which we like to think
That we are sound, substantial flesh and blood —
Again, in spite of that, we call this Friday good.

V

So here I am, in the middle way, having had twenty years —
Twenty years largely wasted, the years of *l'entre deux guerres* —
Trying to learn to use words, and every attempt
Is a wholly new start, and a different kind of failure
Because one has only learnt to get the better of words
For the thing one no longer has to say, or the way in which
One is no longer disposed to say it. And so each venture
Is a new beginning, a raid on the inarticulate
With shabby equipment always deteriorating
In the general mess of imprecision of feeling,
Undisciplined squads of emotion. And what there is to conquer
By strength and submission, has already been discovered
Once or twice, or several times, by men whom one cannot hope
To emulate — but there is no competition —
There is only the fight to recover what has been lost
And found and lost again and again: and now, under conditions
That seem unpropitious. But perhaps neither gain nor loss.
For us, there is only the trying. The rest is not our business.

Home is where one starts from. As we grow older
The world becomes stranger, the pattern more complicated
Of dead and living. Not the intense moment
Isolated, with no before and after,
But a lifetime burning in every moment
And not the lifetime of one man only
But of old stones that cannot be deciphered.
There is a time for the evening under starlight,
A time for the evening under lamplight
(The evening with the photograph album).
Love is most nearly itself
When here and now cease to matter.
Old men ought to be explorers

Here and there does not matter
We must be still and still moving
Into another intensity
For a further union, a deeper communion
Through the dark cold and the empty desolation,
The wave cry, the wind cry, the vast waters
Of the petrel and the porpoise. In my end is my beginning.

The Dry Salvages

(The Dry Salvages — presumably *les trois sauvages* — is a small group
of rocks, with a beacon, off the N.E. coast of Cape Ann, Massachusetts.
Salvages is pronounced to rhyme with *assuages*. *Groaner*: a whistling
buoy.)

I

I do not know much about gods; but I think that the river
Is a strong brown god — sullen, untamed and intractable,
Patient to some degree, at first recognised as a frontier;
Useful, untrustworthy, as a conveyor of commerce;
Then only a problem confronting the builder of bridges.
The problem once solved, the brown god is almost forgotten
By the dwellers in cities — ever, however, implacable,
Keeping his seasons and rages, destroyer, reminder
Of what men choose to forget. Unhonoured, unpropitiated
By worshippers of the machine, but waiting, watching and waiting.
His rhythm was present in the nursery bedroom,
In the rank ailanthus of the April dooryard,
In the smell of grapes on the autumn table,
And the evening circle in the winter gaslight.

The river is within us, the sea is all about us;
The sea is the land's edge also, the granite
Into which it reaches, the beaches where it tosses
Its hints of earlier and other creation:
The starfish, the horseshoe crab, the whale's backbone;
The pools where it offers to our curiosity
The more delicate algae and the sea anemone.
It tosses up our losses, the torn seine,
The shattered lobsterpot, the broken oar
And the gear of foreign dead men. The sea has many voices,
Many gods and many voices.
                                        The salt is on the briar rose,

184

FOUR QUARTETS

The fog is in the fir trees.
                          The sea howl
And the sea yelp, are different voices
Often together heard: the whine in the rigging,
The menace and caress of wave that breaks on water,
The distant rote in the granite teeth,
And the wailing warning from the approaching headland
Are all sea voices, and the heaving groaner
Rounded homewards, and the seagull:
And under the oppression of the silent fog
The tolling bell
Measures time not our time, rung by the unhurried
Ground swell, a time
Older than the time of chronometers, older
Than time counted by anxious worried women
Lying awake, calculating the future,
Trying to unweave, unwind, unravel
And piece together the past and the future,
Between midnight and dawn, when the past is all deception,
The future futureless, before the morning watch
When time stops and time is never ending;
And the ground swell, that is and was from the beginning,
Clangs
The bell.

II

Where is there an end of it, the soundless wailing,
The silent withering of autumn flowers
Dropping their petals and remaining motionless;
Where is there an end to the drifting wreckage,
The prayer of the bone on the beach, the unprayable
Prayer at the calamitous annunciation?

There is no end, but addition: the trailing
Consequence of further days and hours,
While emotion takes to itself the emotionless
Years of living among the breakage
Of what was believed in as the most reliable —
And therefore the fittest for renunciation.

There is the final addition, the failing
Pride or resentment at failing powers,
The unattached devotion which might pass for devotionless,
In a drifting boat with a slow leakage,
The silent listening to the undeniable
Clamour of the bell of the last annunciation.

Where is the end of them, the fishermen sailing
Into the wind's tail, where the fog cowers?
We cannot think of a time that is oceanless
Or of an ocean not littered with wastage
Or of a future that is not liable
Like the past, to have no destination.

We have to think of them as forever bailing,
Setting and hauling, while the North East lowers
Over shallow banks unchanging and erosionless
Or drawing their money, drying sails at dockage;
Not as making a trip that will be unpayable
For a haul that will not bear examination.

There is no end of it, the voiceless wailing,
No end to the withering of withered flowers,
To the movement of pain that is painless and motionless,
To the drift of the sea and the drifting wreckage,
The bone's prayer to Death its God. Only the hardly, barely prayable
Prayer of the one Annunciation.

It seems, as one becomes older,
That the past has another pattern, and ceases to be a mere sequence —
Or even development: the latter a partial fallacy
Encouraged by superficial notions of evolution,
Which becomes, in the popular mind, a means of disowning the past.
The moments of happiness — not the sense of well-being,
Fruition, fulfilment, security or affection,
Or even a very good dinner, but the sudden illumination —
We had the experience but missed the meaning,
And approach to the meaning restores the experience
In a different form, beyond any meaning
We can assign to happiness. I have said before

FOUR QUARTETS

That the past experience revived in the meaning
Is not the experience of one life only
But of many generations — not forgetting
Something that is probably quite ineffable:
The backward look behind the assurance
Of recorded history, the backward half-look
Over the shoulder, towards the primitive terror.
Now, we come to discover that the moments of agony
(Whether, or not, due to misunderstanding,
Having hoped for the wrong things or dreaded the wrong things,
Is not the question) are likewise permanent
With such permanence as time has. We appreciate this better
In the agony of others, nearly experienced,
Involving ourselves, than in our own.
For our own past is covered by the currents of action,
But the torment of others remains an experience
Unqualified, unworn by subsequent attrition.
People change, and smile: but the agony abides.
Time the destroyer is time the preserver,
Like the river with its cargo of dead negroes, cows and chicken coops,
The bitter apple and the bite in the apple.
And the ragged rock in the restless waters,
Waves wash over it, fogs conceal it;
On a halcyon day it is merely a monument,
In navigable weather it is always a seamark
To lay a course by: but in the sombre season
Or the sudden fury, is what it always was.

III

I sometimes wonder if that is what Krishna meant —
Among other things — or one way of putting the same thing:
That the future is a faded song, a Royal Rose or a lavender spray
Of wistful regret for those who are not yet here to regret,
Pressed between yellow leaves of a book that has never been opened.
And the way up is the way down, the way forward is the way back.
You cannot face it steadily, but this thing is sure,
That time is no healer: the patient is no longer here.
When the train starts, and the passengers are settled
To fruit, periodicals and business letters

(And those who saw them off have left the platform)
Their faces relax from grief into relief,
To the sleepy rhythm of a hundred hours.
Fare forward, travellers! not escaping from the past
Into different lives, or into any future;
You are not the same people who left that station
Or who will arrive at any terminus,
While the narrowing rails slide together behind you;
And on the deck of the drumming liner
Watching the furrow that widens behind you,
You shall not think 'the past is finished'
Or 'the future is before us'.
At nightfall, in the rigging and the aerial,
Is a voice descanting (though not to the ear,
The murmuring shell of time, and not in any language)
'Fare forward, you who think that you are voyaging;
You are not those who saw the harbour
Receding, or those who will disembark.
Here between the hither and the farther shore
While time is withdrawn, consider the future
And the past with an equal mind.
At the moment which is not of action or inaction
You can receive this: "on whatever sphere of being
The mind of a man may be intent
At the time of death" — that is the one action
(And the time of death is every moment)
Which shall fructify in the lives of others:
And do not think of the fruit of action.
Fare forward.
                    O voyagers, O seamen,
You who come to port, and you whose bodies
Will suffer the trial and judgement of the sea,
Or whatever event, this is your real destination.'
So Krishna, as when he admonished Arjuna
On the field of battle.
                    Not fare well,
But fare forward, voyagers.

FOUR QUARTETS

IV

Lady, whose shrine stands on the promontory,
Pray for all those who are in ships, those
Whose business has to do with fish, and
Those concerned with every lawful traffic
And those who conduct them.

Repeat a prayer also on behalf of
Women who have seen their sons or husbands
Setting forth, and not returning:
Figlia del tuo figlio,
Queen of Heaven.

Also pray for those who were in ships, and
Ended their voyage on the sand, in the sea's lips
Or in the dark throat which will not reject them
Or wherever cannot reach them the sound of the sea bell's
Perpetual angelus.

V

To communicate with Mars, converse with spirits,
To report the behaviour of the sea monster,
Describe the horoscope, haruspicate or scry,
Observe disease in signatures, evoke
Biography from the wrinkles of the palm
And tragedy from fingers; release omens
By sortilege, or tea leaves, riddle the inevitable
With playing cards, fiddle with pentagrams
Or barbituric acids, or dissect
The recurrent image into pre-conscious terrors —
To explore the womb, or tomb, or dreams; all these are usual
Pastimes and drugs, and features of the press:
And always will be, some of them especially
When there is distress of nations and perplexity
Whether on the shores of Asia, or in the Edgware Road.
Men's curiosity searches past and future
And clings to that dimension. But to apprehend
The point of intersection of the timeless

With time, is an occupation for the saint —
No occupation either, but something given
And taken, in a lifetime's death in love,
Ardour and selflessness and self-surrender.
For most of us, there is only the unattended
Moment, the moment in and out of time,
The distraction fit, lost in a shaft of sunlight,
The wild thyme unseen, or the winter lightning
Or the waterfall, or music heard so deeply
That it is not heard at all, but you are the music
While the music lasts. These are only hints and guesses,
Hints followed by guesses; and the rest
Is prayer, observance, discipline, thought and action.
The hint half guessed, the gift half understood, is Incarnation.
Here the impossible union
Of spheres of existence is actual,
Here the past and future
Are conquered, and reconciled,
Where action were otherwise movement
Of that which is only moved
And has in it no source of movement —
Driven by dæmonic, chthonic
Powers. And right action is freedom
From past and future also.
For most of us, this is the aim
Never here to be realised;
Who are only undefeated
Because we have gone on trying;
We, content at the last
If our temporal reversion nourish
(Not too far from the yew-tree)
The life of significant soil.

Little Gidding

I

Midwinter spring is its own season
Sempiternal though sodden towards sundown,
Suspended in time, between pole and tropic.
When the short day is brightest, with frost and fire,
The brief sun flames the ice, on pond and ditches,
In windless cold that is the heart's heat,
Reflecting in a watery mirror
A glare that is blindness in the early afternoon.
And glow more intense than blaze of branch, or brazier,
Stirs the dumb spirit: no wind, but pentecostal fire
In the dark time of the year. Between melting and freezing
The soul's sap quivers. There is no earth smell
Or smell of living thing. This is the spring time
But not in time's covenant. Now the hedgerow
Is blanched for an hour with transitory blossom
Of snow, a bloom more sudden
Than that of summer, neither budding nor fading,
Not in the scheme of generation.
Where is the summer, the unimaginable
Zero summer?

If you came this way,
Taking the route you would be likely to take
From the place you would be likely to come from,
If you came this way in may time, you would find the hedges
White again, in May, with voluptuary sweetness.
It would be the same at the end of the journey,
If you came at night like a broken king,
If you came by day not knowing what you came for,
It would be the same, when you leave the rough road
And turn behind the pig-sty to the dull façade

And the tombstone. And what you thought you came for
Is only a shell, a husk of meaning
From which the purpose breaks only when it is fulfilled
If at all. Either you had no purpose
Or the purpose is beyond the end you figured
And is altered in fulfilment. There are other places
Which also are the world's end, some at the sea jaws,
Or over a dark lake, in a desert or a city —
But this is the nearest, in place and time,
Now and in England.

                    If you came this way,
Taking any route, starting from anywhere,
At any time or at any season,
It would always be the same: you would have to put off
Sense and notion. You are not here to verify,
Instruct yourself, or inform curiosity
Or carry report. You are here to kneel
Where prayer has been valid. And prayer is more
Than an order of words, the conscious occupation
Of the praying mind, or the sound of the voice praying.
And what the dead had no speech for, when living,
They can tell you, being dead: the communication
Of the dead is tongued with fire beyond the language of the living.
Here, the intersection of the timeless moment
Is England and nowhere. Never and always.

II

Ash on an old man's sleeve
Is all the ash the burnt roses leave.
Dust in the air suspended
Marks the place where a story ended.
Dust inbreathed was a house —
The wall, the wainscot and the mouse.
The death of hope and despair,
     This is the death of air.

There are flood and drouth
Over the eyes and in the mouth,

FOUR QUARTETS

Dead water and dead sand
Contending for the upper hand.
The parched eviscerate soil
Gapes at the vanity of toil,
Laughs without mirth.
  This is the death of earth.

Water and fire succeed
The town, the pasture and the weed.
Water and fire deride
The sacrifice that we denied.
Water and fire shall rot
The marred foundations we forgot,
Of sanctuary and choir.
  This is the death of water and fire.

In the uncertain hour before the morning
 Near the ending of interminable night
 At the recurrent end of the unending
After the dark dove with the flickering tongue
 Had passed below the horizon of his homing
 While the dead leaves still rattled on like tin
Over the asphalt where no other sound was
 Between three districts whence the smoke arose
 I met one walking, loitering and hurried
As if blown towards me like the metal leaves
 Before the urban dawn wind unresisting.
 And as I fixed upon the down-turned face
That pointed scrutiny with which we challenge
 The first-met stranger in the waning dusk
 I caught the sudden look of some dead master
Whom I had known, forgotten, half recalled
 Both one and many; in the brown baked features
The eyes of a familiar compound ghost
 Both intimate and unidentifiable.
 So I assumed a double part, and cried
 And heard another's voice cry: 'What! are *you* here?'
Although we were not. I was still the same,
 Knowing myself yet being someone other —
 And he a face still forming; yet the words sufficed

To compel the recognition they preceded.
 And so, compliant to the common wind,
 Too strange to each other for misunderstanding,
In concord at this intersection time
 Of meeting nowhere, no before and after,
 We trod the pavement in a dead patrol.
I said: 'The wonder that I feel is easy,
 Yet ease is cause of wonder. Therefore speak:
 I may not comprehend, may not remember.'
And he: 'I am not eager to rehearse
 My thoughts and theory which you have forgotten.
 These things have served their purpose: let them be.
So with your own, and pray they be forgiven
 By others, as I pray you to forgive
 Both bad and good. Last season's fruit is eaten
And the fullfed beast shall kick the empty pail.
 For last year's words belong to last year's language
 And next year's words await another voice.
But, as the passage now presents no hindrance
 To the spirit unappeased and peregrine
 Between two worlds become much like each other,
So I find words I never thought to speak
 In streets I never thought I should revisit
 When I left my body on a distant shore.
Since our concern was speech, and speech impelled us
 To purify the dialect of the tribe
 And urge the mind to aftersight and foresight,
Let me disclose the gifts reserved for age
 To set a crown upon your lifetime's effort.
 First, the cold friction of expiring sense
Without enchantment, offering no promise
 But bitter tastelessness of shadow fruit
 As body and soul begin to fall asunder.
Second, the conscious impotence of rage
 At human folly, and the laceration
 Of laughter at what ceases to amuse.
And last, the rending pain of re-enactment
 Of all that you have done, and been; the shame
 Of motives late revealed, and the awareness
 Of things ill done and done to others' harm.

Which once you took for exercise of virtue.
Then fools' approval stings, and honour stains.
From wrong to wrong the exasperated spirit
  Proceeds, unless restored by that refining fire
  Where you must move in measure, like a dancer.'
The day was breaking. In the disfigured street
  He left me, with a kind of valediction,
  And faded on the blowing of the horn.

III

There are three conditions which often look alike
Yet differ completely, flourish in the same hedgerow:
Attachment to self and to things and to persons, detachment
From self and from things and from persons; and, growing between
    them, indifference
Which resembles the others as death resembles life,
Being between two lives — unflowering, between
The live and the dead nettle. This is the use of memory:
For liberation — not less of love but expanding
Of love beyond desire, and so liberation
From the future as well as the past. Thus, love of a country
Begins as attachment to our own field of action
And comes to find that action of little importance
Though never indifferent. History may be servitude,
History may be freedom. See, now they vanish,
The faces and places, with the self which, as it could, loved them,
To become renewed, transfigured, in another pattern.
Sin is Behovely, but
All shall be well, and
All manner of thing shall be well.
If I think, again, of this place,
And of people, not wholly commendable,
Of no immediate kin or kindness,
But some of peculiar genius,
All touched by a common genius,
United in the strife which divided them;
If I think of a king at nightfall,
Of three men, and more, on the scaffold
And a few who died forgotten

In other places, here and abroad,
And of one who died blind and quiet,
Why should we celebrate
These dead men more than the dying?
It is not to ring the bell backward
Nor is it an incantation
To summon the spectre of a Rose.
We cannot revive old factions
We cannot restore old policies
Or follow an antique drum.
These men, and those who opposed them
And those whom they opposed
Accept the constitution of silence
And are folded in a single party.
Whatever we inherit from the fortunate
We have taken from the defeated
What they had to leave us — a symbol:
A symbol perfected in death.
And all shall be well and
All manner of thing shall be well
By the purification of the motive
In the ground of our beseeching.

IV

The dove descending breaks the air
With flame of incandescent terror
Of which the tongues declare
The one discharge from sin and error.
The only hope, or else despair
  Lies in the choice of pyre or pyre —
  To be redeemed from fire by fire.

Who then devised the torment? Love.
Love is the unfamiliar Name
Behind the hands that wove
The intolerable shirt of flame
Which human power cannot remove.
  We only live, only suspire
  Consumed by either fire or fire.

FOUR QUARTETS

V

What we call the beginning is often the end
And to make an end is to make a beginning.
The end is where we start from. And every phrase
And sentence that is right (where every word is at home,
Taking its place to support the others,
The word neither diffident nor ostentatious,
An easy commerce of the old and the new,
The common word exact without vulgarity,
The formal word precise but not pedantic,
The complete consort dancing together)
Every phrase and every sentence is an end and a beginning,
Every poem an epitaph. And any action
Is a step to the block, to the fire, down the sea's throat
Or to an illegible stone: and that is where we start.
We die with the dying:
See, they depart, and we go with them.
We are born with the dead:
See, they return, and bring us with them.
The moment of the rose and the moment of the yew-tree
Are of equal duration. A people without history
Is not redeemed from time, for history is a pattern
Of timeless moments. So, while the light fails
On a winter's afternoon, in a secluded chapel
History is now and England.

With the drawing of this Love and the voice of this Calling

We shall not cease from exploration
And the end of all our exploring
Will be to arrive where we started
And know the place for the first time.
Through the unknown, remembered gate
When the last of earth left to discover
Is that which was the beginning;
At the source of the longest river
The voice of the hidden waterfall
And the children in the apple-tree

FOUR QUARTETS

Not known, because not looked for
But heard, half-heard, in the stillness
Between two waves of the sea.
Quick now, here, now, always —
A condition of complete simplicity
(Costing not less than everything)
And all shall be well and
All manner of thing shall be well
When the tongues of flame are in-folded
Into the crowned knot of fire
And the fire and the rose are one.

OCCASIONAL VERSES

Defence of the Islands

Defence of the Islands cannot pretend to be verse, but its date — just after the evacuation from Dunkirk — and occasion have for me a significance which makes me wish to preserve it. McKnight Kauffer was then working for the Ministry of Information. At his request I wrote these lines to accompany an exhibition in New York of photographs illustrating the war effort of Britain. They were subsequently published in *Britain At War* (the Museum of Modern Art, New York 1941). I now dedicate them to the memory of Edward McKnight Kauffer.

Let these memorials of built stone — music's
enduring instrument, of many centuries of
patient cultivation of the earth, of English
verse

be joined with the memory of this defence of
the islands

and the memory of those appointed to the grey
ships — battleship, merchantman, trawler —
contributing their share to the ages' pavement
of British bone on the sea floor

and of those who, in man's newest form of gamble
with death, fight the power of darkness in air
and fire

and of those who have followed their forebears
to Flanders and France, those undefeated in de-
feat, unalterable in triumph, changing nothing
of their ancestors' ways but the weapons

and those again for whom the paths of glory are
the lanes and the streets of Britain:

to say, to the past and the future generations
of our kin and of our speech, that we took up
our positions, in obedience to instructions.

A Note on War Poetry

A Note on War Poetry was written at the request of Miss Storm Jameson, to be included in a book entitled *London Calling* (Harper Brothers, New York, 1942).

Not the expression of collective emotion
Imperfectly reflected in the daily papers.
Where is the point at which the merely individual
Explosion breaks

In the path of an action merely typical
To create the universal, originate a symbol
Out of the impact? This is a meeting
On which we attend

Of forces beyond control by experiment —
Of Nature and the Spirit. Mostly the individual
Experience is too large, or too small. Our emotions
Are only 'incidents'

In the effort to keep day and night together.
It seems just possible that a poem might happen
To a very young man: but a poem is not poetry —
That is a life.

War is not a life: it is a situation,
One which may neither be ignored nor accepted,
A problem to be met with ambush and stratagem,
Enveloped or scattered.

The enduring is not a substitute for the transient,
Neither one for the other. But the abstract conception
Of private experience at its greatest intensity
Becoming universal, which we call 'poetry',
May be affirmed in verse.

To the Indians who Died in Africa

To the Indians who Died in Africa was written at the request of Miss Cornelia Sorabji for *Queen Mary's Book for India* (Harrap & Co. Ltd., 1943). I dedicate it now to Bonamy Dobree, because he liked it and urged me to preserve it.

A man's destination is his own village,
His own fire, and his wife's cooking;
To sit in front of his own door at sunset
And see his grandson, and his neighbour's grandson
　　Playing in the dust together.

Scarred but secure, he has many memories
Which return at the hour of conversation,
(The warm or the cool hour, according to the climate)
Of foreign men, who fought in foreign places,
　　Foreign to each other.

A man's destination is not his destiny
Every country is home to one man
And exile to another. Where a man dies bravely
At one with his destiny, that soil is his.
　　Let his village remember.

This was not your land, or ours: but a village in the Midlands,
And one in the Five Rivers, may have the same graveyard.
Let those who go home tell the same story of you:
Of action with a common purpose, action
None the less fruitful if neither you nor we
Know, until the judgment after death,
　　What is the fruit of action.

To Walter de la Mare

To Walter de la Mare was written for inclusion in *Tribute to Walter de la Mare* (Faber & Faber Ltd., 1948), a book presented to him on his seventy-fifth birthday.

The children who explored the brook and found
A desert island with a sandy cove
(A hiding place, but very dangerous ground,

For here the water buffalo may rove,
The kinkajou, the mangabey, abound
In the dark jungle of a mango grove,

And shadowy lemurs glide from tree to tree —
The guardians of some long-lost treasure-trove)
Recount their exploits at the nursery tea

And when the lamps are lit and curtains drawn
Demand some poetry, please. Whose shall it be,
At not quite time for bed? . . .

                Or when the lawn
Is pressed by unseen feet, and ghosts return
Gently at twilight, gently go at dawn,
The sad intangible who grieve and yearn;

When the familiar scene is suddenly strange
Or the well known is what we have yet to learn,
And two worlds meet, and intersect, and change;

When cats are maddened in the moonlight dance,
Dogs cower, flitter bats, and owls range
At witches' sabbath of the maiden aunts;

OCCASIONAL VERSES

When the nocturnal traveller can arouse
No sleeper by his call; or when by chance
An empty face peers from an empty house;

By whom, and by what means, was this designed?
The whispered incantation which allows
Free passage to the phantoms of the mind?

By you; by those deceptive cadences
Wherewith the common measure is refined;
By conscious art practised with natural ease;

By the delicate, invisible web you wove —
The inexplicable mystery of sound.

A Dedication to my Wife

To whom I owe the leaping delight
That quickens my senses in our wakingtime
And the rhythm that governs the repose of our sleepingtime,
    The breathing in unison

Of lovers whose bodies smell of each other
Who think the same thoughts without need of speech
And babble the same speech without need of meaning.

No peevish winter wind shall chill
No sullen tropic sun shall wither
The roses in the rose-garden which is ours and ours only

But this dedication is for others to read:
These are private words addressed to you in public.

OLD POSSUM'S BOOK
OF PRACTICAL CATS

The Naming of Cats

The Naming of Cats is a difficult matter,
  It isn't just one of your holiday games;
You may think at first I'm as mad as a hatter
When I tell you, a cat must have THREE DIFFERENT NAMES.
First of all, there's the name that the family use daily,
  Such as Peter, Augustus, Alonzo or James,
Such as Victor or Jonathan, George or Bill Bailey —
  All of them sensible everyday names.
There are fancier names if you think they sound sweeter,
  Some for the gentlemen, some for the dames:
Such as Plato, Admetus, Electra, Demeter —
  But all of them sensible everyday names.
But I tell you, a cat needs a name that's particular,
  A name that's peculiar, and more dignified,
Else how can he keep up his tail perpendicular,
  Or spread out his whiskers, or cherish his pride?
Of names of this kind, I can give you a quorum,
  Such as Munkustrap, Quaxo, or Coricopat,
Such as Bombalurina, or else Jellylorum —
  Names that never belong to more than one cat.
But above and beyond there's still one name left over,
  And that is the name that you never will guess;
The name that no human research can discover —
  But THE CAT HIMSELF KNOWS, and will never confess.
When you notice a cat in profound meditation,
  The reason, I tell you, is always the same:
His mind is engaged in a rapt contemplation
  Of the thought, of the thought, of the thought of his name:
    His ineffable effable
    Effanineffable
Deep and inscrutable singular Name.

The Old Gumbie Cat

I have a Gumbie Cat in mind, her name is Jennyanydots;
Her coat is of the tabby kind, with tiger stripes and leopard spots.
All day she sits upon the stair or on the steps or on the mat:
She sits and sits and sits and sits — and that's what makes a Gumbie
    Cat!

      But when the day's hustle and bustle is done,
      Then the Gumbie Cat's work is but hardly begun.
      And when all the family's in bed and asleep,
      She tucks up her skirts to the basement to creep.
      She is deeply concerned with the ways of the mice —
      Their behaviour's not good and their manners not nice;
      So when she has got them lined up on the matting,
      She teaches them music, crocheting and tatting.

I have a Gumbie Cat in mind, her name is Jennyanydots;
Her equal would be hard to find, she likes the warm and sunny spots.
All day she sits beside the hearth or in the sun or on my hat:
She sits and sits and sits and sits — and that's what makes a Gumbie
    Cat!

      But when the day's hustle and bustle is done,
      Then the Gumbie Cat's work is but hardly begun.
      As she finds that the mice will not ever keep quiet,
      She is sure it is due to irregular diet
      And believing that nothing is done without trying,
      She sets to work with her baking and frying.
      She makes them a mouse-cake of bread and dried peas,
      And a *beautiful* fry of lean bacon and cheese.

I have a Gumbie Cat in mind, her name is Jennyanydots;
The curtain-cord she likes to wind, and tie it into sailor-knots.

She sits upon the window-sill, or anything that's smooth and flat:
She sits and sits and sits and sits — and that's what makes a Gumbie
  Cat!

But when the day's hustle and bustle is done,
Then the Gumbie Cat's work is but hardly begun.
She thinks that the cockroaches just need employment
To prevent them from idle and wanton destroyment.
So she's formed, from that lot of disorderly louts,
A troop of well-disciplined helpful boy-scouts,
With a purpose in life and a good deed to do —
And she's even created a Beetles' Tattoo.

So for Old Gumbie Cats let us now give three cheers —
On whom well-ordered households depend, it appears.

Growltiger's Last Stand

GROWLTIGER was a Bravo Cat, who travelled on a barge:
In fact he was the roughest cat that ever roamed at large.
From Gravesend up to Oxford he pursued his evil aims,
Rejoicing in his title of 'The Terror of the Thames'.

His manners and appearance did not calculate to please;
His coat was torn and seedy, he was baggy at the knees;
One ear was somewhat missing, no need to tell you why,
And he scowled upon a hostile world from one forbidding eye.

The cottagers of Rotherhithe knew something of his fame;
At Hammersmith and Putney people shuddered at his name.
They would fortify the hen-house, lock up the silly goose,
When the rumour ran along the shore: GROWLTIGER'S ON THE LOOSE!

Woe to the weak canary, that fluttered from its cage;
Woe to the pampered Pekinese, that faced Growltiger's rage;
Woe to the bristly Bandicoot, that lurks on foreign ships,
And woe to any Cat with whom Growltiger came to grips!

But most to Cats of foreign race his hatred had been vowed;
To Cats of foreign name and race no quarter was allowed.
The Persian and the Siamese regarded him with fear —
Because it was a Siamese had mauled his missing ear.

Now on a peaceful summer night, all nature seemed at play,
The tender moon was shining bright, the barge at Molesey lay.
All in the balmy moonlight it lay rocking on the tide —
And Growltiger was disposed to show his sentimental side.

His bucko mate, GRUMBUSKIN, long since had disappeared,
For to the Bell at Hampton he had gone to wet his beard;
And his bosun, TUMBLEBRUTUS, he too had stol'n away —
In the yard behind the Lion he was prowling for his prey.

In the forepeak of the vessel Growltiger sate alone,
Concentrating his attention on the Lady GRIDDLEBONE.
And his raffish crew were sleeping in their barrels and their bunks —
As the Siamese came creeping in their sampans and their junks.

Growltiger had no eye or ear for aught but Griddlebone,
And the Lady seemed enraptured by his manly baritone,
Disposed to relaxation, and awaiting no surprise —
But the moonlight shone reflected from a hundred bright blue eyes.

And closer still and closer the sampans circled round,
And yet from all the enemy there was not heard a sound.
The lovers sang their last duet, in danger of their lives —
For the foe was armed with toasting forks and cruel carving knives.

Then GILBERT gave the signal to his fierce Mongolian horde;
With a frightful burst of fireworks the Chinks they swarmed aboard.
Abandoning their sampans, and their pullaways and junks,
They battened down the hatches on the crew within their bunks.

Then Griddlebone she gave a screech, for she was badly skeered;
I am sorry to admit it, but she quickly disappeared.
She probably escaped with ease, I'm sure she was not drowned —
But a serried ring of flashing steel Growltiger did surround.

The ruthless foe pressed forward, in stubborn rank on rank;
Growltiger to his vast surprise was forced to walk the plank.
He who a hundred victims had driven to that drop,
At the end of all his crimes was forced to go ker-flip, ker-flop.

Oh there was joy in Wapping when the news flew through the land;
At Maidenhead and Henley there was dancing on the strand.
Rats were roasted whole at Brentford, and at Victoria Dock,
And a day of celebration was commanded in Bangkok.

The Rum Tum Tugger

The Rum Tum Tugger is a Curious Cat:
If you offer him pheasant he would rather have grouse.
If you put him in a house he would much prefer a flat,
If you put him in a flat then he'd rather have a house.
If you set him on a mouse then he only wants a rat,
If you set him on a rat then he'd rather chase a mouse.
Yes the Rum Tum Tugger is a Curious Cat —
   And there isn't any call for me to shout it:
     For he will do
     As he do do
       And there's no doing anything about it!

The Rum Tum Tugger is a terrible bore:
When you let him in, then he wants to be out;
He's always on the wrong side of every door,
And as soon as he's at home, then he'd like to get about.
He likes to lie in the bureau drawer,
But he makes such a fuss if he can't get out.
Yes the Rum Tum Tugger is a Curious Cat —
   And it isn't any use for you to doubt it:
     For he will do
     As he do do
       And there's no doing anything about it!

The Rum Tum Tugger is a curious beast:
His disobliging ways are a matter of habit.
If you offer him fish then he always wants a feast;
When there isn't any fish then he won't eat rabbit.
If you offer him cream then he sniffs and sneers,
For he only likes what he finds for himself;
So you'll catch him in it right up to the ears,
If you put it away on the larder shelf.
The Rum Tum Tugger is artful and knowing,

The Rum Tum Tugger doesn't care for a cuddle;
But he'll leap on your lap in the middle of your sewing,
For there's nothing he enjoys like a horrible muddle.
Yes the Rum Tum Tugger is a Curious Cat —
   And there isn't any need for me to spout it:
      For he will do
      As he do do
         And there's no doing anything about it!

The Song of the Jellicles

Jellicle Cats come out to-night,
Jellicle Cats come one come all:
The Jellicle Moon is shining bright —
Jellicles come to the Jellicle Ball.

Jellicle Cats are black and white,
Jellicle Cats are rather small;
Jellicle Cats are merry and bright,
And pleasant to hear when they caterwaul.
Jellicle Cats have cheerful faces,
Jellicle Cats have bright black eyes;
They like to practise their airs and graces
And wait for the Jellicle Moon to rise.

Jellicle Cats develop slowly,
Jellicle Cats are not too big;
Jellicle Cats are roly-poly,
They know how to dance a gavotte and a jig.
Until the Jellicle Moon appears
They make their toilette and take their repose:
Jellicles wash behind their ears,
Jellicles dry between their toes.

Jellicle Cats are white and black,
Jellicle Cats are of moderate size;
Jellicles jump like a jumping-jack,
Jellicle Cats have moonlit eyes.
They're quiet enough in the morning hours,
They're quiet enough in the afternoon,
Reserving their terpsichorean powers
To dance by the light of the Jellicle Moon.

Jellicle Cats are black and white,
Jellicle Cats (as I said) are small;

If it happens to be a stormy night
They will practise a caper or two in the hall.
If it happens the sun is shining bright
You would say they had nothing to do at all:
They are resting and saving themselves to be right
For the Jellicle Moon and the Jellicle Ball.

Mungojerrie and Rumpelteazer

Mungojerrie and Rumpelteazer were a very notorious couple of cats.
As knockabout clowns, quick-change comedians, tight-rope walkers and
    acrobats
They had an extensive reputation. They made their home in Victoria
    Grove —
That was merely their centre of operation, for they were incurably given
    to rove.
They were very well known in Cornwall Gardens, in Launceston Place
    and in Kensington Square —
They had really a little more reputation than a couple of cats can very
    well bear.

      If the area window was found ajar
      And the basement looked like a field of war,
      If a tile or two came loose on the roof,
      Which presently ceased to be waterproof,
      If the drawers were pulled out from the bedroom chests,
      And you couldn't find one of your winter vests,
      Or after supper one of the girls
      Suddenly missed her Woolworth pearls:
Then the family would say: 'It's that horrible cat!
It was Mungojerrie — or Rumpelteazer!' — And most of the time they
    left it at that.
Mungojerrie and Rumpelteazer had a very unusual gift of the gab.
They were highly efficient cat-burglars as well, and remarkably smart
    at a smash-and-grab.
They made their home in Victoria Grove. They had no regular
    occupation.
They were plausible fellows, and liked to engage a friendly policeman
    in conversation.

      When the family assembled for Sunday dinner,
      With their minds made up that they wouldn't get thinner

On Argentine joint, potatoes and greens,
And the cook would appear from behind the scenes
And say in a voice that was broken with sorrow:
'I'm afraid you must wait and have dinner *tomorrow*!
For the joint has gone from the oven — like that!'
Then the family would say: 'It's that horrible cat!
It was Mungojerrie — or Rumpelteazer!' — And most of the time they
left it at that.

Mungojerrie and Rumpelteazer had a wonderful way of working
together.
And some of the time you would say it was luck, and some of the time
you would say it was weather.
They would go through the house like a hurricane, and no sober person
could take his oath
Was it Mungojerrie — or Rumpelteazer? or could you have sworn that
it mightn't be both?
And when you heard a dining-room smash
Or up from the pantry there came a loud crash
Or down from the library came a loud *ping*
From a vase which was commonly said to be Ming —
Then the family would say: 'Now which was which cat?
It was Mungojerrie! AND Rumpelteazer!' — And there's nothing at all
to be done about that!

Old Deuteronomy

Old Deuteronomy's lived a long time;
   He's a Cat who has lived many lives in succession.
He was famous in proverb and famous in rhyme
   A long while before Queen Victoria's accession.
Old Deuteronomy's buried nine wives
   And more — I am tempted to say, ninety-nine;
And his numerous progeny prospers and thrives
   And the village is proud of him in his decline.
At the sight of that placid and bland physiognomy,
   When he sits in the sun on the vicarage wall,
The Oldest Inhabitant croaks: 'Well, of all . . .
   Things . . . Can it be . . . really! . . . No! . . . Yes! . . .
     Ho! hi!
     Oh, my eye!
My mind may be wandering, but I confess
I *believe* it is Old Deuteronomy!'

Old Deuteronomy sits in the street,
   He sits in the High Street on market day;
The bullocks may bellow, the sheep they may bleat,
   But the dogs and the herdsmen will turn them away.
The cars and the lorries run over the kerb,
   And the villagers put up a notice: ROAD CLOSED —
So that nothing untoward may chance to disturb
   Deuteronomy's rest when he feels so disposed
Or when he's engaged in domestic economy:
   And the Oldest Inhabitant croaks: 'Well, of all . . .
   Things . . . Can it be . . . really! . . . No! . . . Yes! . . .
     Ho! hi!
     Oh, my eye!
My sight's unreliable, but I can guess
That the cause of the trouble is Old Deuteronomy!'

Old Deuteronomy lies on the floor
　　Of the Fox and French Horn for his afternoon sleep;
And when the men say: 'There's just time for one more,'
　　Then the landlady from her back parlour will peep
And say: 'Now then, out you go, by the back door,
　　For Old Deuteronomy musn't be woken —
I'll have the police if there's any uproar' —
　　And out they all shuffle, without a word spoken.
The digestive repose of that feline's gastronomy
　　Must never be broken, whatever befall:
And the Oldest Inhabitant croaks: 'Well, of all . . .
　　Things . . . Can it be . . . really! . . . Yes! . . . No! . . .
　　　Ho! hi!
　　　Oh, my eye!
My legs may be tottery, I must go slow
And be careful of Old Deuteronomy!'

Of the Awefull Battle
of the Pekes and the Pollicles

*Together with some Account of the Participation
of the Pugs and the Poms, and the Intervention
of the Great Rumpuscat*

The Pekes and the Pollicles, everyone knows,
Are proud and implacable passionate foes;
It is always the same, wherever one goes.
And the Pugs and the Poms, although most people say
That they do not like fighting, yet once in a way,
Or now and again, they join in to the fray
And they
        Bark bark bark bark
        Bark bark BARK BARK
    Until you can hear them all over the Park.

Now on the occasion of which I shall speak
Almost nothing had happened for nearly a week
(And that's a long time for a Pol or a Peke).
The big Police Dog was away from his beat —
I don't know the reason, but most people think
He'd slipped into the Wellington Arms for a drink —
And no one at all was about on the street
When a Peke and a Pollicle happened to meet.
They did not advance, or exactly retreat,
But they glared at each other, and scraped their hind feet,
And started to
        Bark bark bark bark
        Bark bark BARK BARK
    Until you could hear them all over the Park.

Now the Peke, although people may say what they please,
Is no British Dog, but a Heathen Chinese.

222

And so all the Pekes, when they heard the uproar,
Some came to the window, some came to the door;
There were surely a dozen, more likely a score.
And together they started to grumble and wheeze
In their huffery-snuffery Heathen Chinese.
But a terrible din is what Pollicles like,
For your Pollicle Dog is a dour Yorkshire tyke,
And his braw Scottish cousins are snappers and biters,
And every dog-jack of them notable fighters;
And so they stepped out, with their pipers in order,
Playing *When the Blue Bonnets Came Over the Border*.
Then the Pugs and the Poms held no longer aloof,
But some from the balcony, some from the roof,
Joined in
To the din
With a

    Bark bark bark bark
    Bark bark BARK BARK
   Until you could hear them all over the Park.

Now when these bold heroes together assembled,
The traffic all stopped, and the Underground trembled,
And some of the neighbours were so much afraid
That they started to ring up the Fire Brigade.
When suddenly, up from a small basement flat,
Why who should stalk out but the GREAT RUMPUSCAT.
His eyes were like fireballs fearfully blazing,
He gave a great yawn, and his jaws were amazing;
And when he looked out through the bars of the area,
You never saw anything fiercer or hairier.
And what with the glare of his eyes and his yawning,
The Pekes and the Pollicles quickly took warning.
He looked at the sky and he gave a great leap —
And they every last one of them scattered like sheep.

And when the Police Dog returned to his beat,
There wasn't a single one left in the street.

Mr. Mistoffelees

You ought to know Mr. Mistoffelees!
The Original Conjuring Cat —
(There can be no doubt about that).
Please listen to me and don't scoff. All his
Inventions are off his own bat.
There's no such Cat in the metropolis;
He holds all the patent monopolies
For performing surprising illusions
And creating eccentric confusions.
    At prestidigitation
        And at legerdemain
    He'll defy examination
        And deceive you again.
The greatest magicians have something to learn
From Mr. Mistoffelees' Conjuring Turn.
Presto!
    Away we go!
        And we all say: OH!
            Well I never!
            Was there ever
            A Cat so clever
                As Magical Mr. Mistoffelees!

He is quiet and small, he is black
From his ears to the tip of his tail;
He can creep through the tiniest crack
He can walk on the narrowest rail.
He can pick any card from a pack,
He is equally cunning with dice;
He is always deceiving you into believing
That he's only hunting for mice.
    He can play any trick with a cork
        Or a spoon and a bit of fish-paste;

If you look for a knife or a fork
And you think it is merely misplaced —
You have seen it one moment, and then it is *gawn*!
But you'll find it next week lying out on the lawn.
And we all say: OH!
Well I never!
Was there ever
A Cat so clever
As Magical Mr. Mistoffelees!

His manner is vague and aloof,
You would think there was nobody shyer —
But his voice has been heard on the roof
When he was curled up by the fire.
And he's sometimes been heard by the fire
When he was about on the roof —
(At least we all *heard* that somebody purred)
Which is incontestable proof
Of his singular magical powers:
And I have known the family to call
Him in from the garden for hours,
While he was asleep in the hall.
And not long ago this phenomenal Cat
Produced *seven kittens* right out of a hat!
And we all said: OH!
Well I never!
Did you ever
Know a Cat so clever
As Magical Mr. Mistoffelees!

Macavity: the Mystery Cat

Macavity's a Mystery Cat: he's called the Hidden Paw —
For he's the master criminal who can defy the Law.
He's the bafflement of Scotland Yard, the Flying Squad's despair:
For when they reach the scene of crime — *Macavity's not there*!

Macavity, Macavity, there's no one like Macavity,
He's broken every human law, he breaks the law of gravity.
His powers of levitation would make a fakir stare,
And when you reach the scene of crime — *Macavity's not there*!
You may seek him in the basement, you may look up in the air —
But I tell you once and once again, *Macavity's not there*!

Macavity's a ginger cat, he's very tall and thin;
You would know him if you saw him, for his eyes are sunken in.
His brow is deeply lined with thought, his head is highly domed;
His coat is dusty from neglect, his whiskers are uncombed.
He sways his head from side to side, with movements like a snake;
And when you think he's half asleep, he's always wide awake.

Macavity, Macavity, there's no one like Macavity,
For he's a fiend in feline shape, a monster of depravity.
You may meet him in a by-street, you may see him in the square —
But when a crime's discovered, then *Macavity's not there*!

He's outwardly respectable. (They say he cheats at cards.)
And his footprints are not found in any file of Scotland Yard's.
And when the larder's looted, or the jewel-case is rifled,
Or when the milk is missing, or another Peke's been stifled,
Or the greenhouse glass is broken, and the trellis past repair —
Ay, there's the wonder of the thing! *Macavity's not there*!

And when the Foreign Office find a Treaty's gone astray,
Or the Admiralty lose some plans and drawings by the way,

There may be a scrap of paper in the hall or on the stair —
But it's useless to investigate — *Macavity's not there*!
And when the loss has been disclosed, the Secret Service say:
'It *must* have been Macavity!' — but he's a mile away.
You'll be sure to find him resting, or a-licking of his thumbs,
Or engaged in doing complicated long division sums.

Macavity, Macavity, there's no one like Macavity,
There never was a Cat of such deceitfulness and suavity.
He always has an alibi, and one or two to spare:
At whatever time the deed took place — MACAVITY WASN'T THERE!
And they say that all the Cats whose wicked deeds are widely known
(I might mention Mungojerrie, I might mention Griddlebone)
Are nothing more than agents for the Cat who all the time
Just controls their operations: the Napoleon of Crime!

Gus: the Theatre Cat

Gus is the Cat at the Theatre Door.
His name, as I ought to have told you before,
Is really Asparagus. That's such a fuss
To pronounce, that we usually call him just Gus.
His coat's very shabby, he's thin as a rake,
And he suffers from palsy that makes his paw shake.
Yet he was, in his youth, quite the smartest of Cats —
But no longer a terror to mice and to rats.
For he isn't the Cat that he was in his prime;
Though his name was quite famous, he says, in its time.
And whenever he joins his friends at their club
(Which takes place at the back of the neighbouring pub)
He loves to regale them, if someone else pays,
With anecdotes drawn from his palmiest days.
For he once was a Star of the highest degree —
He has acted with Irving, he's acted with Tree.
And he likes to relate his success on the Halls,
Where the Gallery once gave him seven cat-calls.
But his grandest creation, as he loves to tell,
Was Firefrorefiddle, the Fiend of the Fell.

'I have played', so he says, 'every possible part,
And I used to know seventy speeches by heart.
I'd extemporize back-chat, I knew how to gag,
And I knew how to let the cat out of the bag.
I knew how to act with my back and my tail;
With an hour of rehearsal, I never could fail.
I'd a voice that would soften the hardest of hearts,
Whether I took the lead, or in character parts.
I have sat by the bedside of poor Little Nell;
When the Curfew was rung, then I swung on the bell.
In the Pantomime season I never fell flat,
And I once understudied Dick Whittington's Cat.

But my grandest creation, as history will tell,
Was Firefrorefiddle, the Fiend of the Fell.'

Then, if someone will give him a toothful of gin,
He will tell how he once played a part in *East Lynne*.
At a Shakespeare performance he once walked on pat,
When some actor suggested the need for a cat.
He once played a Tiger — could do it again —
Which an Indian Colonel pursued down a drain.
And he thinks that he still can, much better than most,
Produce blood-curdling noises to bring on the Ghost.
And he once crossed the stage on a telegraph wire,
To rescue a child when a house was on fire.
And he says: 'Now, these kittens, they do not get trained
As we did in the days when Victoria reigned.
They never get drilled in a regular troupe,
And they think they are smart, just to jump through a hoop.'
And he'll say, as he scratches himself with his claws,
'Well, the Theatre's certainly not what it was.
These modern productions are all very well,
But there's nothing to equal, from what I hear tell,
    That moment of mystery
    When I made history
As Firefrorefiddle, the Fiend of the Fell.'

Bustopher Jones: the Cat About Town

Bustopher Jones is *not* skin and bones —
In fact, he's remarkably fat.
He doesn't haunt pubs — he has eight or nine clubs,
For he's the St. James's Street Cat!
He's the Cat we all greet as he walks down the street
In his coat of fastidious black:
No commonplace mousers have such well-cut trousers
Or such an impeccable back.
In the whole of St. James's the smartest of names is
The name of this Brummell of Cats;
And we're all of us proud to be nodded or bowed to
By Bustopher Jones in white spats!

His visits are occasional to the *Senior Educational*
And it is against the rules
For any one Cat to belong both to that
And the *Joint Superior Schools*.
For a similar reason, when game is in season
He is found, not at *Fox's*, but *Blimp's*;
But he's frequently seen at the gay *Stage and Screen*
Which is famous for winkles and shrimps.
In the season of venison he gives his ben'son
To the *Pothunter's* succulent bones;
And just before noon's not a moment too soon
To drop in for a drink at the *Drones*.
When he's seen in a hurry there's probably curry
At the *Siamese* — or at the *Glutton*;
If he looks full of gloom then he's lunched at the *Tomb*
On cabbage, rice pudding and mutton.

So, much in this way, passes Bustopher's day —
At one club or another he's found.

It can be no surprise that under our eyes
He has grown unmistakably round.
He's a twenty-five pounder, or I am a bounder,
And he's putting on weight every day:
But he's so well preserved because he's observed
All his life a routine, so he'd say.
Or, to put it in rhyme: 'I shall last out my time'
Is the word for this stoutest of Cats.
It must and it shall be Spring in Pall Mall
While Bustopher Jones wears white spats!

Skimbleshanks: the Railway Cat

There's a whisper down the line at 11.39
When the Night Mail's ready to depart,
Saying 'Skimble where is Skimble has he gone to hunt the thimble?
We must find him or the train can't start.'
All the guards and all the porters and the stationmaster's daughters
They are searching high and low,
Saying 'Skimble where is Skimble for unless he's very nimble
Then the Night Mail just can't go.'
At 11.42 then the signal's overdue
And the passengers are frantic to a man —
Then Skimble will appear and he'll saunter to the rear:
He's been busy in the luggage van!
 He gives one flash of his glass-green eyes
  And the signal goes 'All Clear!'
 And we're off at last for the northern part
  Of the Northern Hemisphere!

You may say that by and large it is Skimble who's in charge
Of the Sleeping Car Express.
From the driver and the guards to the bagmen playing cards
He will supervise them all, more or less.
Down the corridor he paces and examines all the faces
Of the travellers in the First and in the Third;
He establishes control by a regular patrol
And he'd know at once if anything occurred.
He will watch you without winking and he sees what you are thinking
And it's certain that he doesn't approve
Of hilarity and riot, so the folk are very quiet
When Skimble is about and on the move.
 You can play no pranks with Skimbleshanks!
  He's a Cat that cannot be ignored;
 So nothing goes wrong on the Northern Mail
  When Skimbleshanks is aboard.

Oh it's very pleasant when you have found your little den
With your name written up on the door.
And the berth is very neat with a newly folded sheet
And there's not a speck of dust on the floor.
There is every sort of light — you can make it dark or bright;
There's a button that you turn to make a breeze.
There's a funny little basin you're supposed to wash your face in
And a crank to shut the window if you sneeze.
Then the guard looks in politely and will ask you very brightly
'Do you like your morning tea weak or strong?'
But Skimble's just behind him and was ready to remind him.
For Skimble won't let anything go wrong.
   And when you creep into your cosy berth
      And pull up the counterpane,
   You ought to reflect that it's very nice
   To know that you won't be bothered by mice —
   You can leave all that to the Railway Cat,
      The Cat of the Railway Train!

In the watches of the night he is always fresh and bright;
Every now and then he has a cup of tea
With perhaps a drop of Scotch while he's keeping on the watch,
Only stopping here and there to catch a flea.
You were fast asleep at Crewe and so you never knew
That he was walking up and down the station;
You were sleeping all the while he was busy at Carlisle,
Where he greets the stationmaster with elation.
But you saw him at Dumfries, where he summons the police
If there's anything they ought to know about:
When you get to Gallowgate there you do not have to wait —
For Skimbleshanks will help you to get out!
   He gives you a wave of his long brown tail
      Which says: 'I'll see you again!
   You'll meet without fail on the Midnight Mail
      The Cat of the Railway Train.'

The Ad-dressing of Cats

You've read of several kinds of Cat,
And my opinion now is that
You should need no interpreter
To understand their character.
You now have learned enough to see
That Cats are much like you and me
And other people whom we find
Possessed of various types of mind.
For some are sane and some are mad
And some are good and some are bad
And some are better, some are worse —
But all may be described in verse.
You've seen them both at work and games,
And learnt about their proper names,
Their habits and their habitat:
But
    How would you ad-dress a Cat?

So first, your memory I'll jog,
And say: A CAT IS NOT A DOG.

Now Dogs pretend they like to fight;
They often bark, more seldom bite;
But yet a Dog is, on the whole,
What you would call a simple soul.
Of course I'm not including Pekes,
And such fantastic canine freaks.
The usual Dog about the Town
Is much inclined to play the clown,
And far from showing too much pride
Is frequently undignified.
He's very easily taken in —
Just chuck him underneath the chin

Or slap his back or shake his paw,
And he will gambol and guffaw.
He's such an easy-going lout,
He'll answer any hail or shout.

Again I must remind you that
A Dog's a Dog — A CAT'S A CAT.

With Cats, some say, one rule is true:
Don't speak till you are spoken to.
Myself, I do not hold with that —
I say, you should ad-dress a Cat.
But always keep in mind that he
Resents familiarity.
I bow, and taking off my hat,
Ad-dress him in this form: O CAT!
But if he is the Cat next door,
Whom I have often met before
(He comes to see me in my flat)
I greet him with an OOPSA CAT!
I think I've heard them call him James —
But we've not got so far as names.
Before a Cat will condescend
To treat you as a trusted friend,
Some little token of esteem
Is needed, like a dish of cream;
And you might now and then supply
Some caviare, or Strassburg Pie,
Some potted grouse, or salmon paste —
He's sure to have his personal taste.
(I know a Cat, who makes a habit
Of eating nothing else but rabbit,
And when he's finished, licks his paws
So's not to waste the onion sauce.)
A Cat's entitled to expect
These evidences of respect.
And so in time you reach your aim,
And finally call him by his NAME.

So this is this, and that is that:
And there's how you AD-DRESS A CAT.

235

Cat Morgan Introduces Himself

I once was a Pirate what sailed the 'igh seas —
　　But now I've retired as a com-mission-aire:
And that's how you find me a-takin' my ease
　　And keepin' the door in a Bloomsbury Square.

I'm partial to partridges, likewise to grouse,
　　And I favour that Devonshire cream in a bowl;
But I'm allus content with a drink on the 'ouse
　　And a bit o' cold fish when I done me patrol.

I ain't got much polish, me manners is gruff,
　　But I've got a good coat, and I keep meself smart;
And everyone says, and I guess that's enough;
　　'You can't but like Morgan, 'e's got a good 'art.'

I got knocked about on the Barbary Coast,
　　And me voice it ain't no sich melliferous horgan;
But yet I can state, and I'm not one to boast,
　　That some of the gals is dead keen on old Morgan.

So if you 'ave business with Faber — or Faber —
　　I'll give you this tip, and it's worth a lot more:
You'll save yourself time, and you'll spare yourself labour
　　If jist you make friends with the Cat at the door.

　　　　　　　　　　　　　MORGAN.

MURDER IN THE CATHEDRAL

Characters

PART I

A CHORUS OF WOMEN OF CANTERBURY
THREE PRIESTS OF THE CATHEDRAL
A MESSENGER
ARCHBISHOP THOMAS BECKET
FOUR TEMPTERS
ATTENDANTS

The scene is the Archbishop's Hall,
on December 2nd, 1170

PART II

THREE PRIESTS
FOUR KNIGHTS
ARCHBISHOP THOMAS BECKET
CHORUS OF WOMEN OF CANTERBURY
ATTENDANTS

The first scene is in the Archbishop's Hall,
the second scene is in the Cathedral,
on December 29th, 1170

Part I

CHORUS. Here let us stand, close by the cathedral. Here let us wait.
> Are we drawn by danger? Is it the knowledge of safety, that draws
> > our feet
> Towards the cathedral? What danger can be
> For us, the poor, the poor women of Canterbury? what tribulation
> With which we are not already familiar? There is no danger
> For us, and there is no safety in the cathedral. Some presage of an
> > act
> Which our eyes are compelled to witness, has forced our feet
> Towards the cathedral. We are forced to bear witness.

> Since golden October declined into sombre November
> And the apples were gathered and stored, and the land became
> > brown sharp points of death in a waste of water and mud,
> The New Year waits, breathes, waits, whispers in darkness.
> While the labourer kicks off a muddy boot and stretches his hand
> > to the fire,
> The New Year waits, destiny waits for the coming.
> Who has stretched out his hand to the fire and remembered the
> > Saints at All Hallows,
> Remembered the martyrs and saints who wait? and who shall
> Stretch out his hand to the fire, and deny his master? who shall be
> > warm
> By the fire, and deny his master?

> Seven years and the summer is over
> Seven years since the Archbishop left us,
> He who was always kind to his people.
> But it would not be well if he should return.
> King rules or barons rule;
> We have suffered various oppression,
> But mostly we are left to our own devices,
> And we are content if we are left alone.

We try to keep our households in order;
The merchant, shy and cautious, tries to compile a little fortune,
And the labourer bends to his piece of earth, earth-colour, his own
    colour,
Preferring to pass unobserved.
Now I fear disturbance of the quiet seasons:
Winter shall come bringing death from the sea,
Ruinous spring shall beat at our doors,
Root and shoot shall eat our eyes and our ears,
Disastrous summer burn up the beds of our streams
And the poor shall wait for another decaying October.
Why should the summer bring consolation
For autumn fires and winter fogs?
What shall we do in the heat of summer
But wait in barren orchards for another October?
Some malady is coming upon us. We wait, we wait,
And the saints and martyrs wait, for those who shall be martyrs and
    saints.
Destiny waits in the hand of God, shaping the still unshapen:
I have seen these things in a shaft of sunlight.
Destiny waits in the hand of God, not in the hands of statesmen
Who do, some well, some ill, planning and guessing,
Having their aims which turn in their hands in the pattern of time.
Come, happy December, who shall observe you, who shall preserve
    you?
Shall the Son of Man be born again in the litter of scorn?
For us, the poor, there is no action,
But only to wait and to witness.

[*Enter* PRIESTS]

FIRST PRIEST. Seven years and the summer is over.
    Seven years since the Archbishop left us.
SECOND PRIEST. What does the Archbishop do, and our Sovereign
    Lord the Pope
    With the stubborn King and the French King
    In ceaseless intrigue, combinations,
    In conference, meetings accepted, meetings refused,
    Meetings unended or endless
    At one place or another in France?
THIRD PRIEST. I see nothing quite conclusive in the art of temporal
    government,

But violence, duplicity and frequent malversation.
King rules or barons rule:
The strong man strongly and the weak man by caprice.
They have but one law, to seize the power and keep it,
And the steadfast can manipulate the greed and lust of others,
The feeble is devoured by his own.

FIRST PRIEST. Shall these things not end
Until the poor at the gate
Have forgotten their friend, their Father in God, have forgotten
That they had a friend?

[*Enter* MESSENGER]

MESSENGER. Servants of God, and watchers of the temple,
I am here to inform you, without circumlocution:
The Archbishop is in England, and is close outside the city.
I was sent before in haste
To give you notice of his coming, as much as was possible,
That you may prepare to meet him.

FIRST PRIEST. What, is the exile ended, is our Lord Archbishop
Reunited with the King? what reconciliation
Of two proud men?

THIRD PRIEST.   What peace can be found
To grow between the hammer and the anvil?

SECOND PRIEST.   Tell us,
Are the old disputes at an end, is the wall of pride cast down
That divided them? Is it peace or war?

FIRST PRIEST.   Does he come
In full assurance, or only secure
In the power of Rome, the spiritual rule,
The assurance of right, and the love of the people?

MESSENGER. You are right to express a certain incredulity.
He comes in pride and sorrow, affirming all his claims,
Assured, beyond doubt, of the devotion of the people,
Who receive him with scenes of frenzied enthusiasm,
Lining the road and throwing down their capes,
Strewing the way with leaves and late flowers of the season.
The streets of the city will be packed to suffocation,
And I think that his horse will be deprived of its tail,
A single hair of which becomes a precious relic.
He is at one with the Pope, and with the King of France,
Who indeed would have liked to detain him in his kingdom:

But as for our King, that is another matter.

FIRST PRIEST. But again, is it war or peace?

MESSENGER.   Peace, but not the kiss of peace.

A patched up affair, if you ask my opinion.
And if you ask me, I think the Lord Archbishop
Is not the man to cherish any illusions,
Or yet to diminish the least of his pretensions.
If you ask my opinion, I think that this peace
Is nothing like an end, or like a beginning.
It is common knowledge that when the Archbishop
Parted from the King, he said to the King,
My Lord, he said, I leave you as a man
Whom in this life I shall not see again.
I have this, I assure you, on the highest authority;
There are several opinions as to what he meant,
But no one considers it a happy prognostic.

[*Exit*]

FIRST PRIEST. I fear for the Archbishop, I fear for the Church,
I know that the pride bred of sudden prosperity
Was but confirmed by bitter adversity.
I saw him as Chancellor, flattered by the King.
Liked or feared by courtiers, in their overbearing fashion,
Despised and despising, always isolated,
Never one among them, always insecure;
His pride always feeding upon his own virtues,
Pride drawing sustenance from impartiality,
Pride drawing sustenance from generosity,
Loathing power given by temporal devolution,
Wishing subjection to God alone.
Had the King been greater, or had he been weaker
Things had perhaps been different for Thomas.

SECOND PRIEST. Yet our lord is returned. Our lord has come back to
his own again.
We have had enough of waiting, from December to dismal
December.
The Archbishop shall be at our head, dispelling dismay and doubt.
He will tell us what we are to do, he will give us our orders, instruct
us.
Our Lord is at one with the Pope, and also the King of France.
We can lean on a rock, we can feel a firm foothold

Against the perpetual wash of tides of balance of forces of barons
    and landholders.
The rock of God is beneath our feet. Let us meet the Archbishop
    with cordial thanksgiving:
Our lord, our Archbishop returns. And when the Archbishop
    returns
Our doubts are dispelled. Let us therefore rejoice,
I say rejoice, and show a glad face for his welcome.
I am the Archbishop's man. Let us give the Archbishop welcome!
THIRD PRIEST. For good or ill, let the wheel turn.
    The wheel has been still, these seven years, and no good.
    For ill or good, let the wheel turn.
    For who knows the end of good or evil?
    Until the grinders cease
    And the door shall be shut in the street,
    And all the daughters of music shall be brought low.
CHORUS. Here is no continuing city, here is no abiding stay.
    Ill the wind, ill the time, uncertain the profit, certain the danger.
    O late late late, late is the time, late too late, and rotten the year;
    Evil the wind, and bitter the sea, and grey the sky, grey grey grey.
    O Thomas, return, Archbishop; return, return to France.
    Return. Quickly. Quietly. Leave us to perish in quiet.
    You come with applause, you come with rejoicing, but you come
        bringing death into Canterbury:
    A doom on the house, a doom on yourself, a doom on the world.

    We do not wish anything to happen.
    Seven years we have lived quietly,
    Succeeded in avoiding notice,
    Living and partly living.
    There have been oppression and luxury,
    There have been poverty and licence,
    There has been minor injustice.
    Yet we have gone on living,
    Living and partly living.
    Sometimes the corn has failed us,
    Sometimes the harvest is good,
    One year is a year of rain,
    Another a year of dryness,
    One year the apples are abundant,

Another year the plums are lacking.
Yet we have gone on living,
Living and partly living.
We have kept the feasts, heard the masses,
We have brewed beer and cider,
Gathered wood against the winter,
Talked at the corner of the fire,
Talked at the corners of streets,
Talked not always in whispers,
Living and partly living.
We have seen births, deaths and marriages,
We have had various scandals,
We have been afflicted with taxes,
We have had laughter and gossip,
Several girls have disappeared
Unaccountably, and some not able to.
We have all had our private terrors,
Our particular shadows, our secret fears.
But now a great fear is upon us, a fear not of one but of many,
A fear like birth and death, when we see birth and death alone
In a void apart. We
Are afraid in a fear which we cannot know, which we cannot face,
    which none understands,
And our hearts are torn from us, our brains unskinned like the
    layers of an onion, our selves are lost lost
In a final fear which none understands. O Thomas Archbishop,
O Thomas our Lord, leave us and leave us be, in our humble and
    tarnished frame of existence, leave us; do not ask us
To stand to the doom on the house, the doom on the Archbishop,
    the doom on the world.
Archbishop, secure and assured of your fate, unaffrayed among the
    shades, do you realise what you ask, do you realise what it
    means
To the small folk drawn into the pattern of fate, the small folk who
    live among small things,
The strain on the brain of the small folk who stand to the doom of
    the house, the doom of their lord, the doom of the world?
O Thomas, Archbishop, leave us, leave us, leave sullen Dover, and
    set sail for France. Thomas our Archbishop still our
    Archbishop even in France. Thomas Archbishop, set the

white sail between the grey sky and the bitter sea, leave us,
leave us for France.

SECOND PRIEST. What a way to talk at such a juncture!
You are foolish, immodest and babbling women.
Do you not know that the good Archbishop
Is likely to arrive at any moment?
The crowds in the streets will be cheering and cheering,
You go on croaking like frogs in the treetops:
But frogs at least can be cooked and eaten.
Whatever you are afraid of, in your craven apprehension,
Let me ask you at the least to put on pleasant faces,
And give a hearty welcome to our good Archbishop.

[*Enter* THOMAS]

THOMAS. Peace. And let them be, in their exaltation.
They speak better than they know, and beyond your understanding.
They know and do not know, what it is to act or suffer.
They know and do not know, that action is suffering
And suffering is action. Neither does the agent suffer
Nor the patient act. But both are fixed
In an eternal action, an eternal patience
To which all must consent that it may be willed
And which all must suffer that they may will it,
That the pattern may subsist, for the pattern is the action
And the suffering, that the wheel may turn and still
Be forever still.

SECOND PRIEST. O my Lord, forgive me, I did not see you coming,
Engrossed by the chatter of these foolish women.
Forgive us, my Lord, you would have had a better welcome
If we had been sooner prepared for the event.
But your Lordship knows that seven years of waiting,
Seven years of prayer, seven years of emptiness,
Have better prepared our hearts for your coming,
Than seven days could make ready Canterbury.
However, I will have fires laid in all your rooms
To take the chill off our English December,
Your Lordship now being used to a better climate.
Your Lordship will find your rooms in order as you left them.

THOMAS. And will try to leave them in order as I find them.
I am more than grateful for all your kind attentions.
These are small matters. Little rest in Canterbury

With eager enemies restless about us.
Rebellious bishops, York, London, Salisbury,
Would have intercepted our letters,
Filled the coast with spies and sent to meet me
Some who hold me in bitterest hate.
By God's grace aware of their prevision
I sent my letters on another day,
Had fair crossing, found at Sandwich
Broc, Warenne, and the Sheriff of Kent,
Those who had sworn to have my head from me
Only John, the Dean of Salisbury,
Fearing for the King's name, warning against treason,
Made them hold their hands. So for the time
We are unmolested.

FIRST PRIEST.   But do they follow after?

THOMAS. For a little time the hungry hawk
    Will only soar and hover, circling lower,
    Waiting excuse, pretence, opportunity.
    End will be simple, sudden, God-given.
    Meanwhile the substance of our first act
    Will be shadows, and the strife with shadows.
    Heavier the interval than the consummation.
    All things prepare the event. Watch.

[*Enter* FIRST TEMPTER]

FIRST TEMPTER. You see, my Lord, I do not wait upon ceremony:
    Here I have come, forgetting all acrimony,
    Hoping that your present gravity
    Will find excuse for my humble levity
    Remembering all the good time past.
    Your Lordship won't despise an old friend out of favour?
    Old Tom, gay Tom, Becket of London,
    Your Lordship won't forget that evening on the river
    When the King, and you and I were all friends together?
    Friendship should be more than biting Time can sever.
    What, my Lord, now that you recover
    Favour with the King, shall we say that summer's over
    Or that the good time cannot last?
    Fluting in the meadows, viols in the hall,
    Laughter and apple-blossom floating on the water,
    Singing at nightfall, whispering in chambers,

Fires devouring the winter season,
Eating up the darkness, with wit and wine and wisdom!
Now that the King and you are in amity,
Clergy and laity may return to gaiety,
Mirth and sportfulness need not walk warily.

THOMAS. You talk of seasons that are past. I remember
Not worth forgetting.

TEMPTER.   And of the new season.
Spring has come in winter. Snow in the branches
Shall float as sweet as blossoms. Ice along the ditches
Mirror the sunlight. Love in the orchard
Send the sap shooting. Mirth matches melancholy.

THOMAS. We do not know very much of the future
Except that from generation to generation
The same things happen again and again.
Men learn little from others' experience.
But in the life of one man, never
The same time returns. Sever
The cord, shed the scale. Only
The fool, fixed in his folly, may think
He can turn the wheel on which he turns.

TEMPTER. My Lord, a nod is as good as a wink.
A man will often love what he spurns.
For the good times past, that are come again
I am your man.

THOMAS.   Not in this train
Look to your behaviour. You were safer
Think of penitence and follow your master.

TEMPTER. Not at this gait!
If you go so fast, others may go faster.
Your Lordship is too proud!
The safest beast is not the one that roars most loud,
This was not the way of the King our master!
You were not used to be so hard upon sinners
When they were your friends. Be easy, man!
The easy man lives to eat the best dinners.
Take a friend's advice. Leave well alone,
Or your goose may be cooked and eaten to the bone.

THOMAS. You come twenty years too late.

TEMPTER. Then I leave you to your fate.

I leave you to the pleasures of your higher vices,
Which will have to be paid for at higher prices.
Farewell, my Lord, I do not wait upon ceremony,
I leave as I came, forgetting all acrimony,
Hoping that your present gravity
Will find excuse for my humble levity.
If you will remember me, my Lord, at your prayers,
I'll remember you at kissing-time below the stairs.

THOMAS. Leave-well-alone, the springtime fancy,
So one thought goes whistling down the wind.
The impossible is still temptation.
The impossible, the undesirable,
Voices under sleep, waking a dead world,
So that the mind may not be whole in the present.

[*Enter* SECOND TEMPTER]

SECOND TEMPTER. Your Lordship has forgotten me, perhaps. I will
remind you.
We met at Clarendon, at Northampton,
And last at Montmirail, in Maine. Now that I have recalled them,
Let us but set these not too pleasant memories
In balance against other, earlier
And weightier ones: those of the Chancellorship.
See how the late ones rise! You, master of policy
Whom all acknowledged, should guide the state again.

THOMAS. Your meaning?

TEMPTER.   The Chancellorship that you resigned
When you were made Archbishop — that was a mistake
On your part — still may be regained. Think, my Lord,
Power obtained grows to glory,
Life lasting, a permanent possession.
A templed tomb, monument of marble.
Rule over men reckon no madness.

THOMAS. To the man of God what gladness?

TEMPTER.   Sadness
Only to those giving love to God alone.
Shall he who held the solid substance
Wander waking with deceitful shadows?
Power is present. Holiness hereafter.

THOMAS. Who then?

TEMPTER.   The Chancellor, King and Chancellor.

King commands. Chancellor richly rules.
This is a sentence not taught in the schools.
To set down the great, protect the poor,
Beneath the throne of God can man do more?
Disarm the ruffian, strengthen the laws,
Rule for the good of the better cause,
Dispensing justice make all even,
Is thrive on earth, and perhaps in heaven.

THOMAS. What means?

TEMPTER.   Real power
Is purchased at price of a certain submission.
Your spiritual power is earthly perdition.
Power is present, for him who will wield.

THOMAS. Who shall have it?

TEMPTER.   He who will come.

THOMAS. What shall be the month?

TEMPTER.   The last from the first.

THOMAS. What shall we give for it?

TEMPTER.   Pretence of priestly power.

THOMAS. Why should we give it?

TEMPTER.   For the power and the glory.

THOMAS. No!

TEMPTER.   Yes! Or bravery will be broken,
Cabined in Canterbury, realmless ruler,
Self-bound servant of a powerless Pope,
The old stag, circled with hounds.

THOMAS. No!

TEMPTER.   Yes! men must manœuvre. Monarchs also,
Waging war abroad, need fast friends at home.
Private policy is public profit;
Dignity still shall be dressed with decorum.

THOMAS. You forget the bishops
Whom I have laid under excommunication.

TEMPTER. Hungry hatred
Will not strive against intelligent self-interest.

THOMAS. You forget the barons. Who will not forget
Constant curbing of petty privilege.

TEMPTER. Against the barons
Is King's cause, churl's cause, Chancellor's cause.

THOMAS. No! shall I, who keep the keys

Of heaven and hell, supreme alone in England,
Who bind and loose, with power from the Pope,
Descend to desire a punier power?
Delegate to deal the doom of damnation,
To condemn kings, not serve among their servants,
Is my open office. No! Go.
TEMPTER. Then I leave you to your fate.
Your sin soars sunward, covering kings' falcons.
THOMAS. Temporal power, to build a good world,
To keep order, as the world knows order.
Those who put their faith in worldly order
Not controlled by the order of God,
In confident ignorance, but arrest disorder,
Make it fast, breed fatal disease,
Degrade what they exalt. Power with the King —
I *was* the King, his arm, his better reason.
But what was once exaltation
Would now be only mean descent.
[*Enter* THIRD TEMPTER]
THIRD TEMPTER. I am an unexpected visitor.
THOMAS.   I expected you.
TEMPTER. But not in this guise, or for my present purpose.
THOMAS. No purpose brings surprise.
TEMPTER.   Well, my Lord,
I am no trifler, and no politician.
To idle or intrigue at court
I have no skill. I am no courtier.
I know a horse, a dog, a wench;
I know how to hold my estates in order,
A country-keeping lord who minds his own business.
It is we country lords who know the country
And we who know what the country needs.
It is our country. We care for the country.
We are the backbone of the nation.
We, not the plotting parasites
About the King. Excuse my bluntness:
I am a rough straightforward Englishman.
THOMAS. Proceed straight forward.
TEMPTER.   Purpose is plain.
Endurance of friendship does not depend

Upon ourselves, but upon circumstance.
But circumstance is not undetermined.
Unreal friendship may turn to real
But real friendship, once ended, cannot be mended.
Sooner shall enmity turn to alliance.
The enmity that never knew friendship
Can sooner know accord.

THOMAS.   For a countryman
You wrap your meaning in as dark generality
As any courtier.

TEMPTER.   This is the simple fact!
You have no hope of reconciliation
With Henry the King. You look only
To blind assertion in isolation.
That is a mistake.

THOMAS.   O Henry, O my King!

TEMPTER.   Other friends
May be found in the present situation.
King in England is not all-powerful;
King is in France, squabbling in Anjou;
Round him waiting hungry sons.
We are for England. We are in England.
You and I, my Lord, are Normans.
England is a land for Norman
Sovereignty. Let the Angevin
Destroy himself, fighting in Anjou.
He does not understand us, the English barons.
We are the people.

THOMAS. To what does this lead?

TEMPTER.   To a happy coalition
Of intelligent interests.

THOMAS.   But what have you —
If you do speak for barons —

TEMPTER.   For a powerful party
Which has turned its eyes in your direction —
To gain from you, your Lordship asks.
For us, Church favour would be an advantage,
Blessing of Pope powerful protection
In the fight for liberty. You, my Lord,
In being with us, would fight a good stroke

> At once, for England and for Rome,
> Ending the tyrannous jurisdiction
> Of king's court over bishop's court,
> Of king's court over baron's court.

THOMAS. Which I helped to found.

TEMPTER.   Which you helped to found.
> But time past is time forgotten.
> We expect the rise of a new constellation.

THOMAS. And if the Archbishop cannot trust the King,
> How can he trust those who work for King's undoing?

TEMPTER. Kings will allow no power but their own;
> Church and people have good cause against the throne.

THOMAS. If the Archbishop cannot trust the Throne,
> He has good cause to trust none but God alone.
> I ruled once as Chancellor
> And men like you were glad to wait at my door.
> Not only in the court, but in the field
> And in the tilt-yard I made many yield.
> Shall I who ruled like an eagle over doves
> Now take the shape of a wolf among wolves?
> Pursue your treacheries as you have done before:
> No one shall say that I betrayed a king.

TEMPTER. Then, my Lord, I shall not wait at your door.
> And I well hope, before another spring
> The King will show his regard for your loyalty.

THOMAS. To make, then break, this thought has come before,
> The desperate exercise of failing power.
> Samson in Gaza did no more.
> But if I break, I must break myself alone.

[*Enter* FOURTH TEMPTER]

FOURTH TEMPTER. Well done, Thomas, your will is hard to bend.
> And with me beside you, you shall not lack a friend.

THOMAS. Who are you? I expected
> Three visitors, not four.

TEMPTER. Do not be surprised to receive one more.
> Had I been expected, I had been here before.
> I always precede expectation.

THOMAS.   Who are you?

TEMPTER. As you do not know me, I do not need a name,
> And, as you know me, that is why I come.

You know me, but have never seen my face.
To meet before was never time or place.

THOMAS. Say what you come to say.

TEMPTER.   It shall be said at last.
Hooks have been baited with morsels of the past.
Wantonness is weakness. As for the King,
His hardened hatred shall have no end.
You know truly, the King will never trust
Twice, the man who has been his friend.
Borrow use cautiously, employ
Your services as long as you have to lend.
You would wait for trap to snap
Having served your turn, broken and crushed.
As for barons, envy of lesser men
Is still more stubborn than king's anger.
Kings have public policy, barons private profit,
Jealousy raging possession of the fiend.
Barons are employable against each other;
Greater enemies must kings destroy.

THOMAS. What is your counsel?

TEMPTER.   Fare forward to the end.
All other ways are closed to you
Except the way already chosen.
But what is pleasure, kingly rule,
Or rule of men beneath a king,
With craft in corners, stealthy stratagem,
To general grasp of spiritual power?
Man oppressed by sin, since Adam fell —
You hold the keys of heaven and hell.
Power to bind and loose: bind, Thomas, bind,
King and bishop under your heel.
King, emperor, bishop, baron, king:
Uncertain mastery of melting armies,
War, plague, and revolution,
New conspiracies, broken pacts;
To be master or servant within an hour,
This is the course of temporal power.
The Old King shall know it, when at last breath,
No sons, no empire, he bites broken teeth.
You hold the skein: wind, Thomas, wind

    The thread of eternal life and death.

    You hold this power, hold it.

THOMAS.   Supreme, in this land?

TEMPTER. Supreme, but for one.

THOMAS.   That I do not understand.

TEMPTER. It is not for me to tell you how this may be so;

    I am only here, Thomas, to tell you what you know.

THOMAS. How long shall this be?

TEMPTER. Save what you know already, ask nothing of me.

    But think, Thomas, think of glory after death.

    When king is dead, there's another king,

    And one more king is another reign.

    King is forgotten, when another shall come:

    Saint and Martyr rule from the tomb.

    Think, Thomas, think of enemies dismayed,

    Creeping in penance, frightened of a shade;

    Think of pilgrims, standing in line

    Before the glittering jewelled shrine,

    From generation to generation

    Bending the knee in supplication,

    Think of the miracles, by God's grace,

    And think of your enemies, in another place.

THOMAS. I have thought of these things.

TEMPTER.   That is why I tell you.

    Your thoughts have more power than kings to compel you.

    You have also thought, sometimes at your prayers,

    Sometimes hesitating at the angles of stairs,

    And between sleep and waking, early in the morning,

    When the bird cries, have thought of further scorning.

    That nothing lasts, but the wheel turns,

    The nest is rifled, and the bird mourns;

    That the shrine shall be pillaged, and the gold spent,

    The jewels gone for light ladies' ornament,

    The sanctuary broken, and its stores

    Swept into the laps of parasites and whores.

    When miracles cease, and the faithful desert you.

    And men shall only do their best to forget you.

    And later is worse, when men will not hate you

    Enough to defame or to execrate you,

    But pondering the qualities that you lacked

Will only try to find the historical fact.
When men shall declare that there was no mystery
About this man who played a certain part in history.
THOMAS. But what is there to do? what is left to be done?
Is there no enduring crown to be won?
TEMPTER. Yes, Thomas, yes; you have thought of that too.
What can compare with glory of Saints
Dwelling forever in presence of God?
What earthly glory, of king or emperor,
What earthly pride, that is not poverty
Compared with richness of heavenly grandeur?
Seek the way of martyrdom, make yourself the lowest
On earth, to be high in heaven.
And see far off below you, where the gulf is fixed,
Your persecutors, in timeless torment,
Parched passion, beyond expiation.
THOMAS.   No!
Who are you, tempting with my own desires?
Others have come, temporal tempters,
With pleasure and power at palpable price.
What do you offer? what do you ask?
TEMPTER. I offer what you desire. I ask
What you have to give. Is it too much
For such a vision of eternal grandeur?
THOMAS. Others offered real goods, worthless
But real. You only offer
Dreams to damnation.
TEMPTER.   You have often dreamt them.
THOMAS. Is there no way, in my soul's sickness,
Does not lead to damnation in pride?
I well know that these temptations
Mean present vanity and future torment.
Can sinful pride be driven out
Only by more sinful? Can I neither act nor suffer
Without perdition?
TEMPTER. You know and do not know, what it is to act or suffer.
You know and do not know, that action is suffering,
And suffering action. Neither does the agent suffer
Nor the patient act. But both are fixed
In an eternal action, an eternal patience

To which all must consent that it may be willed
And which all must suffer that they may will it,
That the pattern may subsist, that the wheel may turn and still
Be forever still.

CHORUS. There is no rest in the house. There is no rest in the street.
I hear restless movement of feet. And the air is heavy and thick.
Thick and heavy the sky. And the earth presses up against our feet.
What is the sickly smell, the vapour? the dark green light from a
cloud on a withered tree? The earth is heaving to parturition
of issue of hell. What is the sticky dew that forms on the back
of my hand?

THE FOUR TEMPTERS. Man's life is a cheat and a disappointment;
All things are unreal,
Unreal or disappointing:
The Catherine wheel, the pantomime cat,
The prizes given at the children's party,
The prize awarded for the English Essay,
The scholar's degree, the statesman's decoration.
All things become less real, man passes
From unreality to unreality.
This man is obstinate, blind, intent
On self-destruction,
Passing from deception to deception,
From grandeur to grandeur to final illusion,
Lost in the wonder of his own greatness,
The enemy of society, enemy of himself.

THE THREE PRIESTS. O Thomas my Lord do not fight the intractable
tide,
Do not sail the irresistible wind; in the storm,
Should we not wait for the sea to subside, in the night
Abide the coming of day, when the traveller may find his way,
The sailor lay course by the sun?

CHORUS, PRIESTS *and* TEMPTERS *alternately.*

C. Is it the owl that calls, or a signal between the trees?
P. Is the window-bar made fast, is the door under lock and bolt?
T. Is it rain that taps at the window, is it wind that pokes at the door?
C. Does the torch flame in the hall, the candle in the room?
P. Does the watchman walk by the wall?
T. Does the mastiff prowl by the gate?
C. Death has a hundred hands and walks by a thousand ways.

P. He may come in the sight of all, he may pass unseen unheard.

T. Come whispering through the ear, or a sudden shock on the skull.

C. A man may walk with a lamp at night, and yet be drowned in a ditch.

P. A man may climb the stair in the day, and slip on a broken step.

T. A man may sit at meat, and feel the cold in his groin.

CHORUS. We have not been happy, my Lord, we have not been too
     happy.
   We are not ignorant women, we know what we must expect and not
     expect.
   We know of oppression and torture,
   We know of extortion and violence,
   Destitution, disease,
   The old without fire in winter,
   The child without milk in summer,
   Our labour taken away from us,
   Our sins made heavier upon us.
   We have seen the young man mutilated,
   The torn girl trembling by the mill-stream.
   And meanwhile we have gone on living,
   Living and partly living,
   Picking together the pieces,
   Gathering faggots at nightfall,
   Building a partial shelter,
   For sleeping, and eating and drinking and laughter.

   God gave us always some reason, some hope; but now a new terror
     has soiled us, which none can avert, none can avoid, flowing
     under our feet and over the sky;
   Under doors and down chimneys, flowing in at the ear and the
     mouth and the eye.
   God is leaving us, God is leaving us, more pang, more pain than
     birth or death.
   Sweet and cloying through the dark air
   Falls the stifling scent of despair;
   The forms take shape in the dark air:
   Puss-purr of leopard, footfall of padding bear,
   Palm-pat of nodding ape, square hyaena waiting
   For laughter, laughter, laughter. The Lords of Hell are here.
   They curl round you, lie at your feet, swing and wing through the
     dark air.

O Thomas Archbishop, save us, save us, save yourself that we may
    be saved;
Destroy yourself and we are destroyed.

THOMAS. Now is my way clear, now is the meaning plain:
Temptation shall not come in this kind again.
The last temptation is the greatest treason:
To do the right deed for the wrong reason.
The natural vigour in the venial sin
Is the way in which our lives begin.
Thirty years ago, I searched all the ways
That lead to pleasure, advancement and praise.
Delight in sense, in learning and in thought,
Music and philosophy, curiosity,
The purple bullfinch in the lilac tree,
The tiltyard skill, the strategy of chess,
Love in the garden, singing to the instrument,
Were all things equally desirable.
Ambition comes when early force is spent
And when we find no longer all things possible.
Ambition comes behind and unobservable.
Sin grows with doing good. When I imposed the King's law
In England, and waged war with him against Toulouse,
I beat the barons at their own game. I
Could then despise the men who thought me most contemptible,
The raw nobility, whose manners matched their finger-nails.
While I ate out of the King's dish
To become servant of God was never my wish.
Servant of God has chance of greater sin
And sorrow, than the man who serves a king.
For those who serve the greater cause may make the cause serve
    them,
Still doing right: and striving with political men
May make that cause political, not by what they do
But by what they are. I know
What yet remains to show you of my history
Will seem to most of you at best futility,
Senseless self-slaughter of a lunatic,
Arrogant passion of a fanatic.
I know that history at all times draws
The strangest consequence from remotest cause.

But for every evil, every sacrilege,
Crime, wrong, oppression and the axe's edge,
Indifference, exploitation, you, and you,
And you, must all be punished. So must you.
I shall no longer act or suffer, to the sword's end.
Now my good Angel, whom God appoints
To be my guardian, hover over the swords' points.

Interlude

preaches in the Cathedral on Christmas Morning, 1170

' Glory to God in the highest, and on earth peace to men of good will.' *The fourteenth verse of the second chapter of the Gospel according to Saint Luke.* In the Name of the Father, and of the Son, and of the Holy Ghost. Amen.

Dear children of God, my sermon this Christmas morning will be a very short one. I wish only that you should meditate in your hearts the deep meaning and mystery of our masses of Christmas Day. For whenever Mass is said, we re-enact the Passion and Death of Our Lord; and on this Christmas Day we do this in celebration of His Birth. So that at the same moment we rejoice in His coming for the salvation of men, and offer again to God His Body and Blood in sacrifice, oblation and satisfaction for the sins of the whole world. It was in this same night that has just passed, that a multitude of the heavenly host appeared before the shepherds at Bethlehem, saying 'Glory to God in the highest, and on earth peace to men of good will'; at this same time of all the year that we celebrate at once the Birth of Our Lord and His Passion and Death upon the Cross. Beloved, as the World sees, this is to behave in a strange fashion. For who in the World will both mourn and rejoice at once and for the same reason? For either joy will be overborne by mourning, or mourning will be cast out by joy; so it is only in these our Christian mysteries that we can rejoice and mourn at once for the same reason. Now think for a moment about the meaning of this word 'peace'. Does it seem strange to you that the angels should have announced Peace, when ceaselessly the world has been stricken with War and the fear of War? Does it seem to you that the angelic voices were mistaken, and that the promise was a disappointment and a cheat?

Reflect now, how Our Lord Himself spoke of Peace. He said to His disciples, 'Peace I leave with you, my peace I give unto you.' Did He mean peace as we think of it: the kingdom of England at peace with its neighbours, the barons at peace with the King, the householder counting over his peaceful gains, the swept hearth, his best wine for a friend at the table, his wife singing to the children? Those men His disciples knew no such things: they went forth to journey afar, to suffer by land and sea, to know torture, imprisonment, disappointment, to suffer death by martyrdom. What then did He mean? If you ask that, remember then that He said also, 'Not as the world gives, give I unto you.' So then, He gave to His disciples peace, but not peace as the world gives.

Consider also one thing of which you have probably never thought. Not only do we at the feast of Christmas celebrate at once Our Lord's Birth and His Death: but on the next day we celebrate the martyrdom of His first martyr, the blessed Stephen. Is it an accident, do you think, that the day of the first martyr follows immediately the day of the Birth of Christ? By no means. Just as we rejoice and mourn at once, in the Birth and in the Passion of Our Lord; so also, in a smaller figure, we both rejoice and mourn in the death of martyrs. We mourn, for the sins of the world that has martyred them; we rejoice, that another soul is numbered among the Saints in Heaven, for the glory of God and for the salvation of men.

Beloved, we do not think of a martyr simply as a good Christian who has been killed because he is a Christian: for that would be solely to mourn. We do not think of him simply as a good Christian who has been elevated to the company of the Saints: for that would be simply to rejoice: and neither our mourning nor our rejoicing is as the world's is. A Christian martyrdom is never an accident, for Saints are not made by accident. Still less is a Christian martyrdom the effect of a man's will to become a Saint, as a man by willing and contriving may become a ruler of men. A martyrdom is always the design of God, for His love of men, to warn them and to lead them, to bring them back to His ways. It is never the design of man; for the true martyr is he who has become the instrument of God, who has lost his will in the will of God, and who no longer desires anything for himself, not even the glory of being a martyr. So thus as on earth the Church mourns and rejoices at once, in a fashion that the world cannot understand; so in Heaven the Saints are most high, having made themselves most low, and are seen, not as we see them, but in the light of the Godhead from which they draw their being.

I have spoken to you to-day, dear children of God, of the martyrs of the past, asking you to remember especially our martyr of Canterbury, the blessed Archbishop Elphege; because it is fitting, on Christ's birth day, to remember what is that Peace which He brought; and because, dear children, I do not think I shall ever preach to you again; and because it is possible that in a short time you may have yet another martyr, and that one perhaps not the last. I would have you keep in your hearts these words that I say, and think of them at another time. In the Name of the Father, and of the Son, and of the Holy Ghost. Amen.

Part II

CHORUS. Does the bird sing in the South?
Only the sea-bird cries, driven inland by the storm.
What sign of the spring of the year?
Only the death of the old: not a stir, not a shoot, not a breath.
Do the days begin to lengthen?
Longer and darker the day, shorter and colder the night.
Still and stifling the air: but a wind is stored up in the East.
The starved crow sits in the field, attentive; and in the wood
The owl rehearses the hollow note of death.
What signs of a bitter spring?
The wind stored up in the East.
What, at the time of the birth of Our Lord, at Christmastide,
Is there not peace upon earth, goodwill among men?
The peace of this world is always uncertain, unless men keep the
    peace of God.
And war among men defiles this world, but death in the Lord
    renews it,
And the world must be cleaned in the winter, or we shall have
    only
A sour spring, a parched summer, an empty harvest.
Between Christmas and Easter what work shall be done?
The ploughman shall go out in March and turn the same earth
He has turned before, the bird shall sing the same song.
When the leaf is out on the tree, when the elder and may
Burst over the stream, and the air is clear and high,
And voices trill at windows, and children tumble in front of the
    door,
What work shall have been done, what wrong
Shall the bird's song cover, the green tree cover, what wrong
Shall the fresh earth cover? We wait, and the time is short
But waiting is long.
[*Enter the* FIRST PRIEST *with a banner of St. Stephen borne before him.*
The lines sung are in italics.]

263

MURDER IN THE CATHEDRAL

FIRST PRIEST. Since Christmas a day: and the day of St. Stephen, First
    Martyr.

Princes moreover did sit, and did witness falsely against me.

A day that was always most dear to the Archbishop Thomas.

And he kneeled down and cried with a loud voice:

Lord, lay not this sin to their charge.

Princes moreover did sit.

[Introit of St. Stephen is heard]

[Enter the SECOND PRIEST, with a banner of St. John the Apostle borne
before him.]

SECOND PRIEST. Since St. Stephen a day: and the day of St. John the
    Apostle.

In the midst of the congregation he opened his mouth.

That which was from the beginning, which we have heard,

Which we have seen with our eyes, and our hands have handled

Of the word of life; that which we have seen and heard

Declare we unto you.

In the midst of the congregation.

[Introit of St. John is heard]

[Enter the THIRD PRIEST, with a banner of the Holy Innocents borne before
him.]

THIRD PRIEST. Since St. John the Apostle a day: and the day of the
    Holy Innocents.

Out of the mouth of very babes, O God.

As the voice of many waters, of thunder, of harps,

They sang as it were a new song.

The blood of thy saints have they shed like water,

And there was no man to bury them. Avenge, O Lord,

The blood of thy saints. In Rama, a voice heard, weeping.

Out of the mouth of very babes, O God!

[THE PRIESTS stand together with the banners behind them]

FIRST PRIEST. Since the Holy Innocents a day: the fourth day from
    Christmas.

THE THREE PRIESTS. *Rejoice we all, keeping holy day.*

FIRST PRIEST. As for the people, so also for himself, he offereth
    for sins.

He lays down his life for the sheep.

THE THREE PRIESTS. *Rejoice we all, keeping holy day.*

FIRST PRIEST.   To-day?

SECOND PRIEST. To-day, what is to-day? For the day is half gone.

FIRST PRIEST. To-day, what is to-day? but another day, the dusk of
    the year.
SECOND PRIEST. To-day, what is to-day? Another night, and another
    dawn.
THIRD PRIEST. What day is the day that we know that we hope for or
    fear for?
    Every day is the day we should fear from or hope from. One
      moment
    Weighs like another. Only in retrospection, selection,
    We say, that was the day. The critical moment
    That is always now, and here. Even now, in sordid particulars
    The eternal design may appear.
[*Enter the* FOUR KNIGHTS. *The banners disappear*]
FIRST KNIGHT. Servants of the King.
FIRST PRIEST.   And known to us.
    You are welcome. Have you ridden far?
FIRST KNIGHT. Not far to-day, but matters urgent
    Have brought us from France. We rode hard,
    Took ship yesterday, landed last night,
    Having business with the Archbishop.
SECOND KNIGHT. Urgent business.
THIRD KNIGHT.   From the King.
SECOND KNIGHT. By the King's order.
FIRST KNIGHT.   Our men are outside.
FIRST PRIEST. You know the Archbishop's hospitality.
    We are about to go to dinner.
    The good Archbishop would be vexed
    If we did not offer you entertainment
    Before your business. Please dine with us.
    Your men shall be looked after also.
    Dinner before business. Do you like roast pork?
FIRST KNIGHT. Business before dinner. We will roast your pork
    First, and dine upon it after.
SECOND KNIGHT. We must see the Archbishop.
THIRD KNIGHT.   Go, tell the Archbishop
    We have no need of his hospitality.
    We will find our own dinner.
FIRST PRIEST [*to attendant*]. Go, tell His Lordship.
FOURTH KNIGHT. How much longer will you keep us waiting?
[*Enter* THOMAS]

THOMAS [*to* PRIESTS]. However certain our expectation
    The moment foreseen may be unexpected
    When it arrives. It comes when we are
    Engrossed with matters of other urgency.
    On my table you will find
    The papers in order, and the documents signed.
    [*To* KNIGHTS]. You are welcome, whatever your business may be.
    You say, from the King?
FIRST KNIGHT.   Most surely from the King.
    We must speak with you alone.
THOMAS [*to* PRIESTS]   Leave us then alone.
    Now what is the matter?
FIRST KNIGHT.   This is the matter.
THE THREE KNIGHTS. You are the Archbishop in revolt against the
        King; in rebellion to the King and the law of the land;
    You are the Archbishop who was made by the King; whom he set
        in your place to carry out his command.
    You are his servant, his tool, and his jack,
    You wore his favours on your back,
    You had your honours all from his hand; from him you had the
        power, the seal and the ring.
    This is the man who was the tradesman's son: the backstairs brat
        who was born in Cheapside;
    This is the creature that crawled upon the King; swollen with
        blood and swollen with pride.
    Creeping out of the London dirt,
    Crawling up like a louse on your shirt,
    The man who cheated, swindled, lied; broke his oath and betrayed
        his King.
THOMAS. This is not true.
    Both before and after I received the ring
    I have been a loyal subject to the King.
    Saving my order, I am at his command,
    As his most faithful vassal in the land.
FIRST KNIGHT. Saving your order! let your order save you —
    As I do not think it is like to do.
    Saving your ambition is what you mean,
    Saving your pride, envy and spleen.
SECOND KNIGHT. Saving your insolence and greed.
    Won't you ask us to pray to God for you, in your need?

THIRD KNIGHT. Yes, we'll pray for you!

FIRST KNIGHT.   Yes, we'll pray for you!

THE THREE KNIGHTS. Yes, we'll pray that God may help you!

THOMAS. But, gentlemen, your business
        Which you said so urgent, is it only
        Scolding and blaspheming?

FIRST KNIGHT.   That was only
        Our indignation, as loyal subjects.

THOMAS. Loyal? to whom?

FIRST KNIGHT.   To the King!

SECOND KNIGHT.   The King!

THIRD KNIGHT. The King!

THE THREE KNIGHTS.   God bless him!

THOMAS. Then let your new coat of loyalty be worn
        Carefully, so it get not soiled or torn.
        Have you something to say?

FIRST KNIGHT.   By the King's command.
        Shall we say it now?

SECOND KNIGHT.   Without delay,
        Before the old fox is off and away.

THOMAS.   What you have to say
        By the King's command — if it be the King's command —
        Should be said in public. If you make charges,
        Then in public I will refute them.

FIRST KNIGHT.   No! here and now!

[*They make to attack him, but the priests and attendants return and quietly
                    interpose themselves.*]

THOMAS. Now and here!

FIRST KNIGHT. Of your earlier misdeeds I shall make no mention.
        They are too well known. But after dissension
        Had ended, in France, and you were endued
        With your former privilege, how did you show your gratitude?
        You had fled from England, not exiled
        Or threatened, mind you; but in the hope
        Of stirring up trouble in the French dominions.
        You sowed strife abroad, you reviled
        The King to the King of France, to the Pope,
        Raising up against him false opinions.

SECOND KNIGHT. Yet the King, out of his charity,
        And urged by your friends, offered clemency,

Made a pact of peace, and all dispute ended
Sent you back to your See as you demanded.

THIRD KNIGHT. And burying the memory of your transgressions
Restored your honours and your possessions.
All was granted for which you sued:
Yet how, I repeat, did you show your gratitude?

FIRST KNIGHT. Suspending those who had crowned the young prince,
Denying the legality of his coronation.

SECOND KNIGHT. Binding with the chains of anathema.

THIRD KNIGHT. Using every means in your power to evince
The King's faithful servants, every one who transacts
His business in his absence, the business of the nation.

FIRST KNIGHT. These are the facts.
Say therefore if you will be content
To answer in the King's presence. Therefore were we sent.

THOMAS. Never was it my wish
To uncrown the King's son, or to diminish
His honour and power. Why should he wish
To deprive my people of me and keep me from my own
And bid me sit in Canterbury, alone?
I would wish him three crowns rather than one,
And as for the bishops, it is not my yoke
That is laid upon them, or mine to revoke.
Let them go to the Pope. It was he who condemned them.

FIRST KNIGHT. Through you they were suspended.

SECOND KNIGHT.   By you be this amended.

THIRD KNIGHT. Absolve them.

FIRST KNIGHT.   Absolve them.

THOMAS.   I do not deny
That this was done through me. But it is not I
Who can loose whom the Pope has bound.
Let them go to him, upon whom redounds
Their contempt towards me, their contempt towards the Church
    shown.

FIRST KNIGHT. Be that as it may, here is the King's command:
That you and your servants depart from this land.

THOMAS. If that *is* the King's command, I will be bold
To say: seven years were my people without
My presence; seven years of misery and pain.
Seven years a mendicant on foreign charity

I lingered abroad: seven years is no brevity.
I shall not get those seven years back again.
Never again, you must make no doubt,
Shall the sea run between the shepherd and his fold.

FIRST KNIGHT. The King's justice, the King's majesty,
     You insult with gross indignity;
     Insolent madman, whom nothing deters
     From attainting his servants and ministers.

THOMAS. It is not I who insult the King,
     And there is higher than I or the King.
     It is not I, Becket from Cheapside,
     It is not against me, Becket, that you strive.
     It is not Becket who pronounces doom,
     But the Law of Christ's Church, the judgement of Rome.

FIRST KNIGHT. Priest, you have spoken in peril of your life.
SECOND KNIGHT. Priest, you have spoken in danger of the knife.
THIRD KNIGHT. Priest, you have spoken treachery and treason.
THE THREE KNIGHTS. Priest! traitor, confirmed in malfeasance.

THOMAS. I submit my cause to the judgement of Rome.
     But if you kill me, I shall rise from my tomb
     To submit my cause before God's throne.

                                        [*Exit*]

FOURTH KNIGHT. Priest! monk! and servant! take, hold, detain,
     Restrain this man, in the King's name.
FIRST KNIGHT. Or answer with your bodies.
SECOND KNIGHT.   Enough of words.
THE FOUR KNIGHTS. We come for the King's justice, we come with
          swords.

                                      [*Exeunt*]

CHORUS. I have smelt them, the death-bringers, senses are quickened
     By subtile forebodings; I have heard
     Fluting in the night-time, fluting and owls, have seen at noon
     Scaly wings slanting over, huge and ridiculous. I have tasted
     The savour of putrid flesh in the spoon. I have felt
     The heaving of earth at nightfall, restless, absurd. I have heard
     Laughter in the noises of beasts that make strange noises: jackal,
          jackass, jackdaw; the scurrying noise of mouse and jerboa; the
          laugh of the loon, the lunatic bird. I have seen
     Grey necks twisting, rat tails twining, in the thick light of dawn. I
          have eaten

                          269

Smooth creatures still living, with the strong salt taste of living
    things under the sea; I have tasted
The living lobster, the crab, the oyster, the whelk and the prawn;
    and they live and spawn in my bowels, and my bowels dissolve
    in the light of dawn. I have smelt
Death in the rose, death in the hollyhock, sweet pea, hyacinth,
    primrose and cowslip. I have seen
Trunk and horn, tusk and hoof, in odd places;
I have lain on the floor of the sea and breathed with the breathing
    of the sea-anemone, swallowed with ingurgitation of the
    sponge. I have lain in the soil and criticised the worm. In the
    air
Flirted with the passage of the kite, I have plunged with the kite
    and cowered with the wren. I have felt
The horn of the beetle, the scale of the viper, the mobile hard
    insensitive skin of the elephant, the evasive flank of the fish.
I have smelt
Corruption in the dish, incense in the latrine, the sewer in the
    incense, the smell of sweet soap in the woodpath, a hellish
    sweet scent in the woodpath, while the ground heaved. I have
    seen
Rings of light coiling downwards, descending
To the horror of the ape. Have I not known, not known
What was coming to be? It was here, in the kitchen, in the passage,
In the mews in the barn in the byre in the market-place
In our veins our bowels our skulls as well
As well as in the plottings of potentates
As well as in the consultations of powers.
What is woven on the loom of fate
What is woven in the councils of princes
Is woven also in our veins, our brains,
Is woven like a pattern of living worms
In the guts of the women of Canterbury.

I have smelt them, the death-bringers; now is too late
For action, too soon for contrition.
Nothing is possible but the shamed swoon
Of those consenting to the last humiliation.
I have consented, Lord Archbishop, have consented.
Am torn away, subdued, violated,

United to the spiritual flesh of nature,
Mastered by the animal powers of spirit,
Dominated by the lust of self-demolition,
By the final utter uttermost death of spirit,
By the final ecstasy of waste and shame,
O Lord Archbishop, O Thomas Archbishop, forgive us, forgive us,
    pray for us that we may pray for you, out of our shame.

[*Enter* THOMAS]

THOMAS. Peace, and be at peace with your thoughts and visions.
    These things had to come to you and you to accept them,
    This is your share of the eternal burden,
    The perpetual glory. This is one moment,
    But know that another
    Shall pierce you with a sudden painful joy
    When the figure of God's purpose is made complete.
    You shall forget these things, toiling in the household,
    You shall remember them, droning by the fire,
    When age and forgetfulness sweeten memory
    Only like a dream that has often been told
    And often been changed in the telling. They will seem unreal.
    Human kind cannot bear very much reality.

[*Enter* PRIESTS]

PRIESTS [*severally*]. My Lord, you must not stop here. To the minster.
        Through the cloister. No time to waste. They are coming back,
        armed. To the altar, to the altar.

THOMAS. All my life they have been coming, these feet. All my life
    I have waited. Death will come only when I am worthy,
    And if I am worthy, there is no danger.
    I have therefore only to make perfect my will.

PRIESTS. My Lord, they are coming. They will break through
        presently.
    You will be killed. Come to the altar.
    Make haste, my Lord. Don't stop here talking. It is not right.
    What shall become of us, my Lord, if you are killed;
        what shall become of us?

THOMAS. Peace! be quiet! remember where you are, and what is
        happening;
    No life here is sought for but mine,
    And I am not in danger: only near to death.

PRIESTS. My Lord, to vespers! You must not be absent from vespers.

You must not be absent from the divine office. To vespers.
Into the Cathedral!

THOMAS. Go to vespers, remember me at your prayers.

They shall find the shepherd here; the flock shall be spared.

I have had a tremor of bliss, a wink of heaven, a whisper,

And I would no longer be denied; all things

Proceed to a joyful consummation.

PRIESTS. Seize him! force him! drag him!

THOMAS. Keep your hands off!

PRIESTS. To vespers! Hurry.

[*They drag him off. While the* CHORUS *speak, the scene is changed to the cathedral.*]

CHORUS [*while a* Dies Iræ *is sung in Latin by a choir in the distance*].

Numb the hand and dry the eyelid,

Still the horror, but more horror
Than when tearing in the belly.

Still the horror, but more horror
Than when twisting in the fingers,
Than when splitting in the skull.

More than footfall in the passage,
More than shadow in the doorway,
More than fury in the hall.

The agents of hell disappear, the human, they shrink and dissolve
Into dust on the wind, forgotten, unmemorable; only is here
The white flat face of Death, God's silent servant,
And behind the face of Death the Judgement
And behind the Judgement the Void, more horrid than active
    shapes of hell;
Emptiness, absence, separation from God;
The horror of the effortless journey, to the empty land
Which is no land, only emptiness, absence, the Void,
Where those who were men can no longer turn the mind
To distraction, delusion, escape into dream, pretence,
Where the soul is no longer deceived, for there are no objects, no
    tones,
No colours, no forms to distract, to divert the soul
From seeing itself, foully united forever, nothing with nothing,

Not what we call death, but what beyond death is not death,
We fear, we fear. Who shall then plead for me,
Who intercede for me, in my most need?

Dead upon the tree, my Saviour,
Let not be in vain Thy labour;
Help me, Lord, in my last fear.

Dust I am, to dust am bending,
From the final doom impending
Help me, Lord, for death is near.

                        [In the cathedral. THOMAS *and* PRIESTS]

PRIESTS. Bar the door. Bar the door
   The door is barred.
   We are safe. We are safe.
   They dare not break in.
   They cannot break in. They have not the force.
   We are safe. We are safe.
THOMAS. Unbar the doors! throw open the doors!
   I will not have the house of prayer, the church of Christ,
   The sanctuary, turned into a fortress.
   The Church shall protect her own, in her own way, not
   As oak and stone; stone and oak decay,
   Give no stay, but the Church shall endure.
   The Church shall be open, even to our enemies. Open the door!
PRIESTS. My Lord! these are not men, these come not as men come, but
   Like maddened beasts. They come not like men, who
   Respect the sanctuary, who kneel to the Body of Christ,
   But like beasts. You would bar the door
   Against the lion, the leopard, the wolf or the boar,
   Why not more
   Against beasts with the souls of damned men, against men
   Who would damn themselves to beasts. My Lord! My Lord!
THOMAS. You think me reckless, desperate and mad.
   You argue by results, as this world does,
   To settle if an act be good or bad.
   You defer to the fact. For every life and every act
   Consequence of good and evil can be shown.
   And as in time results of many deeds are blended
   So good and evil in the end become confounded.

It is not in time that my death shall be known;
It is out of time that my decision is taken
If you call that decision
To which my whole being gives entire consent.
I give my life
To the Law of God above the Law of Man.
Unbar the door! unbar the door!
We are not here to triumph by fighting, by stratagem, or by
    resistance,
Not to fight with beasts as men. We have fought the beast
And have conquered. We have only to conquer
Now, by suffering. This is the easier victory.
Now is the triumph of the Cross, now
Open the door! I command it. OPEN THE DOOR!

[*The door is opened. The* KNIGHTS *enter, slightly tipsy*]

PRIESTS. This way, my Lord! Quick. Up the stair. To the roof.
      To the crypt. Quick. Come. Force him.

KNIGHTS. Where is Becket, the traitor to the King?
    Where is Becket, the meddling priest?
Come down Daniel to the lions' den,
    Come down Daniel for the mark of the beast.

Are you washed in the blood of the Lamb?
    Are you marked with the mark of the beast?
Come down Daniel to the lions' den,
    Come down Daniel and join in the feast.

Where is Becket the Cheapside brat?
    Where is Becket the faithless priest?
Come down Daniel to the lions' den,
    Come down Daniel and join in the feast.

THOMAS. It is the just man who
    Like a bold lion, should be without fear.
I am here.
No traitor to the King. I am a priest,
A Christian, saved by the blood of Christ,
Ready to suffer with my blood.
This is the sign of the Church always,
The sign of blood. Blood for blood.
His blood given to buy my life,

My blood given to pay for His death,
My death for His death.

FIRST KNIGHT. Absolve all those you have excommunicated.

SECOND KNIGHT. Resign the powers you have arrogated.

THIRD KNIGHT. Restore to the King the money you appropriated.

FIRST KNIGHT. Renew the obedience you have violated.

THOMAS. For my Lord I am now ready to die,
That his Church may have peace and liberty.
Do with me as you will, to your hurt and shame;
But none of my people, in God's name,
Whether layman or clerk, shall you touch.
This I forbid.

KNIGHTS. Traitor! traitor! traitor!

THOMAS. You, Reginald, three times traitor you:
Traitor to me as my temporal vassal,
Traitor to me as your spiritual lord,
Traitor to God in desecrating His Church.

FIRST KNIGHT. No faith do I owe to a renegade,
And what I owe shall now be paid.

THOMAS. Now to Almighty God, to the Blessed Mary ever Virgin, to
the blessed John the Baptist, the holy apostles Peter and Paul,
to the blessed martyr Denys, and to all the Saints, I commend
my cause and that of the Church.

While the KNIGHTS *kill him, we hear the*

CHORUS. Clear the air! clean the sky! wash the wind! take stone from
stone and wash them.

The land is foul, the water is foul, our beasts and ourselves defiled
with blood.

A rain of blood has blinded my eyes. Where is England? where is
Kent? where is Canterbury?

O far far far far in the past; and I wander in a land of barren boughs:
if I break them, they bleed; I wander in a land of dry stones: if
I touch them they bleed.

How how can I ever return, to the soft quiet seasons?

Night stay with us, stop sun, hold season, let the day not come, let
the spring not come.

Can I look again at the day and its common things, and see them
all smeared with blood, through a curtain of falling blood?

We did not wish anything to happen.

We understood the private catastrophe,

275

The personal loss, the general misery,
Living and partly living;
The terror by night that ends in daily action,
The terror by day that ends in sleep;
But the talk in the market-place, the hand on the broom,
The night-time heaping of the ashes,
The fuel laid on the fire at daybreak,
These acts marked a limit to our suffering.
Every horror had its definition,
Every sorrow had a kind of end:
In life there is not time to grieve long.
But this, this is out of life, this is out of time,
An instant eternity of evil and wrong.
We are soiled by a filth that we cannot clean, united to supernatural vermin,
It is not we alone, it is not the house, it is not the city that is defiled,
But the world that is wholly foul.
Clear the air! clean the sky! wash the wind! take the stone from the stone, take the skin from the arm, take the muscle from the bone, and wash them. Wash the stone, wash the bone, wash the brain, wash the soul, wash them wash them!

[*The* KNIGHTS, *having completed the murder, advance to the front of the stage and address the audience.*]

FIRST KNIGHT. We beg you to give us your attention for a few moments. We know that you may be disposed to judge unfavourably of our action. You are Englishmen, and therefore you believe in fair play: and when you see one man being set upon by four, then your sympathies are all with the under dog. I respect such feelings, I share them. Nevertheless, I appeal to your sense of honour. You are Englishmen, and therefore will not judge anybody without hearing both sides of the case. That is in accordance with our long-established principle of Trial by Jury. I am not myself qualified to put our case to you. I am a man of action and not of words. For that reason I shall do no more than introduce the other speakers, who, with their various abilities, and different points of view, will be able to lay before you the merits of this extremely complex problem. I shall call upon our eldest member to speak first, my neighbour in the country: Baron William de Traci.

THIRD KNIGHT. I am afraid I am not anything like such an experienced speaker as my old friend Reginald Fitz Urse would lead you to believe. But there is one thing I should like to say, and I might as well say it at once. It is this: in what we have done, and whatever you may think of it, we have been perfectly disinterested. [*The other* KNIGHTS: 'Hear! hear!'] *We* are not getting anything out of this. We have much more to lose than to gain. We are four plain English-men who put our country first. I dare say that we didn't make a very good impression when we came in just now. The fact is that we knew we had taken on a pretty stiff job; I'll only speak for myself, but I had drunk a good deal — I am not a drinking man ordinarily — to brace myself up for it. When you come to the point, it does go against the grain to kill an Archbishop, especially when you have been brought up in good Church traditions. So if we seemed a bit rowdy, you will understand why it was; and for my part I am awfully sorry about it. We realised this was our duty, but all the same we had to work ourselves up to it. And, as I said, *we* are not getting a penny out of this. We know perfectly well how things will turn out. King Henry — God bless him — will have to say, for reasons of state, that he never meant this to happen; and there is going to be an awful row; and at the best we shall have to spend the rest of our lives abroad. And even when reasonable people come to see that the Archbishop *had* to be put out of the way — and personally I had a tremendous admiration for him — you must have noted what a good show he put up at the end — they won't give *us* any glory. No, we have done for ourselves, there's no mistake about that. So, as I said at the beginning, please give us at least the credit for being completely disinterested in this business. I think that is about all I have to say.

FIRST KNIGHT. I think we will all agree that William de Traci has spoken well and has made a very important point. The gist of his argument is this: that we have been completely disinterested. But our act itself needs more justification than that; and you must hear our other speakers. I shall next call upon Hugh de Morville, who has made a special study of statecraft and constitutional law. Sir Hugh de Morville.

SECOND KNIGHT. I should like first to recur to a point that was very well put by our leader, Reginald Fitz Urse: that you are English-men, and therefore your sympathies are always with the under dog. It is the English spirit of fair play. Now the worthy Archbishop, whose good qualities I very much admired, has throughout been presented as the under dog. But is this really the case? I am going to appeal not to your emotions but to your reason. You are hard-headed sensible people, as I can see, and not to be taken in by emotional clap-trap. I therefore ask you to consider soberly: what were the Archbishop's aims? and what are King Henry's aims? In the answer to these questions lies the key to the problem.

The King's aim has been perfectly consistent. During the reign of the late Queen Matilda and the irruption of the unhappy usurper Stephen, the kingdom was very much divided. Our King saw that the one thing needful was to restore order: to curb the excessive powers of local government, which were usually exercised for selfish and often for seditious ends, and to reform the legal system. He therefore intended that Becket, who had proved himself an ex-tremely able administrator — no one denies that — should unite the offices of Chancellor and Archbishop. Had Becket concurred with the King's wishes, we should have had an almost ideal State: a union of spiritual and temporal administration, under the central government. I knew Becket well, in various official relations; and I may say that I have never known a man so well qualified for the highest rank of the Civil Service. And what happened? The moment that Becket, at the King's instance, had been made Archbishop, he resigned the office of Chancellor, he became more priestly than the priests, he ostentatiously and offensively adopted an ascetic manner of life, he affirmed immediately that there was a higher order than that which our King, and he as the King's servant, had for so many years striven to establish; and that — God knows why — the two orders were incompatible.

You will agree with me that such interference by an Archbishop offends the instincts of a people like ours. So far, I know that I have your approval: I read it in your faces. It is only with the measures we have had to adopt, in order to set matters to rights, that you take issue. No one regrets the necessity for violence more than we do. Unhappily, there are times when violence is the only way in which social justice can be secured. At another time, you would condemn an Archbishop by vote of Parliament and execute him formally as a traitor, and no one would have to bear the burden of being called murderer. And at a later time still, even such temperate measures as these would become unnecessary. But, if you have now arrived at a just subordination of the pretensions of the Church to the welfare of the State, remember that it is we who took the first step. We have been instrumental in bringing about the state of affairs that you approve. We have served your interests; we merit your applause; and if there is any guilt whatever in the matter, you must share it with us.

FIRST KNIGHT. Morville has given us a great deal to think about. It seems to me that he has said almost the last word, for those who have been able to follow his very subtle reasoning. We have, however, one more speaker, who has I think another point of view to express. If there are any who are still unconvinced, I think that Richard Brito, coming as he does of a family distinguished for its loyalty to the Church, will be able to convince them. Richard Brito.

FOURTH KNIGHT. The speakers who have preceded me, to say nothing of our leader, Reginald Fitz Urse, have all spoken very much to the point. I have nothing to add along their particular lines of argument. What I have to say may be put in the form of a question: *Who killed the Archbishop?* As you have been eye-witnesses of this lamentable scene, you may feel some surprise at my putting it in this way. But consider the course of events. I am obliged, very briefly, to go over the ground traversed by the last speaker. While the late Archbishop was Chancellor, no one, under the King, did more to weld the country together, to give it the unity, the stability, order, tranquillity, and justice that it so badly needed. From the moment he became Archbishop, he completely reversed his policy; he showed himself to be utterly indifferent to the fate of the country, to be, in fact, a monster of egotism. This egotism grew upon him, until it became at last an undoubted mania. I have unimpeachable evidence to the effect that before he left France he clearly prophesied, in the presence of numerous witnesses, that he had not long to live, and that he would be killed in England. He used every means of provocation; from his conduct, step by step, there can be no inference except that he had determined upon a death by martyrdom. Even at the last, he could have given us reason: you have seen how he evaded our questions. And when he had deliberately exasperated us beyond human endurance, he could still have easily escaped; he could have kept himself from us long enough to allow our righteous anger to cool. That was just what he did not wish to happen; he insisted, while we were still inflamed with wrath, that the doors should be opened. Need I say more? I think, with these facts before you, you will unhesitatingly render a verdict of Suicide while of Unsound Mind. It is the only charitable verdict you can give, upon one who was, after all, a great man.

FIRST KNIGHT. Thank you, Brito, I think that there is no more to be said; and I suggest that you now disperse quietly to your homes. Please be careful not to loiter in groups at street corners, and do nothing that might provoke any public outbreak.

[*Exeunt* KNIGHTS]

FIRST PRIEST. O father, father, gone from us, lost to us,
How shall we find you, from what far place
Do you look down on us? You now in Heaven,
Who shall now guide us, protect us, direct us?
After what journey through what further dread
Shall we recover your presence? when inherit
Your strength? The Church lies bereft,
Alone, desecrated, desolated, and the heathen shall build on the
    ruins,
Their world without God. I see it. I see it.

THIRD PRIEST. No. For the Church is stronger for this action,
Triumphant in adversity. It is fortified
By persecution: supreme, so long as men will die for it.
Go, weak sad men, lost erring souls, homeless in earth or heaven.
Go where the sunset reddens the last grey rock
Of Brittany, or the Gates of Hercules.
Go venture shipwreck on the sullen coasts
Where blackamoors make captive Christian men;
Go to the northern seas confined with ice
Where the dead breath makes numb the hand, makes dull the brain;
Find an oasis in the desert sun,
Go seek alliance with the heathen Saracen,
To share his filthy rites, and try to snatch
Forgetfulness in his libidinous courts,
Oblivion in the fountain by the date-tree;
Or sit and bite your nails in Aquitaine.
In the small circle of pain within the skull
You still shall tramp and tread one endless round
Of thought, to justify your action to yourselves,
Weaving a fiction which unravels as you weave,
Pacing forever in the hell of make-believe
Which never is belief: this is your fate on earth
And we must think no further of you.

FIRST PRIEST.   O my lord
The glory of whose new state is hidden from us,

Pray for us of your charity.

SECOND PRIEST.   Now in the sight of God

Conjoined with all the saints and martyrs gone before you,
Remember us.

THIRD PRIEST.   Let our thanks ascend

To God, who has given us another Saint in Canterbury.

CHORUS [*while a* Te Deum *is sung in Latin by a choir in the distance*].
> We praise Thee, O God, for Thy glory displayed in all the
> creatures of the earth,

> In the snow, in the rain, in the wind, in the storm; in all of Thy
> creatures, both the hunters and the hunted.

> For all things exist only as seen by Thee, only as known by Thee,
> all things exist

> Only in Thy light, and Thy glory is declared even in that which
> denies Thee; the darkness declares the glory of light.

> Those who deny Thee could not deny, if Thou didst not exist; and
> their denial is never complete, for if it were so, they would not
> exist.

> They affirm Thee in living; all things affirm Thee in living; the
> bird in the air, both the hawk and the finch; the beast on the
> earth, both the wolf and the lamb; the worm in the soil and the
> worm in the belly.

> Therefore man, whom Thou hast made to be conscious of Thee,
> must consciously praise Thee, in thought and in word and in
> deed.

> Even with the hand to the broom, the back bent in laying the fire,
> the knee bent in cleaning the hearth, we, the scrubbers and
> sweepers of Canterbury,

> The back bent under toil, the knee bent under sin, the hands to the
> face under fear, the head bent under grief,

> Even in us the voices of seasons, the snuffle of winter, the song of
> spring, the drone of summer, the voices of beasts and of birds,
> praise Thee.

> We thank Thee for Thy mercies of blood, for Thy redemption by
> blood. For the blood of Thy martyrs and saints

> Shall enrich the earth, shall create the holy places.

> For wherever a saint has dwelt, wherever a martyr has given his
> blood for the blood of Christ,

> There is holy ground, and the sanctity shall not depart from it

> Though armies trample over it, though sightseers come with

guide-books looking over it;
From where the western seas gnaw at the coast of Iona,
To the death in the desert, the prayer in forgotten places by the
    broken imperial column,
From such ground springs that which forever renews the earth
Though it is forever denied. Therefore, O God, we thank Thee
Who hast given such blessing to Canterbury.

Forgive us, O Lord, we acknowledge ourselves as type of the
    common man,
Of the men and women who shut the door and sit by the fire;
Who fear the blessing of God, the loneliness of the night of God,
    the surrender required, the deprivation inflicted;
Who fear the injustice of men less than the justice of God;
Who fear the hand at the window, the fire in the thatch, the fist in
    the tavern, the push into the canal,
Less than we fear the love of God.
We acknowledge our trespass, our weakness, our fault; we
    acknowledge
That the sin of the world is upon our heads; that the blood of the
    martyrs and the agony of the saints
Is upon our heads.
Lord, have mercy upon us.
Christ, have mercy upon us.
Lord, have mercy upon us.
Blessed Thomas, pray for us.

THE FAMILY REUNION

Persons

AMY, DOWAGER LADY MONCHENSEY, IVY, VIOLET, *and* AGATHA,
her younger sisters

COL. THE HON. GERALD PIPER, *and* THE HON. CHARLES PIPER,
brothers of her deceased husband

MARY, *daughter of a deceased cousin of Lady Monchensey*

DENMAN, *a parlourmaid*

HARRY, LORD MONCHENSEY, *Amy's eldest son*

DOWNING, *his servant and chauffeur*

DR. WARBURTON

SERGEANT WINCHELL

THE EUMENIDES

The scene is laid in a country house in the
North of England

PART I

The drawing-room, after tea. An afternoon in late March.

Scene I

AMY, IVY, VIOLET, AGATHA, GERALD, CHARLES, MARY

[DENMAN *enters to draw the curtains*]

AMY. Not yet! I will ring for you. It is still quite light.
　　I have nothing to do but watch the days draw out,
　　Now that I sit in the house from October to June,
　　And the swallow comes too soon and the spring will be over
　　And the cuckoo will be gone before I am out again.
　　O Sun, that was once so warm, O Light that was taken for granted
　　When I was young and strong, and sun and light unsought for
　　And the night unfeared and the day expected
　　And clocks could be trusted, tomorrow assured
　　And time would not stop in the dark!
　　Put on the lights. But leave the curtains undrawn.
　　Make up the fire. Will the spring never come? I am cold.
AGATHA. Wishwood was always a cold place, Amy.
IVY. I have always told Amy she should go south in the winter.
　　Were I in Amy's position, I would go south in the winter.
　　I would follow the sun, not wait for the sun to come here.
　　I would go south in the winter, if I could afford it,
　　Not freeze, as I do, in Bayswater, by a gas-fire counting shillings.
VIOLET. Go south! to the English circulating libraries,
　　To the military widows and the English chaplains,
　　To the chilly deck-chair and the strong cold tea —
　　The strong cold stewed bad Indian tea.
CHARLES. That's not Amy's style at all. We are country-bred people.
　　Amy has been too long used to our ways
　　Living with horses and dogs and guns

285

Ever to want to leave England in the winter.
But a single man like me is better off in London:
A man can be very cosy at his club
Even in an English winter.

GERALD.   Well, as for me,
I'd just as soon be a subaltern again
To be back in the East. An incomparable climate
For a man who can exercise a little common prudence;
And your servants look after you very much better.

AMY. My servants are perfectly competent, Gerald.
I can still see to that.

VIOLET.   Well, as for me,
I would never go south, no, definitely never,
Even could I do it as well as Amy:
England's bad enough, I would never go south,
Simply to see the vulgarest people —
You can keep out of their way at home;
People with money from heaven knows where —

GERALD.   Dividends from aeroplane shares.

VIOLET. They bathe all day and they dance all night
In the absolute *minimum* of clothes.

CHARLES. It's the cocktail-drinking does the harm:
There's nothing on earth so bad for the young.
All that a civilised person needs
Is a glass of dry sherry or two before dinner.
The modern young people don't know what they're drinking,
Modern young people don't care what they're eating;
They've lost their sense of taste and smell
Because of their cocktails and cigarettes.

[*Enter* DENMAN *with sherry and whisky.* CHARLES *takes sherry and*
GERALD *whisky.*]

That's what it comes to.

[*Lights a cigarette*]

IVY.   The younger generation
Are undoubtedly decadent.

CHARLES.   The younger generation
Are not what we were. Haven't the stamina,
Haven't the sense of responsibility.

GERALD. You're being very hard on the younger generation.
I don't come across them very much now, myself;

But I must say I've met some very decent specimens
And some first-class shots — better than you were,
Charles, as I remember. Besides, you've got to make allowances:
We haven't left them such an easy world to live in.
Let the younger generation speak for itself:
It's Mary's generation. What does she think about it?
MARY. Really, Cousin Gerald, if you want information
About the younger generation, you must ask someone else.
I'm afraid that I don't deserve the compliment:
I don't belong to any generation.

[*Exit*]

VIOLET. Really, Gerald, I must say you're very tactless,
And I think that Charles might have been more considerate.
GERALD. I'm very sorry: but why was she upset?
I only meant to draw her into the conversation.
CHARLES. She's a nice girl; but it's a difficult age for her.
I suppose she must be getting on for thirty?
She ought to be married, that's what it is.
AMY. So she should have been, if things had gone as I intended.
Harry's return does not make things easy for her
At the moment: but life may still go right.
Meanwhile, let us drop the subject. The less said the better.
GERALD. That reminds me, Amy,
When are the boys all due to arrive?
AMY. I do not want the clock to stop in the dark.
If you want to know why I never leave Wishwood
That is the reason. I keep Wishwood alive
To keep the family alive, to keep them together,
To keep me alive, and I live to keep them.
You none of you understand how old you are
And death will come to you as a mild surprise,
A momentary shudder in a vacant room.
Only Agatha seems to discover some meaning in death
Which I cannot find.
— I am only certain of Arthur and John,
Arthur in London, John in Leicestershire:
They should both be here in good time for dinner.
Harry telephoned to me from Marseilles,
He would come by air to Paris, and so to London,
And hoped to arrive in the course of the evening.

287

VIOLET. Harry was always the most likely to be late.

AMY. This time, it will not be his fault.

    We are very lucky to have Harry at all.

IVY. And when will you have your birthday cake, Amy,

    And open your presents?

AMY.   After dinner:

    That is the best time.

IVY.   It is the first time

    You have not had your cake and your presents at tea.

AMY. This is a very particular occasion

    As you ought to know. It will be the first time

    For eight years that we have all been together.

AGATHA. It is going to be rather painful for Harry

    After eight years and all that has happened

    To come back to Wishwood.

GERALD.   Why, painful?

VIOLET. Gerald! you know what Agatha means.

AGATHA. I mean painful, because everything is irrevocable,

    Because the past is irremediable,

    Because the future can only be built

    Upon the real past. Wandering in the tropics

    Or against the painted scene of the Mediterranean,

    Harry must often have remembered Wishwood —

    The nursery tea, the school holiday,

    The daring feats on the old pony,

    And thought to creep back through the little door.

    He will find a new Wishwood. Adaptation is hard.

AMY. Nothing is changed, Agatha, at Wishwood.

    Everything is kept as it was when he left it,

    Except the old pony, and the mongrel setter

    Which I had to have destroyed.

    Nothing has been changed. I have seen to that.

AGATHA. Yes. I mean that at Wishwood he will find another Harry.

    The man who returns will have to meet

    The boy who left. Round by the stables,

    In the coach-house, in the orchard,

    In the plantation, down the corridor

    That led to the nursery, round the corner

    Of the new wing, he will have to face him —

    And it will not be a very *jolly* corner.

When the loop in time comes — and it does not come for
    everybody —
The hidden is revealed, and the spectres show themselves.
GERALD. I don't in the least know what you're talking about.
    You seem to be wanting to give us all the hump.
    I must say, this isn't cheerful for Amy's birthday
    Or for Harry's homecoming. Make him feel at home, I say!
    Make him feel that what has happened doesn't matter.
    He's taken his medicine, I've no doubt.
    Let him marry again and carry on at Wishwood.
AMY. Thank you, Gerald. Though Agatha means
    As a rule, a good deal more than she cares to betray,
    I am bound to say that I agree with you.
CHARLES. I never wrote to him when he lost his wife —
    That was just about a year ago, wasn't it?
    Do you think that I ought to mention it now?
    It seems to me too late.
AMY.   Much too late.
    If he wants to talk about it, that's another matter;
    But I don't believe he will. He will wish to forget it.
    I do not mince matters in front of the family:
    You can call it nothing but a blessed relief.
VIOLET. *I* call it providential.
IVY.   Yet it must have been shocking,
    Especially to lose anybody in *that* way —
    Swept off the deck in the middle of a storm,
    And never even to recover the body.
CHARLES. 'Well-known Peeress Vanishes from Liner'.
GERALD. Yes, it's odd to think of her as permanently *missing*.
VIOLET. Had she been drinking?
AMY.   I would never ask him.
IVY. These things are much better not enquired into.
    She may have done it in a fit of temper.
GERALD. I never met her.
AMY.   I am very glad you did not.
    I am very glad that none of you ever met her.
    It will make the situation very much easier
    And is why I was so anxious you should all be here.
    She never would have been one of the family,
    She never wished to be one of the family,

She only wanted to keep him to herself
To satisfy her vanity. That's why she dragged him
All over Europe and half round the world
To expensive hotels and undesirable society
Which she could choose herself. She never wanted
Harry's relations or Harry's old friends;
She never wanted to fit herself to Harry,
But only to bring Harry down to her own level.
A restless shivering painted shadow
In life, she is less than a shadow in death.
You might as well all of you know the truth
For the sake of the future. There can be no grief
And no regret and no remorse.
I would have prevented it if I could. For the sake of the future:
Harry is to take command at Wishwood
And I hope we can contrive his future happiness.
Do not discuss his absence. Please behave only
As if nothing had happened in the last eight years.

GERALD. That will be a little difficult.

VIOLET.   Nonsense, Gerald!
You must see for yourself it's the only thing to do.

AGATHA. Thus with most careful devotion
    Thus with precise attention
    To detail, interfering preparation
    Of that which is already prepared
    Men tighten the knot of confusion
    Into perfect misunderstanding,
    Reflecting a pocket-torch of observation
    Upon each other's opacity
    Neglecting all the admonitions
    From the world around the corner
    The wind's talk in the dry holly-tree
    The inclination of the moon
    The attraction of the dark passage
    The paw under the door.

CHORUS (IVY, VIOLET, GERALD and CHARLES). Why do we feel
        embarrassed, impatient, fretful, ill at ease,
    Assembled like amateur actors who have not been assigned their
        parts?
    Like amateur actors in a dream when the curtain rises, to find

    themselves dressed for a different play, or having rehearsed
      the wrong parts,
    Waiting for the rustling in the stalls, the titter in the dress circle,
      the laughter and catcalls in the gallery?

CHARLES. I might have been in St. James's Street, in a comfortable
    chair rather nearer the fire.

IVY. I might have been visiting Cousin Lily at Sidmouth, if I had not
    had to come to this party.

GERALD. I might have been staying with Compton-Smith, down at his
    place in Dorset.

VIOLET. I should have been helping Lady Bumpus, at the Vicar's
    American Tea.

CHORUS. Yet we are here at Amy's command, to play an unread part in
    some monstrous farce, ridiculous in some nightmare
    pantomime.

AMY. What's that? I thought I saw someone pass the window.
    What time is it?

CHARLES.   Nearly twenty to seven.

AMY. John should be here now, he has the shortest way to come.
    John at least, if not Arthur. Hark, there is someone coming:
    Yes, it must be John.

[*Enter* HARRY]

                Harry!

[HARRY *stops suddenly at the door and stares at the window*]

IVY. Welcome, Harry!

GERALD. Well done!

VIOLET. Welcome home to Wishwood!

CHARLES. Why, what's the matter?

AMY. Harry, if you want the curtains drawn you should let me ring for
    Denman.

HARRY. How can you sit in this blaze of light for all the world to
    look at?
    If you knew how you looked, when I saw you through the window!
    Do you like to be stared at by eyes through a window?

AMY. You forget, Harry, that you are at Wishwood,
    Not in town, where you have to close the blinds.
    There is no one to see you but our servants who belong here,
    And who all want to see you back, Harry.

HARRY. Look there, look there: do you see them?

GERALD. No, I don't see anyone about.

HARRY.   No, no, not there. Look there!
Can't you see them? *You* don't see them, but I see them,
And they see me. This is the first time that I have seen them.
In the Java Straits, in the Sunda Sea,
In the sweet sickly tropical night, I knew they were coming.
In Italy, from behind the nightingale's thicket,
The eyes stared at me, and corrupted that song.
Behind the palm trees in the Grand Hotel
They were always there. But I did not *see* them.
Why should they wait until I came back to Wishwood?
There were a thousand places where I might have met them!
Why here? why here?
                    Many happy returns of the day, mother.
Aunt Ivy, Aunt Violet, Uncle Gerald, Uncle Charles. Agatha.

AMY. We are very glad to have you back, Harry.
Now we shall all be together for dinner.
The servants have been looking forward to your coming:
Would you like to have them in after dinner
Or wait till tomorrow? I am sure you must be tired.
You will find everybody here, and everything the same.
Mr. Bevan — you remember — wants to call tomorrow
On some legal business, a question about taxes —
But I think you would rather wait till you are rested.
Your room is all ready for you. Nothing has been changed.

HARRY. Changed? nothing changed? how can you say that nothing is
    changed?
You all look so withered and young.

GERALD.   We must have a ride tomorrow.
You'll find you know the country as well as ever.
There wasn't an inch of it you didn't know.
But you'll have to see about a couple of new hunters.

CHARLES. And I've a new wine merchant to recommend you;
Your cellar could do with a little attention.

IVY. And you'll really have to find a successor to old Hawkins.
It's really high time the old man was pensioned.
He's let the rock garden go to rack and ruin,
And he's nearly half blind. I've spoken to your mother
Time and time again: she's done nothing about it
Because she preferred to wait for your coming.

VIOLET. And time and time again I have spoken to your mother

About the waste that goes on in the kitchen.
Mrs. Packell is too old to know what she is doing.
It really needs a man in charge of things at Wishwood.

AMY. You see your aunts and uncles are very helpful, Harry.
I have always found them forthcoming with advice
Which I have never taken. Now it is your business.
I have only struggled to keep Wishwood going
And to make no changes before your return.
Now it's for you to manage. I am an old woman.
They can give me no further advice when I'm dead.

IVY. Oh, dear Amy!
No one wants you to die, I'm sure!
Now that Harry's back, is the time to think of living.

HARRY. Time and time and time, and change, no change!
You all of you try to talk as if nothing had happened,
And yet you are talking of nothing else. Why not get to the point
Or if you want to pretend that I am another person —
A person that you have conspired to invent, please do so
In my absence. I shall be less embarrassing to you. Agatha?

AGATHA. I think, Harry, that having got so far —
If you want no pretences, let us have no pretences:
And you must try at once to make us understand,
And we must try to understand you.

HARRY. But how can I explain, how can I explain to *you*?
You will understand less after I have explained it.
All that I could hope to make you understand
Is only events: not what has happened.
And people to whom nothing has ever happened
Cannot understand the unimportance of events.

GERALD. Well, you can't say that nothing has happened to *me*.
I started as a youngster on the North-West Frontier —
Been in tight corners most of my life
And some pretty nasty messes.

CHARLES. And there isn't much would surprise me, Harry;
Or shock me, either.

HARRY.   You are all people
To whom nothing has happened, at most a continual impact
Of external events. You have gone through life in sleep,
Never woken to the nightmare. I tell you, life would be unendurable
If you were wide awake. You do not know

293

The noxious smell untraceable in the drains,
Inaccessible to the plumbers, that has its hour of the night; you do
    not know
The unspoken voice of sorrow in the ancient bedroom
At three o'clock in the morning. I am not speaking
Of my own experience, but trying to give you
Comparisons in a more familiar medium. I am the old house
With the noxious smell and the sorrow before morning,
In which all past is present, all degradation
Is unredeemable. As for what happens —
Of the past you can only see what is past,
Not what is always present. That is what matters.

AGATHA. Nevertheless, Harry, best tell us as you can:
    Talk in your own language, without stopping to debate
    Whether it may be too far beyond our understanding.

HARRY. The sudden solitude in a crowded desert
    In a thick smoke, many creatures moving
    Without direction, for no direction
    Leads anywhere but round and round in that vapour —
    Without purpose, and without principle of conduct
    In flickering intervals of light and darkness;
    The partial anæsthesia of suffering without feeling
    And partial observation of one's own automatism
    While the slow stain sinks deeper through the skin
    Tainting the flesh and discolouring the bone —
    This is what matters, but it is unspeakable,
    Untranslatable: I talk in general terms
    Because the particular has no language. One thinks to escape
    By violence, but one is still alone
    In an over-crowded desert, jostled by ghosts.
    It was only reversing the senseless direction
    For a momentary rest on the burning wheel
    That cloudless night in the mid-Atlantic
    When I pushed her over.

VIOLET.   Pushed her?

HARRY. You would never imagine anyone could sink so quickly.
    I had always supposed, wherever I went
    That she would be with me; whatever I did
    That she was unkillable. It was not like that.
    Everything is true in a different sense.

I expected to find her when I went back to the cabin.
Later, I became excited, I think I made enquiries;
The purser and the steward were extremely sympathetic
And the doctor very attentive.
That night I slept heavily, alone.

AMY.   Harry!

CHARLES. You mustn't indulge such dangerous fancies.
It's only doing harm to your mother and yourself.
Of course we know what really happened, we read it in the papers —
No need to revert to it. Remember, my boy,
I understand, your life together made it seem more horrible.
There's a lot in my own past life that presses on my chest
When I wake, as I do now, early before morning.
I understand these feelings better than you know —
But *you* have no reason to reproach yourself.
Your conscience can be clear.

HARRY.   It goes a good deal deeper
Than what people call their conscience; it is just the cancer
That eats away the self. I knew how you would take it.
First of all, you isolate the single event
As something so dreadful that it couldn't have happened,
Because you could not bear it. So you must believe
That I suffer from delusions. It is not my conscience,
Not my mind, that is diseased, but the world I have to live in.
— I lay two days in contented drowsiness;
Then I recovered. I am afraid of sleep:
A condition in which one can be caught for the last time.
And also waking. She is nearer than ever.
The contamination has reached the marrow
And *they* are always near. Here, nearer than ever.
They are very close here. I had not expected that.

AMY. Harry, Harry, you are very tired
And overwrought. Coming so far
And making such haste, the change is too sudden for you.
You are unused to our foggy climate
And the northern country. When you see Wishwood
Again by day, all will be the same again.
I beg you to go now and rest before dinner.
Get Downing to draw you a hot bath,
And you will feel better.

AGATHA. There are certain points I do not yet understand:
    They will be clear later. I am also convinced
    That you only hold a fragment of the explanation.
    It is only because of what you do not understand
    That you feel the need to declare what you do.
    There is more to understand: hold fast to that
    As the way to freedom.

HARRY.   I think I see what you mean,
    Dimly — as you once explained the sobbing in the chimney
    The evil in the dark closet, which they said was not there,
    Which they explained away, but you explained them
    Or at least, made me cease to be afraid of them.
    I will go and have my bath.

                                                    [*Exit*]

GERALD.   God preserve us!
    I never thought it would be as bad as this.

VIOLET. There is only one thing to be done:
    Harry must see a doctor.

IVY.   But I understand —
    I have heard of such cases before — that people in his condition
    Often betray the most immoderate resentment
    At such a suggestion. They can be very cunning —
    Their malady makes them so. They do not want to be cured
    And they know what you are thinking.

CHARLES. He has probably let this notion grow in his mind,
    Living among strangers, with no one to talk to.
    I suspect it is simply that the wish to get rid of her
    Makes him believe he did. He cannot trust his good fortune.
    I believe that all he needs is someone to talk to,
    To get it off his mind. I'll have a talk to him tomorrow.

AMY. Most certainly not, Charles, you are not the right person.
    I prefer to believe that a few days at Wishwood
    Among his own family, is all that he needs.

GERALD. Nevertheless, Amy, there's something in Violet's suggestion.
    Why not ring up Warburton, and ask him to join us?
    He's an old friend of the family, it's perfectly natural
    That he should be asked. He looked after all the boys
    When they were children. I'll have a word with him.
    He can talk to Harry, and Harry need have no suspicion.
    I'd trust Warburton's opinion.

AMY.   If anyone speaks to Dr. Warburton
  It should be myself. What does Agatha think?
AGATHA. It seems a necessary move
  In an unnecessary action,
  Not for the good that it will do
  But that nothing may be left undone
  On the margin of the impossible.
AMY.   Very well.
  I will ring up the doctor myself.

                                                                    [*Exit*]

CHARLES. Meanwhile, I have an idea. Why not question Downing?
  He's been with Harry ten years, he's absolutely discreet.
  He was with them on the boat. He might be of use.
IVY. Charles! you don't really suppose
  That he might have pushed her over?
CHARLES. In any case, I shouldn't blame Harry.
  I might have done the same thing once, myself.
  Nobody knows what he's likely to do
  Until there's somebody he wants to get rid of.
GERALD. Even so, we don't want Downing to know
  Any more than he knows already.
  And even if he knew, it's very much better
  That he shouldn't know that we knew it also.
  Why not let sleeping dogs lie?
CHARLES. All the same, there's a question or two
                          [*Rings the bell*]
  That I'd like to ask Downing.
                                   He shan't know why I'm asking.
[*Enter* DENMAN]
  Denman, where is Downing? Is he up with his Lordship?
DENMAN. He's out in the garage, Sir, with his Lordship's car.
CHARLES. Tell him I'd like to have a word with him, please.
                                                        [*Exit* DENMAN]
VIOLET. Charles, if you are determined upon this investigation,
  Which I am convinced is going to lead us nowhere,
  And which I am sure Amy would disapprove of —
  I only wish to express my emphatic protest
  Both against your purpose and the means you are employing.
CHARLES. My purpose is, to find out what's wrong with Harry:
  Until we know that, we can do nothing for him.

And as for my means, we can't afford to be squeamish
In taking hold of anything that comes to hand.
If you are interested in helping Harry
You can hardly object to the means.

VIOLET.   I do object.

IVY. And I wish to associate myself with my sister
In her objections —

AGATHA.   I have no objection,
Any more than I object to asking Dr. Warburton:
I only see that this is all quite irrelevant;
We had better leave Charles to talk to Downing
And pursue his own methods.

[Rises]

VIOLET.   I do not agree.
I think there should be witnesses. I intend to remain.
And I wish to be present to hear what Downing says.
I want to know at once, not be told about it later.

IVY. And I shall stay with Violet.

AGATHA.   I shall return
When Downing has left you.

                                [Exit]

CHARLES.   Well, I'm very sorry
You all see it like this: but there simply are times
When there's nothing to do but take the bull by the horns,
And this is one.

[Knock: and enter DOWNING]

CHARLES.   Good evening, Downing.
It's good to see you again, after all these years.
You're well, I hope?

DOWNING.   Thank you, very well indeed, Sir.

CHARLES. I'm sorry to send for you so abruptly,
But I've a question I'd like to put to you,
I'm sure you won't mind, it's about his Lordship.
You've looked after his Lordship for over ten years . . .

DOWNING. Eleven years, Sir, next Lady Day.

CHARLES. Eleven years, and you know him pretty well.
And I'm sure that you've been a good friend to him, too.
We haven't seen him for nearly eight years;
And to tell the truth, now that we've seen him,
We're a little worried about his health.

He doesn't seem to be . . . quite himself.
DOWNING. Quite natural, if I may say so, Sir,
 After what happened.
CHARLES.   Quite so, quite.
 Downing, you were with them on the voyage from New York —
 We didn't learn very much about the circumstances;
 We only knew what we read in the papers —
 Of course, there was a great deal too much in the papers.
 Downing, do you think that it might have been suicide,
 And that his Lordship knew it?
DOWNING. Unlikely, Sir, if I may say so.
 Much more likely to have been an accident.
 I mean, knowing her Ladyship,
 I don't think she had the courage.
CHARLES. Did she ever talk of suicide?
DOWNING. Oh yes, she did, every now and again.
 But in my opinion, it is those that talk
 That are the least likely. To my way of thinking
 She only did it to frighten people.
 If you take my meaning — just for the effect.
CHARLES. I understand, Downing. Was she in good spirits?
DOWNING. Well, always about the same, Sir.
 What I mean is, always up and down.
 Down in the morning, and up in the evening,
 And *then* she used to get rather excited,
 And, in a way, irresponsible, Sir.
 If I may make so bold, Sir,
 I always thought that a very few cocktails
 Went a long way with her Ladyship.
 She wasn't one of those that are *designed* for drinking:
 It's natural for some and unnatural for others.
CHARLES. And how was his Lordship, during the voyage?
DOWNING. Well, you might say depressed, Sir.
 But you know his Lordship was always very quiet:
 Very uncommon that I saw him in high spirits.
 For what my judgment's worth, I always said his Lordship
 Suffered from what they call a kind of repression.
 But what struck me . . . more nervous than usual;
 I mean to say, you could see that he was nervous.
 He behaved as if he thought something might happen.

CHARLES. What sort of thing?

DOWNING.   Well, I don't know, Sir.
But he seemed very anxious about my Lady.
Tried to keep her in when the weather was rough,
Didn't like to see her lean over the rail.
He was in a rare fright, once or twice.
But you know, it is just my opinion, Sir,
That his Lordship is rather psychic, as they say.

CHARLES. Were they always together?

DOWNING.   Always, Sir.
That was just my complaint against my Lady.
It's my opinion that man and wife
Shouldn't see too much of each other, Sir.
Quite the contrary of the usual opinion,
I dare say. She wouldn't leave him alone.
And there's my complaint against these ocean liners
With all their swimming baths and gymnasiums
There's not even a place where a man can go
For a quiet smoke, where the women can't follow him.
She wouldn't leave him out of her sight.

CHARLES. During that evening, did you see him?

DOWNING. Oh yes, Sir, I'm sure I saw him.
I don't mean to say that he had any orders —
His Lordship is always most considerate
About keeping me up. But when I say I saw him,
I mean that I saw him accidental.
You see, Sir, I was down in the Tourist,
And I took a bit of air before I went to bed,
And you could see the corner of the upper deck.
And I remember, there I saw his Lordship
Leaning over the rail, looking at the water —
There wasn't a moon, but I was sure it was him.
While I took my turn about, for near half an hour
He stayed there alone, looking over the rail.
Her Ladyship must have been all right then,
Mustn't she, Sir? or else he'd have known it.

CHARLES. Oh yes . . . quite so. Thank you, Downing,
I don't think we need you any more.

GERALD.   Oh, Downing,
Is there anything wrong with his Lordship's car?

DOWNING. Oh no, Sir, she's in good running order:
    I see to that.
GERALD.   I only wondered
    Why you've been busy about it tonight.
DOWNING. Nothing wrong, Sir:
    Only I like to have her always ready.
    Would there be anything more, Sir?
GERALD.   Thank you, Downing;
    Nothing more.

                          [*Exit* DOWNING]

VIOLET. Well, Charles, I must say, with your investigations,
    You seem to have left matters much as they were —
    Except for having brought Downing into it:
    Of which I disapprove.
CHARLES.   Of which you disapprove.
    But I believe that an unconscious accomplice is desirable.
CHORUS. Why should we stand here like guilty conspirators, waiting
        for some revelation
    When the hidden shall be exposed, and the newsboy shall shout in
        the street?
    When the private shall be made public, the common photographer
    Flashlight for the picture papers: why do we huddle together
    In a horrid amity of misfortune? why should we be implicated,
        brought in and brought together?
IVY. I do not trust Charles with his confident vulgarity, acquired from
        worldly associates.
GERALD. Ivy is only concerned for herself, and her credit among her
    shabby genteel acquaintance.
VIOLET. Gerald is certain to make some blunder, he is useless out of the
    army.
CHARLES. Violet is afraid that her status as Amy's sister will be
    diminished.
CHORUS. We all of us make the pretension
    To be the uncommon exception
    To the universal bondage.
    We like to appear in the newspapers
    So long as we are in the right column.
    We know about the railway accident
    We know about the sudden thrombosis
    And the slowly hardening artery.

We like to be thought well of by others
So that we may think well of ourselves.
And any explanation will satisfy:
We only ask to be reassured
About the noises in the cellar
And the window that should not have been open.
Why do we all behave as if the door might suddenly open, the
      curtains be drawn,
The cellar make some dreadful disclosure, the roof disappear,
And we should cease to be sure of what is real or unreal?
Hold tight, hold tight, we must insist that the world is what we have
      always taken it to be.

AMY'S VOICE. Ivy! Violet! has Arthur or John come yet?

IVY. There is no news of Arthur or John.

[*Enter* AMY *and* AGATHA]

AMY. It is very annoying. They both promised to be here
    In good time for dinner. It is very annoying.
    Now they can hardly arrive in time to dress.
    I do not understand what could have gone wrong
    With both of them, coming from different directions.
    Well, we must go and dress, I suppose. I hope Harry will feel better
    After his rest upstairs.

[*Exeunt, except* AGATHA]

Scene II

[*Enter* MARY *with flowers*]

MARY. The spring is very late in this northern country,
    Late and uncertain, clings to the south wall.
    The gardener had no garden-flowers to give me for this evening.

AGATHA. I always forget how late the spring is, here.

MARY. I had rather wait for our windblown blossoms,
    Such as they are, than have these greenhouse flowers
    Which do not belong here, which do not know
    The wind and rain, as I know them.

AGATHA. I wonder how many we shall be for dinner.

MARY. Seven . . . nine . . . ten surely.
    I hear that Harry has arrived already
    And he was the only one that was uncertain.
    Arthur or John may be late, of course.
    We may have to keep the dinner back . . .

AGATHA. And also Dr. Warburton. At least, Amy has invited him.

MARY. Dr. Warburton? I think she might have told me;
    It is very difficult, having to plan
    For uncertain numbers. Why did she ask him?

AGATHA. She only thought of asking him a little while ago.

MARY. Well, there's something to be said for having an outsider;
    For what is more formal than a family dinner?
    An official occasion of uncomfortable people
    Who meet very seldom, making conversation.
    I am very glad if Dr. Warburton is coming.
    I shall have to sit between Arthur and John.
    Which is worse, thinking of what to say to John,
    Or having to listen to Arthur's chatter
    When he thinks he is behaving like a man of the world?
    Cousin Agatha, I want your advice.

AGATHA.   I should have thought
    You had more than you wanted of that, when at college.

MARY. I might have known you'd throw that up against me.
     I know I wasn't one of your favourite students:
     I only saw you as a hard headmistress
     Who knew the way of dominating timid girls.
     I don't see you any differently now;
     But I really wish that I'd taken your advice
     And tried for a fellowship, seven years ago.
     Now I want your advice, because there's no one else to ask,
     And because you are strong, and because you don't belong here
     Any more than I do. I want to get away.

AGATHA. After seven years?

MARY.   Oh, you don't understand!
     But you do understand. You only want to know
     Whether I understand. You know perfectly well,
     What Cousin Amy wants, she usually gets.
     Why do *you* so seldom come here? *You*'re not afraid of her,
     But I think you must have wanted to avoid collision.
     I suppose I could have gone, if I'd had the moral courage,
     Even against a will like hers. I know very well
     Why she wanted to keep me. She didn't need me:
     She would have done just as well with a hired servant
     Or with none. She only wanted me for Harry —
     Not such a compliment: she only wanted
     To have a tame daughter-in-law with very little money,
     A housekeeper-companion for her and Harry.
     Even when he married, she still held on to me
     Because she couldn't bear to let any project go;
     And even when *she* died: I believed that Cousin Amy —
     I almost believed it — had killed her by willing.
     Doesn't that sound awful? I know that it does.
     Did you ever meet her? What was she like?

AGATHA. I am the only one who ever met her,
     The only one Harry asked to his wedding:
     Amy did not know that. I was sorry for her;
     I could see that she distrusted me — she was frightened of the
          family,
     She wanted to fight them — with the weapons of the weak,
     Which are too violent. And it could not have been easy,
     Living with Harry. It's not what she did to Harry,
     That's important, I think, but what he did to himself.

MARY. But it wasn't till I knew that Harry had returned
 That I felt the strength to go. I know I must go.
 But where? I want a job: and you can help me.
AGATHA. I am very sorry, Mary, I am very sorry for you;
 Though you may not think me capable of such a feeling.
 I would like to help you: but you must not run away.
 Any time before now, it would have shown courage
 And would have been right. Now, the courage is only the moment
 And the moment is only fear and pride. I see more than this,
 More than I can tell you, more than there are words for.
 At this moment, there is no decision to be made;
 The decision will be made by powers beyond us
 Which now and then emerge. You and I, Mary,
 Are only watchers and waiters: not the easiest rôle.
 I must go and change for dinner.

                   [*Exit*]
MARY.   So you will not help me!
 Waiting, waiting, always waiting.
 I think this house *means* to keep us waiting.
[*Enter* HARRY]
HARRY. Waiting? For what?
MARY.   How do you do, Harry.
 You are down very early. I thought you had just arrived.
 Did you have a comfortable journey?
HARRY.   Not very.
 But, at least, it did not last long. How are you, Mary?
MARY. Oh, very well. What are you looking for?
HARRY. I had only just noticed that this room is quite unchanged:
 The same hangings . . . the same pictures . . . even the table,
 The chairs, the sofa . . . all in the same positions.
 I was looking to see if anything was changed,
 But if so, I can't find it.
MARY.   Your mother insisted
 On everything being kept the same as when you left it.
HARRY. I wish she had not done that. It's very unnatural,
 This arresting of the normal change of things:
 But it's very like her. What I might have expected.
 It only makes the changing of people
 All the more manifest.
MARY.   Yes, nothing changes here,
           305

And we just go on . . . drying up, I suppose,
Not noticing the change. But to you, I am sure,
We must seem very altered.

HARRY.   You have hardly changed at all —
And I haven't seen you since you came down from Oxford.

MARY. Well, I must go and change for dinner.
We do change — to that extent.

HARRY.   No, don't go just yet.

MARY. Are you glad to be at home?

HARRY.   There was something
I wanted to ask you. I don't know yet.
All these years I'd been longing to get back
Because I thought I never should. I thought it was a place
Where life was substantial and simplified —
But the simplification took place in my memory,
I think. It seems I shall get rid of nothing,
Of none of the shadows that I wanted to escape;
And at the same time, other memories,
Earlier, forgotten, begin to return
Out of my childhood. I can't explain.
But I thought I might escape from one life to another,
And it may be all one life, with no escape. Tell me,
Were you ever happy here, as a child at Wishwood?

MARY. Happy? not really, though I never knew why:
It always seemed that it must be my own fault,
And never to be happy was always to be naughty.
But there were reasons: I was only a cousin
Kept here because there was nothing else to do with me.
I didn't belong here. It was different for you.
And you seemed so much older. We were rather in awe of you —
At least, I was.

HARRY.   Why were we not happy?

MARY. Well, it all seemed to be imposed upon us;
Even the nice things were laid out ready,
And the treats were always so carefully prepared;
There was never any time to invent our own enjoyments.
But perhaps it was all designed for you, not for us.

HARRY. No, it didn't seem like that. I was part of the design
As well as you. But what was the design?
It never came off. But do you remember

306

MARY. The hollow tree in what we called the wilderness

HARRY. Down near the river. That was the stockade
From which we fought the Indians, Arthur and John.

MARY. It was the cave where we met by moonlight
To raise the evil spirits.

HARRY.   Arthur and John.
Of course we were punished for being out at night
After being put to bed. But at least they never knew
Where we had been.

MARY.   They never found the secret.

HARRY. Not then. But later, coming back from school
For the holidays, after the formal reception
And the family festivities, I made my escape
As soon as I could, and slipped down to the river
To find the old hiding place. The wilderness was gone,
The tree had been felled, and a neat summer-house
Had been erected, 'to please the children'.
It's absurd that one's only memory of freedom
Should be a hollow tree in a wood by the river.

MARY. But when I was a child I took everything for granted,
Including the stupidity of older people —
They lived in another world, which did not touch me.
Just now, I find them very difficult to bear.
They are always assured that you ought to be happy
At the very moment when you are wholly conscious
Of being a misfit, of being superfluous.
But why should I talk about my commonplace troubles?
They must seem very trivial indeed to you.
It's just ordinary hopelessness.

HARRY.   One thing you cannot know:
The sudden extinction of every alternative,
The unexpected crash of the iron cataract.
You do not know what hope is, until you have lost it.
You only know what it is not to hope:
You do not know what it is to have hope taken from you,
Or to fling it away, to join the legion of the hopeless
Unrecognised by other men, though sometimes by each other.

MARY. I know what you mean. That is an experience
I have not had. Nevertheless, however real,
However cruel, it may be a deception.

HARRY.   What I see
    May be one dream or another; if there is nothing else
    The most real is what I fear. The bright colour fades
    Together with the unrecapturable emotion,
    The glow upon the world, that never found its object;
    And the eye adjusts itself to a twilight
    Where the dead stone is seen to be batrachian,
    The aphyllous branch ophidian.

MARY.   You bring your own landscape
    No more real than the other. And in a way you contradict
        yourself:
    That sudden comprehension of the death of hope
    Of which you speak, I know you have experienced it,
    And I can well imagine how awful it must be.
    But in this world another hope keeps springing
    In an unexpected place, while we are unconscious of it.
    You hoped for something, in coming back to Wishwood,
    Or you would not have come.

HARRY.   Whatever I hoped for
    Now that I am here I know I shall not find it.
    The instinct to return to the point of departure
    And start again as if nothing had happened,
    Isn't that all folly? It's like the hollow tree,
    Not there.

MARY.   But surely, what you say
    Only proves that you expected Wishwood
    To be your real self, to do something for you
    That you can only do for yourself.
    What you need to alter is something inside you
    Which you can change anywhere — here, as well as elsewhere.

HARRY. Something inside me, you think, that can be altered!
    And here, indeed! where I have felt them near me,
    Here and here and here — wherever I am not looking,
    Always flickering at the corner of my eye,
    Almost whispering just out of earshot —
    And inside too, in the nightly panic
    Of dreaming dissolution. You do not know,
    You cannot know, you cannot understand.

MARY. I think I could understand, but you would have to be patient
    With me, and with people who have not had your experience.

HARRY. If I tried to explain, you could never understand:
    Explaining would only make a worse misunderstanding;
    Explaining would only set me farther away from you.
    There is only one way for you to understand
    And that is by seeing. They are much too clever
    To admit you into *our* world. Yours is no better.
    They have seen to that: it is part of the torment.
MARY. If you think I am incapable of understanding you —
    But in any case, I must get ready for dinner.
HARRY. No, no, don't go! Please don't leave me
    Just at this moment. I feel it is important.
    Something should have come of this conversation.
MARY. I am not a wise person,
    And in the ordinary sense I don't know you very well,
    Although I remember you better than you think,
    And what is the real you. I haven't much experience,
    But I see something now which doesn't come from tutors
    Or from books, or from thinking, or from observation:
    Something which I did not know I knew.
    Even if, as you say, Wishwood is a cheat,
    Your family a delusion — then it's *all* a delusion,
    Everything you feel — I don't mean what you think,
    But what you feel. You attach yourself to loathing
    As others do to loving: an infatuation
    That's wrong, a good that's misdirected. You deceive yourself
    Like the man convinced that he is paralysed
    Or like the man who believes that he is blind
    While he still sees the sunlight. I know that this is true.
HARRY. I have spent many years in useless travel;
    You have staid in England, yet you seem
    Like someone who comes from a very long distance,
    Or the distant waterfall in the forest,
    Inaccessible, half-heard.
    And I hear your voice as in the silence
    Between two storms, one hears the moderate usual noises
    In the grass and leaves, of life persisting,
    Which ordinarily pass unnoticed.
    Perhaps you are right, though I do not know
    How you should know it. Is the cold spring
    Is the spring not an evil time, that excites us with lying voices?

MARY. The cold spring now is the time
  For the ache in the moving root
  The agony in the dark
  The slow flow throbbing the trunk
  The pain of the breaking bud.
  These are the ones that suffer least:
  The aconite under the snow
  And the snowdrop crying for a moment in the wood.

HARRY. Spring is an issue of blood
  A season of sacrifice
  And the wail of the new full tide
  Returning the ghosts of the dead
  Those whom the winter drowned
  Do not the ghosts of the drowned
  Return to land in the spring?
  Do the dead want to return?

MARY. Pain is the opposite of joy
  But joy is a kind of pain
  I believe the moment of birth
  Is when we have knowledge of death
  I believe the season of birth
  Is the season of sacrifice
  For the tree and the beast, and the fish
  Thrashing itself upstream:
  And what of the terrified spirit
  Compelled to be reborn
  To rise toward the violent sun
  Wet wings into the rain cloud
  Harefoot over the moon?

HARRY. What have we been saying? I think I was saying
  That it seemed as if I had been always here
  And you were someone who had come from a long distance.
  Whether I know what I am saying, or why I say it,
  That does not matter. You bring me news
  Of a door that opens at the end of a corridor,
  Sunlight and singing; when I had felt sure
  That every corridor only led to another,
  Or to a blank wall; that I kept moving
  Only so as not to stay still. Singing and light.
  Stop!

What is that? do you feel it?

MARY.   What, Harry?

HARRY. That apprehension deeper than all sense,
    Deeper than the sense of smell, but like a smell
    In that it is indescribable, a sweet and bitter smell
    From another world. I know it, I know it!
    More potent than ever before, a vapour dissolving
    All other worlds, and me into it. O Mary!
    Don't look at me like that! Stop! Try to stop it!
    I am going. Oh why, now? Come out!
    Come out! Where are you? Let me see you,
    Since I know you are there, I know you are spying on me.
    Why do you play with me, why do you let me go,
    Only to surround me? — When I remember them
    They leave me alone: when I forget them
    Only for an instant of inattention
    They are roused again, the sleepless hunters
    That will not let me sleep. At the moment before sleep
    I always see their claws distended
    Quietly, as if they had never stirred.
    It was only a moment, it was only one moment
    That I stood in sunlight, and thought I might stay there.

MARY. Look at me. You can depend on me.
    Harry! Harry! It's all *right*, I tell you.
    If you will depend on me, it will be all right.

HARRY. Come out!

[*The curtains part, revealing the Eumenides in the window embrasure.*]
    Why do you show yourselves now for the first time?
    When I knew her, I was not the same person.
    I was not any person. Nothing that I did
    Has to do with me. The accident of a dreaming moment,
    Of a dreaming age, when I was someone else
    Thinking of something else, puts me among you.
    I tell you, it is not me you are looking at,
    Not me you are grinning at, not me your confidential looks
    Incriminate, but that other person, if person
    You thought I was: let your necrophily
    Feed upon that carcase. They will not go.

MARY. Harry! There is no one here.
            [*She goes to the window and pulls the curtains across*]

311

HARRY. They were here, I tell you. They are here.
    Are you so imperceptive, have you such dull senses
    That you could not see them? If I had realised
    That you were so obtuse, I would not have listened
    To your nonsense. Can't you help me?
    You're of no use to me. I must face them.
    I must fight them. But they are stupid.
    How can one fight with stupidity?
    Yet I must speak to them.

[*He rushes forward and tears apart the curtains: but the embrasure is empty.*]

MARY.   Oh, Harry!

Scene III

VIOLET. Good evening, Mary: aren't you dressed yet?
How do you think that Harry is looking?
Why, who could have pulled those curtains apart?
[*Pulls them together*]
Very well, I think, after such a long journey;
You know what a rush he had to be here in time
For his mother's birthday.

IVY.   Mary, my dear,
Did you arrange these flowers? Just let me change them.
You don't mind, do you? I know so much about flowers;
Flowers have always been my passion.
You know I had my own garden once, in Cornwall,
When I could afford a garden; and I took several prizes
With my delphiniums. I was rather an authority.

GERALD. Good evening, Mary. You've seen Harry, I see.
It's good to have him back again, isn't it?
We must make him feel at home. And most auspicious
That he could be here for his mother's birthday.

MARY. I must go and change. I came in very late.

[*Exit*]

CHARLES. Now we only want Arthur and John
I'm glad that you'll all be together, Harry;
They need the influence of their elder brother.
Arthur's a bit irresponsible, you know;
You should have a sobering effect upon him.
After all, you're the head of the family.

AMY'S VOICE. Violet! Has Arthur or John come yet?

VIOLET. Neither of them is here yet, Amy.

[*Enter* AMY, *with* DR. WARBURTON]

AMY. It is most vexing. What can have happened?
I suppose it's the fog that is holding them up,

313

So it's no use to telephone anywhere. Harry!
Haven't you seen Dr. Warburton?
You know he's the oldest friend of the family,
And he's known you longer than anybody, Harry.
When he heard that you were going to be here for dinner
He broke an important engagement to come.

WARBURTON. I dare say we've both changed a good deal, Harry.
A country practitioner doesn't get younger.
It takes me back longer than you can remember
To see you again. But you can't have forgotten
The day when you came back from school with measles
And we had such a time to keep you in bed.
You didn't like being ill in the holidays.

IVY. It *was* unpleasant, coming home to have an illness.

VIOLET. It was always the same with your minor ailments
And children's epidemics: you would never stay in bed
Because you were convinced that you would never get well.

HARRY. Not, I think, without some justification:
For what you call restoration to health
Is only incubation of another malady.

WARBURTON. You mustn't take such a pessimistic view
Which is hardly complimentary to my profession.
But I remember, when I was a student at Cambridge,
I used to dream of making some great discovery
To do away with one disease or another.
Now I've had forty years' experience
I've left off thinking in terms of the laboratory.
We're all of us ill in one way or another:
We call it health when we find no symptom
Of illness. Health is a relative term.

IVY. You must have had a very rich experience, Doctor,
In forty years.

WARBURTON.   Indeed, yes.
Even in a country practice. My first patient, now —
You wouldn't believe it, ladies — was a murderer,
Who suffered from an incurable cancer.
How he fought against it! I never saw a man
More anxious to live.

HARRY.   Not at all extraordinary.
It is really harder to believe in murder

Than to believe in cancer. Cancer is here:
The lump, the dull pain, the occasional sickness:
Murder a reversal of sleep and waking.
Murder was there. Your ordinary murderer
Regards himself as an innocent victim.
To himself he is still what he used to be
Or what he would be. He cannot realise
That everything is irrevocable,
The past unredeemable. But cancer, now,
That is something real.

WARBURTON.   Well, let's not talk of such matters.
How did we get onto the subject of cancer?
I really don't know. — But now you're all grown up
I haven't a patient left at Wishwood.
Wishwood was always a cold place, but healthy.
It's only when I get an invitation to dinner
That I ever see your mother.

VIOLET.   Yes, look at your mother!
Except that she can't get about now in winter
You wouldn't think that she was a day older
Than on her birthday ten years ago.

GERALD. Is there any use in waiting for Arthur and John?

AMY. We might as well go in to dinner.
They may come before we finish. Will you take me in, Doctor?
I think we are very much the oldest present —
In fact we are the oldest inhabitants.
As we came first, we will go first, in to dinner.

WARBURTON. With pleasure, Lady Monchensey,
And I hope that next year will bring me the same honour.

                    [*Exeunt* AMY, DR. WARBURTON, HARRY]

CHORUS. I am afraid of all that has happened, and of all that is to come;
Of the things to come that sit at the door, as if they had been there
        always.
And the past is about to happen, and the future was long since
        settled.
And the wings of the future darken the past, the beak and claws
        have desecrated
History. Shamed
The first cry in the bedroom, the noise in the nursery, mutilated
The family album, rendered ludicrous

The tenants' dinner, the family picnic on the moors. Have torn
The roof from the house, or perhaps it was never there.
And the bird sits on the broken chimney. I am afraid.

IVY. This is a most undignified terror, and I must struggle against it.

GERALD. I am used to tangible danger, but only to what I can
understand.

VIOLET. It is the obtuseness of Gerald and Charles and that doctor,
that gets on my nerves.

CHARLES. If the matter were left in my hands, I think I could manage
the situation.

[*Exeunt*]

[*Enter* MARY, *and passes through to dinner. Enter* AGATHA]

AGATHA. The eye is on this house
The eye covers it
There are three together
May the three be separated
May the knot that was tied
Become unknotted
May the crossed bones
In the filled-up well
Be at last straightened
May the weasel and the otter
Be about their proper business
The eye of the day time
And the eye of the night time
Be diverted from this house
Till the knot is unknotted
The crossed is uncrossed
And the crooked is made straight.

[*Exit to dinner*]

END OF PART I

PART II

The library, after dinner.

Scene I

HARRY, WARBURTON

WARBURTON. I'm glad of a few minutes alone with you, Harry.
  In fact, I had another reason for coming this evening
  Than simply in honour of your mother's birthday.
  I wanted a private conversation with you
  On a confidential matter.
HARRY.   I can imagine —
  Though I think it is probably going to be useless,
  Or if anything, make matters rather more difficult.
  But talk about it, if you like.
WARBURTON.   You don't understand me.
  I'm sure you cannot know what is on my mind;
  And as for making matters more difficult —
  It is much more difficult not to be prepared
  For something that is very likely to happen.
HARRY. O God, man, the things that are going to happen
  Have already happened.
WARBURTON.   That is in a sense true,
  But without your knowing it, and what you know
  Or do not know, at any moment
  May make an endless difference to the future.
  It's about your mother . . .
HARRY.   What about my mother?
  Everything has always been referred back to mother.
  When we were children, before we went to school,
  The rule of conduct was simply pleasing mother;
  Misconduct was simply being unkind to mother;

What was wrong was whatever made her suffer,
And whatever made her happy was what was virtuous —
Though never very happy, I remember. That was why
We all felt like failures, before we had begun.
When we came back, for the school holidays,
They were not holidays, but simply a time
In which we were supposed to make up to mother
For all the weeks during which she had not seen us
Except at half-term, and seeing us then
Only seemed to make her more unhappy, and made us
Feel more guilty, and so we misbehaved
Next day at school, in order to be punished,
For punishment made us feel less guilty. Mother
Never punished us, but made us feel guilty.
I think that the things that are taken for granted
At home, make a deeper impression upon children
Than what they are told.

WARBURTON.   Stop, Harry, you're mistaken.
I mean, you don't know what I want to tell you.
You may be quite right, but what we are concerned with
Now, is your mother's happiness in the future,
For the time she has to live: not with the past.

HARRY. Oh, is there any difference!
How can we be concerned with the past
And not with the future? or with the future
And not with the past? What I'm telling you
Is very important. Very important.
You must let me explain, and then you can talk.
I don't know why, but just this evening
I feel an overwhelming need for explanation —
But perhaps I only dream that I am talking
And shall wake to find that I have been silent
Or talked to the stone deaf: and the others
Seem to hear something else than what I am saying.
But if you want to talk, at least you can tell me
Something useful. Do you remember my father?

WARBURTON. Why, yes, of course, Harry, but I really don't see
What that has to do with the present occasion
Or with what I have to tell you.

HARRY.   What you have to tell me

  Is either something that I know already
  Or unimportant, or else untrue.
  But I want to know more about my father.
  I hardly remember him, and I know very well
  That I was kept apart from him, till he went away.
  We never heard him mentioned, but in some way or another
  We felt that he was always here.
  But when we would have grasped for him, there was only a vacuum
  Surrounded by whispering aunts: Ivy and Violet —
  Agatha never came then. Where was my father?
WARBURTON. Harry, there's no good probing for misery.
  There was enough once: but what festered
  Then, has only left a cautery.
  Leave it alone. You know that your mother
  And your father were never very happy together:
  They separated by mutual consent
  And he went to live abroad. You were only a boy
  When he died. You would not remember.
HARRY. But now I do remember. Not Arthur or John,
  They were too young. But now I remember
  A summer day of unusual heat,
  The day I lost my butterfly net;
  I remember the silence, and the hushed excitement
  And the low conversation of triumphant aunts.
  It is the conversations not overheard,
  Not intended to be heard, with the sidewise looks,
  That bring death into the heart of a child.
  That was the day he died. Of course.
  I mean, I suppose, the day on which the news arrived.
WARBURTON. You overinterpret.
  I am sure that your mother always loved him;
  There was never the slightest suspicion of scandal.
HARRY. Scandal? who said scandal? I did not.
  Yes, I see now. That night, when she kissed me,
  I felt the trap close. If you won't tell me,
  I must ask Agatha. I never dared before.
WARBURTON. I advise you strongly, not to ask your aunt —
  I mean, there is nothing she could tell you. But, Harry,
  We can't sit here all the evening, you know;
  You will have to have the birthday celebration,

And your brothers will be here. Won't you let me tell you
What I had to say?

HARRY.   Very well, tell me.

WARBURTON. It's about your mother's health that I wanted to talk to
    you.

I must tell you, Harry, that although your mother
Is still so alert, so vigorous of mind,
Although she seems as vital as ever —
It is only the force of her personality,
Her indomitable will, that keeps her alive.
I needn't go into technicalities
At the present moment. The whole machine is weak
And running down. Her heart's very feeble.
With care, and avoiding all excitement
She may live several years. A sudden shock
Might send her off at any moment.
If she had been another woman
She would not have lived until now.
Her determination has kept her going:
She has only lived for your return to Wishwood,
For you to take command at Wishwood,
And for that reason, it is most essential
That nothing should disturb or excite her.

HARRY.   Well!

WARBURTON. I'm very sorry for you, Harry.
I should have liked to spare you this,
Just now. But there were two reasons
Why you had to know. One is your mother,
To make her happy for the time she has to live.
The other is yourself: the future of Wishwood
Depends on you. I don't like to say this;
But you know that I am a very old friend,
And have always been a party to the family secrets —
You know as well as I do that Arthur and John
Have been a great disappointment to your mother.
John's very steady — but he's not exactly brilliant;
And Arthur has always been rather irresponsible.
Your mother's hopes are all centred on you.

HARRY. Hopes? . . . Tell me
Did you know my father at about my present age?

WARBURTON. Why, yes, Harry, of course I did.

HARRY. What did he look like then? Did he look at all like me?

WARBURTON. Very much like you. Of course there are differences:
But, allowing for the changes in fashion
And your being clean-shaven, very much like you.
And now, Harry, let's talk about yourself.

HARRY. I never saw a photograph. There is no portrait.

WARBURTON. What I want to know is, whether you've been sleeping . . .

[*Enter* DENMAN]

DENMAN. It's Sergeant Winchell is here, my Lord,
And wants to see your Lordship very urgent,
And Dr. Warburton. He says it's very urgent
Or he wouldn't have troubled you.

HARRY.   I'll see him.

                                                [*Exit* DENMAN]

WARBURTON. I wonder what he wants. I hope nothing has happened
To either of your brothers.

HARRY.   Nothing can have happened
To either of my brothers. Nothing can happen —
If Sergeant Winchell is real. But Denman saw him.
But what if Denman saw him, and yet he was not real?
That would be worse than anything that has happened.
What if *you* saw him, and . . .

WARBURTON.   Harry! Pull yourself together.
Something may have happened to one of your brothers.

[*Enter* WINCHELL]

WINCHELL. Good evening, my Lord. Good evening, Doctor.
Many happy . . . Oh, I'm sorry, my Lord,
I was thinking it was your birthday, not her Ladyship's.

HARRY. Her Ladyship's!
        [*He darts at* WINCHELL *and seizes him by the shoulders*]
                              He *is* real, Doctor.
So let us resume the conversation. You, and I
And Winchell. Sit down, Winchell,
And have a glass of port. We were talking of my father.

WINCHELL. Always at your jokes, I see. You don't look a year older
Than when I saw you last, my Lord. But a country sergeant
Doesn't get younger. Thank you, no, my Lord;
I don't find port agrees with the rheumatism.

WARBURTON. For God's sake, Winchell, tell us your business.

His Lordship isn't very well this evening.

WINCHELL.   I understand, Sir.

It'd be the same if it was my birthday —

I beg pardon, I'm forgetting.

If it was my mother's. God rest her soul,

She's been dead these ten years. How is her Ladyship,

If I may ask, my Lord?

HARRY.   Why do you keep asking

About her Ladyship? Do you know or don't you?

I'm not afraid of you.

WINCHELL.   I should hope not, my Lord.

I didn't mean to put myself forward.

But you see, my Lord, I had good reason for asking . . .

HARRY. Well, do you want me to produce her for you?

WINCHELL. Oh no indeed, my Lord, I'd much rather not . . .

HARRY. You mean you think I can't. But I might surprise you;

I think I might be able to give you a shock.

WINCHELL. There's been shock enough for one evening, my Lord:

That's what I've come about.

WARBURTON.   For Heaven's sake, Winchell,

Tell us your business.

WINCHELL.   It's about Mr. John.

HARRY. John!

WINCHELL.   Yes, my Lord, I'm sorry.

I thought I'd better have a word with you quiet,

Rather than phone and perhaps disturb her Ladyship.

So I slipped along on my bike. Mostly walking,

What with the fog so thick, or I'd have been here sooner.

I'd telephoned to Dr. Warburton's,

And they told me he was here, and that you'd arrived.

Mr. John's had a bit of an accident

On the West Road, in the fog, coming along

At a pretty smart pace, I fancy, ran into a lorry

Drawn up round the bend. We'll have the driver up for this:

Says he doesn't know this part of the country

And stopped to take his bearings. We've got him at the Arms —

Mr. John, I mean. By a bit of luck

Dr. Owen was there, and looked him over;

Says there's nothing wrong but some nasty cuts

And a bad concussion; says he'll come round

In the morning, most likely, but he mustn't be moved.
But Dr. Owen was anxious that you should have a look at him.
WARBURTON. Quite right, quite right. I'll go and have a look at him.
We must explain to your mother . . .
AMY'S VOICE.   Harry! Harry!
Who's there with you? Is it Arthur or John?
[*Enter* AMY, *followed severally by* VIOLET, IVY, AGATHA, GERALD and
CHARLES.]
Winchell! what are you here for?
WINCHELL. I'm sorry, my Lady, but I've just told the doctor,
It's really nothing but a minor accident.
WARBURTON. It's John has had the accident, Lady Monchensey:
And Winchell tells me Dr. Owen has seen him
And says it's nothing but a slight concussion,
But he mustn't be moved tonight. I'd trust Owen
On a matter like this. You can trust Owen.
We'll bring him up tomorrow; and a few days' rest,
I've no doubt, will be all that he needs.
AMY. Accident? What sort of an accident?
WINCHELL. Coming along in the fog, my Lady,
And he must have been in rather a hurry.
There was a lorry drawn up where it shouldn't be,
Outside of the village, on the West Road.
AMY. Where is he?
WINCHELL.   At the Arms, my Lady;
Of course, he hasn't come round yet.
Dr. Owen was there, by a bit of luck.
GERALD. I'll go down and see him, Amy, and come back and report to
you.
AMY. I must see for myself. Order the car at once.
WARBURTON. I forbid it, Lady Monchensey.
As your doctor, I forbid you to leave the house tonight.
There is nothing you could do, and out in this weather
At this time of night, I would not answer for the consequences
I am going myself. I will come back and report to you.
AMY. I must see for myself. I do not believe you.
CHARLES. Much better leave it to Warburton, Amy.
Extremely fortunate for us that he's here.
We must put ourselves under Warburton's orders.
WARBURTON. I repeat, Lady Monchensey, that you must not go out.

If you do, I must decline to continue to treat you.

You are only delaying me. I shall return at once.

AMY. Well, I suppose you are right. But can I trust you?

WARBURTON. You have trusted me a good many years, Lady Monchensey;

This is not the time to begin to doubt me.

Come, Winchell. We can put your bicycle

On the back of my car.

[*Exeunt* WARBURTON *and* WINCHELL]

VIOLET.   Well, Harry,

I think that you might have had something to say.

Aren't you sorry for your brother? Aren't you aware

Of what is going on? and what it means to your mother?

HARRY. Oh, of course I'm sorry. But from what Winchell says

I don't think the matter can be very serious.

A minor trouble like a concussion

Cannot make very much difference to John.

A brief vacation from the kind of consciousness

That John enjoys, can't make very much difference

To him or to anyone else. If he was ever really conscious,

I should be glad for him to have a breathing spell:

But John's ordinary day isn't much more than breathing.

IVY. Really, Harry! how can you be so callous?

I always thought you were so fond of John.

VIOLET. And if you don't care what happens to John,

You might show some consideration to your mother.

AMY. I do not know very much:

And as I get older, I am coming to think

How little I have ever known.

But I think your remarks are much more inappropriate

Than Harry's.

HARRY.   It's only when they see nothing

That people can always show the suitable emotions —

And so far as they feel at all, their emotions are suitable.

They don't understand what it is to be awake,

To be living on several planes at once

Though one cannot speak with several voices at once.

I have all of the rightminded feeling about John

That you consider appropriate. Only, that's not the language

That I choose to be talking. I will not talk yours.

AMY. You looked like your father
    When you said that.
HARRY.   I think, mother,
    I shall make you lie down. You must be very tired.
                                [*Exeunt* HARRY *and* AMY]
VIOLET. I really do not understand Harry's behaviour.
AGATHA. I think it is as well to leave Harry to establish
    If he can, some communication with his mother.
VIOLET. I do not seem to be very popular tonight.
CHARLES. Well, there's no sort of use in any of us going —
    On a night like this — it's a good three miles;
    There's nothing we could do that Warburton can't.
    If he's worse than Winchell said, then he'll let us know at once.
GERALD. I am really more afraid of the shock for Amy;
    But I think that Warburton understands *that*.
IVY. You are quite right, Gerald, the one thing that matters
    Is not to let her see that anyone is worried.
    We must carry on as if nothing had happened,
    And have the cake and presents.
GERALD.   But *I*'m worried about Arthur:
    He's much more apt than John to get into trouble.
CHARLES. Oh, but Arthur's a brilliant driver.
    After all the experience he's had at Brooklands,
    He's not likely to get into trouble.
GERALD. A brilliant driver, but more reckless.
IVY. Yet I remember, when they were boys,
    Arthur was always the more adventurous
    But John was the one that had the accidents,
    Somehow, just because he *was* the slow one.
    He was always the one to fall off the pony,
    Or out of a tree — and always on his head.
VIOLET. But a year ago, Arthur took me out in his car,
    And I told him I would never go out with him again.
    Not that I wanted to go with him at all —
    Though of course he meant well — but I think an open car
    Is so undignified: you're blown about so,
    And you feel so conspicuous, lolling back
    And so near the street, and everyone staring;
    And the pace he went at was simply terrifying.
    I said I would rather walk: and I did.

GERALD. Walk? where to?

VIOLET. He started out to take me to Cheltenham;
But I stopped him somewhere in Chiswick, I think.
Anyway, the district was unfamiliar
And I had the greatest trouble in getting home.
I am sure he meant well. But I do think he is reckless.

GERALD. I wonder how much Amy knows about Arthur?

CHARLES. More than she cares to mention, I imagine.

[*Enter* HARRY]

HARRY. Mother is asleep, I think: it's strange how the old
Can drop off to sleep in the middle of calamity
Like children, or like hardened campaigners. She looked
Very much as she must have looked when she was a child.
You've been holding a meeting — the usual family inquest
On the characters of all the junior members?
Or engaged in predicting the minor event,
Engaged in foreseeing the minor disaster?
You go on trying to think of each thing separately,
Making small things important, so that everything
May be unimportant, a slight deviation
From some imaginary course that life ought to take,
That you call normal. What you call the normal
Is merely the unreal and the unimportant.
I was like that in a way, so long as I could think
Even of my own life as an isolated ruin,
A casual bit of waste in an orderly universe.
But it begins to seem just part of some huge disaster,
Some monstrous mistake and aberration
Of all men, of the world, which I cannot put in order.
If you only knew the years that I have had to live
Since I came home, a few hours ago, to Wishwood.

VIOLET. I will make no observations on what you say, Harry;
My comments are not always welcome in this family.

[*Enter* DENMAN]

DENMAN. Excuse me, Miss Ivy. There's a trunk call for you.

IVY. A trunk call? for me? why, who can want me?

DENMAN. He wouldn't give his name, Miss; but it's Mr. Arthur.

IVY. Arthur! Oh dear, I'm afraid *he*'s had an accident.

[*Exeunt* IVY *and* DENMAN]

VIOLET. When it's Ivy that he's asking for, I expect the worst.

AGATHA. Whatever you have learned, Harry, you must remember
    That there is always more: we cannot rest in being
    The impatient spectators of malice or stupidity.
    We must try to penetrate the other private worlds
    Of make-believe and fear. To rest in our own suffering
    Is evasion of suffering. We must learn to suffer more.
VIOLET. Agatha's remarks are invariably pointed.
HARRY. Do you think that I believe what I said just now?
    That was only what I should like to believe.
    I was talking in abstractions: and you answered in abstractions.
    I have a private puzzle. Were they simply outside,
    I might escape somewhere, perhaps. Were they simply inside
    I could cheat them perhaps with the aid of Dr. Warburton —
    Or any other doctor, who would be another Warburton,
    If you decided to set another doctor on me.
    But this is too real for your words to alter.
    Oh, there *must* be another way of talking
    That would get us somewhere. You don't understand me.
    You can't understand me. It's not being alone
    That is the horror — to be alone with the horror.
    What matters is the filthiness. I can clean my skin,
    Purify my life, void my mind,
    But always the filthiness, that lies a little deeper . . .
[*Enter* IVY]
IVY. Where is there an evening paper?
GERALD.   Why, what's the matter.
IVY. Somebody, look for Arthur in the evening paper.
    That was Arthur, ringing up from London:
    The connection was so bad, I could hardly hear him,
    And his voice was very queer. It seems that Arthur too
    Has had an accident. I don't think he's hurt,
    But he says that he hasn't got the use of his car,
    And he missed the last train, so he's coming up tomorrow;
    And he said there was something about it in the paper,
    But it's all a mistake. And not to tell his mother.
VIOLET. What's the use of asking for an evening paper?
    You know as well as I do, at this distance from London
    Nobody's likely to have this evening's paper.
CHARLES. Stop, I think I bought a lunch edition
    Before I left St. Pancras. If I did, it's in my overcoat.

I'll see if it's there. There might be something in that.

[*Exit*]

GERALD. Well, I said that Arthur was every bit as likely
　　To have an accident as John. And it wasn't John's fault,
　　I don't believe. John is unlucky,
　　But Arthur is definitely reckless.

VIOLET. I think these racing cars ought to be prohibited.

[*Re-enter* CHARLES, *with a newspaper*]

CHARLES. Yes, there is a paragraph . . . I'm glad to say
　　It's not very conspicuous . . .

GERALD. There'll have been more in the later editions.
　　You'd better read it to us.

CHARLES [*reads*].

'Peer's Brother in Motor Smash

　　The Hon. Arthur Gerald Charles Piper, younger brother of Lord
　　　Monchensey, who ran into and demolished a roundsman's
　　　cart in Ebury Street early on the morning of January 1st, was
　　　fined £50 and costs to-day, and forbidden to drive a car for the
　　　next twelve months.

　　While trying to extricate his car from the collision, Mr. Piper re-
　　　versed into a shop-window. When challenged, Mr. Piper said:
　　　"I thought it was all open country about here" — '

GERALD. Where?

CHARLES. In Ebury Street. 'The police stated that at the time of the
　　　accident Mr. Piper was being pursued by a patrol, and was
　　　travelling at the rate of 66 miles an hour. When asked why he
　　　did not stop when signalled by the police car, he said: "I
　　　thought you were having a game with me." '

GERALD. This is what the Communists make capital out of.

CHARLES. There's a little more. 'The Piper family . . .' no, we needn't
　　read that.

VIOLET. This is just what I expected. But if Agatha
　　Is going to moralise about it, I shall scream.

GERALD. It's going to be awkward, explaining this to Amy.

IVY. Poor Arthur! I'm sure that you're being much too hard on
　　him.

CHARLES. In my time, these affairs were kept out of the papers;
　　But nowadays, there's no such thing as privacy.

CHORUS. In an old house there is always listening, and more is heard
　　than is spoken.

328

And what is spoken remains in the room, waiting for the future to
    hear it.
And whatever happens began in the past, and presses hard on the
    future.
The agony in the curtained bedroom, whether of birth or of dying,
Gathers in to itself all the voices of the past, and projects them into
    the future.
The treble voices on the lawn
The mowing of hay in summer
The dogs and the old pony
The stumble and the wail of little pain
The chopping of wood in autumn
And the singing in the kitchen
And the steps at night in the corridor
The moment of sudden loathing
And the season of stifled sorrow
The whisper, the transparent deception
The keeping up of appearances
The making the best of a bad job
All twined and tangled together, all are recorded.
There is no avoiding these things
And we know nothing of exorcism
And whether in Argos or England
There are certain inflexible laws
Unalterable, in the nature of music.
There is nothing at all to be done about it,
There is nothing to do about anything,
And now it is nearly time for the news
We must listen to the weather report
And the international catastrophes.

                               [*Exeunt* CHORUS]

Scene II

HARRY. John will recover, be what he always was;
    Arthur again be sober, though not for very long;
    And everything will go on as before. These mild surprises
    Should be in the routine of normal life at Wishwood.
    John is the only one of us I can conceive
    As settling down to make himself at home at Wishwood,
    Make a dull marriage, marry some woman stupider —
    Stupider than himself. He can resist the influence
    Of Wishwood, being unconscious, living in gentle motion
    Of horses, and right visits to the right neighbours
    At the right times; and be an excellent landlord.
AGATHA. What is in your mind, Harry?
    I can guess about the past and what you mean about the future;
    But a present is missing, needed to connect them.
    You may be afraid that I would not understand you,
    You may also be afraid of being understood,
    Try not to regard it as an explanation.
HARRY. I still have to learn exactly what their meaning is.
    At the beginning, eight years ago,
    I felt, at first, that sense of separation,
    Of isolation unredeemable, irrevocable —
    It's eternal, or gives a knowledge of eternity,
    Because it feels eternal while it lasts. That is one hell.
    Then the numbness came to cover it — that is another —
    That was the second hell of not being there,
    The degradation of being parted from my self,
    From the self which persisted only as an eye, seeing.
    All this last year, I could not fit myself together:
    When I was inside the old dream, I felt all the same emotion
    Or lack of emotion, as before: the same loathing
    Diffused, I not a person, in a world not of persons

But only of contaminating presences.
And then I had no horror of my action,
I only felt the repetition of it
Over and over. When I was outside,
I could associate nothing of it with myself,
Though nothing else was real. I thought foolishly
That when I got back to Wishwood, as I had left it,
Everything would fall into place. But *they* prevent it.
I still have to find out what their meaning is.
Here I have been finding
A misery long forgotten, and a new torture,
The shadow of something behind our meagre childhood,
Some origin of wretchedness. Is that what they would show
    me?
And now I want you to tell me about my father.

AGATHA. What do you want to know about your father?

HARRY. If I knew, then I should not have to ask.
You know what I want to know, and that is enough:
Warburton told me that, though he did not mean to.
What I want to know is something I need to know,
And only you can tell me. I know that much.

AGATHA. I had to fight for many years to win my dispossession,
And many years to keep it. What people know me as,
The efficient principal of a women's college —
That is the surface. There is a deeper
Organisation, which your question disturbs.

HARRY. When I know, I know that in some way I shall find
That I have always known it. And that will be better.

AGATHA. I will try to tell you. I hope I have the strength.

HARRY. I have thought of you as the completely strong,
The liberated from the human wheel.
So I looked to you for strength. Now I think it is
A common pursuit of liberation.

AGATHA. Your father might have lived — or so I see him —
An exceptionally cultivated country squire,
Reading, sketching, playing on the flute,
Something of an oddity to his county neighbours,
But not neglecting public duties.
He hid his strength beneath unusual weakness,
The diffidence of a solitary man:

    Where he was weak he recognised your mother's power,
    And yielded to it.

HARRY.   There was no ecstasy.
    Tell me now, who were my parents?

AGATHA. Your father and your mother.

HARRY.   You tell me nothing.

AGATHA. The dead man whom you have assumed to be your father,
    And my sister whom you acknowledge as your mother:
    There is no mystery here.

HARRY.   What then?

AGATHA. You see your mother as identified with this house —
    It was not always so. There were many years
    Before she succeeded in making terms with Wishwood,
    Until she took your father's place, and reached the point where
    Wishwood supported her, and she supported Wishwood.
    At first it was a vacancy. A man and a woman
    Married, alone in a lonely country house together,
    For three years childless, learning the meaning
    Of loneliness. Your mother wanted a sister here
    Always. I was the youngest: I was then
    An undergraduate at Oxford. I came
    Once for a long vacation. I remember
    A summer day of unusual heat
    For this cold country.

HARRY.   And then?

AGATHA. There are hours when there seems to be no past or future,
    Only a present moment of pointed light
    When you want to burn. When you stretch out your hand
    To the flames. They only come once,
    Thank God, that kind. Perhaps there is another kind,
    I believe, across a whole Thibet of broken stones
    That lie, fang up, a lifetime's march. I have believed this.

HARRY. I have known neither.

AGATHA. The autumn came too soon, not soon enough.
    The rain and wind had not shaken your father
    Awake yet. I found him thinking
    How to get rid of your mother. What simple plots!
    He was not suited to the role of murderer.

HARRY. In what way did he wish to murder her?

AGATHA. Oh, a dozen foolish ways, each one abandoned

For something more ingenious. You were due in three months' time;
You would not have been born in that event: I stopped him.
I can take no credit for a little common sense,
He would have bungled it.
                              I did not want to kill *you*!
You to be killed! What were you then? only a thing called 'life' —
Something that should have been *mine*, as I felt then.
Most people would not have felt that compunction
If they felt no other. But I wanted you!
If that had happened, I knew I should have carried
Death in life, death through lifetime, death in my womb.
I felt that you were in some way mine!
And that in any case I should have no other child.

HARRY. And have me. That is the way things happen.
Everything is true in a different sense,
A sense that would have seemed meaningless before.
Everything tends towards reconciliation
As the stone falls, as the tree falls. And in the end
That is the completion which at the beginning
Would have seemed the ruin.
Perhaps my life has only been a dream
Dreamt through me by the minds of others. Perhaps
I only dreamt I pushed her.

AGATHA.   So I had supposed. What of it?
What we have written is not a story of detection,
Of crime and punishment, but of sin and expiation.
It is possible that you have not known what sin
You shall expiate, or whose, or why. It is certain
That the knowledge of it must precede the expiation.
It is possible that sin may strain and struggle
In its dark instinctive birth, to come to consciousness
And so find expurgation. It is possible
You are the consciousness of your unhappy family,
Its bird sent flying through the purgatorial flame.
Indeed it is possible. You may learn hereafter,
Moving alone through flames of ice, chosen
To resolve the enchantment under which we suffer.

HARRY. Look, I do not know why,
I feel happy for a moment, as if I had come home.
It is quite irrational, but now

333

I feel quite happy, as if happiness
Did not consist in getting what one wanted
Or in getting rid of what can't be got rid of
But in a different vision. This is like an end.

AGATHA. And a beginning. Harry, my dear,
I feel very tired, as only the old feel.
The young feel tired at the end of an action —
The old, at the beginning. It is as if
I had been living all these years upon my capital,
Instead of earning my spiritual income daily:
And I am old, to start again to make my living.

HARRY. But you are not unhappy, just now?
AGATHA.   What does the word mean?
There's relief from a burden that I carried,
And exhaustion at the moment of relief.
The burden's yours now, yours
The burden of all the family. And I am a little frightened.

HARRY. You, frightened! I can hardly imagine it.
I wish I had known — but that was impossible.
I only now begin to have some understanding
Of you, and of all of us. Family affection
Was a kind of formal obligation, a duty
Only noticed by its neglect. One had that part to play.
After such training, I could endure, these ten years,
Playing a part that had been imposed upon me;
And I returned to find another one made ready —
The book laid out, lines underscored, and the costume
Ready to be put on. But it is very odd:
When other people seemed so strong, their apparent strength
Stifled my decision. Now I see
I might even become fonder of my mother —
More compassionate at least — by understanding.
But she would not like that. Now I see
I have been wounded in a war of phantoms,
Not by human beings — they have no more power than I.
The things I thought were real are shadows, and the real
Are what I thought were private shadows. O that awful privacy
Of the insane mind! Now I can live in public.
Liberty is a different kind of pain from prison.

AGATHA. I only looked through the little door

When the sun was shining on the rose-garden:
And heard in the distance tiny voices
And then a black raven flew over.
And then I was only my own feet walking
Away, down a concrete corridor
In a dead air. Only feet walking
And sharp heels scraping. Over and under
Echo and noise of feet.
I was only the feet, and the eye
Seeing the feet: the unwinking eye
Fixing the movement. Over and under.

HARRY. In and out, in an endless drift
Of shrieking forms in a circular desert
Weaving with contagion of putrescent embraces
On dissolving bone. In and out, the movement
Until the chain broke, and I was left
Under the single eye above the desert.

AGATHA. Up and down, through the stone passages
Of an immense and empty hospital
Pervaded by a smell of disinfectant,
Looking straight ahead, passing barred windows.
Up and down. Until the chain breaks.

HARRY. To and fro, dragging my feet
Among inner shadows in the smoky wilderness,
Trying to avoid the clasping branches
And the giant lizard. To and fro.
Until the chain breaks.

The chain breaks,
The wheel stops, and the noise of machinery,
And the desert is cleared, under the judicial sun
Of the final eye, and the awful evacuation
Cleanses.

I was not there, you were not there, only our phantasms
And what did not happen is as true as what did happen
O my dear, and you walked through the little door
And I ran to meet you in the rose-garden.

AGATHA. This is the next moment. This is the beginning.
We do not pass twice through the same door
Or return to the door through which we did not pass.
I have seen the first stage: relief from what happened

Is also relief from that unfulfilled craving
Flattered in sleep, and deceived in waking.

You have a long journey.

HARRY. Not yet! not yet! this is the first time that I have been free
From the ring of ghosts with joined hands, from the pursuers,
And come into a quiet place.

Why is it so quiet?

Do you feel a kind of stirring underneath the air?
Do you? don't you? a communication, a scent
Direct to the brain . . . but not just as before,
Not quite like, not the same . . .

[*The* EUMENIDES *appear*]

and this time

You cannot think that I am surprised to see you.
And you shall not think that I am afraid to see you.
This time, you are real, this time, you are outside me,
And just endurable. I know that you are ready,
Ready to leave Wishwood, and I am going with you.
You followed me here, where I thought I should escape you —
No! you were already here before I arrived.
Now I see at last that I am following you,
And I know that there can be only one itinerary
And one destination. Let us lose no time. I will follow.

[*The curtains close.* AGATHA *goes to the window, in a somnambular fashion,
and opens the curtains, disclosing the empty embrasure. She steps into
the place which the* EUMENIDES *had occupied.*]

AGATHA. A curse comes to being
As a child is formed.
In both, the incredible
Becomes the actual
Without our intention
Knowing what is intended.
A curse is like a child, formed
In a moment of unconsciousness
In an accidental bed
Or under an elder tree
According to the phase
Of the determined moon.
A curse is like a child, formed
To grow to maturity:

Accident is design
And design is accident
In a cloud of unknowing.
O my child, my curse,
You shall be fulfilled:
The knot shall be unknotted
And the crooked made straight.

[She moves back into the room]

What have I been saying? I think I was saying
That you have a long journey. You have nothing to stay for.
Think of it as like a children's treasure hunt:
Here you have found a clue, hidden in the obvious place.
Delay, and it is lost. Love compels cruelty
To those who do not understand love.
What you have wished to know, what you have learned
Mean the end of a relation, make it impossible.
You did not intend this, I did not intend it,
No one intended, but . . . You must go.

HARRY. Shall we ever meet again?

AGATHA.   Shall we ever meet again?
And who will meet again? Meeting is for strangers.
Meeting is for those who do not know each other.

HARRY. I know that I have made a decision
In a moment of clarity, and now I feel dull again.
I only know that I made a decision
Which your words echo. I am still befouled,
But I know there is only one way out of defilement —
Which leads in the end to reconciliation.
And I know that I must go.

AGATHA.   You must go.

[Enter AMY]

AMY. What are you saying to Harry? He has only arrived,
And you tell him to go?

AGATHA.   He shall go.

AMY. He shall go? and who are you to say he shall go?
I think I know well enough why you wish him to go.

AGATHA. I wish nothing. I only say what I know must happen.

AMY. You only say what you intended to happen.

HARRY.   Oh, mother,
This is not to do with Agatha, any more than with the rest of you.

My advice has come from quite a different quarter,
But I cannot explain that to you now. Only be sure
That I know what I am doing, and what I must do,
And that it is the best thing for everybody.
But at present, I cannot explain it to anyone:
I do not know the words in which to explain it —
That is what makes it harder. You must just believe me,
Until I come again.

AMY. But why are you going?

HARRY.   I can only speak
And you cannot hear me. I can only speak
So you may not think I conceal an explanation,
And to tell you that I would have liked to explain.

AMY. Why should Agatha know, and I not be allowed to?

HARRY. I do not know whether Agatha knows
Or how much she knows. Any knowledge she may have —
It was not I who told her . . . All this year,
This last year, I have been in flight
But always in ignorance of invisible pursuers.
Now I know that all my life has been a flight
And phantoms fed upon me while I fled. Now I know
That the last apparent refuge, the safe shelter,
That is where one meets them. That is the way of spectres . . .

AMY. There is no one here!
No one, but your family!

HARRY.   And now I know
That my business is not to run away, but to pursue,
Not to avoid being found, but to seek.
I would not have chosen this way, had there been any other!
It is at once the hardest thing, and the only thing possible.
Now they will lead me. I shall be safe with them;
I am not safe here.

AMY.   So you *will* run away.

AGATHA. In a world of fugitives
The person taking the opposite direction
Will appear to run away.

AMY.   I was speaking to Harry.

HARRY. It is very hard, when one has just recovered sanity,
And not yet assured in possession, that is when
One begins to seem the maddest to other people.

It is hard for you too, mother, it is indeed harder,
Not to understand.

AMY.   Where are you going?

HARRY. I shall have to learn. That is still unsettled.
I have not yet had the precise directions.
Where does one go from a world of insanity?
Somewhere on the other side of despair.
To the worship in the desert, the thirst and deprivation,
A stony sanctuary and a primitive altar,
The heat of the sun and the icy vigil,
A care over lives of humble people,
The lesson of ignorance, of incurable diseases.
Such things are possible. It is love and terror
Of what waits and wants me, and will not let me fall.
Let the cricket chirp. John shall be the master.
All I have is his. No harm can come to him.
What would destroy me will be life for John,
I am responsible for him. Why I have this election
I do not understand. It must have been preparing always,
And I see it was what I always wanted. Strength demanded
That seems too much, is just strength enough given.
I must follow the bright angels.

[*Exit*]

Scene III

AMY. I was a fool, to ask you again to Wishwood;
　　　But I thought, thirty-five years is long, and death is an end,
　　　And I thought that time might have made a change in Agatha —
　　　It has made enough in *me*. Thirty-five years ago
　　　You took my husband from me. Now you take my son.
AGATHA. What did I take? nothing that you ever had.
　　　What did I get? thirty years of solitude,
　　　Alone, among women, in a women's college,
　　　Trying not to dislike women. Thirty years in which to think.
　　　Do you suppose that I wanted to return to Wishwood?
AMY. The more rapacious, to take what I never had;
　　　The more unpardonable, to taunt me with not having it.
　　　Had you taken what I had, you would have left me at least a memory
　　　Of something to live upon. You knew that you took everything
　　　Except the walls, the furniture, the acres;
　　　Leaving nothing — but what I could breed for myself,
　　　What I could plant here. Seven years I kept him,
　　　For the sake of the future, a discontented ghost,
　　　In his own house. What of the humiliation,
　　　Of the chilly pretences in the silent bedroom,
　　　Forcing sons upon an unwilling father?
　　　Dare you think what that does to one? Try to think of it.
　　　I *would* have sons, if I could not have a husband:
　　　Then I let him go. I abased myself.
　　　Did I show any weakness, any self-pity?
　　　I forced myself to the purposes of Wishwood;
　　　I even asked you back, for visits, after he was gone,
　　　So that there might be no ugly rumours.
　　　You thought I did not know!
　　　You may be close, but I always saw through *him*.
　　　And now it is my son.

AGATHA.   I know one thing, Amy:
> That you have never changed. And perhaps I have not.
> I thought that I had, until this evening.
> But at least I wanted to. Now I must begin.
> There is nothing more difficult. But you are just the same:
> Just as voracious for what you cannot have
> Because you repel it.

AMY.   I prepared the situation
> For us to be reconciled, because of Harry,
> Because of his mistakes, because of his unhappiness,
> Because of the misery that he has left behind him,
> Because of the waste. I wanted to obliterate
> His past life, and have nothing except to remind him
> Of the years when he had been a happy boy at Wishwood;
> For his future success.

AGATHA.   Success is relative:
> It is what we can make of the mess we have made of things,
> It is what he can make, not what you would make for him.

AMY. Success is one thing, what you would make for him
> Is another. I call it failure. Your fury for possession
> Is only the stronger for all these years of abstinence.
> Thirty-five years ago you took my husband from me
> And now you take my son.

AGATHA. Why should we quarrel for what neither can have?
> If neither has ever had a husband or a son
> We have no ground for argument.

AMY. Who set you up to judge? what, if you please,
> Gives *you* the power to know what is best for Harry?
> What gave you this influence to persuade him
> To abandon his duty, his family and his happiness?
> Who has planned his good? is it you or I?
> Thirty-five years designing his life,
> Eight years watching, without him, at Wishwood,
> Years of bitterness and disappointment.
> What share had you in this? what have you given?
> And now at the moment of success against failure,
> When I felt assured of his settlement and happiness,
> You who took my husband, now you take my son.
> You take him from Wishwood, you take him from me,
> You take him . . .

[*Enter* MARY]

MARY. Excuse me, Cousin Amy. I have just seen Denman.
    She came to tell me that Harry is leaving:
    Downing told her. He has got the car out.
    What is the matter?

AMY.   That woman there,
    She has persuaded him: I do not know how.
    I have been always trying to make myself believe
    That he was not such a weakling as his father
    In the hands of any unscrupulous woman.
    I have no influence over him; *you* can try,
    But you will not succeed: she has some spell
    That works from generation to generation.

MARY. Is Harry really going?

AGATHA.   He is going.
    But that is not my spell, it is none of my doing:
    I have only watched and waited. In this world
    It is inexplicable, the resolution is in another.

MARY. Oh, but it is the danger comes from another!
    Can you not stop him? Cousin Agatha, stop him!
    You do not know what I have seen and what I know!
    He is in great danger, I know that, don't ask me,
    You would not believe me, but I tell you I know.
    You must keep him here, you must not let him leave.
    I do not know what must be done, what can be done,
    Even here, but elsewhere, everywhere, he is in danger.
    I will stay or I will go, whichever is better;
    I do not care what happens to me,
    But Harry must not go. Cousin Agatha!

AGATHA. Here the danger, here the death, here, not elsewhere;
    Elsewhere no doubt is agony, renunciation,
    But birth and life. Harry has crossed the frontier
    Beyond which safety and danger have a different meaning.
    And he cannot return. That is his privilege.
    For those who live in this world, this world only,
    Do you think that I would take the responsibility
    Of tempting them over the border? No one could, no one who
        knows.
    No one who has the least suspicion of what is to be found there.
    But Harry has been led across the frontier: he must follow;

    For him the death is now only on this side,
    For him, danger and safety have another meaning.
    They have made this clear. And I who have seen them must believe
        them.

MARY. Oh! . . . so . . . *you* have seen them too!

AGATHA. We must all go, each in his own direction,
    You, and I, and Harry. You and I,
    My dear, may very likely meet again
    In our wanderings in the neutral territory
    Between two worlds.

MARY.   Then you *will* help me!
    You remember what I said to you this evening?
    I knew that I was right: you made me wait for this —
    Only for this. I suppose I did not really mean it
    Then, but I mean it now. Of course it was much too late
    Then, for anything to come for me: I should have known it;
    It was all over, I believe, before it began;
    But I deceived myself. It takes so many years
    To learn that one is dead! So you must help me.
    I will go. But I suppose it is much too late
    Now, to try to get a fellowship?

AMY.   So you will all leave me!
    An old woman alone in a damned house.
    I will let the walls crumble. Why should I worry
    To keep the tiles on the roof, combat the endless weather,
    Resist the wind? fight with increasing taxes
    And unpaid rents and tithes? nourish investments
    With wakeful nights and patient calculations
    With the solicitor, the broker, agent? Why should I?
    It is no concern of the body in the tomb
    To bother about the upkeep. Let the wind and rain do that.

[*While* AMY *has been speaking,* HARRY *has entered, dressed for departure.*]

HARRY. But, mother, you will always have Arthur and John
    To worry about: not that John is any worry —
    The destined and the perfect master of Wishwood,
    The satisfactory son. And as for me,
    I am the last you need to worry about;
    I have my course to pursue, and I am safe from normal dangers
    If I pursue it. I cannot account for this
    But it is so, mother. Until I come again.

AMY. If you go now, I shall never see you again.

[*Meanwhile* VIOLET, GERALD *and* CHARLES *have entered*]

CHARLES. Where is Harry going? What is the matter?

AMY. Ask Agatha.

GERALD. Why, what's the matter? Where is he going?

AMY. Ask Agatha.

VIOLET. I cannot understand at all. Why is he leaving?

AMY. Ask Agatha.

VIOLET. Really, it sometimes seems to me
    That I am the only sane person in this house.
    Your behaviour all seems to me quite unaccountable.
    What *has* happened, Amy?

AMY. Harry is going away — to become a missionary.

HARRY. But ...!

CHARLES. A missionary! that's never happened in our family!
    And why in such a hurry? Before you make up your mind ...

VIOLET. You can't really think of *living* in a tropical climate!

GERALD. There's nothing wrong with a tropical climate —
    But you have to go in for some sort of training;
    The medical knowledge is the first thing.
    I've met with missionaries, often enough —
    Some of them very decent fellows. A maligned profession.
    They're sometimes very useful, knowing the natives,
    Though occasionally troublesome. But you'll have to learn the
        language
    And several dialects. It means a lot of preparation.

VIOLET. And you need some religious qualification!
    I think you should consult the vicar ...

GERALD. And don't forget
    That you'll need various inoculations —
    That depends on where you're going.

CHARLES. Such a thing
    Has never happened in our family.

VIOLET. I cannot understand it.

HARRY. I never said that I was going to be a missionary.
    I would explain, but you would none of you believe it;
    If you believed it, still you would not understand.
    You can't know why I am going. You have not seen
    What I have seen. Oh why should you make it so ridiculous
    Just now? I only want, please,

344

As little fuss as possible. You must get used to it;
Meanwhile, I apologise for my bad manners.
But if you *could* understand you would be quite happy about it,
So I shall say good-bye, until we meet again.

GERALD. Well, if you are determined, Harry, we must accept it;
But it's a bad night, and you will have to be careful.
You're taking Downing with you?

HARRY. Oh, yes, I'm taking Downing.
You need not fear that I am in any danger
Of such accidents as happen to Arthur and John:
Take care of *them*. My address, mother,
Will be care of the bank in London until you hear from me.
Good-bye, mother.

AMY. Good-bye, Harry.

HARRY. Good-bye.

AGATHA. Good-bye.

HARRY. Good-bye, Mary.

MARY. Good-bye, Harry. Take care of yourself.

[*Exit* HARRY]

AMY. At my age, I only just begin to apprehend the truth
About things too late to mend: and that is to be old.
Nevertheless, I am glad if I can come to know them.
I always wanted too much for my children
More than life can give. And now I am punished for it.
Gerald! you are the stupidest person in this room,
Violet, you are the most malicious in a harmless way;
I prefer your company to that of any of the others
Just to help me to the next room. Where I can lie down.
Then you can leave me.

GERALD. Oh, certainly, Amy.

VIOLET. I do not understand
A single thing that's happened.

[*Exeunt* AMY, VIOLET, GERALD]

CHARLES. It's very odd,
But I am beginning to feel, just beginning to feel
That there is something I *could* understand, if I were told it.
But I'm not sure that I want to know. I suppose I'm getting old:
Old age came softly up to now. I felt safe enough;
And now I don't feel safe. As if the earth should open
Right to the centre, as I was about to cross Pall Mall.

345

I thought that life could bring no further surprises;
But I remember now, that I am always surprised
By the bull-dog in the Burlington Arcade.
What if every moment were like that, if one were awake?
You both seem to know more about this than I do.

[*Enter* DOWNING, *hurriedly, in chauffeur's costume*]

DOWNING. Oh, excuse me, Miss, excuse me, Mr. Charles:
    His Lordship sent me back because he remembered
    He thinks he left his cigarette-case on the table.
    Oh, there it is. Thank you. Good night, Miss; good night,
    Miss Mary; good night, Sir.

MARY. Downing, will you promise never to leave his Lordship
    While you are away?

DOWNING.   Oh, certainly, Miss;
    I'll never leave him so long as he requires me.

MARY. But he will need you. You must never leave him.

DOWNING. You may think it laughable, what I'm going to say —
    But it's not really strange, Miss, when you come to look at it:
    After all these years that I've been with him
    I think I understand his Lordship better than anybody;
    And I have a kind of feeling that his Lordship won't need me
    Very long now. I can't give you any reasons.
    But to show you what I mean, though you'd hardly credit it,
    I've always said, whatever happened to his Lordship
    Was just a kind of preparation for something else.
    I've no gift of language, but I'm sure of what I mean:
    We most of us seem to live according to circumstance,
    But with people like him, there's something inside them
    That accounts for what happens to them. You get a feeling of it.
    So I seem to know beforehand, when something's going to happen,
    And it seems quite natural, being his Lordship.
    And that's why I say now, I have a feeling
    That he won't want me long, and he won't want anybody.

AGATHA. And, Downing, if his behaviour seems unaccountable
    At times, you mustn't worry about that.
    He is every bit as sane as you or I,
    He sees the world as clearly as you or I see it,
    It is only that he has seen a great deal more than that,
    And we have seen them too — Miss Mary and I.

DOWNING. I understand you, Miss. And if I may say so,

Now that you've raised the subject, I'm most relieved —
If you understand my meaning. I thought that was the reason
We was off tonight. In fact, I half expected it,
So I had the car all ready. You mean them ghosts, Miss!
I wondered when his Lordship would get round to seeing them —
And so you've seen them too! They must have given you a turn!
They did me, at first. You soon get used to them.
Of course, I knew they was to do with his Lordship,
And not with me, so I could see them cheerful-like,
In a manner of speaking. There's no harm in *them*,
I'll take my oath. Will that be all, Miss?

AGATHA. That will be all, thank you, Downing. We mustn't keep you;
His Lordship will be wondering why you've been so long.

[*Exit* DOWNING. *Enter* IVY]

IVY. Where is Downing going? where is Harry?
Look. Here's a telegram come from Arthur;

[*Enter* GERALD *and* VIOLET]

I wonder why he sent it, after telephoning.
Shall I read it to you? I was wondering
Whether to show it to Amy or not.

[*Reads*]

'Regret delayed business in town many happy returns see you to-
morrow many happy returns hurrah love Arthur.'
I mean, after what we know of what did happen,
Do you think Amy ought to see it?

VIOLET.   No, certainly not.
You do not know what has been going on, Ivy.
And if you did, you would not understand it.
I do not understand, so how could you? Amy is not well;
And she is resting.

IVY.   Oh, I'm sorry. But can't you explain?
Why do you all look so peculiar? I think I might be allowed
To know what has happened.

AMY'S VOICE.   Agatha! Mary! come!
The clock has stopped in the dark!

[*Exeunt* AGATHA *and* MARY. *Pause. Enter* WARBURTON]

WARBURTON. Well! it's a filthy night to be out in.
That's why I've been so long, going and coming.
But I'm glad to say that John is getting on nicely;
It wasn't so serious as Winchell made out,

And we'll have him up here in the morning.

I hope Lady Monchensey hasn't been worrying?

I'm anxious to relieve her mind. Why, what's the trouble?

[*Enter* MARY]

MARY. Dr. Warburton!

WARBURTON.   Excuse me.

[*Exeunt* MARY *and* WARBURTON]

CHORUS. We do not like to look out of the same window, and see quite a
      different landscape.

We do not like to climb a stair, and find that it takes us down.

We do not like to walk out of a door, and find ourselves back in the
      same room.

We do not like the maze in the garden, because it too closely
      resembles the maze in the brain.

We do not like what happens when we are awake, because it too
      closely resembles what happens when we are asleep.

We understand the ordinary business of living,

We know how to work the machine,

We can usually avoid accidents,

We are insured against fire,

Against larceny and illness,

Against defective plumbing,

But not against the act of God.

We know various spells and enchantments.

And minor forms of sorcery,

Divination and chiromancy,

Specifics against insomnia,

Lumbago, and the loss of money.

But the circle of our understanding

Is a very restricted area.

Except for a limited number

Of strictly practical purposes

We do not know what we are doing;

And even, when you think of it,

We do not know much about thinking.

What is happening outside of the circle?

And what is the meaning of happening?

What ambush lies beyond the heather

And behind the Standing Stones?

Beyond the Heaviside Layer

And behind the smiling moon?
And what is being done to us?
And what are we, and what are we doing?
To each and all of these questions
There is no conceivable answer.
We have suffered far more than a personal loss —
We have lost our way in the dark.

IVY. I shall have to stay till after the funeral: will my ticket to London
still be valid?

GERALD. I do not look forward with pleasure to dealing with Arthur
and John in the morning.

VIOLET. We must wait for the will to be read. I shall send a wire in the
morning.

CHARLES. I fear that my mind is not what it was — or was it? — and
yet I think that I might understand.

ALL. But we must adjust ourselves to the moment: we must do the right
thing.

[*Exeunt*]

[*Enter, from one door,* AGATHA *and* MARY, *and set a small portable table.
From another door, enter* DENMAN *carrying a birthday cake with
lighted candles, which she sets on the table. Exit* DENMAN. AGATHA
and MARY *walk slowly in single file round and round the table, clock-
wise. At each revolution they blow out a few candles, so that their last
words are spoken in the dark.*]

AGATHA. A curse is slow in coming
To complete fruition
It cannot be hurried
And it cannot be delayed

MARY. It cannot be diverted
An attempt to divert it
Only implicates others
At the day of consummation

AGATHA. A curse is a power
Not subject to reason
Each curse has its course
Its own way of expiation
Follow follow

MARY. Not in the day time
And in the hither world
Where we know what we are doing

349

There is not its operation
                Follow follow
AGATHA. But in the night time
        And in the nether world
        Where the meshes we have woven
        Bind us to each other
                Follow follow
MARY. A curse is written
        On the under side of things
        Behind the smiling mirror
        And behind the smiling moon
                Follow follow
AGATHA. This way the pilgrimage
        Of expiation
        Round and round the circle
        Completing the charm
        So the knot be unknotted
        The crossed be uncrossed
        The crooked be made straight
        And the curse be ended
        By intercession
        By pilgrimage
        By those who depart
        In several directions
        For their own redemption
        And that of the departed —
                May they rest in peace.

THE COCKTAIL PARTY

Persons

EDWARD CHAMBERLAYNE

JULIA (MRS. SHUTTLETHWAITE)

CELIA COPLESTONE

ALEXANDER MACCOLGIE GIBBS

PETER QUILPE

AN UNIDENTIFIED GUEST, *later identified as*
    SIR HENRY HARCOURT-REILLY

LAVINIA CHAMBERLAYNE

A NURSE-SECRETARY

TWO CATERER'S MEN

The scene is laid in London

Act One. Scene 1

The drawing-room of the Chamberlaynes' London flat. Early evening.
EDWARD CHAMBERLAYNE, JULIA SHUTTLETHWAITE, CELIA
COPLESTONE, PETER QUILPE, ALEXANDER MACCOLGIE GIBBS,
and an UNIDENTIFIED GUEST.

ALEX. You've missed the point completely, Julia:
    There *were* no tigers. *That* was the point.
JULIA. Then what were you doing, up in a tree:
    You and the Maharaja?
ALEX.   My dear Julia!
    It's perfectly hopeless. You haven't been listening.
PETER. You'll have to tell us all over again, Alex.
ALEX. I never tell the same story twice.
JULIA. But I'm still waiting to know what happened.
    I know it started as a story about tigers.
ALEX. I said there were no tigers.
CELIA.   Oh do stop wrangling,
    Both of you. It's your turn, Julia.
    Do tell us that story you told the other day, about Lady Klootz and
        the wedding cake.
PETER. And how the butler found her in the pantry, rinsing her mouth
        out with champagne.
    I like that story.
CELIA.   I love that story.
ALEX.   *I'm* never tired of hearing that story.
JULIA. Well, you all seem to know it.
CELIA.   Do we all know it?
    But we're never tired of hearing *you* tell it.
    I don't believe everyone here knows it.
    [*To the* UNIDENTIFIED GUEST] You don't know it, do you?
UNIDENTIFIED GUEST.   No, I've never heard it.
CELIA. Here's one new listener for you, Julia;

And I don't believe that Edward knows it.

EDWARD. I may have heard it, but I don't remember it.

CELIA. And Julia's the only person to tell it.

She's such a good mimic.

JULIA.   Am I a good mimic?

PETER. You *are* a good mimic. You never miss anything.

ALEX. She never misses anything unless she wants to.

CELIA. Especially the Lithuanian accent.

JULIA. Lithuanian? Lady Klootz?

PETER. I thought she was Belgian.

ALEX. Her father belonged to a Baltic family —

One of the *oldest* Baltic families

With a branch in Sweden and one in Denmark.

There were several very lovely daughters:

I wonder what's become of them now.

JULIA. Lady Klootz was very lovely, once upon a time.

What a life she led! I used to say to her: 'Greta!

You have too much vitality.' But she enjoyed herself.

[*To the* UNIDENTIFIED GUEST] Did *you* know Lady Klootz?

UNIDENTIFIED GUEST.   No, I never met her.

CELIA. Go on with the story about the wedding cake.

JULIA. Well, but it really isn't my story.

I heard it first from Delia Verinder

Who was there when it happened.

[*To the* UNIDENTIFIED GUEST] Do *you* know Delia Verinder?

UNIDENTIFIED GUEST. No, I don't know her.

JULIA.   Well, one can't be too careful

Before one tells a story.

ALEX.   Delia Verinder?

Was she the one who had three brothers?

JULIA. How many brothers? Two, I think.

ALEX. No, there were three, but you wouldn't know the third one:

They kept him rather quiet.

JULIA.   Oh, you mean *that* one.

ALEX. He was feeble-minded.

JULIA.   Oh, not feeble-minded:

He was only harmless.

ALEX.   Well then, harmless.

JULIA. He was very clever at repairing clocks;

And he had a remarkable sense of hearing —

The only man I ever met who could hear the cry of bats.

PETER. Hear the cry of bats?

JULIA.   He could hear the cry of bats.

CELIA. But how do you know he could hear the cry of bats?

JULIA. Because he said so. And I believed him.

CELIA. But if he was so . . . harmless, how could you believe him?
    He might have imagined it.

JULIA.   My darling Celia,
    You needn't be so sceptical. I stayed there once
    At their castle in the North. How he suffered!
    They had to find an island for him
    Where there were no bats.

ALEX.   And is he still there?
    Julia is really a mine of information.

CELIA. There isn't much that Julia doesn't know.

PETER. Go on with the story about the wedding cake.

                                    [EDWARD *leaves the room*]

JULIA. No, we'll wait until Edward comes back into the room.
    Now I want to relax, Are there any more cocktails?

PETER. But do go on. Edward wasn't listening anyway.

JULIA. No, he wasn't listening, but he's such a strain —
    Edward without Lavinia! He's quite impossible!
    Leaving it to me to keep things going.
    What a host! And nothing fit to eat!
    The only reason for a cocktail party
    For a gluttonous old woman like me
    Is a really nice tit-bit. I can drink at home.

                    [EDWARD *returns with a tray*]

    Edward, give me another of those delicious olives.
    What's that? Potato crisps? No, I can't endure them.
    Well, I started to tell you about Lady Klootz.
    It was at the Vincewell wedding. Oh, so many years ago!
    [*To the* UNIDENTIFIED GUEST] Did *you* know the Vincewells?

UNIDENTIFIED GUEST.   No, I don't know the Vincewells.

JULIA. Oh, they're both dead now. But I wanted to know.
    If they'd been friends of yours, I couldn't tell the story.

PETER. Were they the parents of Tony Vincewell?

JULIA. Yes. Tony was the product, but not the solution.
    He only made the situation more difficult.
    You know Tony Vincewell? You knew him at Oxford?

PETER. No, I never knew him at Oxford:

    I came across him last year in California.

JULIA. I've always wanted to go to California.

    Do tell us what you were doing in California.

CELIA. Making a film.

PETER.   Trying to make a film.

JULIA. Oh, what film was it? I wonder if I've seen it.

PETER. No, you wouldn't have seen it. As a matter of fact

    It was never produced. They did a film

    But they used a different scenario.

JULIA. Not the one you wrote?

PETER.   Not the one I wrote:

    But I had a very enjoyable time.

CELIA. Go on with the story about the wedding cake.

JULIA. Edward, do sit down for a moment.

    I know you're always the perfect host,

    But just try to pretend you're another guest

    At Lavinia's party. There are so many questions

    I want to ask you. It's a golden opportunity

    Now Lavinia's away. I've always said:

    'If I could only get Edward alone

    And have a really *serious* conversation!'

    I said so to Lavinia. She agreed with me.

    She said: 'I wish you'd try.' And this is the first time

    I've ever seen you without Lavinia

    Except for the time she got locked in the lavatory

    And couldn't get out. I know what you're thinking!

    I know you think I'm a silly old woman

    But I'm really very serious. Lavinia takes me seriously.

    I believe that's the reason why she went away —

    So that I could make you talk. Perhaps she's in the pantry

    Listening to all we say!

EDWARD.   No, she's not in the pantry.

CELIA. Will she be away for some time, Edward?

EDWARD. I really don't know until I hear from her.

    If her aunt is very ill, she may be gone some time.

CELIA. And how will you manage while she is away?

EDWARD. I really don't know. I may go away myself.

CELIA. Go away yourself!

JULIA.   Have you an aunt too?

EDWARD. No, I haven't any aunt. But I might go away.

CELIA. But, Edward . . . what was I going to say?
It's dreadful for old ladies alone in the country,
And almost impossible to get a nurse.

JULIA. Is that her Aunt Laura?

EDWARD.   No; another aunt
Whom you wouldn't know. Her mother's sister
And rather a recluse.

JULIA.   Her favourite aunt?

EDWARD. Her aunt's favourite niece. And she's rather difficult.
When she's ill, she insists on having Lavinia.

JULIA. I never heard of her being ill before.

EDWARD. No, she's always very strong. That's why when she's ill
She gets into a panic.

JULIA.   And sends for Lavinia.
I quite understand. Are there any prospects?

EDWARD. No, I think she put it all into an annuity.

JULIA. So it's very unselfish of Lavinia
Yet very like her. But really, Edward,
Lavinia may be away for weeks,
Or she may come back and be called away again.
I understand these tough old women —
I'm one myself. I feel as if I knew
All about that aunt in Hampshire.

EDWARD.   Hampshire?

JULIA. Didn't you say Hampshire?

EDWARD.   No, I didn't say Hampshire.

JULIA. Did you say Hampstead?

EDWARD.   No, I didn't say Hampstead.

JULIA. But she must live somewhere.

EDWARD.   She lives in Essex.

JULIA. Anywhere near Colchester? Lavinia loves oysters.

EDWARD. No. In the *depths* of Essex.

JULIA.   Well, we won't probe into it.
You have the address, and the telephone number?
I might run down and see Lavinia
On my way to Cornwall. But let's be sensible:
Now you must let me be *your* maiden aunt —
Living on an annuity, of course.
I am going to make you dine alone with me

On Friday, and talk to me about everything.

EDWARD. Everything?

JULIA. Oh, you know what I mean.

The next election. And the secrets of your cases.

EDWARD. Most of my secrets are quite uninteresting.

JULIA. Well, you shan't escape. You dine with me on Friday.

I've already chosen the people you're to meet.

EDWARD. But you asked me to dine with you alone.

JULIA. Yes, alone!

Without Lavinia! You'll like the other people —

But you're to talk to me. So that's all settled.

And now I must be going.

EDWARD. Must you be going?

PETER. But won't you tell the story about Lady Klootz?

JULIA. What Lady Klootz?

CELIA. And the wedding cake.

JULIA. Wedding cake? I wasn't at her wedding.

Edward, it's been a delightful evening:

The potato crisps were really excellent.

Now let me see. Have I got everything?

It's such a nice party, I hate to leave it.

It's such a nice party, I'd like to repeat it.

Why don't you *all* come to dinner on Friday?

No, I'm afraid my good Mrs. Batten

Would give me notice. And now I must be going.

ALEX. I'm afraid *I* ought to be going.

PETER. Celia —

May I walk along with you?

CELIA. No, I'm sorry, Peter;

I've got to take a taxi.

JULIA. You come with me, Peter:

You can get *me* a taxi, and then I can drop you.

I expect you on Friday, Edward. And Celia —

I must see you very soon. Now don't all go

Just because I'm going. Good-bye, Edward.

EDWARD. Good-bye, Julia.

[*Exeunt* JULIA *and* PETER]

CELIA. Good-bye, Edward.

Shall I see you soon?

EDWARD. Perhaps. I don't know.

CELIA. Perhaps you don't know? Very well, good-bye.

EDWARD. Good-bye, Celia.

ALEX.   Good-bye, Edward. I do hope
    You'll have better news of Lavinia's aunt.

EDWARD. Oh . . . yes . . . thank you. Good-bye, Alex,
    It was nice of you to come.

                              [*Exeunt* ALEX *and* CELIA]
    [*To the* UNIDENTIFIED GUEST] Don't go yet.
    Don't go yet. We'll finish the cocktails.
    Or would you rather have whisky?

UNIDENTIFIED GUEST.   Gin.

EDWARD. Anything in it?

UNIDENTIFIED GUEST. A drop of water.

EDWARD. I want to apologise for this evening.
    The fact is, I tried to put off this party:
    These were only the people I couldn't put off
    Because I couldn't get at them in time;
    And I didn't know that *you* were coming.
    I thought that Lavinia had told me the names
    Of all the people she said she'd invited.
    But it's only that dreadful old woman who mattered —
    I shouldn't have minded anyone else,
        [*The doorbell rings.* EDWARD *goes to the door, saying:*]
    But she always turns up when she's least wanted.
                    [*Opens the door*]
    Julia!

[*Enter* JULIA]

JULIA.   Edward! How lucky that it's raining!
    It made me remember my umbrella,
    And there it is! Now what are you two plotting?
    How very lucky it was my umbrella,
    And not Alexander's — *he's* so inquisitive!
    But *I* never poke into other people's business.
    Well, good-bye again. I'm off at last.

                                        [*Exit*]

EDWARD. I'm sorry. I'm afraid I don't know your name.

UNIDENTIFIED GUEST. I ought to be going.

EDWARD.   Don't go yet.
    I very much want to talk to somebody;
    And it's easier to talk to a person you don't know.

The fact is, that Lavinia has left me.

UNIDENTIFIED GUEST. Your wife has left you?

EDWARD.   Without warning, of course;
    Just when she'd arranged a cocktail party.
    She'd gone when I came in, this afternoon.
    She left a note to say that she was leaving me;
    But I don't know where she's gone.

UNIDENTIFIED GUEST.   This is an occasion.
    May I take another drink?

EDWARD.   Whisky?

UNIDENTIFIED GUEST.   Gin.

EDWARD. Anything in it?

UNIDENTIFIED GUEST. Nothing but water.
    And I recommend you the same prescription . . .
    Let me prepare it for you, if I may . . .
    Strong . . . but sip it slowly . . . and drink it sitting down.
    Breathe deeply, and adopt a relaxed position.
    There we are. Now for a few questions.
    How long married?

EDWARD.   Five years.

UNIDENTIFIED GUEST.   Children?

EDWARD. No.

UNIDENTIFIED GUEST. Then look at the brighter side.
    You say you don't know where she's gone?

EDWARD.   No, I do not.

UNIDENTIFIED GUEST. Do you know who the man is?

EDWARD.   There was no other man —
    None that I know of.

UNIDENTIFIED GUEST. Or another woman
    Of whom she thought she had cause to be jealous?

EDWARD. She had nothing to complain of in my behaviour.

UNIDENTIFIED GUEST. Then no doubt it's all for the best.
    With another man, she might have made a mistake
    And want to come back to you. If another woman,
    She might decide to be forgiving
    And gain an advantage. If there's no other woman
    And no other man, then the reason may be deeper
    And you've ground for hope that she won't come back at all.
    If another man, then you'd want to re-marry
    To prove to the world that somebody wanted you;

If another woman, you might have to marry her —
You might even imagine that you wanted to marry her.

EDWARD. But I want my wife back.

UNIDENTIFIED GUEST. That's the natural reaction.
It's embarrassing, and inconvenient.
It was inconvenient, having to lie about it
Because you can't tell the truth on the telephone.
It will all take time that you can't well spare;
But I put it to you . . .

EDWARD. Don't put it to me.

UNIDENTIFIED GUEST. Then I suggest . . .

EDWARD. And please don't suggest.
I have often used these terms in examining witnesses,
So I don't like them. May I put it to *you*?
I know that I invited this conversation:
But I don't know who you are. This is not what I expected.
I only wanted to relieve my mind
By telling someone what I'd been concealing.
I don't think I want to know who you are;
But, at the same time, unless you know my wife
A good deal better than I thought, or unless you know
A good deal more about us than appears —
I think your speculations rather offensive.

UNIDENTIFIED GUEST. I know you as well as I know your wife;
And I knew that all you wanted was the luxury
Of an intimate disclosure to a stranger.
Let me, therefore, remain the stranger.
But let me tell you, that to approach the stranger
Is to invite the unexpected, release a new force,
Or let the genie out of the bottle.
It is to start a train of events
Beyond your control. So let me continue.
I will say then, you experience some relief
Of which you're not aware. It will come to you slowly:
When you wake in the morning, when you go to bed at night,
That you are beginning to enjoy your independence;
Finding your life becoming cosier and cosier
Without the consistent critic, the patient misunderstander
Arranging life a little better than you like it,
Preferring not quite the same friends as yourself,

Or making your friends like her better than you;
And, turning the past over and over,
You'll wonder only that you endured it for so long.
And perhaps at times you will feel a little jealous
That she saw it first, and had the courage to break it —
Thus giving herself a permanent advantage.

EDWARD. It might turn out so, yet . . .

UNIDENTIFIED GUEST.   Are you going to say, you love her?

EDWARD. Why, I thought we took each other for granted.
I never thought I should be any happier
With another person. Why speak of love?
We were used to each other. So her going away
At a moment's notice, without explanation,
Only a note to say that she had gone
And was not coming back — well, I can't understand it.
Nobody likes to be left with a mystery:
It's so . . . unfinished.

UNIDENTIFIED GUEST. Yes, it's unfinished;
And nobody likes to be left with a mystery.
But there's more to it than that. There's a loss of personality;
Or rather, you've lost touch with the person
You thought you were. You no longer feel quite human.
You're suddenly reduced to the status of an object —
A living object, but no longer a person.
It's always happening, because one is an object
As well as a person. But we forget about it
As quickly as we can. When you've dressed for a party
And are going downstairs, with everything about you
Arranged to support you in the role you have chosen,
Then sometimes, when you come to the bottom step
There is one step more than your feet expected
And you come down with a jolt. Just for a moment
You have the experience of being an object
At the mercy of a malevolent staircase.
Or, take a surgical operation.
In consultation with the doctor and the surgeon,
In going to bed in the nursing home,
In talking to the matron, you are still the subject,
The centre of reality. But, stretched on the table,
You are a piece of furniture in a repair shop

For those who surround you, the masked actors;
All there is of you is your body
And the 'you' is withdrawn. May I replenish?

EDWARD. Oh, I'm sorry. What were you drinking?
Whisky?

UNIDENTIFIED GUEST. Gin.

EDWARD.   Anything with it?

UNIDENTIFIED GUEST.   Water.

EDWARD. To what does this lead?

UNIDENTIFIED GUEST.   To finding out
What you really are. What you really feel.
What you really are among other people.
Most of the time we take ourselves for granted,
As we have to, and live on a little knowledge
About ourselves as we were. Who are you now?
You don't know any more than I do,
But rather less. You are nothing but a set
Of obsolete responses. The one thing to do
Is to do nothing. Wait.

EDWARD.   Wait!
But waiting is the one thing impossible.
Besides, don't you see that it makes me ridiculous?

UNIDENTIFIED GUEST. It will do you no harm to find yourself
ridiculous.
Resign yourself to be the fool you are.
That's the best advice that *I* can give you.

EDWARD. But how can I wait, not knowing what I'm waiting for?
Shall I say to my friends, 'My wife has gone away'?
And they answer 'Where?' and I say 'I don't know';
And they say, 'But when will she be back?'
And I reply 'I don't know that she *is* coming back'.
And they ask 'But what are you going to do?'
And I answer 'Nothing'. They will think me mad
Or simply contemptible.

UNIDENTIFIED GUEST.   All to the good.
You will find that you survive humiliation.
And that's an experience of incalculable value.

EDWARD. Stop! I agree that much of what you've said
Is true enough. But that is not all.
Since I saw her this morning when we had breakfast

I no longer remember what my wife is like.
I am not quite sure that I could describe her
If I had to ask the police to search for her.
I'm sure I don't know what she was wearing
When I saw her last. And yet I want her back.
And I *must* get her back, to find out what has happened
During the five years that we've been married.
I must find out who she is, to find out who I am.
And what is the use of all your analysis
If I am to remain always lost in the dark?

UNIDENTIFIED GUEST. There is certainly no purpose in remaining in
the dark
Except long enough to clear from the mind
The illusion of having ever been in the light.
The fact that you can't give a reason for wanting her
Is the best reason for believing that you want her.

EDWARD. I want to see her again — here.

UNIDENTIFIED GUEST.   You shall see her again — here.

EDWARD. Do you mean to say that you know where she is?

UNIDENTIFIED GUEST. That question is not worth the trouble of an
answer.
But if I bring her back it must be on one condition:
That you promise to ask her no questions
Of where she has been.

EDWARD.   I will not ask them.
And yet — it seems to me — when we began to talk
I was not sure I wanted her; and now I want her.
Do I want her? Or is it merely your suggestion?

UNIDENTIFIED GUEST. We do not know yet. In twenty-four hours
She will come to you here. You will be here to meet her.

                    [*The doorbell rings*]

EDWARD. I must answer the door.

                    [EDWARD *goes to the door*]
                              So it's you again, Julia!

[*Enter* JULIA *and* PETER]

JULIA. Edward, I'm so glad to find you.
Do you know, I must have left my glasses here,
And I simply can't see a thing without them.
I've been dragging Peter all over town
Looking for them everywhere I've been.

Has anybody found them? You can tell if they're mine —
Some kind of a plastic sort of frame —
I'm afraid I don't remember the colour,
But I'd know them, because one lens is missing.

UNIDENTIFIED GUEST [*Sings*].

> *As I was drinkin' gin and water,*
> *And me bein' the One Eyed Riley,*
> *Who came in but the landlord's daughter*
> *And she took my heart entirely.*

You will keep our appointment?

EDWARD.   I shall keep it.

UNIDENTIFIED GUEST [*Sings*].

> *Tooryooly toory-iley,*
> *What's the matter with One Eyed Riley?*

[*Exit*]

JULIA. Edward, who *is* that dreadful man?
I've never been so insulted in my life.
It's very lucky that I left my spectacles:
This is what I call an adventure!
Tell me about him. You've been *drinking* together!
So this is the kind of friend you have
When Lavinia is out of the way! Who is he?

EDWARD. *I* don't know.

JULIA.   *You* don't know?

EDWARD.   I never saw him before in my life.

JULIA. But how did he come here?

EDWARD.   *I* don't know.

JULIA. *You* don't know! And what's his name?
Did I hear him say his name was Riley?

EDWARD. I don't know his name.

JULIA.   You don't know his *name*?

EDWARD. I tell you I've no idea who he is
Or how he got here.

JULIA.   But what did you talk about
Or were you singing songs all the time?
There's altogether too much mystery
About this place to-day.

EDWARD.   I'm very sorry.

JULIA. No, I love it. But that reminds me
About my glasses. That's the greatest mystery.

365

Peter! Why aren't you looking for them?
Look on the mantelpiece. Where was I sitting?
Just turn out the bottom of that sofa —
No, this chair. Look under the cushion.

EDWARD. Are you quite sure they're not in your bag?

JULIA. Why no, of course not: that's where I keep them.
Oh, here they are! Thank you, Edward;
That really was very clever of you;
I'd never have found them but for you.
The next time I lose *anything*, Edward,
I'll come straight to you, instead of to St. Anthony.
And now I must fly. I've kept the taxi waiting.
Come along, Peter.

PETER.   I hope you won't mind
If I don't come with you, Julia? On the way back
I remembered something I had to say to Edward . . .

JULIA. Oh, about Lavinia?

PETER.   No, not about Lavinia.
It's something I want to consult him about,
And I could do it now.

JULIA.   Of course I don't mind.

PETER. Well, at least you must let me take you down in the lift.

JULIA. No, you stop and talk to Edward. I'm not helpless yet.
And besides, I like to manage the machine myself —
In a lift I can meditate. Good-bye then.
And thank you — both of you — very much.

                                                    [*Exit*]

PETER. I hope I'm not disturbing you, Edward.

EDWARD. I seem to have been disturbed already;
And I did rather want to be alone.
But what's it all about?

PETER.   I want your help.
I was going to telephone and try to see you later;
But this seemed an opportunity.

EDWARD.   And what's your trouble?

PETER. This evening I felt I could bear it no longer.
That awful party! I'm sorry, Edward;
Of course it was really a very nice party
For everyone but me. And that wasn't your fault.
I don't suppose you noticed the situation.

EDWARD. I did think I noticed one or two things;
 But I don't pretend I was aware of everything.
PETER. Oh, I'm very glad that you didn't notice:
 I must have behaved rather better than I thought.
 If you didn't notice, I don't suppose the others did,
 Though I'm rather afraid of Julia Shuttlethwaite.
EDWARD. Julia is certainly observant,
 But I think she had some other matter on her mind.
PETER. It's about Celia. Myself and Celia.
EDWARD. Why, what could there be about yourself and Celia?
 Have you anything in common, do you think?
PETER. It seemed to me we had a great deal in common.
 We're both of us artists.
EDWARD.   I never thought of that.
 What arts do you practise?
PETER.   You won't have seen my novel,
 Though it had some very good reviews.
 But it's more the cinema that interests both of us.
EDWARD. A common interest in the moving pictures
 Frequently brings young people together.
PETER. Now you're only being sarcastic:
 Celia was interested in the art of the film.
EDWARD. As a possible profession?
PETER.   She might make it a profession;
 Though she had her poetry.
EDWARD.   Yes, I've seen her poetry —
 Interesting if one is interested in Celia.
 Apart, of course, from its literary merit
 Which I don't pretend to judge.
PETER.   Well, I can judge it,
 And I think it's very good. But that's not the point.
 The point is, I thought we had a great deal in common
 And I think she thought so too.
EDWARD.   How did you come to know her?
[*Enter* ALEX]
ALEX. Ah, there you are, Edward! Do you know why *I*'ve looked in?
EDWARD. I'd like to know first how you *got* in, Alex.
ALEX. Why, I came and found that the door was open
 And so I thought I'd slip in and see if anyone was with you.
PETER. Julia must have left it open.

EDWARD.   Never mind;
    So long as you both shut it when you go out.

ALEX. Ah, but you're coming with me, Edward.
    I thought, Edward may be all alone this evening,
    And I know that he hates to spend an evening alone,
    So you're going to come out and have dinner with me.

EDWARD. That's very thoughtful of you, Alex, I'm sure;
    But I rather *want* to be alone, this evening.

ALEX. But you've got to have some dinner. Are you going
      out?
    Is there anyone here to get dinner for you?

EDWARD. No, I shan't want much, and I'll get it myself.

ALEX. Ah, in that case I know what I'll do.
    I'm going to give you a little surprise:
    You know, I'm rather a famous cook.
    I'm going straight to your kitchen now
    And I shall prepare you a nice little dinner
    Which you can have alone. And then we'll leave you.
    Meanwhile, you and Peter can go on talking
    And I shan't disturb you.

EDWARD.   My dear Alex,
    There'll be nothing in the larder worthy of your cooking.
    I couldn't think of it.

ALEX.   Ah, but that's my special gift —
    Concocting a toothsome meal out of nothing.
    Any scraps you have will do. I learned that in the East.
    With a handful of rice and a little dried fish
    I can make half a dozen dishes. Don't say a word.
    I shall begin at once.

                                  [Exit to kitchen]

EDWARD.   Well, where did you leave off?

PETER. You asked me how I came to know Celia.
    I met her here, about a year ago.

EDWARD. At one of Lavinia's amateur Thursdays?

PETER. A Thursday. Why do you say amateur?

EDWARD. Lavinia's attempts at starting a salon,
    Where I entertained the minor guests
    And dealt with the misfits, Lavinia's mistakes.
    But you were one of the minor successes
    For a time at least.

PETER. I wouldn't say that.
But Lavinia was awfully kind to me
And I owe her a great deal. And then I met Celia.
She was different from any girl I'd ever known
And not easy to talk to, on that occasion.

EDWARD. Did you see her often?

ALEX'S VOICE. Edward, have you a double boiler?

EDWARD. I suppose there must be a double boiler:
Isn't there one in every kitchen?

ALEX'S VOICE. I can't find it.
There goes *that* surprise. I must think of another.

PETER. Not very often.
And when I did, I got no chance to talk to her.

EDWARD. You and Celia were asked for different purposes.
Your role was to be one of Lavinia's discoveries;
Celia's, to provide society and fashion.
Lavinia always had the ambition
To establish herself in two worlds at once —
But she herself had to be the link between them.
That is why, I think, her Thursdays were a failure.

PETER. You speak as if everything was finished.

EDWARD. Oh no, no, everything is left unfinished.
But you haven't told me how you came to know Celia.

PETER. I saw her again a few days later
Alone at a concert. And I was alone.
I've always gone to concerts alone —
At first, because I knew no one to go with,
And later, I found I preferred to go alone.
But a girl like Celia, it seemed very strange,
Because I thought of her merely as a name
In a society column, to find her there alone.
Anyway, we got into conversation
And I found that she went to concerts alone
And to look at pictures. So we often met
In the same way, and sometimes went together.
And to be with Celia, that was something different
From company or solitude. And we sometimes had tea
And once or twice dined together.

EDWARD. And after that
Did she ever introduce you to her family

369

Or to any of her friends?

PETER. No, but once or twice she spoke of them
    And about their lack of intellectual interests.

EDWARD. And what happened after that?

PETER. Oh, nothing happened.
    But I thought that she really cared about me.
    And I was so happy when we were together —
    So . . . contented, so . . . at peace: I can't express it;
    I had never imagined such quiet happiness.
    I had only experienced excitement, delirium,
    Desire for possession. It was not like that at all.
    It was something very strange. There was such . . . tranquillity . . .

EDWARD. And what interrupted this interesting affair?

[*Enter* ALEX *in shirtsleeves and an apron*]

ALEX. Edward, I can't find any curry powder.

EDWARD. There isn't any curry powder. Lavinia hates curry.

ALEX. There goes another surprise, then. I must think.
    I didn't expect to find any mangoes,
    But I *did* count upon curry powder.

[*Exit*]

PETER. That is exactly what I want to know.
    She has simply faded — into some other picture —
    Like a film effect. She doesn't want to see me;
    Makes excuses, not very plausible,
    And when I do see her, she seems preoccupied
    With some secret excitement which I cannot share.

EDWARD. Do you think she has simply lost interest in you?

PETER. You put it just wrong. I think of it differently.
    It is not her interest in *me* that I miss —
    But those moments in which we seemed to share some perception,
    Some feeling, some indefinable experience
    In which we were both unaware of ourselves.
    In your terms, perhaps, she's lost interest in me.

EDWARD. That is all very normal. If you could only know
    How lucky you are. In a little while
    This might have become an ordinary affair
    Like any other. As the fever cooled
    You would have found that she was another woman
    And that you were another man. I congratulate you
    On a timely escape.

PETER.   I should prefer to be spared
Your congratulations. I had to talk to someone.
And I have been telling you of something real —
My first experience of reality
And perhaps it is the last. And you don't understand.

EDWARD. My dear Peter, I have only been telling you
What would have happened to you with Celia
In another six months' time. There it is.
You can take it or leave it.

PETER.   But what am I to do?

EDWARD. Nothing. Wait. Go back to California.

PETER. But I must see Celia.

EDWARD.   Will it be the same Celia?
Better be content with the Celia you remember.
Remember! I say it's already a memory.

PETER. But I must see Celia at least to make her tell me
What has happened, in her terms. Until I know that
I shan't know the truth about even the memory.
Did we really share these interests? Did we really feel the
    same
When we heard certain music? Or looked at certain
    pictures?
There was something real. But what is the reality . . .
                    [*The telephone rings*]

EDWARD. Excuse me a moment.
                    [*Into telephone*]
                         Hello! . . . I can't talk now . . .
Yes, there is . . . Well then, I'll ring you
As soon as I can.
[*To* PETER] I'm sorry. You were saying?

PETER. I was saying, what is the reality
Of experience between two unreal people?
If I can only hold to the memory
I can bear any future. But I must find out
The truth about the past, for the sake of the memory.

EDWARD. There's no memory you can wrap in camphor
But the moths will get in. So you want to see Celia.
I don't know why I should be taking all this trouble
To protect you from the fool you are.
What do you want me to do?

371

PETER.   See Celia for me.

> You know her in a different way from me
> And you are so much older.

EDWARD.   So much older?

PETER. Yes, I'm sure that she would listen to you
> As someone disinterested.

EDWARD.   Well, I will see Celia.

PETER. Thank you, Edward. It's very good of you.

[*Enter* ALEX, *with his jacket on*]

ALEX. Oh, Edward! I've prepared you such a treat!
> I really think that of all my triumphs
> This is the greatest. To make something out of
>> nothing!
> Never, even when travelling in Albania,
> Have I made such a supper out of so few materials
> As I found in your refrigerator. But of course
> I was lucky to find half-a-dozen eggs.

EDWARD. What! You used all those eggs! Lavinia's aunt
> Has just sent them from the country.

ALEX.   Ah, so the aunt

> Really exists. A substantial proof.

EDWARD. No, no . . . I mean, this is another aunt.

ALEX. I understand. The real aunt. But you'll be grateful.
> There are very few peasants in Montenegro
> Who can have the dish that you'll be eating, nowadays.

EDWARD. But what about my breakfast?

ALEX.   Don't worry about breakfast.

> All you should want is a cup of black coffee
> And a little dry toast. I've left it simmering.
> Don't leave it longer than another ten minutes.
> Now I'll be going, and I'll take Peter with me.

PETER. Edward, I've taken too much of your time,
> And you want to be alone. Give my love to Lavinia
> When she comes back . . . but, if you don't mind,
> I'd rather you didn't tell *her* what I've told you.

EDWARD. I shall not say anything about it to Lavinia.

PETER. Thank you, Edward. Good night.

EDWARD.   Good night, Peter,

> And good night, Alex. Oh, and if you don't mind,
> Please *shut the door after you,* so that it latches.

ALEX. Remember, Edward, not more than ten minutes,
　　Twenty minutes, and my work will be ruined.

　　　　　　　　　　　　　　[*Exeunt* ALEX *and* PETER]

　　　　[EDWARD *picks up the telephone, and dials a number*]

EDWARD. Is Miss Celia Coplestone in? . . . How long ago? . . .
　　No, it doesn't matter.

　　　　　　　　CURTAIN

Act One. Scene 2

The same room: a quarter of an hour later. EDWARD *is alone, playing Patience. The doorbell rings, and he goes to answer it.*

CELIA'S VOICE. Are you alone?
[EDWARD *returns with* CELIA]
EDWARD.   Celia! Why have you come back?
　　I said I would telephone as soon as I could:
　　And I tried to get you a short while ago.
CELIA. If there had happened to be anyone with you
　　I was going to say I'd come back for my umbrella. . . .
　　I must say you don't seem very pleased to see me.
　　Edward, I understand what has happened
　　But I could not understand your manner on the telephone.
　　It did not seem like you. So I felt I must see you.
　　Tell me it's all right, and then I'll go.
EDWARD. But how can you say you understand what has happened?
　　I don't know what has happened, or what is going to happen;
　　And to try to understand it, I want to be alone.
CELIA. I should have thought it was perfectly simple.
　　Lavinia has left you.
EDWARD.   Yes, that *was* the situation.
　　I suppose it was pretty obvious to everyone.
CELIA. It was obvious that the aunt was a pure invention
　　On the spur of the moment, and not a very good one.
　　You should have been prepared with something better, for Julia;
　　But it doesn't really matter. They will know soon enough.
　　Doesn't that settle all our difficulties?
EDWARD. It has only brought to light the real difficulties.
CELIA. But surely, these are only temporary.
　　You know I accepted the situation
　　Because a divorce would ruin your career;
　　And we thought that Lavinia would never want to leave you.
　　Surely you don't hold to that silly convention

That the husband must always be the one to be divorced?
And if she chooses to give *you* the grounds . . .

EDWARD. I see. But it is not like that at all.
Lavinia is coming back.

CELIA.   Lavinia coming back!
Do you mean to say that she's laid a trap for us?

EDWARD. No. If there is a trap, we are all in the trap,
We have set it for ourselves. But I do not know
What kind of a trap it is.

CELIA.   Then what has happened?
                    [*The telephone rings*]

EDWARD. Damn the telephone. I suppose I must answer it.
Hello . . . oh, hello! . . . No. I mean yes, Alex;
Yes, of course . . . it was marvellous.
I've never tasted anything like it . . .
Yes, that's very interesting. But I just wondered
Whether it mightn't be rather indigestible? . . .
Oh, no, Alex, don't bring me any cheese;
I've got some cheese . . . No, not Norwegian;
But I don't really want cheese . . . Slipper what? . . .
Oh, from Jugoslavia . . . prunes and alcohol?
No, really, Alex, I don't want anything.
I'm very tired. Thanks awfully, Alex.
Good night.

CELIA.   What on earth was that about?

EDWARD. That was Alex.

CELIA.   I know it was Alex.
But what was he talking of?

EDWARD.   I had quite forgotten.
He made his way in, a little while ago,
And insisted on cooking me something for supper;
And he said I must eat it within ten minutes.
I suppose it's still cooking.

CELIA.   You suppose it's still cooking!
I thought I noticed a peculiar smell:
Of course it's still cooking — or doing *something*.
I must go and investigate.
                    [*Starts to leave the room*]

EDWARD.   For heaven's sake, don't bother!
                    [*Exit* CELIA]

375

Suppose someone came and found you in the kitchen?

[EDWARD *goes over to the table and inspects his game of Patience. He moves a card. The doorbell rings repeatedly. Re-enter* CELIA, *in an apron.*]

CELIA. You'd better answer the door, Edward.

It's the best thing to do. Don't lose your head.

You see, I really did leave my umbrella;

And I'll say I found you here starving and helpless

And had to do something. Anyway, I'm *staying*

And I'm not going to hide.

[*Returns to kitchen. The bell rings again.* EDWARD *goes to front door, and is heard to say:*]

Julia!

What have you come back for?

[*Enter* JULIA]

JULIA.   I've had an inspiration!

[*Enter* CELIA *with saucepan*]

CELIA. Edward, it's ruined!

EDWARD.   What a good thing.

CELIA. But it's ruined the saucepan too.

EDWARD.   *And* half a dozen eggs:

I wanted one for breakfast. A boiled egg.

It's the only thing I know how to cook.

JULIA. Celia! I see you've had the same inspiration

That I had. Edward must be fed.

He's under such a strain. We must keep his strength up.

Edward! Don't you realise how lucky you are

To have *two* Good Samaritans? I never heard of that before.

EDWARD. The man who fell among thieves was luckier than I:

He was left at an inn.

JULIA.   Edward, how ungrateful.

What's in that saucepan?

CELIA.   Nobody knows.

EDWARD. It's something that Alex came and prepared for me.

He *would* do it. Three Good Samaritans.

I forgot all about it.

JULIA.   But you mustn't touch it.

EDWARD. Of course I shan't touch it.

JULIA.   My dear, I should have warned you:

Anything that Alex makes is absolutely deadly.

I could tell such tales of his poisoning people.

Now, my dear, you give me that apron
And we'll see what I can do. You stay and talk to Edward.

                                  [*Exit* JULIA]

CELIA. But what has happened, Edward? What has happened?

EDWARD. Lavinia is coming back, I think.

CELIA. You think! Don't you know?

EDWARD. No, but I believe it. That man who was here —

CELIA. Yes, who was that man? I was rather afraid of him;
    He has some sort of power.

EDWARD.   I don't know who he is.
    But I had some talk with him, when the rest of you had left,
    And he said he would bring Lavinia back, tomorrow.

CELIA. But why should that man want to bring her back —
    Unless he is the Devil! I could believe he was.

EDWARD. Because I asked him to.

CELIA.   Because you asked him to!
    Then he *must* be the Devil! He must have bewitched you.
    How did he persuade you to want her back?

        [*A popping noise is heard from the kitchen*]

EDWARD. What the devil's that?

[*Re-enter* JULIA, *in apron, with a tray and three glasses*]

JULIA.   I've had an inspiration!
    There's nothing in the place fit to eat:
    I've looked high and low. But I found some champagne —
    Only a half-bottle, to be sure,
    And of course it isn't chilled. But it's so refreshing;
    And I thought, we are all in need of a stimulant
    After this disaster. Now I'll propose a health.
    Can you guess whose health I'm going to propose?

EDWARD. No, I can't. But I won't drink to Alex's.

JULIA. Oh, it isn't Alex's. Come, I give you
    Lavinia's aunt! You might have guessed it.

EDWARD *and* CELIA. Lavinia's aunt.

JULIA.   Now, the next question
    Is, what's to be done. That's very simple.
    It's too late, or too early, to go to a restaurant.
    You must both come home with me.

EDWARD.   No, I'm sorry, Julia.
    I'm too tired to go out, and I'm not at all hungry.
    I shall have a few biscuits.

JULIA.   But you, Celia?
    You must come and have a light supper with me —
    Something very light.
CELIA.   Thank you, Julia.
    I think I will, if I may follow you
    In about ten minutes? Before I go, there's something
    I want to say to Edward.
JULIA.   About Lavinia?
    Well, come on quickly. And take a taxi.
    You know, you're looking absolutely famished.
    Good night, Edward.

                                              [*Exit* JULIA]

CELIA.   Well, how did he persuade you?
EDWARD. How did he persuade me? Did he persuade me?
    I have a very clear impression
    That he tried to persuade me it was all for the best
    That Lavinia had gone; that I ought to be thankful.
    And yet, the effect of all his argument
    Was to make me see that I wanted her back.
CELIA. That's the Devil's method! So you want Lavinia back!
    Lavinia! So the one thing you care about
    Is to avoid a break — anything unpleasant!
    No, it can't be that. I won't think it's that.
    I think it is just a moment of surrender
    To fatigue. And panic. You can't face the trouble.
EDWARD. No, it is not that. It is not only that.
CELIA. It cannot be simply a question of vanity:
    That you think the world will laugh at you
    Because your wife has left you for another man?
    I shall soon put that right, Edward,
    When you are free.
EDWARD.   No, it is not that.
    And all these reasons were suggested to me
    By the man I call Riley — though his name is not Riley;
    It was just a name in a song he sang . . .
CELIA. He sang you a song about a man named Riley!
    Really, Edward, I think you are mad —
    I mean, you're on the edge of a nervous breakdown.
    Edward, if I go away now
    Will you promise me to see a very great doctor

Whom I have heard of — and his name *is* Reilly!

EDWARD. It would need someone greater than the greatest doctor
   To cure *this* illness.

CELIA.   Edward, if I go now,
   Will you assure me that everything is right,
   That you do not mean to have Lavinia back
   And that you do mean to gain your freedom,
   And that everything is all right between us?
   That's all that matters. Truly, Edward,
   If that is right, everything else will be,
   I promise you.

EDWARD.   No, Celia.
   It has been very wonderful, and I'm very grateful,
   And I think you are a very rare person.
   But it was too late. And I should have known
   That it wasn't fair to you.

CELIA.   It wasn't fair to *me*!
   You can stand there and talk about being fair to *me*!

EDWARD. But for Lavinia leaving, this would never have arisen.
   What future had you ever thought there could be?

CELIA. What had I thought that the future could be?
   I abandoned the future before we began,
   And after that I lived in a present
   Where time was meaningless, a private world of *ours*,
   Where the word 'happiness' had a different meaning
   Or so it seemed.

EDWARD.   I have heard of that experience.

CELIA. A dream. I was happy in it till to-day,
   And then, when Julia asked about Lavinia
   And it came to me that Lavinia had left you
   And that you would be free — then I suddenly discovered
   That the dream was not enough; that I wanted something
      more
   And I waited, and wanted to run to tell you.
   Perhaps the dream was better. It seemed the real reality,
   And if this is reality, it is very like a dream.
   Perhaps it was I who betrayed my own dream
   All the while; and to find I wanted
   This world as well as that . . . well, it's humiliating.

EDWARD. There is no reason why you should feel humiliated . . .

379

CELIA. Oh, don't think that you can humiliate me!
    Humiliation — it's something I've done to myself.
    I am not sure even that you seem real enough
    To humiliate me. I suppose that most women
    Would feel degraded to find that a man
    With whom they thought they had shared something wonderful
    Had taken them only as a passing diversion.
    Oh, I dare say that you deceived yourself:
    But that's what it was, no doubt.

EDWARD. I *didn't* take you as a passing diversion!
    If you want to speak of passing diversions
    How did you take Peter?

CELIA.   Peter? Peter who?

EDWARD. Peter Quilpe, who was here this evening. *He* was in a
        dream
    And now he is simply unhappy and bewildered.

CELIA. I simply don't know what you are talking about.
    Edward, this is really too crude a subterfuge
    To justify yourself. There was never anything
    Between me and Peter.

EDWARD.   Wasn't there? *He* thought so.
    He came back this evening to talk to me about it.

CELIA. But this is ridiculous! I never gave Peter
    Any reason to suppose I cared for him.
    I thought he had talent; I saw that he was lonely;
    I thought that I could help him. I took him to concerts.
    But then, as he came to make more acquaintances,
    I found him less interesting, and rather conceited.
    But why should we talk about Peter? All that matters
    Is, that you think you want Lavinia.
    And if that is the sort of person you are —
    Well, you had better have her.

EDWARD.   It's not like that.
    It is not that I am in love with Lavinia.
    I don't think I was ever really in love with her.
    If I have ever been in love — and I think that I have —
    I have never been in love with anyone but you,
    And perhaps I still am. But this can't go on.
    It never could have been . . . a permanent thing:
    You should have a man . . . nearer your own age.

CELIA. I don't think I care for advice from you, Edward:
    You are not entitled to take any interest
    Now, in *my* future. I only hope you're competent
    To manage your own. But if you are not in love
    And never have been in love with Lavinia,
    What is it that you want?

EDWARD.   I am not sure.
    The one thing of which I am relatively certain
    Is, that only since this morning
    I have met myself as a middle-aged man
    Beginning to know what it is to feel old.
    That is the worst moment, when you feel that you have lost
    The desire for all that was most desirable,
    Before you are contented with what you can desire;
    Before you know what is left to be desired;
    And you go on wishing that you could desire
    What desire has left behind. But you cannot understand.
    How could *you* understand what it is to feel old?

CELIA. But I want to understand you. I could understand.
    And, Edward, please believe that whatever happens
    I shall not loathe you. I shall only feel sorry for you.
    It's only myself I am in danger of loathing.
    But what will your life be? I cannot bear to think of it.
    Oh, Edward! Can you be happy with Lavinia?

EDWARD. No — not happy: or, if there is any happiness,
    Only the happiness of knowing
    That the misery does not feed on the ruin of loveliness,
    That the tedium is not the residue of ecstasy.
    I see that my life was determined long ago
    And that the struggle to escape from it
    Is only a make-believe, a pretence
    That what is, is not, or could be changed.
    The self that can say 'I want this — or want that' —
    The self that wills — he is a feeble creature;
    He has to come to terms in the end
    With the obstinate, the tougher self; who does not speak,
    Who never talks, who cannot argue;
    And who in some men may be the *guardian* —
    But in men like me, the dull, the implacable,
    The indomitable spirit of mediocrity.

The willing self can contrive the disaster
Of this unwilling partnership — but can only flourish
In submission to the rule of the stronger partner.

CELIA. I am not sure, Edward, that I understand you;
And yet I understand as I never did before.
I think — I believe — you are being yourself
As you never were before, with me.
Twice you have changed since I have been looking at you.
I looked at your face: and I thought that I knew
And loved every contour; and as I looked
It withered, as if I had unwrapped a mummy.
I listened to your voice, that had always thrilled me,
And it became another voice — no, not a voice:
What I heard was only the noise of an insect,
Dry, endless, meaningless, inhuman —
You might have made it by scraping your legs together —
Or however grasshoppers do it. I looked,
And listened for your heart, your blood;
And saw only a beetle the size of a man
With nothing more inside it than what comes out
When you tread on a beetle.

EDWARD. Perhaps that is what I am.
Tread on me, if you like.

CELIA. No, I won't tread on you.
That is not what you are. It is only what was left
Of what I had thought you were. I see another person,
I see you as a person whom I never saw before.
The man I saw before, he was only a projection —
I see that now — of something that I wanted —
No, not *wanted* — something I aspired to —
Something that I desperately wanted to exist.
It must happen somewhere — but what, and where is it?
Edward, I see that I was simply making use of you.
And I ask you to forgive me.

EDWARD. You . . . ask me to forgive *you*!

CELIA. Yes, for two things. First . . .

[*The telephone rings*]

EDWARD. Damn the telephone.
I suppose I had better answer it.

CELIA. Yes, better answer it.

EDWARD. Hello! . . . Oh, Julia: what is it now?
    Your spectacles again . . . where did you leave them?
    Or have we . . . have I got to hunt all over?
    Have you looked in your bag? . . . Well, don't snap my head off . . .
    You're sure, in the kitchen? Beside the champagne bottle?
    You're quite sure? . . . Very well, hold on if you like;
    We . . . I'll look for them.
CELIA.   Yes, you look for them.
    I shall never go into your kitchen again.

          [*Exit* EDWARD. *He returns with the spectacles and a bottle*]

EDWARD. She was right for once.
CELIA.   She is always right.
    But why bring an empty champagne bottle?
EDWARD. It isn't empty. It may be a little flat —
    But why did she say that it was a half-bottle?
    It's one of my best: and I have no half-bottles.
    Well, I hoped that you would drink a final glass with me.
CELIA. What should we drink to?
EDWARD.   Whom shall we drink to?
CELIA. To the Guardians.
EDWARD.   To the Guardians?
CELIA. To the Guardians. It was you who spoke of guardians.

          [*They drink*]

    It may be that even Julia is a guardian.
    Perhaps she is *my* guardian. Give me the spectacles.
    Good night, Edward.
EDWARD.   Good night . . . Celia.

                      [*Exit* CELIA]

              Oh!

    [*He snatches up the receiver*]

    Hello, Julia! are you there? . . .
    Well, I'm awfully sorry to have kept you waiting;
    But we . . . I had to hunt for them . . . No, I found them.
    . . . Yes, she's bringing them now . . . Good night.

CURTAIN

Act One. Scene 3

The same room: late afternoon of the next day. EDWARD *alone. He goes to
answer the doorbell.*

EDWARD. Oh ... good evening.
[*Enter the* UNIDENTIFIED GUEST]
UNIDENTIFIED GUEST. Good evening, Mr. Chamberlayne.
EDWARD. Well. May I offer you some gin and water?
UNIDENTIFIED GUEST. No, thank you. This is a different occasion.
EDWARD. I take it that as you have come alone
    You have been unsuccessful.
UNIDENTIFIED GUEST.   Not at all.
    I have come to remind you — you have made a decision.
EDWARD. Are you thinking that I may have changed my mind?
UNIDENTIFIED GUEST. No. You will not be ready to change your mind
    Until you recover from having made a decision.
    No. I have come to tell you that you will change your mind,
    But that it will not matter. It will be too late.
EDWARD. I have half a mind to change my mind now
    To show you that I am free to change it.
UNIDENTIFIED GUEST. You will change your mind, but you are not
       free.
    Your moment of freedom was yesterday.
    You made a decision. You set in motion
    Forces in your life and in the lives of others
    Which cannot be reversed. That is one consideration.
    And another is this: it is a serious matter
    To bring someone back from the dead.
EDWARD.   From the dead?
    That figure of speech is somewhat ... dramatic,
    As it was only yesterday that my wife left me.
UNIDENTIFIED GUEST. Ah, but we die to each other daily.
    What we know of other people
    Is only our memory of the moments

During which we knew them. And they have changed since
then.
To pretend that they and we are the same
Is a useful and convenient social convention
Which must sometimes be broken. We must also remember
That at every meeting we are meeting a stranger.

EDWARD. So you want me to greet my wife as a stranger?
That will not be easy.

UNIDENTIFIED GUEST. It is very difficult.
But it is perhaps still more difficult
To keep up the pretence that you are not strangers.
The affectionate ghosts: the grandmother,
The lively bachelor uncle at the Christmas party,
The beloved nursemaid — those who enfolded
Your childhood years in comfort, mirth, security —
If they returned, would it not be embarrassing?
What would you say to them, or they to you
After the first ten minutes? You would find it difficult
To treat them as strangers, but still more difficult
To pretend that you were not strange to each other.

EDWARD. You can hardly expect me to obliterate
The last five years.

UNIDENTIFIED GUEST. I ask you to forget nothing.
To try to forget is to try to conceal.

EDWARD. There are certainly things I should like to forget.

UNIDENTIFIED GUEST. And persons also. But you must not forget
them.
You must face them all, but meet them as strangers.

EDWARD. Then I myself must also be a stranger.

UNIDENTIFIED GUEST. And to yourself as well. But remember,
When you see your wife, you must ask no questions
And give no explanations. I have said the same to her.
Don't strangle each other with knotted memories.
Now I shall go.

EDWARD.   Stop! Will you come back with her?

UNIDENTIFIED GUEST. No, I shall not come with her.

EDWARD.   I don't know why,
But I think I should like you to bring her yourself.

UNIDENTIFIED GUEST. Yes, I know you would. And for definite
reasons

Which I am not prepared to explain to you
I must ask you not to speak of me to her;
And she will not mention me to you.

EDWARD. I promise.

UNIDENTIFIED GUEST. And now you must await your visitors.

EDWARD. Visitors? What visitors?

UNIDENTIFIED GUEST.   Whoever comes. The strangers.
As for myself, I shall take the precaution
Of leaving by the service staircase.

EDWARD. May I ask one question?

UNIDENTIFIED GUEST.   You may ask it.

EDWARD. Who are you?

UNIDENTIFIED GUEST. I also am a stranger.

[*Exit. A pause.* EDWARD *moves about restlessly. The bell rings, and he goes
to the front door.*]

EDWARD. Celia!

CELIA.   Has Lavinia arrived?

EDWARD.   Celia! Why have you come?
I expect Lavinia at any moment.
You must not be here. Why have you come here?

CELIA. Because Lavinia asked me.

EDWARD.   Because Lavinia asked you!

CELIA. Well, not directly. Julia had a telegram
Asking her to come, and to bring me with her.
Julia was delayed, and sent me on ahead.

EDWARD. It seems very odd. And not like Lavinia.
I suppose there is nothing to do but wait.
Won't you sit down?

CELIA.   Thank you.
                    [*Pause*]

EDWARD. Oh, my God, what shall we talk about?
We can't sit here in silence.

CELIA.   Oh, I could.
Just looking at you. Edward, forgive my laughing.
You look like a little boy who's been sent for
To the headmaster's study; and is not quite sure
What he's been found out in. I never saw you so before.
This is really a ludicrous situation.

EDWARD. I'm afraid I can't see the humorous side of it.

CELIA. I'm not really laughing at *you*, Edward.

I couldn't have laughed at anything, yesterday;
But I've learnt a lot in twenty-four hours.
It wasn't a very pleasant experience.
Oh, I'm glad I came!
I can see you at last as a human being.
Can't you see me that way too, and laugh about it?

EDWARD. I wish I could. I wish I understood anything.
    I'm completely in the dark.

CELIA.   But it's all so simple.
    Can't you see that . . .
              [*The doorbell rings*]

EDWARD.   There's Lavinia.
              [*Goes to front door*]
                      Peter!

[*Enter* PETER]

PETER. Where's Lavinia?

EDWARD.   Don't tell me that Lavinia
    Sent you a telegram . . .

PETER.   No, not to me,
    But to Alex. She told him to come here
    And to bring me with him. He'll be here in a minute.
    Celia! Have you heard from Lavinia too?
    Or am I interrupting?

CELIA.   I've just explained to Edward —
    I only got here this moment myself —
    That she telegraphed to Julia to come and bring me with her.

EDWARD. I wonder whom else Lavinia has invited.

PETER. Why, I got the impression that Lavinia intended
    To have yesterday's cocktail party to-day.
    So I don't suppose her aunt can have died.

EDWARD. What aunt?

PETER.   The aunt you told us about.
    But Edward — you remember our conversation yesterday?

EDWARD. Of course.

PETER.   I hope you've done nothing about it.

EDWARD. No, I've done nothing.

PETER.   I'm so glad.
    Because I've changed my mind. I mean, I've decided
    That it's all no use. I'm going to California.

CELIA. You're going to California!

PETER. Yes, I have a new job.

EDWARD. And how did that happen, overnight?

PETER. Why, it's a man Alex put me in touch with
And we settled everything this morning.
Alex is a wonderful person to know,
Because, you see, he knows everybody, everywhere.
So what I've really come for is to say good-bye.

CELIA. Well, Peter, I'm awfully glad, for your sake,
Though of course we . . . I shall miss you;
You know how I depended on you for concerts,
And picture exhibitions — more than you realised.
It *was* fun, wasn't it! But now you'll have a chance,
I hope, to realise your ambitions.
I shall miss you.

PETER. It's nice of you to say so;
But you'll find someone better, to go about with.

CELIA. I don't think that I shall be going to concerts.
I am going away too.

[LAVINIA *lets herself in with a latch-key*]

PETER. You're going abroad?

CELIA. I don't know. Perhaps.

EDWARD. You're both going away!

[*Enter* LAVINIA]

LAVINIA. Who's going away? Well, Celia. Well, Peter.
I didn't expect to find either of you here.

PETER *and* CELIA. But the telegram!

LAVINIA. What telegram?

CELIA. The one you sent to Julia.

PETER. And the one you sent to Alex.

LAVINIA. I don't know what you mean.
Edward, have you been sending telegrams?

EDWARD. Of course I haven't sent any telegrams.

LAVINIA. This is some of Julia's mischief.
And is *she* coming?

PETER. Yes, and Alex.

LAVINIA. Then I shall ask *them* for an explanation.
Meanwhile, I suppose we might as well sit down.
What shall we talk about?

EDWARD. Peter's going to America.

PETER. Yes, and I would have rung you up tomorrow

And come in to say good-bye before I left.

LAVINIA. And Celia's going too? Was that what I heard?
I congratulate you both. To Hollywood, of course?
How exciting for you, Celia! Now you'll have a chance
At last, to realise your ambitions.
You're going together?

PETER.   We're not going together.
Celia told us she was going away,
But I don't know where.

LAVINIA.   You don't know where?
And do you know where you are going, yourself?

PETER. Yes, of course, I'm going to California.

LAVINIA. Well, Celia, why don't you go to California?
Everyone says it's a wonderful climate:
The people who go there never want to leave it.

CELIA. Lavinia, I think I understand about Peter . . .

LAVINIA. I have no doubt you do.

CELIA.   And why he is going . . .

LAVINIA. I don't doubt that either.

CELIA.   And I believe he is right to go.

LAVINIA. Oh, so you advised him?

PETER.   She knew nothing about it.

CELIA. But now that I may be going away — somewhere —
I should like to say good-bye — as friends.

LAVINIA. Why, Celia, but haven't we always been friends?
I thought you were one of my dearest friends —
At least, in so far as a girl *can* be a friend
Of a woman so much older than herself.

CELIA.   Lavinia,
Don't put me off. I may not see you again.
What I want to say is this: I should like you to remember me
As someone who wants you and Edward to be happy.

LAVINIA. You are very kind, but very mysterious.
I'm sure that we shall manage somehow, thank you,
As we have in the past.

CELIA.   Oh, not as in the past!
              [*The doorbell rings, and* EDWARD *goes to answer it*]
Oh, I'm afraid that all this sounds rather silly!
But . . .

[EDWARD *re-enters with* JULIA]

JULIA.   There you are, Lavinia! I'm sorry to be late.

But your telegram was a bit unexpected.

I dropped everything to come. And how is the dear aunt?

LAVINIA. So far as I know, she is very well, thank you.

JULIA. She must have made a marvellous recovery.

I said so to myself, when I got your telegram.

LAVINIA. But where, may I ask, was this telegram sent from?

JULIA. Why, from Essex, of course.

LAVINIA.   And why from Essex?

JULIA. Because you've been in Essex.

LAVINIA.   Because I've been in Essex!

JULIA. Lavinia! Don't say you've had a lapse of memory!

Then that accounts for the aunt — and the telegram.

LAVINIA. Well, perhaps I was in Essex. I really don't know.

JULIA. You don't know where you were? Lavinia!

Don't tell me you were abducted! Tell us

I'm thrilled . . .

[*The doorbell rings.* EDWARD *goes to answer it. Enter* ALEX]

ALEX. Has Lavinia arrived?

EDWARD.   Yes.

ALEX.   Welcome back, Lavinia!

When I got your telegram . . .

LAVINIA.   Where from?

ALEX.   Dedham.

LAVINIA. Dedham is in Essex. So it was from Dedham.

Edward, have *you* any friends in Dedham?

EDWARD. No, *I* have no connections in Dedham.

JULIA. Well, it's all delightfully mysterious.

ALEX. But what is the mystery?

JULIA.   Alex, *don't* be inquisitive.

Lavinia has had a lapse of memory,

And so, of course, she sent us telegrams:

And now I don't believe she really wants us.

I can see that she is quite worn out

After her anxiety about her aunt —

Who, you'll be glad to hear, has quite recovered, Alex —

And after that long journey on the old Great Eastern,

Waiting at junctions. And I suppose she's famished.

ALEX. Ah, in that case I know what I'll do . . .

JULIA.   No, Alex.

We must leave them alone, and let Lavinia rest.
Now we'll all go back to *my* house. Peter, call a taxi.

[Exit PETER]

We'll have a cocktail party at *my* house to-day.

CELIA. Well, I'll go now. Good-bye, Lavinia.
Good-bye, Edward.
EDWARD.   Good-bye, Celia.
CELIA. Good-bye, Lavinia.
LAVINIA.   Good-bye, Celia.

[Exit CELIA]

JULIA. And now, Alex, you and I should be going.
EDWARD. Are you sure you haven't left anything, Julia?
JULIA. Left anything? Oh, you mean my spectacles.
No, they're here. Besides, they're no use to me.
I'm not coming back again *this* evening.
LAVINIA. Stop! I want you to explain the telegram.
JULIA. Explain the telegram? What do you think, Alex?
ALEX. No, Julia, *we* can't explain the telegram.
LAVINIA. I am sure that you could explain the telegram.
I don't know why. But it seems to me that yesterday
I started some machine, that goes on working,
And I cannot stop it; no, it's not like a machine —
Or if it's a machine, someone else is running it.
But who? Somebody is always interfering . . .
I don't feel free . . . and yet I started it . . .
JULIA. Alex, do you think we could explain *anything*?
ALEX. I think not, Julia. She must find out for herself:
That's the only way.
JULIA.   How right you are!
Well, my dears, I shall see you very soon.
EDWARD. *When* shall we see you?
JULIA.   Did I say you'd see me?
Good-bye. I believe . . . I haven't left anything.
[Enter PETER]
PETER. I've got a taxi, Julia.
JULIA.   Splendid! Good-bye!

[Exeunt JULIA, ALEX *and* PETER]

LAVINIA. I must say, you don't seem very pleased to see me.
EDWARD. I can't say that I've had much opportunity
To seem anything. But of course I'm glad to see you.

391

LAVINIA. Yes, that was a silly thing to say.

Like a schoolgirl. Like Celia. I don't know why I said it.

Well, here I am.

EDWARD.   I am to ask no questions.

LAVINIA. And I know I am to give no explanations.

EDWARD. And I am to give no explanations.

LAVINIA. And I am to ask no questions. And yet . . . why not?

EDWARD. I don't know why not. So what are we to talk about?

LAVINIA. There is one thing I ought to know, because of other people

And what to do about them. It's about that party.

I suppose you won't believe I forgot all about it!

I let you down badly. What did you do about it?

I only remembered after I had left.

EDWARD. I telephoned to everyone I knew was coming

But I couldn't get everyone. And so a few came.

LAVINIA. Who came?

EDWARD.   Just those who were here this evening . . .

LAVINIA. That's odd.

EDWARD.   . . . and one other. I don't know who he was,

But *you* ought to know.

LAVINIA.   Yes, I think I know.

But I'm puzzled by Julia. That woman is the devil.

She knows by instinct when something's going to happen.

Trust her not to miss any awkward situation!

And what did you tell them?

EDWARD.   I invented an aunt

Who was ill in the country, and had sent for you.

LAVINIA. Really, Edward! You had better have told the truth:

Nothing less than the truth could deceive Julia.

But how did the aunt come to live in Essex?

EDWARD. Julia compelled me to make her live somewhere.

LAVINIA. I see. So Julia made her live in Essex;

And made the telegrams come from Essex.

Well, I shall have to tell Julia the truth.

I shall always tell the truth now.

We have wasted such a lot of time in lying.

EDWARD. I don't quite know what you mean.

LAVINIA.   Oh, Edward!

The point is, that since I've been away

I see that I've taken you much too seriously.

392

And now I can see how absurd you are.

EDWARD. That is a very serious conclusion
 To have arrived at in . . . how many? . . . thirty-two hours.

LAVINIA. Yes, a very important discovery,
 Finding that you've spent five years of your life
 With a man who has no sense of humour;
 And that the effect upon me was
 That I lost all sense of humour myself.
 That's what came of always giving in to you.

EDWARD. I was unaware that you'd always given in to me.
 It struck me very differently. As we're on the subject,
 I thought that it was I who had given in to *you*.

LAVINIA. I know what you mean by giving in to *me*:
 You mean, leaving all the practical decisions
 That you should have made yourself. I remember —
 Oh, I ought to have realised what was coming —
 When we were planning our honeymoon,
 I couldn't make you say where you wanted to go . . .

EDWARD. But I wanted *you* to make that decision.

LAVINIA. But how could I tell where I wanted to go
 Unless you suggested some other place first?
 And I remember that finally in desperation
 I said: 'I suppose you'd as soon go to Peacehaven' —
 And you said 'I don't mind'.

EDWARD.   Of course I didn't mind.
 I meant it as a compliment.

LAVINIA.   You meant it as a compliment!
 And you were so considerate, people said;
 And you thought you were unselfish. It was only passivity;
 You only wanted to be bolstered, encouraged. . . .

EDWARD. Encouraged? To what?

LAVINIA.   To think well of yourself.
 You know it was I who made you work at the Bar . . .

EDWARD. You nagged me because I didn't get enough work
 And said that I ought to meet more people:
 But when the briefs began to come in —
 And they didn't come through any of *your* friends —
 You suddenly found it inconvenient
 That I should be always too busy or too tired
 To be of use to you socially . . .

LAVINIA. I *never* complained.

EDWARD. No; and it was perfectly infuriating,
The way you *didn't* complain . . .

LAVINIA. It was you who complained
Of seeing nobody but solicitors and clients . . .

EDWARD. And you were never very sympathetic.

LAVINIA. Well, but I tried to do something about it.
That was why I took so much trouble
To have those Thursdays, to give you the chance
Of talking to intellectual people . . .

EDWARD. You would have given me about as much opportunity
If you had hired me as your butler:
Some of your guests may have thought I *was* the butler.

LAVINIA. And on several occasions, when somebody was coming
Whom I particularly wanted you to meet,
You didn't arrive until just as they were leaving.

EDWARD. Well, at least, *they* can't have thought I was the butler.

LAVINIA. Everything I tried only made matters worse,
And the moment you were offered something that you wanted
You wanted something else. I shall treat you very differently
In future.

EDWARD. Thank you for the warning. But tell me,
Since this is how you see me, why did you come back?

LAVINIA. Frankly, I don't know. I was warned of the danger,
Yet something, or somebody, compelled me to come.
And why did you want me?

EDWARD. I don't know either.
You say you were trying to 'encourage' me:
Then why did you always make me feel insignificant?
I may not have known what life I wanted,
But it wasn't the life you chose for me.
You wanted your husband to be *successful*,
You wanted me to supply a public background
For your kind of public life. You wished to be a hostess
For whom my career would be a support.
Well, I tried to be accommodating. But, in future,
I shall behave, I assure you, very differently.

LAVINIA. Bravo! Edward. This is surprising.
Now who could have taught you to answer back like that?

EDWARD. I have had quite enough humiliation

394

Lately, to bring me to the point
At which humiliation ceases to humiliate.
You get to the point at which you cease to feel
And then you speak your mind.

LAVINIA.   That will be a novelty
To find that you have a mind to speak.
Anyway, I'm prepared to take you as you are.

EDWARD. You mean, you are prepared to take me
As I was, or as you think I am.
But what do you think I am?

LAVINIA.   Oh, what you always were.
As for me, I'm rather a different person
Whom you must get to know.

EDWARD.   This is very interesting:
But you seem to assume that you've done all the changing —
Though I haven't yet found it a change for the better.
But doesn't it occur to you that possibly
I may have changed too?

LAVINIA.   Oh, Edward, when you were a little boy,
I'm sure you were always getting yourself measured
To prove how you had grown since the last holidays.
You were always intensely concerned with yourself;
And if other people grow, well, you want to grow too.
In what way have you changed?

EDWARD.   The change that comes
From seeing oneself through the eyes of other people.

LAVINIA. That must have been very shattering for you.
But never mind, you'll soon get over it
And find yourself another little part to play,
With another face, to take people in.

EDWARD. One of the most infuriating things about you
Has always been your perfect assurance
That you understood me better than I understood myself.

LAVINIA. And the most infuriating thing about you
Has always been your placid assumption
That I wasn't worth the trouble of understanding.

EDWARD. So here we are again. Back in the trap,
With only one difference, perhaps — we can fight each
    other,
Instead of each taking his corner of the cage.

Well, it's a better way of passing the evening
Than listening to the gramophone.

LAVINIA.   We have very good records;
But I always suspected that you really hated music
And that the gramophone was only your escape
From talking to me when we had to be alone.

EDWARD. I've often wondered why you married me.

LAVINIA. Well, you really were rather attractive, you know;
And you kept on *saying* that you were in love with me —
I believe you were trying to persuade yourself you were.
I seemed always on the verge of some wonderful experience
And then it never happened. I wonder now
How you could have thought you were in love with me.

EDWARD. Everybody told me that I was;
And they told me how well suited we were.

LAVINIA. It's a pity that you had no opinion of your own.
Oh, Edward, I should like to be good to you —
Or if that's impossible, at least be horrid to you —
Anything but nothing, which is all you seem to want of me.
But I'm sorry for you . . .

EDWARD.   Don't say you are sorry for me!
I have had enough of people being sorry for me.

LAVINIA. Yes, because they can never be so sorry for you
As you are for yourself. And that's hard to bear.
I thought that there might be some way out for you
If I went away. I thought that if I died
To you, I who had been only a ghost to you,
You might be able to find the road back
To a time when you were real — for you must have been real
At some time or other, before you ever knew me:
Perhaps only when you were a child.

EDWARD. I don't want you to make yourself responsible for me:
It's only another kind of contempt.
And I do not want you to explain me to myself.
You're still trying to invent a personality for me
Which will only keep me away from myself.

LAVINIA. You're complicating what is in fact very simple.
But there is one point which I see clearly:
We are not to relapse into the kind of life we led
Until yesterday morning.

EDWARD. There was a door
And I could not open it. I could not touch the handle.
Why could I not walk out of my prison?
What is hell? Hell is oneself,
Hell is alone, the other figures in it
Merely projections. There is nothing to escape from
And nothing to escape to. One is always alone.

LAVINIA. Edward, what *are* you talking about?
Talking to yourself. Could you bear, for a moment,
To think about *me*?

EDWARD. It was only yesterday
That damnation took place. And now I must live with it
Day by day, hour by hour, for ever and ever.

LAVINIA. I think you're on the edge of a nervous breakdown!

EDWARD. Don't say that!

LAVINIA. I must say it.
I know . . . of a doctor who I think could help you.

EDWARD. If I go to a doctor, I shall make my own choice;
Not take one whom you choose. How do I know
That you wouldn't see him first, and tell him all about me
From *your* point of view? But I don't need a doctor.
I am simply in hell. Where there are no doctors —
At least, not in a professional capacity.

LAVINIA. One can be practical, even in hell:
And you know I am much more practical than you are.

EDWARD. I ought to know by now what you consider practical.
Practical! I remember, on our honeymoon,
You were always wrapping things up in tissue paper
And then had to unwrap everything again
To find what you wanted. And I never could teach you
How to put the cap on a tube of tooth-paste.

LAVINIA. Very well, then, I shall not try to press you.
You're much too divided to know what you want.
But, being divided, you will tend to compromise,
And your sort of compromise will be the old one.

EDWARD. You don't understand me. Have I not made it clear
That in future you will find me a different person?

LAVINIA. Indeed. And has the difference nothing to do
With Celia going to California?

EDWARD. Celia? Going to California?

LAVINIA.   Yes, with Peter.
    Really, Edward, if you were human
    You would burst out laughing. But you won't.

EDWARD. O God, O God, if I could return to yesterday
    Before I thought that I had made a decision.
    What devil left the door on the latch
    For these doubts to enter? And then you came back, you
    The angel of destruction — just as I felt sure.
    In a moment, at your touch, there is nothing but ruin.
    O God, what have I done? The python. The octopus.
    Must I become after all what you would make me?

LAVINIA. Well, Edward, as I am unable to make you laugh,
    And as I can't persuade you to see a doctor,
    There's nothing else at present that I can do about it.
    I ought to go and have a look in the kitchen.
    I know there are some eggs. But we must go out for dinner.
    Meanwhile, my luggage is in the hall downstairs:
    Will you get the porter to fetch it up for me?

CURTAIN

398

Act Two

SIR HENRY HARCOURT-REILLY'S *consulting room in London. Morning: several weeks later.* SIR HENRY *alone at his desk. He presses an electric button. The* NURSE-SECRETARY *enters, with Appointment Book.*

REILLY. About those three appointments this morning, Miss
      Barraway:
    I should like to run over my instructions again.
    You understand, of course, that it is important
    To avoid any meeting?
NURSE-SECRETARY.   You made that clear, Sir Henry:
    The first appointment at eleven o'clock.
    He is to be shown into the small waiting-room;
    And you will see him almost at once.
REILLY. I shall see him at once. And the second?
NURSE-SECRETARY. The second to be shown into the other room
    Just as usual. She arrives at a quarter past;
    But you may keep her waiting.
REILLY.   Or she may keep me waiting;
    But I think she will be punctual.
NURSE-SECRETARY.   I telephone through
    The moment she arrives. I leave her there
    Until you ring three times.
REILLY.   And the third patient?
NURSE-SECRETARY. The third one to be shown into the small room;
    And I need not let you know that she has arrived.
    Then, when you ring, I show the others out;
    And only after they have left the house. . . .
REILLY. Quite right, Miss Barraway. That's all for the moment.
NURSE-SECRETARY. Mr. Gibbs is here, Sir Henry.
REILLY.   Ask him to come straight in.
                      [*Exit* NURSE-SECRETARY]

[ALEX *enters almost immediately*]

ALEX. When is Chamberlayne's appointment?

REILLY.   At eleven o'clock,

 The conventional hour. We have not much time.

 Tell me now, did you have any difficulty

 In convincing him I was the man for his case?

ALEX. Difficulty? No! He was only impatient

 At having to wait four days for the appointment.

REILLY. It was necessary to delay his appointment

 To lower his resistance. But what I mean is,

 Does he trust your judgement?

ALEX.   Yes, implicitly.

 It's not that he regards me as very intelligent,

 But he thinks I'm well informed: the sort of person

 Who would know the right doctor, as well as the right
  shops.

 Besides, he was ready to consult any doctor

 Recommended by anyone except his wife.

REILLY. I had already impressed upon her

 That she was not to mention my name to him.

ALEX. With your usual foresight. Now, he's quite triumphant

 Because he thinks he's stolen a march on her.

 And when you've sent him to a sanatorium

 Where she can't get at him — then, he believes,

 She will be very penitent. He's enjoying his illness.

REILLY. Illness offers him a double advantage:

 To escape from himself — and get the better of his wife.

ALEX. Not to escape from her?

REILLY.   He doesn't want to escape from her.

ALEX. He is staying at his club.

REILLY.   Yes, that is where he wrote from.

    [*The house-telephone rings*]

 Hello! Yes, show him up.

ALEX.   You will have a busy morning!

 I will go out by the service staircase

 And come back when they've gone.

REILLY. Yes, when they've gone.

       [*Exit* ALEX *by side door*]

[EDWARD *is shown in by* NURSE-SECRETARY]

EDWARD. Sir Henry Harcourt-Reilly —

    [*Stops and stares at* REILLY]

400

REILLY [*without looking up from his papers*]. Good morning, Mr.
    Chamberlayne.
    Please sit down. I won't keep you a moment.
    — Now, Mr. Chamberlayne?
EDWARD.   It came into my mind
    Before I entered the door, that you might be the same person:
    But I dismissed that as just another symptom.
    Well, I should have known better than to come here
    On the recommendation of a man who did not know you.
    Yet Alex is so plausible. And his recommendations
    Of shops, have always been satisfactory.
    I beg your pardon. But he *is* a blunderer.
    I should like to know . . . but what is the use!
    I suppose I might as well go away at once.
REILLY. No. If you please, sit down, Mr. Chamberlayne.
    You are not going away, so you might as well sit down.
    You were going to ask a question.
EDWARD.   When you came to my flat
    Had you been invited by my wife as a guest
    As I supposed? . . . Or did she *send* you?
REILLY. I cannot say that I had been invited;
    And Mrs. Chamberlayne did not know that I was coming.
    But I knew you would be there, and whom I should find with you.
EDWARD. But you had seen my wife?
REILLY.   Oh yes, I had seen her.
EDWARD. So this *is* a trap!
REILLY.   Let's not call it a trap.
    But if it is a trap, then you cannot escape from it:
    And so . . . you might as well sit down.
    I think that you will find that chair comfortable.
EDWARD.   You knew,
    Before I began to tell you, what had happened?
REILLY. That is so, that is so. But all in good time.
    Let us dismiss that question for the moment.
    Tell me first, about the difficulties
    On which you want my professional opinion.
EDWARD. It's not for me to blame you for bringing my wife back,
    I suppose. You seemed to be trying to persuade me
    That I was better off without her. But didn't you realise
    That I was in no state to make a decision?

REILLY. If I had not brought your wife back, Mr. Chamberlayne,
　　Do you suppose that things would be any better — now?

EDWARD. I don't know, I'm sure. They could hardly be worse.

REILLY. They might be much worse. You might have ruined three lives
　　By your indecision. Now there are only two —
　　Which you still have the chance of redeeming from ruin.

EDWARD. You talk as if I was capable of action:
　　If I were, I should not need to consult you
　　Or anyone else. I came here as a patient.
　　If you take no interest in my case, I can go elsewhere.

REILLY. You have reason to believe that you are very ill?

EDWARD. I should have thought a doctor could see that for himself.
　　Or at least that he would enquire about the symptoms.
　　Two people advised me recently,
　　Almost in the same words, that I ought to see a doctor.
　　They said — again, in almost the same words —
　　That I was on the edge of a nervous breakdown.
　　I didn't know it then myself — but if they saw it
　　I should have thought that a doctor could see it.

REILLY. 'Nervous breakdown' is a term I never use:
　　It can mean almost anything.

EDWARD. 　　　　　　　　　　And since then, I have realised
　　That mine is a very unusual case.

REILLY. All cases are unique, and very similar to others.

EDWARD. Is there a sanatorium to which you send such patients
　　As myself, under your personal observation?

REILLY. You are very impetuous, Mr. Chamberlayne.
　　There are several kinds of sanatoria
　　For several kinds of patient. And there are also patients
　　For whom a sanatorium is the worst place possible.
　　We must first find out what is wrong with you
　　Before we decide what to do with you.

EDWARD. I doubt if you have ever had a case like mine:
　　I have ceased to believe in my own personality.

REILLY. Oh, dear yes; this is serious. A very common malady.
　　Very prevalent indeed.

EDWARD. 　　　　.　　　　I remember, in my childhood . . .

REILLY. I always begin from the immediate situation
　　And then go back as far as I find necessary.
　　You see, your memories of childhood —

I mean, in your present state of mind —
Would be largely fictitious; and as for your dreams,
You would produce amazing dreams, to oblige me.
I could make you dream any kind of dream I suggested,
And it would only go to flatter your vanity
With the temporary stimulus of feeling interesting.

EDWARD. But I am obsessed by the thought of my own insignificance.

REILLY. Precisely. And I could make you feel important,
And you would imagine it a marvellous cure;
And you would go on, doing such amount of mischief
As lay within your power — until you came to grief.
Half of the harm that is done in this world
Is due to people who want to feel important.
They don't mean to do harm — but the harm does not interest
    them.
Or they do not see it, or they justify it
Because they are absorbed in the endless struggle
To think well of themselves.

EDWARD.   If I am like that
I must have done a great deal of harm.

REILLY. Oh, not so much as you would like to think:
Only, shall we say, within your modest capacity.
Try to explain what has happened since I left you.

EDWARD. I see now why I wanted my wife to come back.
It was because of what she had made me into.
We had not been alone again for fifteen minutes
Before I felt, and still more acutely —
Indeed, acutely, perhaps, for the first time,
The whole oppression, the unreality
Of the role she had always imposed upon me
With the obstinate, unconscious, sub-human strength
That some women have. Without her, it was vacancy.
When I thought she had left me, I began to dissolve,
To cease to exist. That was what she had done to me!
I cannot live with her — that is now intolerable;
I cannot live without her, for she has made me incapable
Of having any existence of my own.
That is what she has done to me in five years together!
She has made the world a place I cannot live in
Except on her terms. I must be alone,

403

But not in the same world. So I want you to put me
Into your sanatorium. I could be alone there?
                    [*House-telephone rings*]
REILLY [*into telephone*]. Yes.
     [*To* EDWARD] Yes, you could be alone there.
EDWARD.   I wonder
     If you have understood a word of what I have been saying.
REILLY. You must have patience with me, Mr. Chamberlayne:
     I learn a good deal by merely observing you,
     And letting you talk as long as you please,
     And taking note of what you do not say.
EDWARD. I once experienced the extreme of physical pain,
     And now I know there is suffering worse than that.
     It is surprising, if one had time to be surprised:
     I am not afraid of the death of the body,
     But this death is terrifying. The death of the spirit —
     Can you understand what I suffer?
REILLY.   I understand what you mean.
EDWARD. I can no longer act for myself.
     Coming to see you — that's the last decision
     I was capable of making. I am in your hands.
     I cannot take any further responsibility.
REILLY. Many patients come in that belief.
EDWARD. And now will you send me to the sanatorium?
REILLY. You have nothing else to tell me?
EDWARD.   What else can I tell you?
     You didn't want to hear about my early history.
REILLY. No, I did not want to hear about your *early* history.
EDWARD. And so will you send me to the sanatorium?
     I can't go home again. And at my club
     They won't let you keep a room for more than seven days;
     I haven't the courage to go to a hotel,
     And besides, I need more shirts — you can get my wife
     To have my things sent on: whatever I shall need.
     But of course you mustn't tell her where I am.
     Is it far to go?
REILLY.   You might say, a long journey.
     But before I treat a patient like yourself
     I need to know a great deal more about him,
     Than the patient himself can always tell me.

Indeed, it is often the case that my patients
Are only pieces of a total situation
Which I have to explore. The single patient
Who is ill by himself, is rather the exception.
I have recently had another patient
Whose situation is much the same as your own.
            [*Presses the bell on his desk three times*]
You must accept a rather unusual procedure:
I propose to introduce you to the other patient.

EDWARD. What do you mean? Who is this other patient?
    I consider this very unprofessional conduct —
    I will not discuss my case before another patient.

REILLY. On the contrary. That is the only way
    In which it can be discussed. You have told me nothing.
    You have had the opportunity, and you have said enough
    To convince me that you have been making up your case
    So to speak, as you went along. A barrister
    Ought to know his brief before he enters the court.

EDWARD. I am at least free to leave. And I propose to do so.
    My mind is made up. I shall go to a hotel.

REILLY. It is just because you are not free, Mr. Chamberlayne,
    That you have come to me. It is for me to give you that —
    Your freedom. That is my affair.

[LAVINIA *is shown in by the* NURSE-SECRETARY]
    But here is the other patient.

EDWARD.   Lavinia!

LAVINIA.   Well, Sir Henry!
    I said I would come to talk about my husband:
    I didn't say I was prepared to meet him.

EDWARD. And I did not expect to meet *you*, Lavinia.
    I call this a very dishonourable trick.

REILLY. Honesty before honour, Mr. Chamberlayne.
    Sit down, please, both of you. Mrs. Chamberlayne,
    Your husband wishes to enter a sanatorium,
    And that is a question which naturally concerns
            you.

EDWARD. I am not going to any sanatorium.
    I am going to a hotel. And I shall ask you, Lavinia,
    To be so good as to send me on some clothes.

LAVINIA. Oh, to what hotel?

EDWARD.   I don't know — I mean to say,
 That doesn't concern you.
LAVINIA.   In that case, Edward,
 I don't think your clothes concern me either.
 [*To* REILLY] I presume you will send him to the same sanatorium
 To which you sent me? Well, he needs it more than I did.
REILLY. I am glad that you have come to see it in that light —
 At least, for the moment. But, Mrs. Chamberlayne,
 You have never visited my sanatorium.
LAVINIA. What do you mean? I asked to be sent
 And you took me there. If that was not a sanatorium
 What was it?
REILLY.   A kind of hotel. A retreat
 For people who imagine that they need a respite
 From everyday life. They return refreshed;
 And if they believe it to be a sanatorium
 That is good reason for not sending them to one.
 The people who need my sort of sanatorium
 Are not easily deceived.
LAVINIA.   Are you a devil
 Or merely a lunatic practical joker?
EDWARD. I incline to the second explanation
 Without the qualification 'lunatic'.
 Why should *you* go to a sanatorium?
 I have never known anyone in my life
 With fewer mental complications than you;
 You're stronger than a . . . battleship. That's what drove me mad.
 I am the one who needs a sanatorium —
 But I'm not going there.
REILLY.   You are right, Mr. Chamberlayne.
 You are no case for my sanatorium:
 You are much too ill.
EDWARD.   Much too ill?
 Then I'll go and be ill in a suburban boarding-house.
LAVINIA. That would never suit you, Edward. Now I know of a hotel
 In the New Forest . . .
EDWARD.   How like you, Lavinia.
 You always know of something better.
LAVINIA. It's only that I have a more practical mind
 Than you have, Edward. You do know that.

EDWARD. Only because you've told me so often.
I'd like to see *you* filling up an income-tax form.
LAVINIA. Don't be silly, Edward. When I say practical,
I mean practical in the things that really matter.
REILLY. May I interrupt this interesting discussion?
I say you are both too ill. There are several symptoms
Which must occur together, and to a marked degree,
To qualify a patient for *my* sanatorium:
And one of them is an honest mind.
That is one of the causes of their suffering.
LAVINIA. No one can say my husband has an honest mind.
EDWARD. And I could not honestly say that of *you*, Lavinia.
REILLY. I congratulate you both on your perspicacity.
Your sympathetic understanding of each other
Will prepare you to appreciate what I have to say to you.
I do not trouble myself with the common cheat,
Or with the insuperably, innocently dull:
My patients such as you are the self-deceivers
Taking infinite pains, exhausting their energy,
Yet never quite successful. You have both of you pretended
To be consulting me; both, tried to impose upon me
Your own diagnosis, and prescribe your own cure.
But when you put yourselves into hands like mine
You surrender a great deal more than you meant to.
This is the consequence of trying to lie to me.
LAVINIA. I did not come here to be insulted.
REILLY. You have come where the word 'insult' has no meaning;
And you must put up with that. All that you have told me —
Both of you — was true enough: you described your feelings —
Or some of them — omitting the important facts.
Let me take your husband first.
[*To* EDWARD]   You were lying to me
By concealing your relations with Miss Coplestone.
EDWARD. This is monstrous! My wife knew nothing about it.
LAVINIA. Really, Edward! Even if I'd been blind
There were plenty of people to let me know about it.
I wonder if there was anyone who didn't know.
REILLY. There was one, in fact. But you, Mrs. Chamberlayne,
Tried to make me believe that it was this discovery
Precipitated what you called your nervous breakdown.

LAVINIA. But it's true! I was completely prostrated;
  Even if I have made a partial recovery.
REILLY. Certainly, you were completely prostrated,
  And certainly, you have somewhat recovered.
  But you failed to mention that the cause of your distress
  Was the defection of your lover — who suddenly
  For the first time in his life, fell in love with someone,
  And with someone of whom you had reason to be jealous.
EDWARD. Really, Lavinia! This is very interesting.
  You seem to have been much more successful at concealment
  Than I was. Now I wonder who it could have been.
LAVINIA. Well, tell him if you like.
REILLY.   A young man named Peter.
EDWARD. Peter? Peter who?
REILLY.   Mr. Peter Quilpe
  Was a frequent guest.
EDWARD.   Peter Quilpe.
  Peter Quilpe! Really Lavinia!
  I congratulate you. You could not have chosen
  Anyone I was less likely to suspect.
  And then he came to *me* to confide about Celia!
  I have never heard anything so utterly ludicrous:
  This is the best joke that ever happened.
LAVINIA. I never knew you had such a sense of humour.
REILLY. It is the first more hopeful symptom.
LAVINIA. How did you know all this?
REILLY.   That I cannot disclose.
  I have my own method of collecting information
  About my patients. You must not ask me to reveal it —
  That is a matter of professional etiquette.
LAVINIA. I have not noticed much professional etiquette
  About your behaviour to-day.
REILLY.   A point well taken.
  But permit me to remark that my revelations
  About each of you, to one another,
  Have not been of anything that you confided to me.
  The information I have exchanged between you
  Was all obtained from outside sources.
  Mrs. Chamberlayne, when you came to me two months ago
  I was dissatisfied with your explanation

Of your obvious symptoms of emotional strain
And so I made enquiries.

EDWARD.   It was two months ago
That your breakdown began! and I never noticed it.

LAVINIA. You wouldn't notice anything. You never noticed *me*.

REILLY. Now, I want to point out to both of you
How much you have in common. Indeed, I consider
That you are exceptionally well-suited to each other.
Mr. Chamberlayne, when you thought your wife had left you,
You discovered, to your surprise and consternation,
That you were not really in love with Miss Coplestone . . .

LAVINIA. My husband has never been in love with anybody.

REILLY. And were not prepared to make the least sacrifice
On her account. This injured your vanity.
You liked to think of yourself as a passionate lover.
Then you realised, what your wife has justly remarked,
That you had never been in love with anybody;
Which made you suspect that you were incapable
Of loving. To men of a certain type
The suspicion that they are incapable of loving
Is as disturbing to their self-esteem
As, in cruder men, the fear of impotence.

LAVINIA. You *are* cold-hearted, Edward.

REILLY.   So you say, Mrs. Chamberlayne.
And now, let us turn to your side of the problem.
When you discovered that your young friend
(Though you knew, in your heart, that he was not in love with you,
And were always humiliated by the awareness
That you had forced him into this position) —
When, I say, you discovered that your young friend
Had actually fallen in love with Miss Coplestone,
It took you some time, I have no doubt,
Before you would admit it. Though perhaps you knew it
Before he did. You pretended to yourself,
I suspect, and for as long as you could,
That he was aiming at a higher social distinction
Than the honour conferred by being *your* lover.
When you had to face the fact that his feelings towards her
Were different from any you had aroused in him —
It was a shock. You had wanted to be loved;

409

You had come to see that no one had ever loved you.
Then you began to fear that no one *could* love you.

EDWARD. I'm beginning to feel very sorry for you, Lavinia.
You know, you really are exceptionally unlovable,
And I never quite knew why. I thought it was *my* fault.

REILLY. And now you begin to see, I hope,
How much you have in common. The same isolation.
A man who finds himself incapable of loving
And a woman who finds that no man can love her.

LAVINIA. It seems to me that what we have in common
Might be just enough to make us loathe one another.

REILLY. See it rather as the bond which holds you together.
While still in a state of unenlightenment,
You could always say: 'he could not love any woman;'
You could always say: 'no man could love her.'
You could accuse each other of your own faults,
And so could avoid understanding each other.
Now, you have only to reverse the propositions
And put them together.

LAVINIA. Is that possible?

REILLY. If I had sent either of you to the sanatorium
In the state in which you came to me — I tell you this:
It would have been a horror beyond your imagining,
For you would have been left with what you brought with you:
The shadow of desires of desires. A prey
To the devils who arrive at their plenitude of power
When they have you to themselves.

LAVINIA. Then what can we do
When we can go neither back nor forward? Edward!
What can we do?

REILLY. You have answered your own question,
Though you do not know the meaning of what you have
said.

EDWARD. Lavinia, we must make the best of a bad job.
That is what he means.

REILLY. When you find, Mr. Chamberlayne,
The best of a bad job is all any of us make of it —
Except of course, the saints — such as those who go
To the sanatorium — you will forget this phrase,
And in forgetting it will alter the condition.

LAVINIA. Edward, there *is* that hotel in the New Forest
    If you want to go there. The proprietor
    Who has just taken over, is a friend of Alex's.
    I could go down with you, and then leave you there
    If you want to be alone . . .
EDWARD.   But I can't go away!
    I have a case coming on next Monday.
LAVINIA. Then will you stop at your club?
EDWARD.   No, they won't let me.
    I must leave tomorrow — but how did you know
    I was staying at the club?
LAVINIA.   Really, Edward!
    I have *some* sense of responsibility.
    I was going to leave some shirts there for you.
EDWARD. It seems to me that I might as well go home.
LAVINIA. Then we can share a taxi, and be economical.
    Edward, have you anything else to ask him
    Before we go?
EDWARD.   Yes, I have.
    But it's difficult to say.
LAVINIA.   But I wish you would say it.
    At least, there is something I would like you to ask.
EDWARD. It's about the future of . . . the others.
    I don't want to build on other people's ruins.
LAVINIA. Exactly. And I have a question too.
    Sir Henry, was it you who sent those telegrams?
REILLY. I think I will dispose of your husband's problem.
    [*To* EDWARD] Your business is not to clear your conscience
    But to learn how to bear the burdens on your conscience.
    With the future of the others you are not concerned.
LAVINIA. I think you have answered my question too.
    They had to tell us, themselves, that they had made their decision.
EDWARD. Have you anything else to say to us, Sir Henry?
REILLY. No. Not in this capacity.
       [EDWARD *takes out his cheque-book.* REILLY *raises his hand*]
    My secretary will send you my account.
    Go in peace. And work out your salvation with diligence.
                         [*Exeunt* EDWARD *and* LAVINIA]
[REILLY *goes to the couch and lies down. The house-telephone rings. He
gets up and answers it.*]

REILLY. Yes? . . . Yes. Come in.

[*Enter* JULIA *by side door*]

                                 She's waiting downstairs.

JULIA. I know that, Henry. I brought her here myself.

REILLY. Oh? You didn't let her know you were seeing me first?

JULIA. Of course not. I dropped her at the door
    And went on in the taxi, round the corner;
    Waited a moment, and slipped in by the back way.
    I only came to tell you, I am sure she is ready
    To make a decision.

REILLY.   Was she reluctant?
    Was that why you brought her?

JULIA.   Oh no, not reluctant:
    Only diffident. She cannot believe
    That you will take her seriously.

REILLY.   That is not uncommon.

JULIA. Or that she deserves to be taken seriously.

REILLY. That is most uncommon.

JULIA.   Henry, get up.
    You can't be as tired as that. I shall wait in the next room,
    And come back when she's gone.

REILLY.   Yes, when she's gone.

JULIA. Will Alex be here?

REILLY.   Yes, he'll be here.

                               [*Exit* JULIA *by side door*]

    [REILLY *presses button.* NURSE-SECRETARY *shows in* CELIA]

REILLY. Miss Celia Coplestone? . . . Won't you sit down?
    I believe you are a friend of Mrs. Shuttlethwaite.

CELIA. Yes, it was Julia . . . Mrs. Shuttlethwaite
    Who advised me to come to you. — But I've met you before,
    Haven't I, somewhere? . . . Oh, of course.
    But I didn't know . . .

REILLY.   There is nothing you need to know.
    I was there at the instance of Mrs. Shuttlethwaite.

CELIA. That makes it even more perplexing. However,
    I don't want to waste your time. And I'm awfully afraid
    That you'll think that I am wasting it anyway.
    I suppose most people, when they come to see you,
    Are obviously ill, or can give good reasons
    For wanting to see you. Well, I can't.

I just came in desperation. And I shan't be offended
If you simply tell me to go away again.

REILLY. Most of my patients begin, Miss Coplestone,
By telling me exactly what is the matter with them,
And what I am to do about it. They are quite sure
They have had a nervous breakdown — that is what they call it —
And usually they think that someone else is to blame.

CELIA. I at least have no one to blame but myself.

REILLY. And after that, the prologue to my treatment
Is to try to show them that they are mistaken
About the nature of their illness, and lead them to see
That it's not so interesting as they had imagined.
When I get as far as that, there is something to be done.

CELIA. Well, I can't pretend that my trouble is interesting;
But I shan't begin that way. I feel perfectly well.
I could lead an active life — if there's anything to work for;
I don't imagine that I am being persecuted;
I don't hear any voices, I have no delusions —
Except that the world I live in seems all a delusion!
But oughtn't I first to tell you the circumstances?
I'd forgotten that you know nothing about me;
And with what I've been going through, these last weeks,
I somehow took it for granted that I needn't explain myself.

REILLY. I know quite enough about you for the moment:
Try first to describe your present state of mind.

CELIA. Well, there are two things I can't understand,
Which you might consider symptoms. But first I must tell you
That I should really *like* to think there's something wrong with
     me —
Because, if there isn't, then there's something wrong,
Or at least, very different from what it seemed to be,
With the world itself — and that's much more frightening!
That would be terrible. So I'd rather believe
There is something wrong with me, that could be put right.
I'd do anything you told me, to get back to normality.

REILLY. We must find out about you, before we decide
What *is* normality. You say there are two things:
What is the first?

CELIA.   An awareness of solitude.
But that sounds so flat. I don't mean simply

413

That there's been a crash: though indeed there has been.
It isn't simply the end of an illusion
In the ordinary way, or being ditched.
Of course that's something that's always happening
To all sorts of people, and they get over it
More or less, or at least they carry on.
No. I mean that what has happened has made me aware
That I've always been alone. That one always is alone.
Not simply the ending of one relationship,
Not even simply finding that it never existed —
But a revelation about my relationship
With *everybody*. Do you know —
It no longer seems worth while to *speak* to anyone!

REILLY. And what about your parents?

CELIA.   Oh, they live in the country,
Now they can't afford to have a place in town.
It's all they can do to keep the country house going:
But it's been in the family so long, they won't leave it.

REILLY. And you live in London?

CELIA.   I share a flat
With a cousin: but she's abroad at the moment,
And my family want me to come down and stay with them.
But I just can't face it.

REILLY.   So you want to see no one?

CELIA. No . . . it isn't that I *want* to be alone,
But that everyone's alone — or so it seems to me.
They make noises, and think they are talking to each other;
They make faces, and think they understand each other.
And I'm sure that they don't. Is that a delusion?

REILLY. A delusion is something we must return from.
There are other states of mind, which we take to be delusion,
But which we have to accept and go on from.
And the second symptom?

CELIA.   That's stranger still.
It sounds ridiculous — but the only word for it
That I can find, is a sense of sin.

REILLY. You suffer from a sense of sin, Miss Coplestone?
This is most unusual.

CELIA.   It seemed to *me* abnormal.

REILLY. We have yet to find what would be normal

For *you*, before we use the term 'abnormal'.
Tell me what you mean by a sense of sin.
CELIA. It's much easier to tell you what I don't mean:
    I don't mean sin in the ordinary sense.
REILLY. And what, in your opinion, is the ordinary sense?
CELIA. Well ... I suppose it's being immoral —
    And I don't feel as if I was immoral:
    In fact, aren't the people one thinks of as immoral
    Just the people who we say have no moral sense?
    I've never noticed that immorality
    Was accompanied by a sense of sin:
    At least, I have never come across it.
    I suppose it is wicked to hurt other people
    If you know that you're hurting them. I haven't hurt
      her.
    I wasn't taking anything away from her —
    Anything she wanted. I may have been a fool:
    But I don't mind at all having been a fool.
REILLY. And what is the point of view of your family?
CELIA. Well, my bringing up was pretty conventional —
    I had always been taught to disbelieve in sin.
    Oh, I don't mean that it was ever mentioned!
    But anything wrong, from our point of view,
    Was either bad form, or was psychological.
    And bad form always led to disaster
    Because the people one knew disapproved of it.
    I don't worry much about form, myself —
    But when everything's bad form, or mental kinks,
    You either become bad form, and cease to care,
    Or else, if you care, you must be kinky.
REILLY. And so you suppose you have what you call a 'kink'?
CELIA. But everything seemed so right, at the time!
    I've been thinking about it, over and over;
    I can see now, it was all a mistake:
    But I don't see why mistakes should make one feel sinful!
    And yet I can't find any other word for it.
    It must be some kind of hallucination;
    Yet, at the same time, I'm frightened by the fear
    That it is more real than anything I believed in.
REILLY. What is more real than anything you believed in?

CELIA. It's not the feeling of anything I've ever *done*,
　　Which I might get away from, or of anything in me
　　I could get rid of — but of emptiness, of failure
　　Towards someone, or something, outside of myself;
　　And I feel I must . . . *atone* — is that the word?
　　Can you treat a patient for such a state of mind?
REILLY. What had you believed were your relations with this man?
CELIA. Oh, you'd guessed that, had you? That's clever of you.
　　No, perhaps I made it obvious. You don't need to know
　　About him, do you?
REILLY.　　　　　　No.
CELIA.　　　　　　　　　Perhaps I'm only typical.
REILLY. There are different types. Some are rarer than others.
CELIA. Oh, I thought that I was giving him so much!
　　And he to me — and the giving and the taking
　　Seemed so right: not in terms of calculation
　　Of what was good for the persons we had been
　　But for the new person, *us*. If I could feel
　　As I did then, even now it would seem right.
　　And then I found we were only strangers
　　And that there had been neither giving nor taking
　　But that we had merely made use of each other
　　Each for his purpose. That's horrible. Can we only love
　　Something created by our own imagination?
　　Are we all in fact unloving and unlovable?
　　Then one *is* alone, and if one is alone
　　Then lover and belovèd are equally unreal
　　And the dreamer is no more real than his dreams.
REILLY. And this man. What does he now seem like, to you?
CELIA. Like a child who has wandered into a forest
　　Playing with an imaginary playmate
　　And suddenly discovers he is only a child
　　Lost in a forest, wanting to go home.
REILLY. Compassion may be already a clue
　　Towards finding your own way out of the forest.
CELIA. But even if I find my way out of the forest
　　I shall be left with the inconsolable memory
　　Of the treasure I went into the forest to find
　　And never found, and which was not there
　　And perhaps is not anywhere? But if not anywhere,

Why do I feel guilty at not having found it?

REILLY. Disillusion can become itself an illusion
    If we rest in it.

CELIA.   I cannot argue.
    It's not that I'm afraid of being hurt again:
    Nothing again can either hurt or heal.
    I have thought at moments that the ecstasy is real
    Although those who experience it may have no reality.
    For what happened is remembered like a dream
    In which one is exalted by intensity of loving
    In the spirit, a vibration of delight
    Without desire, for desire is fulfilled
    In the delight of loving. A state one does not know
    When awake. But what, or whom I loved,
    Or what in me was loving, I do not know.
    And if that is all meaningless, I want to be cured
    Of a craving for something I cannot find
    And of the shame of never finding it.
    Can you cure me?

REILLY.   The condition is curable.
    But the form of treatment must be your own choice:
    I cannot choose for you. If that is what you wish,
    I can reconcile you to the human condition,
    The condition to which some who have gone as far as you
    Have succeeded in returning. They may remember
    The vision they have had, but they cease to regret it,
    Maintain themselves by the common routine,
    Learn to avoid excessive expectation,
    Become tolerant of themselves and others,
    Giving and taking, in the usual actions
    What there is to give and take. They do not repine;
    Are contented with the morning that separates
    And with the evening that brings together
    For casual talk before the fire
    Two people who know they do not understand each other,
    Breeding children whom they do not understand
    And who will never understand them.

CELIA.   Is that the best life?

REILLY. It is a good life. Though you will not know how good
    Till you come to the end. But you will want nothing else,

THE COCKTAIL PARTY

And the other life will be only like a book
You have read once, and lost. In a world of lunacy,
Violence, stupidity, greed . . . it is a good life.

CELIA. I know I ought to be able to accept that
If I might still have it. Yet it leaves me cold.
Perhaps that's just a part of my illness,
But I feel it would be a kind of surrender —
No, not a surrender — more like a betrayal.
You see, I think I really had a vision of something
Though I don't know what it is. I don't want to forget it.
I want to live with it. I could do without everything,
Put up with anything, if I might cherish it.
In fact, I think it would really be dishonest
For me, now, to try to make a life with *any*body!
I couldn't give anyone the kind of love —
I wish I could — which belongs to that life.
Oh, I'm afraid this sounds like raving!
Or just cantankerousness . . . still,
If there's no other way . . . then I feel just hopeless.

REILLY. There *is* another way, if you have the courage.
The first I could describe in familiar terms
Because you have seen it, as we all have seen it,
Illustrated, more or less, in lives of those about us.
The second is unknown, and so requires faith —
The kind of faith that issues from despair.
The destination cannot be described;
You will know very little until you get there;
You will journey blind. But the way leads towards possession
Of what you have sought for in the wrong place.

CELIA. That sounds like what I want. But what is my duty?

REILLY. Whichever way you choose will prescribe its own duty.

CELIA. Which way is better?

REILLY.   Neither way is better.
Both ways are necessary. It is also necessary
To make a choice between them.

CELIA.   Then I choose the second.

REILLY. It is a terrifying journey.

CELIA.   I am not frightened
But glad. I suppose it is a lonely way?

REILLY. No lonelier than the other. But those who take the other

418

Can forget their loneliness. You will not forget yours.
Each way means loneliness — and communion.
Both ways avoid the final desolation
Of solitude in the phantasmal world
Of imagination, shuffling memories and desires.

CELIA. That is the hell I have been in.

REILLY.   It isn't hell
Till you become incapable of anything else.
Now — do you feel quite sure?

CELIA.   I want your second way.
So what am I to do?

REILLY.   You will go to the sanatorium.

CELIA. Oh, what an anti-climax! I have known people
Who have been to your sanatorium, and come back again —
I don't mean to say they weren't much better for it —
That's why I came to you. But they returned . . .
Well . . . I mean . . . to everyday life.

REILLY. True. But the friends you have in mind
Cannot have been to this sanatorium.
I am very careful whom I send there:
Those who go do not come back as these did.

CELIA. It sounds like a prison. But they can't *all* stay there!
I mean, it would make the place so over-crowded.

REILLY. Not very many go. But I said they did not come back
In the sense in which your friends came back.
I did not say they stayed there.

CELIA.   What becomes of them?

REILLY. They choose, Miss Coplestone. Nothing is forced on them.
Some of them return, in a physical sense;
No one disappears. They lead very active lives
Very often, in the world.

CELIA.   How soon will you send me there?

REILLY. How soon will you be ready?

CELIA.   Tonight, by nine o'clock.

REILLY. Go home then, and make your preparations.
Here is the address for you to give your friends;
                    [*Writes on a slip of paper*]
You had better let your family know at once.
I will send a car for you at nine o'clock.

CELIA. What do I need to take with me?

419

REILLY.   Nothing.

Everything you need will be provided for you,

And you will have no expenses at the sanatorium.

CELIA. I don't in the least know what I am doing

Or why I am doing it. There is nothing else to do:

That is the only reason.

REILLY.   It is the best reason.

CELIA. But I know it is I who have made the decision:

I must tell you that. Oh, I almost forgot —

May I ask what your fee is?

REILLY.   I have told my secretary

That there is no fee.

CELIA.   But . . .

REILLY.   For a case like yours

There is no fee.

[*Presses button*]

CELIA.   You have been very kind.

REILLY. Go in peace, my daughter.

Work out your salvation with diligence.

[NURSE-SECRETARY *appears at door. Exit* CELIA. REILLY *dials on house-telephone.*]

REILLY [*into telephone*]. It is finished. You can come in now.

[*Enter* JULIA *by side door*]

She will go far, that one.

JULIA.   Very far, I think.

You do not need to tell me. I knew from the beginning.

REILLY. It's the other ones I am worried about.

JULIA. Nonsense, Henry. *I* shall keep an eye on them.

REILLY. To send them back: what have they to go back to?

To the stale food mouldering in the larder,

The stale thoughts mouldering in their minds.

Each unable to disguise his own meanness

From himself, because it is known to the other.

It's not the knowledge of the mutual treachery

But the knowledge that the other understands the motive —

Mirror to mirror, reflecting vanity.

I have taken a great risk.

JULIA.   We must always take risks.

That is our destiny. Since you question the decision

What possible alternative can you imagine?

REILLY. None.

JULIA. Very well then. We must take the risk.
All we could do was to give them the chance.
And now, when they are stripped naked to their souls
And can choose, whether to put on proper costumes
Or huddle quickly into new disguises,
They have, for the first time, somewhere to start from.
Oh, of course, they might just murder each other!
But I don't think they will do that. We shall see.
It's the thought of Celia that weighs upon my mind.

REILLY. Of Celia?

JULIA. Of Celia.

REILLY. But when I said just now
That she would go far, you agreed with me.

JULIA. Oh yes, she will go far. And we know where she is going.
But what do we know of the terrors of the journey?
You and I don't know the process by which the human is
Transhumanised: what do we know
Of the kind of suffering they must undergo
On the way of illumination?

REILLY. Will she be frightened
By the first appearance of projected spirits?

JULIA. Henry, you simply do not understand innocence.
She will be afraid of nothing; she will not even know
That there is anything there to be afraid of.
She is too humble. She will pass between the scolding hills,
Through the valley of derision, like a child sent on an errand
In eagerness and patience. Yet she must suffer.

REILLY. When I express confidence in anything
You always raise doubts; when I am apprehensive
Then you see no reason for anything but confidence.

JULIA. That's one way in which I am so useful to you.
You ought to be grateful.

REILLY. And when I say to one like her
'Work out your salvation with diligence', I do not understand
What I myself am saying.

JULIA. You must accept your limitations.
— But how much longer will Alex keep us waiting?

REILLY. He should be here by now. I'll speak to Miss Barraway.

[*Takes up house-telephone*]

421

Miss Barraway, when Mr. Gibbs arrives . . .

Oh, very good.

[*To* JULIA] He's on his way up.

[*Into telephone*]

You may bring the tray in now, Miss Barraway.

[*Enter* ALEX]

ALEX. Well! Well! and how have we got on?

JULIA.   Everything is in order.

ALEX. The Chamberlaynes have chosen?

REILLY.   They accept their destiny.

ALEX. And *she* has made the choice?

REILLY.   She will be fetched this evening.

[NURSE-SECRETARY *enters with a tray, a decanter and three glasses, and exit.* REILLY *pours drinks.*]

And now we are ready to proceed to the libation.

ALEX. The words for the building of the hearth.

[*They raise their glasses*]

REILLY. Let them build the hearth

Under the protection of the stars.

ALEX. Let them place a chair each side of it.

JULIA. May the holy ones watch over the roof,

May the moon herself influence the bed.

[*They drink*]

ALEX. The words for those who go upon a journey.

REILLY. Protector of travellers

Bless the road.

ALEX. Watch over her in the desert.

Watch over her in the mountain.

Watch over her in the labyrinth.

Watch over her by the quicksand.

JULIA.

Protect her from the Voices

Protect her from the Visions

Protect her in the tumult

Protect her in the silence.

[*They drink*]

REILLY. There is one for whom the words cannot be spoken.

ALEX. They can not be spoken yet.

JULIA.   You mean Peter Quilpe.

REILLY. He has not yet come to where the words are valid.

JULIA. Shall we ever speak them?

ALEX.   Others, perhaps, will speak them.
   You know, I have connections — even in California.

CURTAIN

Act Three

The drawing-room of the Chamberlaynes' London flat. Two years later.
A late afternoon in July. A CATERER'S MAN *is arranging a buffet*
table. LAVINIA *enters from side door.*

CATERER'S MAN. Have you any further orders for us, Madam?

LAVINIA. You could bring in the trolley with the glasses
    And leave them ready.

CATERER'S MAN.   Very good, Madam.

[*Exit.* LAVINIA *looks about the room critically and moves a bowl of flowers.*]
[*Re-enter* CATERER'S MAN *with trolley*]

LAVINIA. There, in that corner. That's the most convenient;
    You can get in and out. Is there anything you need
    That you can't find in the kitchen?

CATERER'S MAN.   Nothing, Madam.
    Will there be anything more you require?

LAVINIA. Nothing more, I think, till half past six.

                                        [*Exit* CATERER'S MAN]

[EDWARD *lets himself in at the front door*]

EDWARD. I'm in good time, I think. I hope you've not been worrying.

LAVINIA. Oh no. I did in fact ring up your chambers,
    And your clerk told me you had already left.
    But all I rang up for was to reassure you . . .

EDWARD [*smiling*]. That you hadn't run away?

LAVINIA.   Now Edward, that's unfair!
    You know that we've given *several* parties
    In the last two years. And I've attended *all* of them.
    I hope you're not too tired?

EDWARD.   Oh no, a quiet day.
    Two consultations with solicitors
    On quite straightforward cases. It's you who should be tired.

LAVINIA. I'm not tired yet. But I know that I'll be glad
    When it's all over.

EDWARD.   I like the dress you're wearing:

424

I'm glad you put on that one.

LAVINIA. Well, Edward!
Do you know it's the first time you've paid me a compliment
Before a party? And that's when one needs them.

EDWARD. Well, you deserve it. — We asked too many people.

LAVINIA. It's true, a great many more accepted
Than we thought would want to come. But what can you do?
There's usually a lot who don't want to come
But all the same would be bitterly offended
To hear we'd given a party without asking them.

EDWARD. Perhaps we ought to have arranged to have two parties
Instead of one.

LAVINIA. That's never satisfactory.
Everyone who's asked to either party
Suspects that the other one was more important.

EDWARD. That's true. You have a very practical mind.

LAVINIA. But you know, I don't think that you need worry:
They won't all come, out of those who accepted.
You know we said, 'we can ask twenty more
Because they will be going to the Gunnings instead'.

EDWARD. I know, that's what we said at the time;
But I'd forgotten what the Gunnings' parties were like.
Their guests will get just enough to make them thirsty;
They'll come on to us later, roaring for drink.
Well, let's hope that those who come to us early
Will be going on to the Gunnings afterwards,
To make room for those who come from the Gunnings.

LAVINIA. And if it's very crowded, they can't get at the
cocktails,
And the man won't be able to take the tray about,
So they'll go away again. Anyway, at that stage
There's nothing whatever you can do about it:
And everyone likes to be seen at a party
Where everybody else is, to show they've been invited.
That's what makes it a success. Is that picture straight?

EDWARD. Yes, it is.

LAVINIA. No, it isn't. Do please straighten it.

EDWARD. Is it straight now?

LAVINIA. Too much to the left.

EDWARD. How's that now?

LAVINIA.   No, I meant the right.
   That will do. I'm too tired to bother.
EDWARD. After they're all gone, we will have some champagne,
   Just ourselves. You lie down now, Lavinia
   No one will be coming for at least half an hour;
   So just stretch out.
LAVINIA.   You must sit beside me,
   Then I can relax.
EDWARD.   This is the best moment
   Of the whole party.
LAVINIA.   Oh no, Edward.
   The best moment is the moment it's over;
   And then to remember, it's the end of the season
   And no more parties.
EDWARD.   And no more committees.
LAVINIA. Can we get away soon?
EDWARD.   By the end of next week
   I shall be quite free.
LAVINIA.   And we can be alone.
   I love that house being so remote.
EDWARD. That's why we took it. And I'm really thankful
   To have that excuse for not seeing people;
   And you do need to rest now.

                    [*The doorbell rings*]
LAVINIA.   Oh, bother!
   Now who would come so early? I simply *can't* get up.
CATERER'S MAN. Mrs. Shuttlethwaite!
LAVINIA.   Oh, it's Julia!
[*Enter* JULIA]
JULIA. Well, my dears, and here I am!
   I seem *literally* to have caught you napping!
   I know I'm much too early; but the fact is, my dears,
   That I have to go on to the Gunnings' party —
   And you know what *they* offer in the way of food and drink!
   And I've had to miss my tea, and I'm simply ravenous
   And dying of thirst. What can Parkinson's do for me?
   Oh yes, I know this is a Parkinson party;
   I recognised one of their men at the door —
   An old friend of mine, in fact. But I'm forgetting!
   I've got a surprise: I've brought Alex with me!

426

He only got back this morning from somewhere —
One of his mysterious expeditions,
And we're going to get him to tell us all about it.
But what's become of him?

[*Enter* ALEX]

EDWARD.   Well, Alex!
Where on earth do you turn up from?

ALEX. Where on earth? From the East. From Kinkanja —
An island that you won't have heard of
Yet. Got back this morning. I heard about your party
And, as I thought you might be leaving for the country,
I said, I must not miss the opportunity
To see Edward and Lavinia.

LAVINIA.   How are you, Alex?

ALEX. I did try to get you on the telephone
After lunch, but my secretary couldn't get through to you.
Never mind, I said — to myself, not to her —
Never mind: the unexpected guest
Is the one to whom they give the warmest welcome.
I know them well enough for that.

JULIA.   But tell us, Alex.
What were you doing in this strange place —
What's it called?

ALEX.   Kinkanja.

JULIA.   What were you doing
In Kinkanja? Visiting some Sultan?
You were shooting tigers?

ALEX.   There are no tigers, Julia,
In Kinkanja. And there are no sultans.
I have been staying with the Governor.
Three of us have been out on a tour of inspection
Of local conditions.

JULIA.   What about? Monkey nuts?

ALEX. That was a nearer guess than you think.
No, not monkey nuts. But it had to do with monkeys —
Though whether the monkeys are the core of the problem
Or merely a symptom, I am not so sure.
At least, the monkeys have become the pretext
For general unrest amongst the natives.

EDWARD. But how do the monkeys create unrest?

ALEX. To begin with, the monkeys are very destructive . . .

JULIA. You don't need to tell me that monkeys are destructive.
  I shall never forget Mary Mallington's monkey,
  The horrid little beast — stole my ticket to Mentone
  And I had to travel in a very slow train
  And in a *couchette*. She was very angry
  When I told her the creature ought to be destroyed.

LAVINIA. But can't they exterminate these monkeys
  If they are a pest?

ALEX.   Unfortunately,
  The majority of the natives are heathen:
  They hold these monkeys in peculiar veneration
  And do not want them killed. So they blame the Government
  For the damage that the monkeys do.

EDWARD. That seems unreasonable.

ALEX.   It is unreasonable,
  But characteristic. And that's not the worst of it.
  Some of the tribes are Christian converts,
  And, naturally, take a different view.
  They trap the monkeys. And they eat them.
  The young monkeys are extremely palatable:
  I've cooked them myself . . .

EDWARD.   And did anybody eat them
  When you cooked them?

ALEX.   Oh yes, indeed.
  I invented for the natives several new recipes.
  But you see, what with eating the monkeys
  And what with protecting their crops from the monkeys
  The Christian natives prosper exceedingly:
  And that creates friction between them and the others.
  And that's the real problem. I hope I'm not boring you?

EDWARD. No indeed: we are anxious to learn the solution.

ALEX. I'm not sure that there *is* any solution.
  But even this does not bring us to the heart of the matter.
  There are also foreign agitators,
  Stirring up trouble . . .

LAVINIA.   Why don't you expel them?

ALEX. They are citizens of a friendly neighbouring state
  Which we have just recognised. You see, Lavinia,
  These are very deep waters.

EDWARD.   And the agitators;
     How do they agitate?
ALEX.   By convincing the heathen
     That the slaughter of monkeys has put a curse on them
     Which can only be removed by slaughtering the Christians.
     They have even been persuading some of the converts —
     Who, after all, prefer not to be slaughtered —
     To relapse into heathendom. So, instead of eating monkeys
     They are eating Christians.
JULIA.   Who have eaten monkeys.
ALEX. The native is not, I fear, very logical.
JULIA. I wondered where you were taking us, with your
          monkeys.
     I thought I was going to dine out on those monkeys:
     But one can't dine out on eating Christians —
     Even among pagans!
ALEX.   Not on the *whole* story.
EDWARD. And have any of the English residents been murdered?
ALEX. Yes, but they are not usually eaten.
     When these people have done with a European
     He is, as a rule, no longer fit to eat.
EDWARD. And what has your commission accomplished?
ALEX. We have just drawn up an interim report.
EDWARD. Will it be made public?
ALEX.   It cannot be, at present:
     There are too many international complications.
     Eventually, there may be an official publication.
EDWARD. But when?
ALEX.   In a year or two.
EDWARD.   And meanwhile?
ALEX. Meanwhile the monkeys multiply.
LAVINIA.   And the Christians?
ALEX. Ah, the Christians! Now, I think I ought to tell you
     About someone you know — or knew ...
JULIA.   Edward!
     Somebody must have walked over my grave:
     I'm feeling so chilly. Give me some gin.
     Not a cocktail. I'm freezing — in July!
CATERER'S MAN. Mr. Quilpe!
EDWARD.   Now who ...

[*Enter* PETER]

Why, it's Peter!

LAVINIA. Peter!

PETER.   Hullo, everybody!

LAVINIA.   When did you arrive?

PETER. I flew over from New York last night —
   I left Los Angeles three days ago.
   I saw Sheila Paisley at lunch to-day
   And she told me you were giving a party —
   She's coming on later, after the Gunnings —
   So I said, I really must crash in:
   It's my only chance to see Edward and Lavinia.
   I'm only over for a week, you see,
   And I'm driving down to the country this evening,
   So I knew you wouldn't mind my looking in so early.
   It does seem ages since I last saw any of you!
   And how are you, Alex? And dear old Julia!

LAVINIA. So you've just come from New York.

PETER.   Yes, from New York.
   The Bologolomskys saw me off.
   You remember Princess Bologolomsky
   In the old days? We dined the other night
   At the Saffron Monkey. That's the place to go now.

ALEX. How very odd. *My* monkeys are saffron.

PETER. Your monkeys, Alex? I always said
   That Alex knew everybody. But I didn't know
   That he knew any monkeys.

JULIA.   But give us your news;
   Give us your news of the world, Peter.
   We lead such a quiet life, here in London.

PETER. You always did enjoy a leg-pull, Julia:
   But you all know I'm working for Pan-Am-Eagle?

EDWARD. No. Tell us, what is Pan-Am-Eagle?

PETER. You must have been living a quiet life!
   Don't you go to the movies?

LAVINIA.   Occasionally.

PETER.   Alex knows.
   Did you see my last picture, Alex?

ALEX. I knew about it, but I didn't see it.
   There is no cinema in Kinkanja.

PETER. Kinkanja? Where's that? They don't have pictures?
Pan-Am-Eagle must look into this.
Perhaps it would be a good place to make one.
— Alex knows all about Pan-Am-Eagle:
It was he who introduced me to the great Bela.

JULIA. And who is the great Bela?

PETER.   Why, Bela Szogody —
He's my boss. I thought everyone knew *his* name.

JULIA. Is he your connection in California, Alex?

ALEX. Yes, we have sometimes obliged each other.

PETER. Well, it was Bela sent me over
Just for a week. And I have my hands full
I'm going down tonight, to Boltwell.

JULIA. To stay with the Duke?

PETER.   And do him a good turn.
We're making a film of English life
And we want to use Boltwell.

JULIA.   But I understood that Boltwell
Is in a very decayed condition.

PETER. Exactly. It is. And that's why we're interested.
The most decayed noble mansion in England!
At least, of any that are still inhabited.
We've got a team of experts over
To study the decay, so as to reproduce it.
Then we build another Boltwell in California.

JULIA. But what is your position, Peter?
Have you become an expert on decaying houses?

PETER. Oh dear no! I've written the script of this film,
And Bela is very pleased with it.
He thought I should see the original Boltwell;
And besides, he thought that as I'm English
I ought to know the best way to handle a duke.
Besides that, we've got the casting director:
He's looking for some typical English faces —
Of course, only for minor parts —
And I'll help him decide what faces are typical.

JULIA. Peter, I've thought of a wonderful idea!
I've always wanted to go to California:
Couldn't you persuade your casting director
To take us all over? We're all very typical.

PETER. No, I'm afraid . . .

CATERER'S MAN.   Sir Henry Harcourt-Reilly!

JULIA. Oh, I forgot! I'd another surprise for you.

[*Enter* REILLY]

    I want you to meet Sir Henry Harcourt-Reilly —

EDWARD. We're delighted to see him. But we *have* met before.

JULIA. Then if you know him already, you won't be afraid of him.

    You know, I was afraid of him at first:

    He looks so forbidding . . .

REILLY.   My dear Julia,

    You are giving me a very bad introduction —

    Supposing that an introduction was necessary.

JULIA. My dear Henry, you are interrupting me.

LAVINIA. If you can interrupt Julia, Sir Henry,

    You are the perfect guest we've been waiting for.

REILLY. I should not dream of trying to interrupt Julia . . .

JULIA. But you're both interrupting!

REILLY.   Who is interrupting now?

JULIA. Well, you shouldn't interrupt my interruptions:

    That's really worse than interrupting.

    Now my head's fairly spinning. I must have a cocktail.

EDWARD. [*To* REILLY]. And will you have a cocktail?

REILLY.   Might I have a glass of water?

EDWARD. Anything with it?

REILLY.   Nothing, thank you.

LAVINIA. May I introduce Mr. Peter Quilpe?

    Sir Henry Harcourt-Reilly. Peter's an old friend

    Of my husband and myself. Oh, I forgot —

                      [*Turning to* ALEX]

    I rather assumed that you knew each other —

    I don't know why I should. Mr. MacColgie Gibbs.

ALEX. Indeed, yes, we have met.

REILLY.   On several commissions.

JULIA. We've been having such an interesting conversation.

    Peter's just over from California

    Where he's something very important in films.

    He's making a film of English life

    And he's going to find parts for all of us. Think of it!

PETER. But, Julia, I was just about to explain —

    I'm afraid I can't find parts for anybody

In *this* film — it's not my business;
And that's not the way we do it.

JULIA.   But, Peter;
If you're taking Boltwell to California
Why can't you take me?

PETER.   We're not taking Boltwell.
We reconstruct a Boltwell.

JULIA.   Very well, then:
Why not reconstruct *me*? It's very much cheaper.
Oh, dear, I can see you're determined not to have me:
So good-bye to my hopes of seeing California.

PETER. You know you'd never come if we invited you.
But there's someone I wanted to ask about,
Who did really want to get into films,
And I always thought she could make a success of it
If she only got the chance. It's Celia Coplestone.
She always wanted to. And now I could help her.
I've already spoken to Bela about her,
And I want to introduce her to our cast'ng director.
I've got an idea for another film.
Can you tell me where she is? I couldn't find her
In the telephone directory.

JULIA.   Not in the directory,
Or in any directory. You can tell them now, Alex.

LAVINIA. What does Julia mean?

ALEX.   I was about to speak of her
When you came in, Peter. I'm afraid you can't have Celia.

PETER. Oh . . . Is she married?

ALEX.   Not married, but dead.

LAVINIA. Celia?

ALEX.   Dead.

PETER.   Dead. That knocks the bottom out of it.

EDWARD. Celia dead.

JULIA.   You had better tell them, Alex,
The news that you bring back from Kinkanja.

LAVINIA. Kinkanja? What was Celia doing in Kinkanja?
We heard that she had joined some nursing order . . .

ALEX. She had joined an order. A very austere one.
And as she already had experience of nursing . . .

LAVINIA. Yes, she had been a V.A.D. I remember.

ALEX. She was directed to Kinkanja,
Where there are various endemic diseases
Besides, of course, those brought by Europeans,
And where the conditions are favourable to plague.

EDWARD. Go on.

ALEX. It seems that there were three of them —
Three sisters at this station, in a Christian village;
And half the natives were dying of pestilence.
They must have been overworked for weeks.

EDWARD. And then?

ALEX. And then, the insurrection broke out
Among the heathen, of which I was telling you.
They knew of it, but would not leave the dying natives.
Eventually, two of them escaped:
One died in the jungle, and the other
Will never be fit for normal life again.
But Celia Coplestone, she was taken.
When our people got there, they questioned the villagers —
Those who survived. And then they found her body,
Or at least, they found the traces of it.

EDWARD. But before that . . .

ALEX. It was difficult to tell.
But from what we know of local practices
It would seem that she must have been crucified
Very near an ant-hill.

LAVINIA. But Celia! . . . Of all people . . .

EDWARD. And just for a handful of plague-stricken natives
Who would have died anyway.

ALEX. Yes, the patients died anyway;
Being tainted with the plague, they were not eaten.

LAVINIA. Oh, Edward, I'm so sorry — what a feeble thing to say!
But you know what I mean.

EDWARD. And you know what I'm thinking.

PETER. I don't understand at all. But then I've been away
For two years, and I don't know what happened
To Celia, during those two years.
Two years! Thinking about Celia.

EDWARD. It's the waste that I resent.

PETER. You know more than I do:
For *me*, it's everything else that's a waste.

Two years! And it was all a mistake.
Julia! Why don't *you* say anything?

JULIA. You gave her those two years, as best you could.

PETER. When did she . . . take up this career?

JULIA.   Two years ago.

PETER. Two years ago! I tried to forget about her,
Until I began to think myself a success
And got a little more self-confidence;
And then I thought about her again. More and more.
At first I did not want to know about Celia
And so I never asked. Then I wanted to know
And did not dare to ask. It took all my courage
To ask you about her just now; but I never thought
Of anything like this. I suppose I didn't know her,
I didn't understand her. I understand nothing.

REILLY. You understand your *métier*, Mr. Quilpe —
Which is the most that any of us can ask for.

PETER. And what a *métier*! I've tried to believe in it
So that I might believe in myself.
I thought I had ideas to make a revolution
In the cinema, that no one could ignore —
And here I am, making a second-rate film!
But I thought it was going to lead to something better,
And that seemed possible, while Celia was alive.
I wanted it, believed in it, for Celia.
And, of course, I wanted to do something for Celia —
But what mattered was, that Celia was alive.
And now it's all worthless. Celia's not alive.

LAVINIA. No, it's not all worthless, Peter. You've only just begun.
I mean, this only brings you to the point
At which you *must* begin. You were saying just now
That you never knew Celia. We none of us did.
What you've been living on is an image of Celia
Which you made for yourself, to meet your own needs.
Peter, please don't think I'm being unkind . . .

PETER. No, I don't think you're being unkind, Lavinia;
And I know that you're right.

LAVINIA.   And perhaps what I've been saying
Will seem less unkind if I can make you understand
That in fact I've been talking about myself.

435

EDWARD. Lavinia is right. This is where you start from.
　　　If you find out now, Peter, things about yourself
　　　That you don't like to face: well, just remember
　　　That some men have to learn much worse things
　　　About themselves, and learn them later
　　　When it's harder to recover, and make a new beginning.
　　　It's not so hard for you. You're naturally good.
PETER. I'm sorry. I don't believe I've taken in
　　　All that you've been saying. But I'm grateful all the same.
　　　You know, all the time that you've been talking,
　　　One thought has been going round and round in my head —
　　　That I've only been interested in myself:
　　　And that isn't good enough for Celia.
JULIA. You must have learned how to look at people, Peter,
　　　When you look at them with an eye for the films:
　　　That is, when you're not concerned with yourself
　　　But just being an eye. You will come to think of Celia
　　　Like that, one day. And then you'll understand her
　　　And be reconciled, and be happy in the thought of her.
LAVINIA. Sir Henry, there is something I want to say to you.
　　　While Alex was telling us what had happened to Celia
　　　I was looking at your face. And it seemed from your expression
　　　That the way in which she died did not disturb you
　　　Or the fact that she died because she would not leave
　　　A few dying natives.
REILLY. 　　　　　　　Who knows, Mrs. Chamberlayne,
　　　The difference that made to the natives who were dying
　　　Or the state of mind in which they died?
LAVINIA. I'm willing to grant that. What struck me, though,
　　　Was that your face showed no surprise or horror
　　　At the way in which she died. I don't know if you knew her.
　　　I suspect that you did. In any case you knew *about* her.
　　　Yet I thought your expression was one of . . . satisfaction!
REILLY. Mrs. Chamberlayne, I must be very transparent
　　　Or else you are very perceptive.
JULIA. 　　　　　　　　　　　Oh, Henry!
　　　Lavinia is much more observant than you think.
　　　I believe that she has forced you to a show-down.
REILLY. You state the position correctly, Julia.
　　　Do you mind if I quote poetry, Mrs. Chamberlayne?

LAVINIA. Oh no, I should love to hear you speaking poetry . . .
JULIA. She has made a point, Henry.
LAVINIA.   . . . if it answers my question.
REILLY.   *Ere Babylon was dust*

> *The magus Zoroaster, my dead child,*
> *Met his own image walking in the garden.*
> *That apparition, sole of men, he saw.*
> *For know there are two worlds of life and death:*
> *One that which thou beholdest; but the other*
> *Is underneath the grave, where do inhabit*
> *The shadows of all forms that think and live*
> *Till death unite them and they part no more!*

> When I first met Miss Coplestone, in this room,
> I saw the image, standing behind her chair,
> Of a Celia Coplestone whose face showed the astonishment
> Of the first five minutes after a violent death.
> If this strains your credulity, Mrs. Chamberlayne,
> I ask you only to entertain the suggestion
> That a sudden intuition, in certain minds,
> May tend to express itself at once in a picture.
> That happens to me, sometimes. So it was obvious
> That here was a woman under sentence of death.
> That was her destiny. The only question
> Then was, what sort of death? *I* could not know;
> Because it was for her to choose the way of life
> To lead to death, and, without knowing the end
> Yet choose the form of death. We know the death she chose.
> I did not know that she would die in this way;
> *She* did not know. So all that I could do
> Was to direct her in the way of preparation.
> That way, which she accepted, led to this death.
> And if that is not a happy death, what death is happy?

EDWARD. Do you mean that having chosen this form of death
> She did not suffer as ordinary people suffer?
REILLY. Not at all what I mean. Rather the contrary.
> I'd say that she suffered all that we should suffer
> In fear and pain and loathing — all these together —
> And reluctance of the body to become a *thing*.
> I'd say she suffered more, because more conscious

Than the rest of us. She paid the highest price
In suffering. That is part of the design.

LAVINIA. Perhaps she had been through greater agony beforehand.
I mean — I know nothing of her last two years.

REILLY. That shows some insight on your part, Mrs. Chamberlayne;
But such experience can only be hinted at
In myths and images. To speak about it
We talk of darkness, labyrinths, Minotaur terrors.
But that world does not take the place of this one.
Do you imagine that the Saint in the desert
With spiritual evil always at his shoulder
Suffered any less from hunger, damp, exposure,
Bowel trouble, and the fear of lions,
Cold of the night and heat of the day, than we should?

EDWARD. But if this was right — if this was right for Celia —
There must be something else that is terribly wrong,
And the rest of us are somehow involved in the wrong.
I should only speak for myself. I'm sure that *I* am.

REILLY. Let me free your mind from one impediment:
You must try to detach yourself from what you still feel
As your responsibility.

EDWARD.   I cannot help the feeling
That, in some way, my responsibility
Is greater than that of a band of half-crazed savages.

LAVINIA. Oh, Edward, I knew! I knew what you were thinking!
Doesn't it help you, that I feel guilty too?

REILLY. If we all were judged according to the consequences
Of all our words and deeds, beyond the intention
And beyond our limited understanding
Of ourselves and others, we should all be condemned.
Mrs. Chamberlayne, I often have to make a decision
Which may mean restoration or ruin to a patient —
And sometimes I have made the wrong decision.
As for Miss Coplestone, because you think her death was waste
You blame yourselves, and because you blame yourselves
You think her life was wasted. It was triumphant.
But I am no more responsible for the triumph —
And just as responsible for her death as you are.

LAVINIA. Yet I know I shall go on blaming myself
For being so unkind to her . . . so spiteful.

I shall go on seeing her at the moment
When she said good-bye to us, two years ago.

EDWARD. Your responsibility is nothing to mine, Lavinia.

LAVINIA. I'm not sure about that. If I had understood you
Then I might not have misunderstood Celia.

REILLY. You will have to live with these memories and make them
Into something new. Only by acceptance
Of the past will you alter its meaning.

JULIA. Henry, I think it is time that *I* said something:
Everyone makes a choice, of one kind or another,
And then must take the consequences. Celia chose
A way of which the consequence was Kinkanja.
Peter chose a way that leads him to Boltwell:
And he's got to go there . . .

PETER.   I see what you mean.
I wish I didn't have to. But the car will be waiting,
And the experts — I'd almost forgotten them.
I realise that I can't get out of it —
And what else can I do?

ALEX.   It is your film.
And I know that Bela expects great things of it.

PETER. So now I'll be going.

EDWARD.   Shall we see you again, Peter,
Before you leave England?

LAVINIA.   Do try to come to see us.
You know, I think it would do us all good —
You and me and Edward . . . to talk about Celia.

PETER. Thanks very much. But not this time —
I simply shan't be able to.

EDWARD.   But on your next visit?

PETER. The next time I come to England, I promise you.
I really do want to see you both, very much.
Good-bye, Julia. Good-bye, Alex. Good-bye, Sir Henry.   [*Exit*]

JULIA. . . . And now the consequence of the Chamberlaynes' choice
Is a cocktail party. They must be ready for it.
Their guests may be arriving at any moment.

REILLY. Julia, you are right. It is also right
That the Chamberlaynes should now be giving a party.

LAVINIA. And I have been thinking, for these last five minutes,
How I could face my guests. I wish it was over.

I mean ... I am glad you came ... I am glad Alex told us ...
And Peter had to know ...

EDWARD.   Now I think I understand ...

LAVINIA. Then I hope you will explain it to me!

EDWARD.   Oh, it isn't much
That I understand yet! But Sir Henry has been saying,
I think, that every moment is a fresh beginning;
And Julia, that life is only keeping on;
And somehow, the two ideas seem to fit together.

LAVINIA. But all the same ... I don't want to see these people.

REILLY. It is your appointed burden. And as for the party,
I am sure it will be a success.

JULIA.   And I think, Henry,
That we should leave before the party begins.
They will get on better without us. You too, Alex.

LAVINIA. We don't *want* you to go!

ALEX.   We have another engagement.

REILLY. And on this occasion I shall not be unexpected.

JULIA. Now, Henry. Now, Alex. We're going to the Gunnings.

                              [*Exeunt* JULIA, REILLY *and* ALEX]

LAVINIA. Edward, how am I looking?

EDWARD.   Very well.
I might almost say, your best. But you always look your best.

LAVINIA. Oh, Edward, that spoils it. No woman can believe
That she always looks her best. You're rather transparent,
You know, when you're trying to cheer me up.
To say I always look my best can only mean the worst.

EDWARD. I never shall learn how to pay a compliment.

LAVINIA. What you should have done was to admire my dress.

EDWARD. But I've already told you how much I like it.

LAVINIA. But so much has happened since then. And besides,
One sometimes likes to hear the same compliment twice.

EDWARD. And now for the party.

LAVINIA.   Now for the party.

EDWARD. It will soon be over.

LAVINIA.   I wish it would begin.

EDWARD. There's the doorbell.

LAVINIA.   Oh, I'm glad. It's begun.

CURTAIN

The tune of *One-eyed Riley* (page 137), as scored from the author's dictation by Miss Mary Trevelyan.

The Cast of the First Production
at the
Edinburgh Festival,
August 22–27, 1949

Edward Chamberlayne	ROBERT FLEMYNG
Julia (Mrs. Shuttlethwaite)	CATHLEEN NESBITT
Celia Coplestone	IRENE WORTH
Alexander MacColgie Gibbs	ERNEST CLARK
Peter Quilpe	DONALD HOUSTON
An Unidentified Guest, *later identified* as Sir Henry Harcourt-Reilly	ALEC GUINNESS
Lavinia Chamberlayne	URSULA JEANS
A Nurse-Secretary	CHRISTINA HORNIMAN
Two Caterer's Men	{ DONALD BAIN MARTIN BECKWITH

Directed by E. MARTIN BROWNE
Settings designed by ANTHONY HOLLAND
Produced by SHEREK PLAYERS LTD.
in association with THE ARTS COUNCIL

THE CONFIDENTIAL CLERK

Characters

SIR CLAUDE MULHAMMER
EGGERSON
COLBY SIMPKINS
B. KAGHAN
LUCASTA ANGEL
LADY ELIZABETH MULHAMMER
MRS. GUZZARD

Act One

The Business Room on the first floor of SIR CLAUDE MULHAMMER'S
London house. Early afternoon. SIR CLAUDE *writing at desk. Enter*
EGGERSON.

SIR CLAUDE. Ah, there you are, Eggerson! Punctual as always.
I'm sorry to have to bring you up to London
All the way from Joshua Park, on an errand like this.
But you know my wife wouldn't like anyone to meet her
At Northolt, but you. And I couldn't send Colby.
That's not the way to arrange their first meeting,
On her return from Switzerland.
EGGERSON.   Impossible, Sir Claude!
A very delicate situation —
Her first meeting with Mr. Simpkins.
But I was glad of the excuse for coming up to London:
I've spent the morning shopping! Gardening tools.
The number of things one needs for a garden!
And I thought, now's the moment to buy some new tools
So as not to lose a moment at the end of the winter
And I matched some material for Mrs. E.,
Which she's been wanting. So *she*'ll be pleased.
Then I lunched at the store — they have a restaurant;
An excellent lunch, and cheap, for nowadays.
But where's Mr. Simpkins? Will he be here?
SIR CLAUDE. I had to send him to the City this morning,
But he'll be back, I hope, before you leave.
EGGERSON. And how's he getting on? Swimmingly, I'm sure,
As I've heard nothing since the last time I came.
SIR CLAUDE. Well, of course, Eggerson, you're irreplaceable . . .
EGGERSON. Oh, Sir Claude, you shouldn't say that!
Mr. Simpkins is far better qualified than I was
To be your confidential clerk.
He was finding his feet, very quickly,

445

    During the time we worked together.
    All he needs is confidence.

SIR CLAUDE.   And experience.
    With a young man, some readjustment is necessary.
    But I'm satisfied that he's getting the hang of things,
    And I think he's beginning to take a keen interest.

EGGERSON. And getting over his disappointment?
    Of course, I never mentioned that:
    It's only what you told me.

SIR CLAUDE.   About his music.
    Yes, I think so. I understand his feelings.
    He's like me, Eggerson. The same disappointment
    In a different form. He won't forget
    That his great ambition was to be an organist,
    Just as I can't forget . . . no matter.
    The great thing was to find something else
    He could do, and do well. And I think he's found it,
    Just as I did. I shall tell him about myself.
    But so far, I've left him to his own devices:
    I thought he would fall into this way of life more quickly
    If we started on a purely business basis.

EGGERSON. No doubt that's best. While he's still living
    With his aunt in Teddington, and coming up daily
    Just as I used to. And the flat in the mews?
    How soon will that be ready for him?

SIR CLAUDE. They have still to do the walls. And then it must be
        furnished.
    I'm trying to find him a really good piano.

EGGERSON. A piano? Yes, I'm sure he'll feel at home
    When he has a piano. You think of everything.
    But if I might make a suggestion: window boxes!
    He's expressed such an interest in my garden
    That I think he ought to have window boxes.
    Some day, he'll want a garden of his own. And yes, a bird bath!

SIR CLAUDE. A bird bath? In the mews? What's the point of that?

EGGERSON. He told me he was very fond of bird watching.

SIR CLAUDE. But there won't be any birds — none worth watching.

EGGERSON. I don't know, Sir Claude. Only the other day
    I read a letter in *The Times* about wild birds seen in London:
    And I'm sure Mr. Simpkins will find them if anybody.

SIR CLAUDE. Well, we'll leave that for the present. As we have a little
time
    Before you start for Northolt — the car will be ready —
    Let's think what you're to say to Lady Elizabeth,
    Coming back from the airport, about Colby.
    I think, you ought to give her warning
    Of whom she is to meet on her arrival.

EGGERSON. How would you like me to approach the subject?

SIR CLAUDE. Of course, she knows you were wanting to retire,
    As we had some discussion about replacing you.
    But you know she regards you — well, completely
    As one of the household.

EGGERSON.   That's a great compliment.

SIR CLAUDE. And well deserved; but rather inconvenient
    When it comes to appointing a successor.
    Makes it very difficult to replace you.
    She thinks she ought to have a hand in the choosing;
    And besides, she is convinced that she, of all people,
    Is a better judge of character than I am.

EGGERSON. Oh, I wouldn't say that, Sir Claude!
    She has too much respect for your business genius.
    But it's true she believes she has what she calls 'guidance'.

SIR CLAUDE. Guidance. That's worse than believing in her judgment:
    We could argue about that. You can't argue with guidance.
    But if she appears to be puzzled, or annoyed
    At my making the appointment during her absence,
    You must say you had to leave under medical orders.
    She's always been concerned about your state of health,
    So she'll be sympathetic. And as for Colby —
    Say that Mr. Simpkins was highly recommended,
    And say that I had to make a quick decision
    Because he'd had another very tempting offer.
    Something like that. Don't make too much of it.
    And I rather hope that she will take to him at once:
    If so, she is certain to come to believe
    That she chose him herself. By the way, don't forget
    To let her know that he's very musical.
    She can take him to concerts. But don't overdo it!

EGGERSON. I'll remember that. Music.

SIR CLAUDE.   And by the way,

How much have you actually told him about her?
You remember, I asked you to prepare him a little;
There are some things you could say better than I could,
And ways in which you could reassure him
Better than I. He's more at ease with you
Than he is with me.

EGGERSON.   Oh, you mustn't say that!
Though I've done my best to gain his confidence.
I did mention her interest in Light from the East.

SIR CLAUDE. And the Book of Revelation? And the Wisdom of
    Atlantis?

EGGERSON. Well, to tell the truth, Sir Claude, I only touched on these
    matters,
They're much too deep for me. And I thought, Mr. Simpkins,
He's highly educated. He'll soon begin to grasp them.
No, I haven't told him much about Lady Elizabeth.
But there's one thing I should like to know —
If you don't mind — before I go to meet her.
How soon do you propose to . . . *explain* Mr. Simpkins?
Regularize his position in the household?
You told me that was your eventual intention.

SIR CLAUDE. When — or indeed whether — I reveal his identity
Depends on how she takes to him. This afternoon
She will only learn that you have finally retired
And that you have a young successor,
A Mr. Colby Simpkins.

EGGERSON.   Merely Mr. Simpkins.

SIR CLAUDE. The reasons for starting him during her absence
Are perfectly clear. But beyond that point
I haven't yet explained my plans to you.
Why I've never told her about him,
The reason for meeting him as merely Mr. Simpkins,
Is, that she has a strong maternal instinct . . .

EGGERSON. I realise that.

SIR CLAUDE.   Which has always been thwarted.

EGGERSON. I'm sure it's been a grief to both of you
That you've never had children.

SIR CLAUDE.   No worse, Eggerson,
Than for you and your wife, to have had a son
Lost in action, and his grave unknown.

EGGERSON. And you're thinking no doubt that Lady Elizabeth
 Would be put in mind of the child *she* lost.
SIR CLAUDE. In a very different way, yes. You might say *mislaid*,
 Since the father is dead, and there's no way of tracing it.
 Yes, I was thinking of her missing child:
 In the circumstances, that might make her jealous.
 I've explained all this to Colby — Mr. Simpkins.
EGGERSON. I see what you mean.
SIR CLAUDE.   She must get to like him first:
 And then, Eggerson, I am not unhopeful
 That, under the impression that he is an orphan,
 She will want us to adopt him.
EGGERSON.   Adopt him! Yes, indeed,
 That would be the solution. Yes, quite ideal.
SIR CLAUDE. I'm glad you agree. Your support will be helpful.
EGGERSON. I'm sure I shall be very happy to commend him.
SIR CLAUDE. You mustn't overdo it! But your approval matters.
 You know she thinks the world of your opinion.
EGGERSON. Well, I believe that once or twice, perhaps . . .
 But I'm afraid you overrate my influence.
 I have never been able to make her like Miss Angel;
 She becomes abstracted, whenever I mention her.
SIR CLAUDE. But she knew about Lucasta — Miss Angel, from the
  start.
 That was one difficulty. And there are others.
 For one, they're both of them women.
EGGERSON.   True.
SIR CLAUDE. But I don't think she takes much notice of Miss Angel.
 She just doesn't see her. And Miss Angel
 Will soon be getting married, I expect.
EGGERSON. And so I hope. A most suitable arrangement.
 But will you tell me this: if it comes to the point
 At which Lady Elizabeth wants to adopt him —
 An admirable solution — then what follows?
 Will you let her know, then, that Mr. Simpkins
 Is actually your son?
SIR CLAUDE.   That's where I'm in the dark.
 I simply can't guess what her reaction would be.
 There's a lot I don't understand about my wife.
 There's always something one's ignorant of

449

About anyone, however well one knows them;
And that may be something of the greatest importance.
It's when you're sure you understand a person
That you're liable to make the worst mistake about him.
As a matter of fact, there's a lot I don't know
About you, Eggerson, although we worked together
For nearly thirty years.

EGGERSON.   Nearly thirty-one.
But now you put it so convincingly,
I must admit there's a lot that *I* don't understand
About my wife.

SIR CLAUDE. And just as much
She doesn't know about you. And just as much
You don't know about me — I'm not so sure of that!
My rule is to remember that I understand nobody,
But on the other hand never to be sure
That they don't understand me — a good deal better
Than I should care to think, perhaps.

EGGERSON.   And do I infer
That you're not sure you understand Mr. Simpkins, either?

SIR CLAUDE. A timely reminder. You may have to repeat it.
But he should be back by now. And then I'll leave you.
I must telephone to Amsterdam, and possibly to Paris.
But when you return with Lady Elizabeth
I'll be ready waiting to introduce him.

[*Enter* COLBY SIMPKINS *with briefcase*]

SIR CLAUDE. Ah, Colby, I was just saying to Eggerson
It was time you were back. Was your morning satisfactory?

COLBY. I've got what you wanted, Sir Claude. Good afternoon,
Mr. Eggerson. I was afraid I'd miss you.

EGGERSON. I'm off in half an hour, Mr. Simpkins.

SIR CLAUDE. I'll leave you now. But when Eggerson comes back
With Lady Elizabeth, I will rejoin you.

[*Exit* SIR CLAUDE]

COLBY. I'm glad you don't have to leave just yet.
I'm rather nervous about this meeting.
You've told me very little about Lady Elizabeth,
And Sir Claude himself hasn't told me very much:
So I've no idea how I ought to behave.
B. Kaghan has told me something about her,

But that's rather alarming.

EGGERSON.   Mr. Kaghan is prejudiced.
He's never hit it off with Lady Elizabeth.
Don't listen to him. He understands Sir Claude,
And he's always been very grateful to Sir Claude,
As he ought to be. Sir Claude picked him out
And gave him his start. And he's made the most of it —
That I will say. An encouraging example
For you, Mr. Simpkins. He'll be a power in the City!
And he has a heart of gold. But not to beat about the bush,
He's rather a rough diamond. Very free and easy ways;
And Lady Elizabeth has never taken to him.
But you, Mr. Simpkins, that's very different.

COLBY. I don't know why it should be so different.
I like B. Kaghan. I've found him very helpful
And very good company apart from business.

EGGERSON. Oh yes, Mr. Kaghan is very good company.
He makes me laugh sometimes. I don't laugh easily.
Quite a humorist, he is. In fact, Mrs. E.
Sometimes says to me: 'Eggerson, why can't you make me laugh
The way B. Kaghan did?' She's only met him once;
But do you know, he began addressing her as Muriel —
Within the first ten minutes! I was horrified.
But she actually liked it. Muriel *is* her name.
He has a way with the ladies, you know.
But with Lady Elizabeth he wasn't so successful.
She once referred to him as 'undistinguished';
But with you, as I said, it will be very different.
She'll see at once that you're a man of culture;
And besides, she's very musical.

COLBY.   Thank you for the warning!

EGGERSON. So if you don't mind, I shall mention at once
That you are a musician.

COLBY.   I'll be on my guard.

EGGERSON. Your music will certainly be a great asset
With Lady Elizabeth. I envy you that.
I've always sung in our voluntary choir
And at the carol service. But I wish I was musical.

COLBY. I still don't feel very well prepared for meeting her.
[*A loud knock. Enter* B. KAGHAN]

KAGHAN. Enter B. Kaghan. Hello Colby!
     And hello Eggers! I'm glad to find you here.
     It's lucky for Colby.

EGGERSON.   How so Mr. Kaghan?

KAGHAN. Because Lucasta's with me! The usual catastrophe.
     She's come to pry some cash from the money-box.
     Bankrupt again! So I thought I'd better bring her
     And come upstairs ahead, to ease the shock for Colby.
     But as you're here, Eggers, I can just relax.
     I'm going to enjoy the game from the sidelines.

[*Enter* LUCASTA ANGEL]

LUCASTA. Eggy, I've lost my job!

EGGERSON.   Again, Miss Angel?

LUCASTA. Yes, again! And serve them right!

EGGERSON. You have been, I presume, persistently unpunctual.

LUCASTA. You're wrong, Eggy. It's rank injustice.
     Two months I'd gone on filing those papers
     Which no one ever wanted — at least, not till yesterday.
     Then, just by bad luck, the boss did want a letter
     And I couldn't find it. And then he got suspicious
     And asked for things I'm sure he didn't want —
     Just to make trouble! And I couldn't find one of them.
     But they're all filed somewhere, I'm sure, so why bother?
     But who's this, Eggy? Is it Colby Simpkins?
     Introduce him, one or the other of you.

EGGERSON. Mr. Simpkins, Miss Angel. As you know, Miss Angel,
     Mr. Simpkins has taken over my duties.

LUCASTA. And does he know that *I'm* one of his duties?
     Have you prepared him for taking *me* over?
     Did you know that, Colby? I'm Lucasta.
     It's only Eggy calls me Miss Angel,
     Just to annoy me. Don't you agree
     That Lucasta suits me better?

COLBY. I'm sure they both suit you.

LUCASTA. Snubbed again! I suppose I asked for it.
     That's what comes of being cursed with a name like Angel.
     I'm thinking of changing it. But, Colby,
     Do you know that I'm one of your responsibilities?

COLBY. No, I'm afraid I didn't know that.

EGGERSON. You mustn't give way to her, Mr. Simpkins.

I never do. I always say
That if you give Miss Angel an inch
She'll take an ell.

LUCASTA.   L. for Lucasta.
Go on, Eggy. Don't mind him, Colby.
Colby, are you married?

COLBY.   No, I'm not married.

LUCASTA. Then I don't mind being seen with you in public.
You may take me out to dinner. A working girl like me
Is often very hungry — living on a pittance —
Cooking a sausage on a gas ring . . .

EGGERSON. You mustn't believe a word she says.

LUCASTA. *Mr.* Simpkins is going to believe all I say,
Mr. Eggerson. And I know he'll be nice to me
When you're out of the way. Why don't you let him speak?
Eggy's really quite human, Colby.
It's only that he's terrified of Mrs. Eggerson;
That's why he's never asked me out to lunch.

EGGERSON. We will leave Mrs. Eggerson out of this, Miss Angel.

LUCASTA. That's what he always says, Colby,
When I mention Mrs. Eggerson. He never fails to rise.
B.! What have you told Colby about me?

KAGHAN. It's no use telling anybody about you:
Nobody'd ever believe in your existence
Until they met you. Colby's still reeling.
It's going to be my responsibility,
As your fiancé, to protect Colby from you.
But first, let's cope with the financial crisis.

LUCASTA. Yes, Eggy, will you break the sad news to Claude?
Meanwhile, you'll have to raid the till for me. I'm starving.

KAGHAN. I've just given her lunch. The problem with Lucasta
Is how to keep her fed between meals.

LUCASTA. B., you're a beast. I've a very small appetite.
But the point is, that I'm penniless.

KAGHAN. She's had a week's salary in lieu of notice.

LUCASTA. B., remember you're only my fiancé on approval.
Can I have some money, Eggy?

EGGERSON.   I'm no longer in charge
And that duty has *not* devolved on Mr. Simpkins:
Sir Claude intends to deal with these matters himself.

THE CONFIDENTIAL CLERK

You will have to ask Sir Claude. But I'll speak to him
When I return from Northolt.
LUCASTA.   You're going to meet Lizzie?
EGGERSON. I am meeting Lady Elizabeth at Northolt.
LUCASTA. Well, I don't propose to be on the scene when *she*
          comes.
KAGHAN. And I don't propose to leave you with Colby.
          He's had enough for one day. Take my advice, Colby.
          Never allow Lucasta the slightest advantage
          Or she'll exploit it. You have to be tough with her;
          She's hard as nails. Now I'll take her off your hands.
          I'll show you how it's done. Come along, Lucasta,
          I'm going to make a day of it, and take you out to tea.
LUCASTA. I'm dying for my tea. The strain of this crisis
          Has been too much for me. Another time, Colby.
          I'll ring you up, and let you take me out to lunch.

                                                    [*Exit* LUCASTA]

KAGHAN. Take it easy, Colby. You'll get used to her.

                                                    [*Exit* KAGHAN]

COLBY. Egg . . . Mr. Eggerson!
EGGERSON.   Yes, Mr. Simpkins?
COLBY. You seem to me sane. And I think I am.
EGGERSON. I have no doubt on either point, none at all.
COLBY. And B. Kaghan has always seemed to me sane.
EGGERSON. I should call him the very picture of sanity.
COLBY. But you never warned me about Miss Angel.
          What about *her*?
EGGERSON.   Oh, Miss Angel.
          She's rather flighty. But she has a good heart.
COLBY. But does she address Sir Claude Mulhammer
          As Claude? To his face?
EGGERSON.   She does indeed.
COLBY. And does she call Lady Elizabeth *Lizzie*?
EGGERSON. Well, not in her presence. Not when I've been there.
          No, I don't think she would. But she does call her Lizzie,
          Sometimes, to Sir Claude. And do you know —
          I think it amuses him.
COLBY.   Well, perhaps I'll be amused.
          But it did make my head spin — all those first names
          The first time I met her. I'm not used to it.

454

EGGERSON. You'll soon get used to it. You'll be calling me Eggers
    Before you know it!

COLBY.   I shouldn't wonder.
    I nearly did, a moment ago.
    Then I'd have been certain I'd lost my reason:
    Her influence is perfectly frightening.
    But tell me about Lu . . . Miss Angel:
    What's her connection with this household?

EGGERSON. Well. A kind of fiduciary relationship.
    No, I don't think that's quite the right term.
    She's no money of her own, as you may have gathered;
    But I think her father was a friend of Sir Claude's,
    And he's made himself responsible for her.
    In any case, he's behaved like a father —
    A very generous man, is Sir Claude.
    To tell the truth, she's something of a thorn in his flesh,
    Always losing her jobs, because she won't stick to them.
    He gives her an allowance — very adequate indeed,
    Though she's always in debt. But you needn't worry
    About her, Mr. Simpkins. She'll marry Mr. Kaghan
    In the end. He's a man who gets his own way,
    And I think he can manage her. If anyone can.

COLBY. But is she likely to be a nuisance?

EGGERSON. Not unless you give her encouragement.
    I have never encouraged her.

COLBY.   But you have Mrs. Eggerson.

EGGERSON. Yes, she's a great protection. And I have my garden
    To protect me against Mrs. E. That's my joke.

COLBY. Well, I've never met anyone like Miss Angel.

EGGERSON. You'll get used to her, Mr. Simpkins.
    Time works wonders, that's what I always say.
    But I don't expect you'll have to see much of her:
    That responsibility's not on your shoulders.
    Lady Elizabeth, now, that's different.

COLBY. At least, I don't suppose Lady Elizabeth
    Can be quite so unusual as Miss Angel.

EGGERSON. O yes, Mr. Simpkins, much more unusual.

COLBY. Oh!

EGGERSON. Well, as I told you, she really is a lady,
    Rather a *grande dame*, as the French say.

That's what Sir Claude admires about her.
He said to me once, in a moment of confidence —
He'd just come back from a public luncheon —
'Eggerson', he said, 'I wanted a lady,
And I'm perfectly satisfied with the bargain.'
Of course it's true that her family connections
Have sometimes been useful. But he didn't think of that:
He's not petty-minded — though nothing escapes him.
And such a generous heart! He's rather a Socialist.
I'm a staunch Conservative, myself.

COLBY. But is Lady Elizabeth very unusual
In any other way, besides being a lady?

EGGERSON. Why, yes, indeed, I must admit she is.
Most of her oddities are perfectly harmless.
You'll soon get used to them. That's what Sir Claude said:
'Humour her, Eggerson,' he said, 'humour her.'
But she has one trait that I think I did touch on:
She's very absent-minded.

COLBY.   I hope you don't mean,
She has lapses of memory?

EGGERSON.   I didn't mean that.
No. She hasn't very much memory to lose,
Though she sometimes remembers when you least expect it.
But she does forget things. And she likes to travel,
Mostly for her health. And when she's abroad
She is apt to buy a house. And then goes away
And forgets all about it. That can be complicated
And very costly. I've had some rare adventures!
I remember long ago, saying to Mrs. E.,
When we'd bought our house in Joshua Park
(On a mortgage, of course) 'now we've settled down
All the travel *I* want is up to the City
And back to Joshua Park in the evening,
And once a year our holiday at Dawlish'.
And to think that was only the beginning of my travels!
It's been a very unusual privilege
To see as much of Europe as I have,
Getting Lady Elizabeth out of her difficulties.

COLBY. Perhaps she won't even arrive by this plane.

EGGERSON. Oh, that could happen. She sometimes gets lost,

Or loses her ticket, or even her passport.
But let's not be crossing any bridges
Until we come to them. That's what *I* always say.
And I'm sure you'll like her. She's *such* a lady!
And what's more, she has a good heart.

COLBY. Everybody seems to be kind-hearted.
But there's one thing I do believe, Mr. Eggerson:
That *you* have a kind heart. And I'm convinced
That you always contrive to think the best of everyone.

EGGERSON. You'll come to find that I'm right, I assure you.

[*Enter* SIR CLAUDE]

SIR CLAUDE. Hello! Still here? It's time you were off.

EGGERSON. I'm just going. There's plenty of time.

[*Looks at his watch*]

I'll arrive at the airport with minutes to spare,
And besides, there's the Customs. That'll take her a time,
From my experience.

LADY ELIZABETH MULHAMMER's *voice off*.* Just open that case, I
    want something out of it.
Unwrap that — It's a bottle of medicine.
Now, Parkman, will you give it to the driver?
He tells me that he suffers from chronic catarrh.

SIR CLAUDE. Hello! What's that?

[*Opens door on to landing and listens*]

She's here, Eggerson! That's her voice.
Where is she? Oh, she's gone out again.

[*Goes to the window and looks down on the street*]

She's having a conversation with the cabman.
What can they be talking about? She's coming in!

LADY ELIZABETH MULHAMMER's *voice off*.* No, Gertrude, I haven't
    had any lunch,
And I don't want it now. Just bring me some tea.
Nothing with it. No, I forgot:
You haven't learned yet how to make tea properly.
A cup of black coffee. Is Sir Claude at home?
I'll speak to him first.

SIR CLAUDE. Good heavens, Eggerson, what *can* have happened?

EGGERSON. It's perfectly amazing. Let *me* go down to meet her.

* *Lady Elizabeth's words off stage are not intended to be heard distinctly by an
audience in the theatre.*

SIR CLAUDE. Where ought we to be? What ought we to be doing?

EGGERSON [*at the open door*]. She's speaking to the parlourmaid. She's coming up.

SIR CLAUDE. Colby, sit at the desk, and pick up some papers.
We must look as if we'd been engaged in business.

[*Enter* LADY ELIZABETH MULHAMMER]

EGGERSON & SIR CLAUDE [*simultaneously*]. Lady Elizabeth!
Elizabeth!

SIR CLAUDE. What on earth has happened?

EGGERSON. Lady Elizabeth! This is most surprising.

LADY ELIZABETH. What's surprising, Eggerson? I've arrived, that's all.

EGGERSON. I was just starting for Northolt to meet you.

LADY ELIZABETH. That was very thoughtful of you, Eggerson,
But quite unnecessary. And besides,
I didn't come by air. I arrived at Victoria.

SIR CLAUDE. Do you mean to say that you changed your ticket?

EGGERSON. Yes, how did you manage to change your ticket?

LADY ELIZABETH. I went to the agency and got them to change it.
I can't understand why you're both so surprised.
You know I'm a very experienced traveller.

SIR CLAUDE. Oh yes, of course we know that, Elizabeth.
But why did you change your plans?

LADY ELIZABETH.   Because of Mildred Deverell.
She's been having the treatment with me,
And she can't go by air — she says it makes her sea-sick;
So we took the night train, and did the Channel crossing.
But who is this young man? His face is familiar.

SIR CLAUDE. This young man is Eggerson's successor.
You know that Eggerson's been meaning to retire . . .

EGGERSON. Under medical orders, Lady Elizabeth:
The doctor made it very imperative . . .

SIR CLAUDE. Mr. Simpkins had very strong recommendations . . .

EGGERSON. And at the same time, he had another tempting offer:
So we had to make a quick decision.

SIR CLAUDE. I didn't want to bother you, during your treatment . . .

EGGERSON. And Mr. Simpkins is much more highly qualified
Than I am, to be a confidential clerk.
Besides, he's very musical.

LADY ELIZABETH.   Musical?
Isn't this the young man I interviewed

And recommended to Sir Claude? Of course it is.
I remember saying: 'He has a good aura.'
I remember people's auras almost better than their faces.
What did you say his name was?

SIR CLAUDE.   Colby Simpkins.

LADY ELIZABETH [*counting on her fingers*]. Thirteen letters. That's very
      auspicious —
Contrary to what most people think.
You should be artistic. But you look rather frail.
I must give you lessons in the art of health.
Where is your home, Mr. Colby?

COLBY.   Simpkins.

EGGERSON. Mr. Colby Simpkins.

LADY ELIZABETH.   I prefer Colby.
Where are you living?

SIR CLAUDE.   His home's outside London.
But I want to have him closer at hand —
You know what a bother it's been for Eggerson —
So I'm having the flat in the mews done over.

LADY ELIZABETH. But all in the wrong colours, I'm sure. My husband
Does not understand the importance of colour
For our spiritual life, Mr. Colby.
Neither, I regret to say, does Eggerson.
What colour have you chosen, between you?

SIR CLAUDE. I thought a primrose yellow would be cheerful.

LADY ELIZABETH. Just what I expected. A primrose yellow
Would be absolutely baneful to Mr. Colby.
He needs a light mauve. I shall see about that.
But not today. I shall go and rest now.
In a sleeping-car it is quite impossible
To get one's quiet hour. A quiet hour a day
Is most essential, Dr. Rebmann says.

SIR CLAUDE. Rebmann? I thought it was a Dr. Leroux.

LADY ELIZABETH. Dr. Leroux is in Lausanne.
I have been in Zürich, under Dr. Rebmann.

SIR CLAUDE. But you were going out to Dr. Leroux
In Lausanne. What made you go to Zürich?

LADY ELIZABETH. Why, I'd no sooner got to Lausanne
Than whom should I meet but Mildred Deverell.
She was going on to Zürich. So she said: 'Come to Zürich!

459

There's a wonderful doctor who teaches mind control.'
So on I went to Zürich.

SIR CLAUDE.   So on you went to Zürich.
But I thought that the doctor in Lausanne taught mind control?

LADY ELIZABETH. No, Claude, he only teaches *thought* control.
Mind control is a different matter:
It's more advanced. But I wrote you all about it.

SIR CLAUDE. It's true, you did send me postcards from Zürich;
But you know that I can't decipher your writing.
I like to have the cards, just to know where you are
By reading the postmark.

LADY ELIZABETH.   But Claude, I'm glad to find
That you've taken my advice.

SIR CLAUDE.   Your advice? About what?

LADY ELIZABETH. To engage Mr. Colby. I really am distressed!
This is not the first sign that I've noticed
Of your memory failing. I must persuade you
To have a course of treatment with Dr. Rebmann —
No, at your stage, I think, with Dr. Leroux.
Don't you remember, I said before I left:
'Trust my guidance for once, and engage that young man?'
Well, that was Mr. Colby.

SIR CLAUDE.   Oh, I see.
Yes, now I am beginning to remember.
I must have acted on your guidance.

LADY ELIZABETH. I must explain to you, Mr. Colby,
That I am to share you with my husband.
You shall have tea with me tomorrow,
And then I shall tell you about my committees.
I must go and rest now.

SIR CLAUDE.   Yes, you go and rest.
I'm in the middle of some business with Mr. . . .

LADY ELIZABETH.   Colby!

[*Exit* LADY ELIZABETH]

SIR CLAUDE. She actually went and changed her own ticket.
It's something unheard of.

EGGERSON.   Amazing, isn't it!

SIR CLAUDE. If this is what the doctor in Zürich has done for her,
I give him full marks. Well, Eggerson,
I seem to have brought you up to London for nothing.

EGGERSON. Oh, not for nothing! I wouldn't have missed it.
    And besides, as I told you, I've done some shopping.
    But I'd better be off now. Mr. Simpkins —
    I: anything *should* turn up unexpected
    And you find yourself non-plussed, you must get me on the phone.
    If I'm not in the house, I'll be out in the garden.
    And I'll slip up to town any day, if you want me.
    In fact, Mrs. E. said: 'I wish he'd ring us up!
    I'm sure he has a very cultivated voice.'
COLBY. Thank you very much, I will. It's reassuring
    To know that I have you always at my back
    If I get into trouble. But I hope
    That I shan't have to call upon you often.
EGGERSON. Oh, and I forgot . . . Mrs. E. keeps saying:
    'Why don't you ask him out to dinner one Sunday?'
    But I say: 'We couldn't ask him to come
    All the way to Joshua Park, at this time of year!'
    I said: 'Let's think about it in the Spring
    When the garden will really be a treat to look at.'
    Well, I'll be going.
SIR CLAUDE.   Goodbye, and thank you, Eggerson.
EGGERSON. Good day, Sir Claude. Good day, Mr. Simpkins.
                                    [*Exit* EGGERSON]
SIR CLAUDE. Well, Colby! I've been calling you Mr. Simpkins
    In public, till now, as a matter of prudence.
    As we arranged. But after two months —
    And as my wife insists upon your being Mr. Colby —
    I shall begin to call you Colby with everyone.
COLBY. I'm sure that will make it easier for both of us.
SIR CLAUDE. Her sudden arrival was very disconcerting:
    As you gather, such a thing never happened before.
    So the meeting didn't go quite the way I'd intended;
    And yet I believe that it's all for the best.
    It went off very well. It's very obvious
    That she took to you at once.
COLBY.   Did she really think
    That she had seen me before?
SIR CLAUDE.   Impossible to tell.
    The point is that she's taken a fancy to you
    And so she lays claim to you. That's very satisfactory.

461

> She's taken it for granted that you should have the flat —
> By tomorrow she'll be sure it was she who proposed it.
> So I feel pretty confident that, before long,
> We can put matters onto a permanent basis.

COLBY. I must confess, that up to this point
> I haven't been able to feel very settled.
> And what you've had in mind still seems to me
> Like building my life upon a deception.
> Do you really believe that Lady Elizabeth
> Can ever accept me as if I was her son?

SIR CLAUDE. As if you were her son? If she comes to think of you
> As the kind of man that her son would have been —
> And I believe she will: though I'm perfectly convinced
> That *her* son would have been a different type of person —
> Then you *will* become her son, in her eyes. She's like that.
> Why, it wouldn't surprise me if she came to believe
> That you really are her son, instead of being mine.
> She has always lived in a world of make-believe,
> And the best one can do is to guide her delusions
> In the right direction.

COLBY.   It doesn't seem quite honest.
> If we all have to live in a world of make-believe,
> Is that good for us? Or a kindness to her?

SIR CLAUDE. If you haven't the strength to impose your own terms
> Upon life, you must accept the terms it offers you.
> But tell me first — I've a reason for asking —
> How do you like your work? You don't find it uncongenial?
> I'm not changing the subject: I'm coming back to it.
> You know I've deliberately left you alone,
> And so far we've discussed only current business,
> Thinking that you might find it easier
> To start by a rather formal relationship
> In adapting yourself to a new situation.

COLBY. I'm very grateful to you, for that:
> It is indeed a new and strange situation,
> And nothing about it is real to me yet.

SIR CLAUDE. But now I want it to be different. It's odd, Colby.
> I didn't realise, till you started with me here,
> That we hardly know each other at all.

COLBY. I suppose there hasn't been the opportunity.

SIR CLAUDE. When you were a child, you belonged to your aunt,
    Or so she made me feel. I never saw you alone.
    And then when I sent you both over to Canada
    In the war — that was perhaps a mistake,
    Though it seemed to have such obvious advantages
    That I had no doubts at the time — that's five years;
    And then your school, and your military service,
    And then your absorption in your music . . .
COLBY. You started by asking me how I found this work.
SIR CLAUDE. Yes, how do you find it?
COLBY.   In a way, exhilarating.
    To find there is something that I can do
    So remote from my previous interests.
    It gives me, in a way, a kind of self-confidence
    I've never had before. Yet at the same time
    It's rather disturbing. I don't mean the work:
    I mean, about myself. As if I was becoming
    A different person. Just as, I suppose,
    If you learn to speak a foreign language fluently,
    So that you can think in it — you feel yourself to be
    Rather a different person when you're talking it.
    I'm not at all sure that I like the other person
    That I feel myself becoming — though he fascinates me.
    And yet from time to time, when I least expect it,
    When my mind is cleared and empty, walking in the street
    Or waking in the night, then the former person,
    The person I used to be, returns to take possession:
    And I am again the disappointed organist,
    And for a moment the thing I cannot do,
    The art that I could never excel in,
    Seems the one thing worth doing, the one thing
    That I want to do. I have to fight that person.
SIR CLAUDE. I understand what you are saying
    Much better than you think. It's my own experience
    That you are repeating.
COLBY.   Your own experience?
SIR CLAUDE. Yes, I did not want to be a financier.
COLBY. What did you want to do?
SIR CLAUDE.   I wanted to be a potter.
COLBY. A potter!

463

SIR CLAUDE.   A potter. When I was a boy
    I loved to shape things. I loved form and colour
    And I loved the material that the potter handles.
    Most people think that a sculptor or a painter
    Is something more excellent to be than a potter.
    Most people think of china or porcelain
    As merely for use, or for decoration —
    In either case, an inferior art.
    For me, they are neither 'use' nor 'decoration' —
    That is, decoration as a background for living;
    For me, they are life itself. To be among such things,
    If it is an escape, is escape into living,
    Escape from a sordid world to a pure one.
    Sculpture and painting — I have some good things —
    But they haven't this . . . remoteness I have always longed for.
    I want a world where the form is the reality,
    Of which the substantial is only a shadow.
    It's strange. I have never talked of this to anyone.
    Never until now. Do you feel at all like that
    When you are alone with your music?

COLBY.   Just the same.
    All the time you've been speaking, I've been translating
    Into terms of music. But may I ask,
    With this passion for . . . ceramics, how did it happen
    That you never made it your profession?

SIR CLAUDE. Family pressure, in the first place.
    My father — your grandfather — built up this business
    Starting from nothing. It was *his* passion.
    He loved it with the same devotion
    That I gave to clay, and what could be done with it —
    What I hoped I could do with it. I thought I despised him
    When I was young. And yet I was in awe of him.
    I was wrong, in both. I loathed this occupation
    Until I began to feel my power in it.
    The life changed me, as it is changing you:
    It begins as a kind of make-believe
    And the make-believing makes it real.
    That's not the whole story. My father knew I hated it:
    That was a grief to him. He knew, I am sure,
    That I cherished for a long time a secret reproach:

But after his death, and then it was too late,
I knew that he was right. And all my life
I have been atoning. To a dead father,
Who had always been right. I never understood him.
I was too young. And when I was mature enough
To understand him, he was not there.

COLBY. You've still not explained why you came to think
That your father had been right.

SIR CLAUDE.   Because I came to see
That I should never have become a first-rate potter.
I didn't have it in me. It's strange, isn't it,
That a man should have a consuming passion
To do something for which he lacks the capacity?
Could a man be said to have a vocation
To be a second-rate potter? To be, at best,
A competent copier, possessed by the craving
To create, when one is wholly uncreative?
I don't think so. For I came to see
That I had always known, at the secret moments,
That I didn't have it in me. There are occasions
When I am transported — a different person,
Transfigured in the vision of some marvellous creation,
And I feel what the man must have felt when he made it.
But nothing *I* made ever gave me that contentment —
That state of utter exhaustion and peace
Which comes in dying to give something life . . .
I intend that you shall have a good piano. The best.
And when you are alone at your piano, in the evening,
I believe you will go through the private door
Into the real world, as I do, sometimes.

COLBY. Indeed, I have felt, while you've been talking,
That it's my own feelings you have expressed,
Although the medium is different. I know
I should never have become a great organist,
As I aspired to be. I'm not an executant;
I'm only a shadow of the great composers.
Always, when I play to myself,
I hear the music I should like to have written,
As the composer heard it when it came to him;
But when I played before other people

I was always conscious that what *they* heard
Was not what I hear when I play to myself.
What I hear is a great musician's music,
What they hear is an inferior rendering.
So I've given up trying to play to other people:
I am only happy when I play to myself.

SIR CLAUDE. You shall play to yourself. And as for me,
I keep my pieces in a private room.
It isn't that I don't want anyone to see them!
But when I am alone, and look at one thing long enough,
I sometimes have that sense of identification
With the maker, of which I spoke — an agonising ecstasy
Which makes life bearable. It's all I have.
I suppose it takes the place of religion:
Just as my wife's investigations
Into what she calls the life of the spirit
Are a kind of substitute for religion.
I dare say truly religious people —
I've never known any — can find some unity.
Then there are also the men of genius.
There are others, it seems to me, who have at best to live
In two worlds — each a kind of make-believe.
That's you and me. Some day, perhaps,
I will show you my collection.

COLBY.   Thank you.

SIR CLAUDE. And perhaps, some time, you will let me hear you play.
I shan't mention it again. I'll wait until you ask me.
Do you understand now what I meant when I spoke
Of accepting the terms life imposes upon you
Even to the point of accepting . . . make-believe?

COLBY. I think I do. At least, I understand *you* better
In learning to understand the conditions
Which life has imposed upon you. But . . . something in me
Rebels against accepting such conditions.
It would be so much simpler if you *weren't* my father!
I was struck by what you said, a little while ago,
When you spoke of never having understood your father
Until it was too late. And you spoke of atonement.
Even your failure to understand him,
Of which you spoke — that was a relationship

466

Of father and son. It must often happen.
And the reconcilement, after his death,
That perfects the relation. You have always been his son
And he is still your father. I only wish
That I had something to atone for!
There's something lacking, between you and me,
That you had, and have, and always will have, with your
    father.
I begin to see how I have always thought of you —
As a kind of protector, a generous provider:
Rather as a patron than a father —
The father who was missing in the years of childhood.
Those years have gone forever. The empty years.
Oh, I'm terribly sorry to be saying this;
But it goes to explain what I said just now
About rebelling against the terms
That life has imposed.

SIR CLAUDE.   It's my own fault.
I was always anxious to avoid the mistakes
My father made with me. And yet I seem
To have made a greater mistake than he did.

COLBY. I know that I'm hurting you and I know
That I hate myself for hurting you.

SIR CLAUDE.   You mustn't think of that.

COLBY. I'm very grateful for all you've done for me;
And I want to do my best to justify your kindness
By the work I do.

SIR CLAUDE.   As my confidential clerk.

COLBY. I'm really interested by the work I'm doing
And eager for more. I don't want my position
To be, in any way, a make-believe.

SIR CLAUDE. It shan't be. Meanwhile, we must simply wait to
    learn
What new conditions life will impose on us.
Just when we think we have settled our account
Life presents a new one, more difficult to pay.
— I shall go now, and sit for a while with my china.

COLBY. Excuse me, but I must remind you:
You have that meeting in the City
Tomorrow morning. You asked me to prepare

Some figures for you. I've got them here.

SIR CLAUDE. Much depends on my wife. Be patient with her, Colby.

— Oh yes, that meeting. We must run through the figures.

CURTAIN

Act Two

The flat in the mews a few weeks later. COLBY *is seated at the piano;* LUCASTA *in an armchair. The concluding bars of a piece of music are heard as the curtain rises.*

LUCASTA. *I* think you play awfully well, Colby —
　　Not that *my* opinion counts for anything:
　　You know that. But I'd like to learn about music.
　　I wish you would teach me how to appreciate it.
COLBY. I don't think that you'll need much teaching;
　　Not at this stage, anyway. All you need at first
　　Is to hear more music. And to find out what you like.
　　When you know what you like, and begin to know it well,
　　Then you will want to learn about its structure
　　And the various forms, and the different ways of playing it.
LUCASTA. But suppose I only like the wrong things?
COLBY. No, I'm sure you'll prefer the right things, when you hear them.
　　I've given you a test. Several of the pieces
　　That I've just played you were very second-rate,
　　And you didn't like them. You liked the right ones.
LUCASTA. Colby, I didn't know you were so artful!
　　So the things I liked were the right ones to like?
　　Still, I'm awfully ignorant. Can you believe
　　That I've never been to a concert in my life?
　　I only go to shows when somebody invites me,
　　And no one has ever asked me to a concert.
　　I've been to the Opera, of course, several times,
　　But I'm afraid I never really listened to the music:
　　I just enjoyed going — to see the other people,
　　And to be seen there! And because you feel out of it
　　If you never go to the Opera, in the season.
　　Though I've always felt out of it. And can you realise
　　That nobody has ever played to me before?
COLBY. And this is the first time I've played to anyone . . .

LUCASTA. Don't be such a fraud. You know you told me
    The piano was only delivered this week
    And you had it tuned yesterday. Still, I'm flattered
    To be your first visitor in this flat
    And to be the first to hear you play *this* piano.
COLBY. That's not what I meant. I mean that I've not played
    To anyone, since I came to the conclusion
    That I should never become a musician.
LUCASTA. Did you find it a strain, then, playing to me?
COLBY. As a matter of fact, I think I played better.
    I can't bring myself to play to other people,
    And when I'm alone I can't forget
    That it's only myself to whom I'm playing.
    But with you, it was neither solitude nor . . . people.
LUCASTA. I'm glad I'm not people. Will you play to me again
    And teach me about music?
COLBY.   Yes, of course I will.
    But I'm sure that when you learn about music —
    And that won't take you long — and hear good performers,
    You'll very quickly realise how bad my playing is.
LUCASTA. Really, Colby, you do make difficulties!
    But what about taking me to a concert?
COLBY. Only the other day, I invited you . . .
LUCASTA. To go to see that American Musical!
COLBY. Well, I'd heard you say you wanted to see it.
LUCASTA. But not with you!
COLBY.   You made that very clear.
  But why not with me?
LUCASTA.   Because you don't like them —
    American Musicals. Do you think it's any compliment
    To invite a woman to something she would like
    When she knows *you* wouldn't like it? That's not a compliment:
    That's just being . . . patronising. But if you invite me
    To something you like — that *is* a compliment.
    It shows you want to educate me.
COLBY.   But I didn't know
    That you wanted to be educated.
LUCASTA.   Neither did I.
    But I wanted you to want to educate me;
    And now I'm beginning to believe that I want it.

COLBY. Well, I'm going to invite you to the next concert . . .

LUCASTA. The next that you want to go to *yourself*.

COLBY. And perhaps you'll let me tell you beforehand
    About the programme — or the things I want to hear.
    I'll play you the themes, so you'll recognise them.
    Better still, I'll play you the gramophone records.

LUCASTA. I'd rather you played me bits yourself, and explained them.
    We'll begin my education at once.

COLBY. I suspect that it's you who are educating *me*.

LUCASTA. Colby, you really are full of surprises!
    I've never met a man so ignorant as you
    Yet knowing so much that one wouldn't suspect.
    Perhaps that's why I like you.

COLBY.   That's not quite the reason.

LUCASTA. Oh, so you believe that I like you?
    I didn't know that you were so conceited.

COLBY. No, it's not conceit — the reason that I'm thinking of.
    It's something quite simple.

LUCASTA.   Then I wish you'd tell me.
    Because *I* don't know.

COLBY.   The first time we met
    You were trying very hard to give a false impression.
    And then you came to see that you hadn't succeeded.

LUCASTA. Oh, so I was trying to give a false impression?
    What sort of impression was I trying to give?

COLBY. That doesn't really matter. But, for some reason,
    You thought I'd get a false impression anyway.
    You preferred it to be one of your own creation
    Rather than wait to see what happened.
    I hope you don't mind: I know it sounds impertinent.

LUCASTA. Well, there's one thing you haven't learnt yet,
    And that is, to know when you're paying a compliment.
    That was a compliment. And a very clever one.

COLBY. I admit that at first I was very bewildered
    By you . . . and B.

LUCASTA.   Oh, by me . . . and B.

COLBY.   Only afterwards,
    When I had seen you a number of times,
    I decided that was only your kind of self-defence.

LUCASTA. What made you think it was self-defence?

COLBY. Because you couldn't wait to see what happened.
You're afraid of what would happen if you left things to themselves.
You jump — because you're afraid of being pushed.
I think that you're brave — and I think that you're frightened.
Perhaps you've been very badly hurt, at some time.
Or at least, there may have been something in your life
To rob you of any sense of security.

LUCASTA. And I'm sure you have *that* — the sense of security.

COLBY. No, I haven't either.

LUCASTA. There, I don't believe you.
What did I think till now? Oh, it's strange, isn't it,
That as one gets to know a person better
One finds them in some ways very like oneself,
In unexpected ways. And then you begin
To discover differences inside the likeness.
You may *feel* insecure, in some ways —
But your insecurity is nothing like mine.

COLBY. In what way is it different?

LUCASTA. It's hard to explain.
Perhaps it's something that your music stands for.
There's one thing I know. When you first told me
What a disaster it was in your life
When you found that you'd never be a good musician —
Of course, *I* don't know whether you were right.
For all I can tell, you may have been mistaken,
And perhaps you could be a very great musician:
But that's not the point. You'd convinced yourself;
And you felt that your life had all collapsed
And that you must learn to do something different.
And so you applied for Eggerson's position,
And made up your mind to go into business
And be someone like Claude . . . or B. I was sorry,
Very sorry for you. I admired your courage
In facing facts — or the facts as you saw them.
And yet, all the time, I found I *envied* you
And I didn't know why! And now I think I know.
It's awful for a man to have to give up,
A career that he's set his heart on, I'm sure:
But it's only the outer world that you've lost:
You've still got your inner world — a world that's more real.

That's why you're different from the rest of us:
You have your secret garden; to which you can retire
And lock the gate behind you.

COLBY.   And lock the gate behind me?
Are you sure that you haven't your own secret garden
Somewhere, if you could find it?

LUCASTA.   If I could find it!
No, my only garden is . . . a dirty public square
In a shabby part of London — like the one where I lived
For a time, with my mother. I've no garden.
I hardly feel that I'm even a person:
Nothing but a bit of living matter
Floating on the surface of the Regent's Canal.
Floating, that's it.

COLBY.   You're very much a person.
I'm sure that there is a garden somewhere for you —
For anyone who wants one as much as you do.

LUCASTA. And *your* garden is a garden
Where you hear a music that no one else could hear,
And the flowers have a scent that no one else could smell.

COLBY. You may be right, up to a point.
And yet, you know, it's not quite real to me —
Although it's as real to me as . . . this world.
But that's just the trouble. They seem so unrelated.
I turn the key, and walk through the gate,
And there I am . . . alone, in my 'garden'.
Alone, that's the thing. That's why it's not real.
You know, I think that Eggerson's garden
Is more real than mine.

LUCASTA.   Eggerson's garden?
What makes you think of Eggerson — of all people?

COLBY. Well, he retires to his garden — literally,
And also in the same sense that I retire to mine.
But he doesn't feel alone there. And when he comes out
He has marrows, or beetroot, or peas . . . for Mrs. Eggerson.

LUCASTA. Are you laughing at me?

COLBY.   I'm being very serious.
What I mean is, my garden's no less unreal to me
Than the world outside it. If you have two lives
Which have nothing whatever to do with each other —

Well, they're both unreal. But for Eggerson
His garden is a part of one single world.

LUCASTA. But what do you want?

COLBY.   Not to be alone there.
If I were religious, God would walk in my garden
And that would make the world outside it real
And acceptable, I think.

LUCASTA.   You sound awfully religious.
Is there no other way of making it real to you?

COLBY. It's simply the fact of being alone there
That makes it unreal.

LUCASTA.   Can no one else enter?

COLBY. It can't be done by issuing invitations:
They would just have to come. And I should not see them coming.
I should not hear the opening of the gate.
They would simply . . . be there suddenly,
Unexpectedly. Walking down an alley
I should become aware of someone walking with me.
That's the only way I can think of putting it.

LUCASTA. How afraid one is of . . . being hurt!

COLBY. It's not the hurting that one would mind
But the sense of desolation afterwards.

LUCASTA. I know what you mean. Then the flowers would fade
And the music would stop. And the walls would be broken.
And you would find yourself in a devastated area —
A bomb-site . . . willow-herb . . . a dirty public square.
But I can't imagine that happening to you.
You seem so secure, to me. Not only in your music —
That's just its expression. You don't seem to me
To need anybody.

COLBY.   That's quite untrue.

LUCASTA. But you've something else, that I haven't got:
Something of which the music is a . . . symbol.
I really would like to understand music,
Not in order to be able to talk about it,
But . . . partly, to enjoy it . . . and because of what it stands for.
You know, I'm a little jealous of your music!
When I see it as a means of contact with a world
More real than any *I've* ever lived in.
And I'd like to understand *you*.

COLBY.   I believe you do already,
Better than . . . other people. And I want to understand *you*.
Does one ever come to understand anyone?

LUCASTA. I think you're being very discouraging:
Are you doing it deliberately?

COLBY.   That's not what I meant.
I meant, there's no end to understanding a person.
All one can do is to understand them better,
To keep up with them; so that as the other changes
You can understand the change as soon as it happens,
Though you couldn't have predicted it.

LUCASTA.   I think I'm changing.
I've changed quite a lot in the last two hours.

COLBY. And I think I'm changing too. But perhaps what we call
change . . .

LUCASTA. Is understanding better what one really is.
And the reason why that comes about, perhaps . . .

COLBY. Is, beginning to understand another person.

LUCASTA. Oh Colby, now that we begin to understand,
I'd like you to know a little more about me.
You must have wondered.

COLBY.   Must have wondered?
No, I haven't wondered. It's all a strange world
To me, you know, in which I find myself.
But if you mean, wondered about your . . . background:
No. I've been curious to know what you *are*,
But not who you are, in the ordinary sense.
Is that what you mean? I've just accepted you.

LUCASTA. Oh, that's so wonderful, to be accepted!
No one has ever 'just accepted' me before.
Of course the facts don't matter, in a sense.
But now we've got to this point — you might as well know
them.

COLBY. I'd gladly tell you everything about myself;
But you know most of what there is to say
Already, either from what I've told you
Or from what I've told B.; or from Sir Claude.

LUCASTA. Claude hasn't told me anything about you;
He doesn't tell me much. And as for B. —
I'd much rather hear it from yourself.

COLBY. There's only one thing I can't tell you.

At least, not yet. I'm not allowed to tell.

And that's about my parents.

LUCASTA.   Oh, I see.

Well, I can't believe that matters.

But I can tell you all about *my* parents:

At least, I'm going to.

COLBY.   Does that matter, either?

LUCASTA. In one way, it matters. A little while ago

You said, very cleverly, that when we first met

You saw I was trying to give a false impression.

I want to tell you now, why I tried to do that.

And it's always succeeded with people before:

I got into the habit of giving that impression.

That's where B. has been such a help to me —

He fosters the impression. He half believes in it.

But he knows all about me, and he knows

That what some men have thought about me wasn't true.

COLBY. What wasn't true?

LUCASTA.   That I was Claude's mistress —

Or had been his mistress, palmed off on B.

COLBY. I never thought of such a thing!

LUCASTA.   You never thought of such a thing!

There are not many men who wouldn't have thought it.

I don't know about B. He's very generous.

I don't think he'd have minded. But he's very clever too;

And he guessed the truth from the very first moment.

COLBY. But what is there to know?

LUCASTA.   You'll laugh when I tell you:

I'm only Claude's daughter.

COLBY.   His daughter!

LUCASTA. His daughter. Oh, it's a sordid story.

I hated my mother. I never could see

How Claude had ever liked her. Oh, that childhood —

Always living in seedy lodgings

And being turned out when the neighbours complained.

Oh of course Claude gave her money, a regular allowance;

But it wouldn't have mattered how much he'd given her:

It was always spent before the end of the quarter

On gin and betting, I should guess.

And I knew how she supplemented her income
When I was sent out. I've been locked in a cupboard!
I was only eight years old
When she died of an 'accidental overdose'.
Then Claude took me over. That was lucky.
But I was old enough to remember . . . too much.

COLBY. You are Claude's daughter!

LUCASTA.   Oh, there's no doubt of that.
I'm sure he wished there had been. He's been good to me
In his way. But I'm always a reminder to him
Of something he would prefer to forget.

                    [*A pause*]

But why don't you say something? Are you shocked?

COLBY. Shocked? No. Yes. You don't understand.
I want to explain. But I can't, just yet.
Oh, why did I ever come into this house!
Lucasta . . .

LUCASTA.   I can see well enough you *are* shocked.
You ought to see your face! I'm disappointed.
I suppose that's all. I believe you're more shocked
Than if I'd told you I *was* Claude's mistress.
Claude has always been ashamed of me:
Now *you're* ashamed of me. I thought you'd understand.
Little you know what it's like to be a bastard
And wanted by nobody. I know why you're shocked:
Claude has just accepted me like a debit item
Always in his cash account. I don't like myself.
I don't like the person I've forced myself to be;
And I liked you because you didn't like that person either,
And I thought you'd come to see me as the real kind of person
That I want to be. That I know I am.
That was new to me. I suppose I was flattered.
And I thought, now, perhaps, if someone else sees me
As I really am, I might become myself.

COLBY. Oh Lucasta, I'm not shocked. Not by you,
Not by anything you think. It's to do with myself.

LUCASTA. Yourself, indeed! Your precious self!
Why don't you shut yourself up in that garden
Where you like to be alone with yourself?
Or perhaps you think it would be bad for your prospects

Now that you're Claude's white-headed boy.
Perhaps he'll adopt you, and make you his heir
And you'll marry another Lady Elizabeth.
But in that event, Colby, you'll have to accept me
As your sister! Even if I am a guttersnipe . . .

COLBY. You mustn't use such words! You don't know how it's hurting.

LUCASTA. I could use words much stronger than that,
And I will, if I choose. Oh, I'm sorry:
I suppose it's my mother coming out in me.
You know, Colby, I'm truly disappointed.
I was sure, when I told you all I did,
That you wouldn't mind at all. That you might be sorry for me.
But now I don't want you to be sorry, thank you.
Why, I'd actually thought of telling you before,
And I postponed telling you, just for the fun of it:
I thought, when I tell him, it will be so wonderful
All in a moment. And now there's nothing,
Nothing at all. It's far worse than ever.
Just when you think you're on the point of release
From loneliness, then loneliness swoops down upon you;
When you think you're getting out, you're getting further in,
And you know at last that there's no escape.
Well, I'll be going.

COLBY.   You mustn't go yet!
There's something else that I want to explain,
And now I'm going to. I'm breaking a promise. But . . .

LUCASTA. I don't believe there's anything to explain
That could explain anything away. I shall never
Never forget that look on your face
When I told you about Claude and my mother.
I may be a bastard, but I have some self-respect.
Well, there's always B. I think that now
I'm just beginning to appreciate B.

COLBY. Lucasta, wait!

[*Enter* B. KAGHAN]

KAGHAN.   Enter B. Kaghan.
To see the new flat. And here's Lucasta.
I knew I should find she'd got in first!
Trust Kaghan's intuitions! I'm your guardian angel,
Colby, to protect you from Lucasta.

LUCASTA. You're *my* guardian angel at the moment, B.
  You're to take me out to dinner. And I'm dying for a drink.
KAGHAN. I told Colby, never learn to mix cocktails,
  If you don't want women always dropping in on you.
  And between a couple of man-eating tigers
  Like you and Lizzie, he's got to have protection.
LUCASTA. Colby doesn't need your protection racket
  So far as I'm concerned, B. And as for Lizzie,
  You'd better not get in *her* way when she's hunting.
  But all that matters now is, that I'm hungry,
  And you've got to give me a very good dinner.
KAGHAN. You shall be fed. All in good time.
  I've come to inspect the new bachelor quarters,
  And to wish Colby luck. I've always been lucky,
  And I always bring luck to other people.
COLBY. Will you have a glass of sherry?
KAGHAN.   Yes, I'll have a glass of sherry,
  To drink success to the flat. Lucasta too:
  Much better for you than cocktails, Lucasta.
LUCASTA. You know I don't like sherry.
KAGHAN.   You've got to drink it,
  To Colby, and a happy bachelor life!
  Which depends, of course, on preventing Lizzie
  From always interfering. Be firm with her, Colby;
  Assert your right to a little privacy.
  Now's the moment for firmness. Don't let her cross the threshold.
LUCASTA. As if you weren't as afraid of her as anybody!
KAGHAN. Well, at least, I've always managed to escape her.
LUCASTA. Only because she's never wanted to pursue you.
KAGHAN. Yes, I made a bad impression at the start:
  I saw that it was necessary. I'm afraid Colby
  Has made a good impression; which he'll have to live down.
  — I must say, I like the way you've had the place done up.
COLBY. It was Lady Elizabeth chose the decorations.
KAGHAN. Then I'm not sure I like them. You must change the colours.
  It's all a bit too dim. You need something brighter.
  But otherwise, it looks pretty comfortable.
  If I was as snug as Colby is, Lucasta,
  I'd never have thought of changing my condition.
LUCASTA. You're always free to think again.

KAGHAN. Marriage is a gamble. But I'm a born gambler
    And I've put my shirt . . . no, not quite the right expression —
    Lucasta's the most exciting speculation
    I've ever thought of investing in.
    Colby's more cautious. You know, Colby,
    You and I ought to be in business together.
    I'm a good guesser. But I sometimes guess wrong.
    I make decisions on the spur of the moment,
    But you'd never take a leap in the dark;
    You'd keep me on the rails.

COLBY.   That's just nonsense.
    You only pretend that you're a gambler.
    You've got as level a head as anyone,
    And you never get involved in anything risky.
    You like to pretend to other people
    That you're a gambler. I don't believe you ever gamble
    On anything that isn't a certainty.

KAGHAN. Well, there's something in that. You know, Lucasta,
    Colby is a good judge of character.

LUCASTA. You'd need to be a better judge of character
    Yourself, before you said that of Colby.

KAGHAN. Oh, I'm a good judge. Now, I'll tell you the difference
    Between ourselves and Colby. You and me —
    The one thing *we* want is security
    And respectability! Now Colby
    Doesn't really care about being respectable —
    He was born and bred to it. I wasn't, Colby.
    Do you know, I was a foundling? You didn't know that!
    Never had any parents. Just adopted, from nowhere.
    That's why I want to be a power in the City,
    On the boards of all the solidest companies:
    Because I've no background — no background at all.
    That's one thing I like about Lucasta:
    She doesn't despise me.

LUCASTA.   Nobody could despise you.
    And what's more important, you don't despise *me*.

KAGHAN. Nobody could despise *you*, Lucasta;
    And we want the same things. But as for Colby,
    He's the sort of fellow who might chuck it all
    And go to live on a desert island.

But I hope you won't do that. We need you where you are.

COLBY. I'm beginning to believe you've a pretty shrewd insight
Into things that have nothing to do with business.

KAGHAN. And you have a very sound head for business.
Maybe you're a better financier than I am!
That's why we ought to be in business together.

LUCASTA. You're both very good at paying compliments;
But I remarked that I was hungry.

KAGHAN.   You can't want dinner yet.
It's only six o'clock. We can't dine till eight;
Not at any restaurant that *you* like.
— For a change, let's talk about Lucasta.

LUCASTA [*rising*]. If you want to discuss *me* . . .
[*A knock at the door. Enter* LADY ELIZABETH]

LADY ELIZABETH.   Oh, good evening.
Good evening, Mr. Kaghan. Good evening, Lucasta.
Have you just arrived, or are you just leaving?

LUCASTA. We're on the point of leaving, Lady Elizabeth.

LADY ELIZABETH. I've come over to have a look at the flat
Now that you've moved in. Because you can't tell
Whether a scheme of decoration
Is *right*, until the place has been lived in
By the person for whom it was designed.
So I have to see you in it. Did you say you were leaving?

KAGHAN. We're going out to dinner. Lucasta's very hungry.

LADY ELIZABETH. Hungry? At six o'clock? Where will you get dinner?
Oh, I know. It's a chance to try that Herbal Restaurant
I recommended to you. You can have dinner early:
Most of its patrons dine at half past six.
They have the most delicious salads!
And I told you, Mr. Kaghan, you're the type of person
Who needs to eat a great deal of salad.
You remember, I made you take a note of the address;
And I don't believe that you've been there yet.

KAGHAN. Why no, as a matter of fact, I haven't.
I've kept meaning to. Shall we go there, Lucasta?

LUCASTA. I'm so hungry, I could even eat a herbal salad.

LADY ELIZABETH. That's right. Just mention my name, Mr. Kaghan,
And ask for the table in the left hand corner:
It has the best waitress. Good night.

LUCASTA.   Good night.

KAGHAN. And thank you so much. You give such good advice.

                              [*Exeunt* KAGHAN *and* LUCASTA]

LADY ELIZABETH. Were those young people here by appointment?
    Or did they come in unexpectedly?

COLBY. I'd invited Lucasta. She had asked me to play to her.

LADY ELIZABETH. You call her Lucasta? Young people nowadays
    Seem to have dropped the use of surnames altogether.
    But, Colby, I hope you won't mind a gentle hint.
    I feared it was possible you might become too friendly
    With Mr. Kaghan and Miss Angel.
    I can see you've lived a rather sheltered life,
    And I've noticed them paying you a good deal of attention.
    You see, you're rather a curiosity
    To both of them — you're not the sort of person
    They ever meet in their kind of society.
    So naturally, they want to take you up.
    I can speak more freely, as an elderly person.

COLBY. But, Lady Elizabeth . . .

LADY ELIZABETH.   Well, older than you are,
    And a good deal wiser in the ways of the world.

COLBY. But, Lady Elizabeth, what is it you object to?
    They're both intelligent . . . and kind.

LADY ELIZABETH. Oh, I don't say they're not intelligent and kind.
    I'm not making any malicious suggestions:
    But they are rather worldly and materialistic,
    And . . . well, rather vulgar. They're not your sort at all.

COLBY. I shouldn't call them vulgar. Perhaps I'm vulgar too.
    But what, do you think, *is* my sort?
    I don't know, myself. And I should like to know.

LADY ELIZABETH. In the first place, you ought to mix with people of
        breeding.
    I said to myself, when I first saw you,
    'He is very well bred'. I knew nothing about you,
    But one doesn't need to know, if one knows what breeding is.
    And, second, you need intellectual society.
    Now, that already limits your acquaintance:
    Because, what's surprising, well-bred people
    Are sometimes far from intellectual;
    And — what's less surprising — intellectual people

Are often ill-bred. But that's not all.
You need intellectual, well-bred people
Of spirituality — and that's the rarest.

COLBY. That would limit my acquaintance to a very small number,
And I don't know where to find them.

LADY ELIZABETH.   They can be found.
But I came to have a look at the flat
To see if the colour scheme really suited you.
I believe it does. The walls; and the curtains;
And most of the furniture. But, that writing-table!
Where did that writing-table come from?

COLBY. It's an office desk. Sir Claude got it for me.
I said I needed a desk in my room:
You see, I shall do a good deal of my work here.

LADY ELIZABETH. And what is that shrouded object on it?
Don't tell me it's a typewriter.

COLBY.   It is a typewriter.
I've already begun to work here. At the moment
I'm working on a company report.

LADY ELIZABETH. I hadn't reckoned on reports and typewriters
When I designed this room.

COLBY.   It's the sort of room I wanted.

LADY ELIZABETH [*rising*]. And I see a photograph in a silver
      frame.
I'm afraid I shall have to instruct you, Colby.
Photographic portraits — even in silver frames —
Are much too intimate for the sitting-room.
May I remove it? Surely your bedroom
Is the proper place for photographic souvenirs.
            [*She sits down, holding the portrait*]
What was I going to say? Oh, I know.
Do you believe in reincarnation?

COLBY. No, I don't. I mean, I've never thought about it.

LADY ELIZABETH. I can't say that *I* believe in it.
I did, for a time. I studied the doctrine.
But I was going to say, *if* I believed in it
I should have said that we had known each other
In some previous incarnation. — Is this your mother?

COLBY. No, that is my aunt. I never knew my mother.
She died when I was born.

483

LADY ELIZABETH.   She died when you were born.
　　Have you other near relatives? Brothers or sisters?
COLBY. No brothers or sisters. No. As for other relatives,
　　I never knew any, when I was a child.
　　I suppose I've never been interested . . . in relatives.
LADY ELIZABETH. You did not want to know your relatives!
　　I understand exactly how you felt.
　　How I disliked my parents! I had a governess;
　　Several, in fact. And I loathed them all.
　　Were you brought up by a governess?
COLBY.   No. By my aunt.
LADY ELIZABETH. And did you loathe her? No, of course not.
　　Or you wouldn't have her portrait. If you never knew your
　　　　parents . . .
　　But was your father living?
COLBY.   I never knew my father.
LADY ELIZABETH. Then, if you never had a governess,
　　And if you never knew either of your parents,
　　You can't understand what loathing really is.
　　Yet we must have *some* similarity of background.
COLBY. But you had parents. And no doubt, many relatives.
LADY ELIZABETH. Oh, swarms of relatives! And such unpleasant
　　　　people!
　　I thought of myself as a dove in an eagle's nest.
　　They were so carnivorous. Always killing things and eating them.
　　And yet our childhood must have been similar.
　　These are only superficial differences:
　　You must have been a lonely child, having no relatives —
　　No brothers or sisters — and I was lonely
　　Because they were so numerous — and so uncongenial.
　　They made me feel an outcast. And yet they were so commonplace.
　　Do you know, Colby, when I was a child
　　I had three obsessions, and I never told anyone.
　　I wonder if *you* had the same obsessions?
COLBY. What were they?
LADY ELIZABETH.   The first was, that I was very ugly
　　And didn't know it. Then, that I was feeble-minded
　　And didn't know it. Finally,
　　That I was a foundling, and didn't know it.
　　Of course, I was terrified of being ugly,

And of being feeble-minded: though my family made me think so.
But you know, I actually *liked* to believe
That I was a foundling — or do I mean 'changeling'?
COLBY. I don't know which you mean.
LADY ELIZABETH. However that may be,
I didn't want to belong there. I refused to believe
That my father could have been an ordinary earl!
And I couldn't believe that my mother *was* my mother.
These were foolish fancies. I was a silly girl,
And very romantic. But it goes to show
How different I felt myself to be
And then I took up the Wisdom of the East
And believed, for a while, in reincarnation.
That seemed to explain it all. I don't believe it now.
That was only a phase. But it made it all so simple!
To be able to think that one's earthly parents
Are only the means that we have to employ
To become reincarnate. And that one's real ancestry
Is one's previous existences. Of course, there's something in us,
In all of us, which isn't just heredity,
But something unique. Something we have been
From eternity. Something . . . straight from God.
That means that we are nearer to God than to anyone.
— Where did you live, as a child?
COLBY. In Teddington.
LADY ELIZABETH. Teddington? In what county?
COLBY. It's very close to London.
LADY ELIZABETH. Still, you were brought up, like me, in the country.
Teddington. I seem to have heard of it.
Was it a large house?
COLBY. No, a very small one.
LADY ELIZABETH. But you had your aunt. And she was devoted to
you,
I have no doubt. What is your aunt's name?
Is it Simpkins?
COLBY. No, a married aunt.
A widow. Her name is Mrs. Guzzard.
LADY ELIZABETH. Guzzard? Did you say Guzzard? An unusual name.
Guzzard, did you say? The name means something to me.
Yes. Guzzard. *That* is the name I've been hunting for!

COLBY. You may have come across the name before;
    Although, as you say, it is an uncommon one.
    You couldn't have known my aunt.
LADY ELIZABETH.   No. I never met . . . your aunt.
    But the name is familiar. How old are you, Colby?
COLBY. I'm twenty-five.
LADY ELIZABETH.   Twenty-five. What became of your father?
COLBY. Well . . . I didn't have a father.
    You see . . . I was an illegitimate child.
LADY ELIZABETH. Oh yes. An illegitimate child.
    So that the only relative you knew
    Was Mrs. Guzzard. And you always called her 'aunt'?
COLBY. Why not? She was my aunt.
LADY ELIZABETH.   And as for your mother —
    Mrs. Guzzard's sister, I suppose . . .
COLBY. Her sister — which makes Mrs. Guzzard my aunt.
LADY ELIZABETH. And are you quite sure that Mrs. Guzzard's sister —
    Who you say was your mother — really was your mother?
COLBY. Why, Lady Elizabeth! Why should I doubt it?
    That is not the kind of story my aunt would invent.
LADY ELIZABETH. Not if she *is* your aunt. Did Mrs. Guzzard
    And Mr. Guzzard — have any children?
COLBY. They had no children of their own.
    That is to say, they had had one little boy
    Who died when I was very young indeed.
    I don't remember him. I was told about him.
    But I can't help wondering why you are so interested:
    There's nothing very interesting about my background —
    I assure you there isn't.
LADY ELIZABETH.   It may be more interesting
    Than you are aware of. Colby . . .
               [*A knock on the door*]
                   Who's that?

[*Enter* SIR CLAUDE]
SIR CLAUDE. Elizabeth! I was told that you were here with Colby.
    So I came over instead of telephoning,
    Just to give him these notes. They're notes for my speech
    At the dinner of the Potters' Company.
COLBY. That's tomorrow night, I believe.
SIR CLAUDE.   Yes it is.

But you know that I'll have to have my speech written out
And then memorise it. I can't use notes:
It's got to sound spontaneous. I've jotted down some headings.
Just see if you can develop them for me
With a few striking phrases. It should last about ten minutes.
And then we'll go over it tomorrow.

COLBY [*looking at the notes*].   I'll try.

SIR CLAUDE. It's just in ways like this, Elizabeth,
That Colby can be of greater help than Eggerson.
I couldn't have asked Eggerson to write a speech for me.
Oh, by the way, Colby, how's the piano?

COLBY. It's a wonderful piano. I've never played
On such an instrument. It's much too good for me.

SIR CLAUDE. You need a good piano. You'll play all the better.

LADY ELIZABETH. Claude!

SIR CLAUDE.   What is it, Elizabeth?

LADY ELIZABETH. I've just made a startling discovery!
All through a name — and intuition.
But it shall be proved. The truth has come out.
It's Colby. Colby is my lost child!

SIR CLAUDE. What? Your child, Elizabeth? What on earth makes
you think so?

LADY ELIZABETH. I must see this Mrs. Guzzard. I must confront her.
This couldn't possibly be a coincidence.
It seems incredible, doesn't it, Claude?
And yet it would be still more incredible
If it were only a coincidence.
Perhaps I ought not to believe it yet,
Perhaps it is wrong of me to feel so sure,
But it seems that Providence has brought you back to me,
And you, Claude, and Eggerson have been the instruments.
I must be right. Claude, tell me I am right.

SIR CLAUDE. But Elizabeth, what has led you to believe
That Colby is your son?

LADY ELIZABETH.   Oh, I forgot
In my excitement: you arrived the very moment
When the truth dawned on me. Mrs. Guzzard!
Claude, Colby was brought up by a Mrs. Guzzard.

SIR CLAUDE. I know that. But why should that make him your son?

LADY ELIZABETH. It's the name I've been hunting for all these years —

That, and the other name, *Teddington*:
Mrs. Guzzard of Teddington. That was all I knew.
Then Tony was killed, as you know, in Africa,
And I had lost the name. Mrs. Guzzard.

SIR CLAUDE. I'm beginning now to piece it together.
You've been asking Colby about his family . . .

LADY ELIZABETH. And when he mentioned *Teddington,* there was a
faint echo —
And then Mrs. Guzzard! It must be true.

SIR CLAUDE. It is certainly a remarkable coincidence —
If it is a coincidence. But I'm afraid, Elizabeth,
What has happened is that, brooding on the past,
You began to think of Colby as what your son would be,
And then you began to see him as your son,
And then — any name you heard would have seemed the right one.

LADY ELIZABETH. Oh Claude, how can you be so sceptical!
We must see this Mrs. Guzzard, and get her to confess it.

SIR CLAUDE. I'm sorry, Elizabeth. If Mrs. Guzzard comes
To make her confession, it will be very different
From what you expect. I'm afraid, Colby,
It seems to me that we must let her know the truth.

COLBY. It seems to me . . . there is nothing for me —
Absolutely nothing — for me to say about it.
I must leave that to you.

SIR CLAUDE.   I should have told you one day.
I've always loathed keeping such a thing from you.
I see now I might as well have told you before,
But I'd hoped — and now it seems a silly thought . . .
What happens is so like what one had planned for,
And yet such a travesty of all one's plans —
I'd hoped that you would become fond of Colby,
And that he might come to take the place of your own child,
If you got to know him first — and that you'd want to adopt him.

LADY ELIZABETH. But of course I want to adopt him, Claude!
That is, if one's allowed to adopt one's own child.

SIR CLAUDE. That's not what I meant. Elizabeth,
Colby is *my* son.

LADY ELIZABETH. Quite impossible, Claude!
You have a daughter. Now you want a son.

SIR CLAUDE. I'd never want to take your son away from you.

Perhaps you have a son. But it isn't Colby.
I ought to have told you, years ago.
I told you about Lucasta, and you told me
About your own . . . misfortune. And I almost told you
About Colby. I didn't. For such a foolish reason.
Absurd it sounds now. One child each —
That seemed fair enough — though yours had been lost,
And mine I couldn't lose. But if I had another
I thought you might think — 'and how many more?'
You might have suspected any number of children!
That seems grotesque now. But it influenced me.
And I found a better reason for keeping silent.
I came to see how you longed for a son of your own,
And I thought, I'll wait for children of *our* own,
And tell her then. And they never came.
And now I regret the decision bitterly.
I ought to have told you that I had a son.

LADY ELIZABETH. But why do you think that Colby is your son?

SIR CLAUDE. Colby is the son of Mrs. Guzzard's sister,
Who died when he was born. Mrs. Guzzard brought him up,
And I provided for his education.
I have watched him grow. And Mrs. Guzzard
Knows he is my son.

LADY ELIZABETH.   But where were you, Claude,
When Colby was born?

SIR CLAUDE.   Where was I? In Canada.
My father had sent me on a business tour
To learn about his overseas investments.

LADY ELIZABETH. Then how do you know that the sister had a child?
Perhaps Mrs. Guzzard invented the story. . . .

SIR CLAUDE. Why should she invent it? The child was expected.

LADY ELIZABETH. In order to get money from you, perhaps.
No, I shouldn't say that. But she had a child
Left on her hands. The father had died
And she'd never been told the name of the mother;
And the mother had forgotten the name of Mrs. Guzzard,
And I was the mother and the child was Colby;
And Mrs. Guzzard thought you would be happy
To think you had a son, and would do well by him —
Because you *did* care for the girl, didn't you?

SIR CLAUDE. Yes, I did care. Very much. I had never
    Been in love before.
LADY ELIZABETH.   Very well then.
    That is the way it must have happened.
    Oh, Claude, you know I'm rather weak in the head
    Though I try to be clever. Do try to help me.
SIR CLAUDE. It could have happened. But I'm sure it didn't.
LADY ELIZABETH. Oh, Colby, doesn't your instinct tell you?
SIR CLAUDE. Yes, tell us everything that's in your mind.
    I know this situation must be more of an agony
    To you, than it can be even to . . . us.
COLBY. I only wish it was more acute agony:
    I don't know whether I've been suffering or not
    During this conversation. I only feel . . . numb.
    If there's agony, it's part of a total agony
    Which I can't begin to feel yet. I'm simply indifferent.
    And all the time that you've been talking
    I've only been thinking: 'What does it matter
    Whose son I am?' You don't understand
    That when one has lived without parents, as a child,
    There's a gap that never can be filled. Never.
    I like you both, I could even come to love you —
    But as friends . . . older friends. Neither, as a parent.
    I am sorry. But that's why I say it doesn't matter
    To me, which of you should be my parent.
LADY ELIZABETH. But a mother, Colby, isn't that different?
    There should always be a bond between mother and son,
    No matter how long they have lost each other.
COLBY. No, Lady Elizabeth. The position is the same
    Or crueller. Suppose I am your son.
    Then it's merely a fact. Better not know
    Than to know the fact and know it means nothing.
    At the time I was born, you might have been my mother,
    But you chose not to be. I don't blame you for that:
    God forbid! but we must take the consequences.
    At the time when I was born, your being my mother —
    If you are my mother — was a living fact.
    Now, it is a dead fact, and out of dead facts
    Nothing living can spring. Now, it is too late.
    I never wanted a parent till now —

I never thought about it. Now, you have made me think,
And I wish that I could have had a father and a mother.

LADY ELIZABETH. Stop, Colby! Something has come to me.
Claude! I don't want to take away from you
The son you thought was yours. And I know from what you said,
That you would rather he was *ours* than only *yours*.
Why should we make any further enquiries?
Let us regard him as being *our* son:
It won't be the same as what we had wanted —
But in some ways better! And prevent us both
From making unreasonable claims upon you, Colby.
It's a good idea! Why should we not be happy,
All of us? Already, Claude,
I feel as if this brought us closer together.

SIR CLAUDE. I should be contented with such an understanding;
And indeed, it's not so far from what I had intended.
Could you accept us both in that way, Colby?

COLBY. I can only say what I feel at the moment:
And yet I believe I shall always feel the same.

SIR CLAUDE. Well?

COLBY.   It would be easier, I think,
To accept you both in the place of parents
If neither of you could be. If it was pure fiction —
One can live on a fiction — but not on such a mixture
Of fiction and fact. Already, it's been hard
For me, who have never known the feelings of a son,
To be disputed between two parents.
But, if we followed your suggestion,
I know, I know I should always be haunted
By the miserable ghosts of the other parents!
It's strange enough to have two parents —
But I should have four! What about those others?
I should have to live with those ghosts, one indignant
At being cheated of his — or her — parenthood,
The other indignant at the imputation
Of false parenthood. Both mocked at.

SIR CLAUDE. Then what do you want, Colby? What do you want?
Think of the future. When you marry
You will want parents, for the sake of your children.

COLBY. I don't feel, tonight, that I ever want to marry.

You may be right. I can't take account of that.
But now I want to know whose son I am.

SIR CLAUDE. Then the first thing is: we must see Mrs. Guzzard.

LADY ELIZABETH. Oh Claude! I am terribly sorry for you.
I believe that if I had known of your . . . delusion
I would never have undeceived you.

SIR CLAUDE.   And as for me,
If I could have known what was going to happen,
I would gladly have surrendered Colby to you.
But we must see Mrs. Guzzard. I'll arrange to get her here.

LADY ELIZABETH. And I think you ought to get Eggerson as well.

SIR CLAUDE [rising]. Oh, of course, Eggerson! He knows all about it.
Let us say no more tonight. Now, Colby,
Can you find some consolation at the piano?

COLBY. I don't think, tonight, the piano would help me:
At the moment, I never want to touch it again.
But there's another reason. I must remind you
About your speech for the Potters' Company
Tomorrow night. I must get to work on it.

SIR CLAUDE. Tomorrow night. Must I go to that dinner
Tomorrow night?

COLBY.   I was looking at your notes —
Before you brought me into the conversation —
And I found one note I couldn't understand.
'Reminiscent mood.' I can't develop that
Unless you can tell me — reminiscent of what?

SIR CLAUDE. Reminiscent of what? Reminiscent of what?
'Tonight I feel in a reminiscent mood' —
Oh yes. To say something of my early ambitions
To be a potter. Not that the Members
Of the Potters' Company know anything at all
About ceramics . . . or any other art.
No, I don't think I shall be in a reminiscent mood.
Cross that out. It would only remind me
Of things that would surprise the Potters' Company
If I told them what I was really remembering.
Come, Elizabeth.

LADY ELIZABETH.   My poor Claude!

[*Exeunt* SIR CLAUDE *and* LADY ELIZABETH]

CURTAIN

Act Three

The Business Room, as in Act 1. Several mornings later. SIR CLAUDE *is moving chairs about. Enter* LADY ELIZABETH.

LADY ELIZABETH. Claude, what are you doing?

SIR CLAUDE.   Settling the places.
It's important, when you have a difficult meeting,
To decide on the seating arrangements beforehand.
I don't think you and I should be near together.
Will you sit there, beside the desk?

LADY ELIZABETH. On the other side, with the light behind me:
But won't you be sitting at the desk yourself?

SIR CLAUDE. No, that would look too formal. I thought it would be
        better
To put Eggerson there, behind the desk.
You see, I want him to be a sort of chairman.

LADY ELIZABETH. That's a good idea.

SIR CLAUDE.   On the other hand,
We mustn't look like a couple of barristers
Ready to cross-examine a witness.
It's very awkward. We don't want to start
By offending Mrs. Guzzard. That's why I thought
That Eggerson should put the first questions.
He's very good at approaching a subject
In a roundabout way. But where shall we place her?

LADY ELIZABETH. Over there, with the light full on her:
I want to be able to watch her expression.

SIR CLAUDE. But not in this chair! She must have an armchair . . .

LADY ELIZABETH. Not such a low one. Leave that in the corner
For Colby. He won't want to be conspicuous,
Poor boy!

SIR CLAUDE. After all, it was he who insisted
On this . . . investigation. But perhaps you're right.

LADY ELIZABETH. Claude, I've been thinking things over and over —

All through the night. I hardly slept at all.
I wish that Colby, somehow, might prove to be *your* son
Instead of mine. Really, I do!
It would be so much fairer. If he is mine —
As I am sure he is — then you never had a son;
While, if he were yours . . . he could still take the place
Of my son: and so he could be *our* son.
Oh dear, what do I want? I should like him to be mine,
But for you to believe that he is yours!
So I hope Mrs. Guzzard will say he is your son
And I needn't believe her. I don't believe in facts.
You do. That is the difference between us.

SIR CLAUDE. I'm not so sure of that. I've tried to believe in facts;
And I've always acted as if I believed in them.
I thought it was facts that my father believed in;
I thought that what he cared for was power and wealth;
And I came to see that what I had interpreted
In this way, was something else to *him* —
An idea, an inspiration. What he wanted to transmit to me
Was that idea, that inspiration,
Which to him was life. To me, it was a burden.
You can't communicate an inspiration,
Like that, by force of will. He was a great financier —
And I am merely a successful one.
I might have been truer to my father's inspiration
If I had done what I wanted to do.

LADY ELIZABETH. You've never talked like this to me before!
Why haven't you? I don't suppose I understand
And I know you don't think I understand anything,
And perhaps I don't. But I wish you would talk
Sometimes to me as if I did understand,
And perhaps I might come to understand better.
What did you want to do?

SIR CLAUDE.   To be a potter.
Don't laugh.

LADY ELIZABETH. I'm not laughing. I was only thinking
How strange to have lived with you, all these years,
And now you tell me, you'd have liked to be a potter!
You really mean, to make jugs and jars
Like those in your collection?

SIR CLAUDE. That's what I mean.

LADY ELIZABETH. But I should have loved you to be a potter!
Why have you never told me?

SIR CLAUDE. I didn't think
That you would be interested. More than that.
I took it for granted that what you wanted
Was a husband of importance. I thought you would despise me
If you knew what I'd really wanted to be.

LADY ELIZABETH. And I took it for granted that you were not
interested
In anything but financial affairs;
And that you needed me chiefly as a hostess.
It's a great mistake, I do believe,
For married people to take anything for granted.

SIR CLAUDE. That was a very intelligent remark.
Perhaps I have taken too much for granted
About you, Elizabeth. What did *you* want?

LADY ELIZABETH. To inspire an artist. Don't laugh.

SIR CLAUDE. I'm not laughing.
So what you wanted was to inspire an artist!

LADY ELIZABETH. Or to inspire a poet. I thought Tony was a poet.
Because he wrote me poems. And he was so beautiful.
I know now that poets don't look like poets:
And financiers, it seems, don't look like potters —
Is that what I mean? I'm getting confused.
I thought I was escaping from a world that I loathed
In Tony — and then, too late, I discovered
He belonged to the world I wanted to escape from.
He was so commonplace! I wanted to forget him,
And so, I suppose, I wanted to forget
Colby. But Colby is an artist.

SIR CLAUDE. A musician.
I am a disappointed craftsman,
And Colby is a disappointed composer.
I should have been a second-rate potter,
And he would have been a second-rate organist.
We have both chosen . . . obedience to the facts.

LADY ELIZABETH. I believe that was what *I* was trying to do.
It's very strange, Claude, but this is the first time
I have talked to you, without feeling very stupid.

495

You always made me feel that I wasn't worth talking to.

SIR CLAUDE. And you always made me feel that *your* interests
Were much too deep for discussion with *me*:
Health cures. And modern art — so long as it was modern —
And dervish dancing.

LADY ELIZABETH. Dervish dancing!
Really, Claude, how absurd you are!
Not that there isn't a lot to be learnt,
I don't doubt, from the dervish rituals.
But it doesn't matter what Mrs. Guzzard tells us,
If it satisfies Colby. Whatever happens
He shall be *our* son.

[*A knock on the door. Enter* EGGERSON]

SIR CLAUDE. Good morning, Eggerson.

EGGERSON. Good morning, Sir Claude. And Lady Elizabeth!

SIR CLAUDE. I'm sorry, Eggerson, to bring you up to London
At such short notice.

EGGERSON. Don't say that, Sir Claude.
It's true, I haven't much nowadays to bring me;
But Mrs. E. wishes I'd come up oftener!
Isn't that like the ladies! She used to complain
At my being up in London five or six days a week:
But now she says: 'You're becoming such a countryman!
You're losing touch with public affairs.'
The fact is, she misses the contact with London,
Though she doesn't admit it. She misses my news
When I came home in the evening. And the late editions
Of the papers that I picked up at Liverpool Street.
But I've so much to do, in Joshua Park —
Apart from the garden — that I've not an idle moment.
And really, now, I'm quite lost in London.
Every time I come, I notice the traffic
Has got so much worse.

SIR CLAUDE. Yes, it's always getting worse.

LADY ELIZABETH. — I hope Mrs. Eggerson is well?

EGGERSON. Pretty well.
She's always low-spirited, around this season,
When we're getting near the anniversary.

SIR CLAUDE. The anniversary? Of your son's death?

EGGERSON. Of the day we got the news. We don't often speak of it;

Yet I know what's on her mind, for days beforehand.
But here I am, talking about ourselves!
And we've more important business, I imagine.

SIR CLAUDE. Eggerson, I'm expecting Mrs. Guzzard.

EGGERSON. Indeed! Mrs. Guzzard! And why are we expecting
her?

SIR CLAUDE. I have asked her to come. Lady Elizabeth
Is sure that she knows the name of Mrs. Guzzard.

LADY ELIZABETH. Mrs. Guzzard, of Teddington.

EGGERSON.   Ah, indeed!
I shouldn't have expected her name to be known to you.

SIR CLAUDE. She'd been questioning Colby about himself,
And he mentioned the name of his aunt, Mrs. Guzzard.
Now she's convinced that Mrs. Guzzard
Of Teddington is the name of the person
To whom her own child was entrusted.

EGGERSON. What an amazing coincidence!

SIR CLAUDE.   That's what it is,
Unless she is mistaken . . .

LADY ELIZABETH.   Now, Claude!

SIR CLAUDE. And she came to the conclusion that her child must be
Colby,
So I told her the truth. But she cannot believe it.

LADY ELIZABETH. Claude, that's not quite right. Let me explain.
I am convinced that Sir Claude is mistaken,
Or has been deceived, and that Colby is my son.
I feel sure he is. But I don't want to know:
I am perfectly content to leave things as they are,
So that we may regard him as *our* son.

SIR CLAUDE. That is perfectly correct. It is Colby
Who is not satisfied with that solution.
He insists upon the facts. And that is why
I have asked Mrs. Guzzard here. *She* doesn't know that.

EGGERSON. A natural line for Mr. Simpkins to take,
If I may say so. Of course, we might discover
Another Mrs. Guzzard . . .

LADY ELIZABETH.   *Two* Mrs. Guzzards?

EGGERSON. I agree, it is a most uncommon name,
But stranger things have happened.

LADY ELIZABETH.   And both in Teddington?

EGGERSON. I agree, that would be most surprising.
  And at the same address?

LADY ELIZABETH.   I don't know the address.
  Mrs. Guzzard of Teddington, that's all I know,
  And that I could swear to.

EGGERSON.   It does seem unlikely
  That there should be two Mrs. Guzzards in Teddington.
  But assuming, for the moment, only one Mrs. Guzzard,
  Could there not have been two babies?

LADY ELIZABETH. *Two* babies, Eggerson?

EGGERSON.   I was only suggesting
  That perhaps Mrs. Guzzard made a profession
  Of . . . looking after other people's children?
  In a manner of speaking, it's perfectly respectable.

SIR CLAUDE. You're suggesting that she ran a baby farm.
  That's most unlikely, nowadays.
  Besides, I should have noticed it. I visited her house
  Often. I never saw more than one baby.

EGGERSON. She might have taken in another one
  As a temporary accommodation —
  On suitable terms. But if she did that,
  We must enquire what became of the other one.

SIR CLAUDE. But *this* baby was Colby.

LADY ELIZABETH.   Of course it was Colby.

SIR CLAUDE. But Eggerson, you really can't ask me to believe
  That she took two babies, and got them mixed.

LADY ELIZABETH. That seems to be what happened. And now we must find out
  What became of your child, Claude.

SIR CLAUDE.   What became of *my* child!
  The mother of *my* child was Mrs. Guzzard's sister.
  She wouldn't dispose of *him*. It's your child, Elizabeth,
  Whom we must try to trace.

EGGERSON.   If there was another child
  Then we must try to trace it. Certainly, Sir Claude:
  Our first step must be to question Mrs. Guzzard.

SIR CLAUDE. And that's what we are here for. She will be here shortly.
  And when she arrives I will summon Colby.
  I wanted you here first, to explain the situation:
  And I thought I would like you to conduct the proceedings.

Will you sit at the desk?

EGGERSON.   If you wish, Sir Claude.
I do feel more at ease when I'm behind a desk:
It's second nature.

SIR CLAUDE.   And put the case to her.
Don't let her think that *I* have any doubts:
You are putting the questions on behalf of my wife.

EGGERSON. I understand, Sir Claude: I understand completely.

[*A knock on the door*]

SIR CLAUDE. Good Lord, she's here already! Well . . . Come in!

[*Enter* LUCASTA]

LUCASTA. Is this a meeting? I came to speak to Colby.
I'm sorry.

SIR CLAUDE. Colby will be here.
But you're not involved in this meeting, Lucasta.
Won't it do another time?

LUCASTA.   I came to apologise
To Colby. No matter. It'll do another time.
Oh, I'm glad you're here, Eggy! You're such a support.
In any case, I've an announcement to make,
And I might as well make it now. If you'll listen.

SIR CLAUDE. Of course I'll listen. But we haven't much time.

LUCASTA. It won't take much time. I'm going to marry B.

SIR CLAUDE. To marry B.! But I thought that was all settled.

LUCASTA. Yes, of course, Claude. You thought everything settled.
That was just the trouble. You made it so obvious
That this would be the ideal solution
From your point of view. To get me off your hands.
Oh, I know what a nuisance you've always found me!
And I haven't made it easier. I didn't try to.
And knowing that you wanted me to marry B.
Made me determined that I wouldn't. Just to spite you,
I dare say. That was why I took an interest
In Colby. Because you thought he was too good for me.

SIR CLAUDE. In Colby!

LUCASTA.   Why not? That's perfectly natural.
But I'm grateful to Colby. But for Colby
I'd never have come to appreciate B.

SIR CLAUDE. But Colby! Lucasta, if I'd suspected this
I would have explained. Colby is your brother.

499

EGGERSON. Half-brother, Miss Angel.

SIR CLAUDE.   Yes, half-brother.

LUCASTA. What do you mean?

SIR CLAUDE.   Colby is my son.

LADY ELIZABETH. That is what Sir Claude believes. Claude, let me
    explain.

SIR CLAUDE. No, I'll explain. There's been some misunderstanding.
    My wife believes that Colby is *her* son.

    That is the reason for this meeting today.

    We're awaiting Mrs. Guzzard — Colby's aunt.

LUCASTA. Colby's aunt? You make my brain reel.

SIR CLAUDE. I ought to have made things clear to you
    At the time when he came here. But I didn't trust you
    To keep a secret. There were reasons for that
    Which no longer exist. But I ought to have told you.

LUCASTA. Well, I don't understand. What I do understand
    Is Colby's behaviour. If he knew it.

SIR CLAUDE.   He knew it.

LUCASTA. Why didn't he tell me? Perhaps he was about to.
    Anyway, I *knew* there had been some mistake.
    You don't know at all what I'm talking about!
    But if he knew that he was your son
    He must have been staggered when I said I was your daughter!
    I came to thank him for the shock he'd given me.
    He made me see what I really wanted.
    B. makes me feel safe. And that's what I want.
    And somehow or other, I've something to give him —
    Something that he needs. Colby doesn't need me,
    He doesn't need anyone. He's fascinating,
    But he's undependable. He has his own world,
    And he might vanish into it at any moment —
    At just the moment when you needed him most!
    And he doesn't depend upon other people, either.
    B. needs me. He's been hurt by life, just as I have,
    And we can help each other. Oh, I know you think of him
    Simply as a business man. As you thought of me
    Simply as a nuisance. We're suited to each other:
    You thought so too, Claude, but for the wrong reasons,
    And that put me off. So I'm grateful to Colby.

SIR CLAUDE. I don't know what's happened, but nevertheless

I'm sure that you have made the right decision.

LUCASTA. But the reasons why you think so are the wrong ones.

LADY ELIZABETH. And I'm sure too, Lucasta, you have made a wise
    decision.

LUCASTA. And I know very well why *you* think so:
    You think we're suited because we're both common.
    B. knows you think him common. And so he pretends
    To be very common, because he knows you think so.
    You gave us our parts. And we've shown that we can play them.

LADY ELIZABETH. I don't think you ought to say that, Lucasta;
    I have always been a person of liberal views —
    That's why I never got on with my family.

LUCASTA. Well, I'm not a person of liberal views.
    I'm very conventional. And I'm not ashamed of it.

SIR CLAUDE. Perhaps you are right. I'm not sure of anything.
    Perhaps, as you say, I've misunderstood B.,
    And I've never thought that I understood *you*;
    And I certainly fail to understand Colby.

LADY ELIZABETH. But you and I, Claude, can understand each other,
    No matter how late. And perhaps that will help us
    To understand other people. I hope so.
    Lucasta, I regard you as a . . . step-daughter;
    And shall be happy to accept Mr. Kaghan as a son-in-law.

LUCASTA. Thank you. I'm sure he'll appreciate *that*.
    But that reminds me. He's waiting downstairs.
    I don't suppose you want *us* at your meeting.

EGGERSON. Allow me. May I make a suggestion?
    Though first of all I must take the occasion
    To wish Miss Angel every happiness.
    And I'm sure she will be happy. Mr. Kaghan
    Is one of the most promising young men in the City,
    And he has a heart of gold. So have you, Miss Angel.
    We have this very important interview,
    But I'm sure that we want to greet the happy pair.
    It's all in the family. Why not let them wait downstairs
    And come back after Mrs. Guzzard has left?

SIR CLAUDE. That's not a bad idea. If Colby agrees.

LUCASTA. I trust you, Eggy. And I want to make my peace with him.

SIR CLAUDE. We'll get him now.

                [Reaches for the telephone]

501

[*A knock. Enter* COLBY]

COLBY. Have I come too soon?

I'm afraid I got impatient of waiting.

LUCASTA. Colby! I've not come to interrupt your meeting.

I've been told what it's about. But I did come to see you.

I came to apologise for my behaviour

The other afternoon.

COLBY. Apologise?

SIR CLAUDE. I've told her.

COLBY. But why should you apologise?

LUCASTA. Oh, because I knew

That I must have misunderstood your reaction.

It wouldn't have been like you — the way I thought it was.

You're much too . . . detached, ever to be shocked

In the way I thought you were. I was ashamed

Of what I was telling you, and so I was expecting

What I thought I got. But I couldn't believe it!

It isn't like you, to despise people:

You don't care enough.

COLBY. I don't care enough?

LUCASTA. No. You're either above caring,

Or else you're insensible — I don't mean insensitive!

But you're terribly cold. Or else you've some fire

To warm you, that isn't the same kind of fire

That warms other people. You're either an egotist

Or something so different from the rest of us

That we can't judge you. That's you, Colby.

COLBY. That's me, is it? I simply don't know.

Perhaps you know me better than I know myself.

But now that you know what I am . . .

LUCASTA. *Who* you are,

In the sense I've been told that you're my brother;

Which makes it more difficult to know *what* you are.

It may be there's no one so hard to understand

As one's brother . . .

COLBY. Or sister . . .

LUCASTA. What's so difficult

Is to recognise the limits of one's understanding.

It may be that understanding, as a brother and a sister,

Will come, in time. Perhaps, one day

We may understand each other. And accept the fact
That we're not necessary to each other
In the way we might have been. But a different way
That reveals itself in time. And perhaps — who knows? —
We might become more necessary to each other,
As a brother and a sister, than we could have been
In any other form of relationship.

COLBY. I want you to be happy.

LUCASTA.   I shall be happy,
If you will accept me as a sister
For the happiness that relationship may bring us
In twenty or thirty or forty years' time.
I shall be happy. I'm going to marry B.
I know you like B.

COLBY.   I'm very fond of him;
And I'm glad to think he'll be my brother-in-law.
I shall need you, both of you, Lucasta!

LUCASTA. We'll mean something to you. But you don't *need* anybody.

EGGERSON. And now may I interrupt, Miss Angel?
Why shouldn't you and Mr. Kaghan wait downstairs
And rejoin us when this interview is over?
I'm sure Mr. Simpkins will concur in this proposal.

COLBY. Of course I'd like them . . . Can't B. come up now?

EGGERSON. Better wait till afterwards.

SIR CLAUDE.   Quite right, Eggerson.

LUCASTA. Good-bye, Colby.

COLBY.   Why do you say good-bye?

LUCASTA. Good-bye to Colby as Lucasta knew him,
And good-bye to the Lucasta whom Colby knew.
We've changed since then: as you said, we're always changing.
When I come back, we'll be brother and sister —
Or so I hope. Yes, in any event,
Good-bye, Colby.

                                        [*Exit* LUCASTA]

COLBY.   Good-bye then, Lucasta.

EGGERSON. And now, how soon are we expecting Mrs. Guzzard?

SIR CLAUDE [*looking at his watch*]. She ought to be here now! It's
        surprising,
I hadn't been aware how the time was passing,
What with Lucasta's unexpected visit.

She ought to be here. It wouldn't be like her
To be late for an appointment. She always mentioned it
If *I* was late when I went to see her.

[*Enter* LUCASTA]

LUCASTA. I'm sorry to come back. It's an anti-climax.
But there seems to be nobody to answer the door.
I've just let someone in. It's the Mrs. Guzzard
Whom you are expecting. She looks rather formidable.

SIR CLAUDE. It's Parkman's day off. But where's the parlourmaid?

LUCASTA. I thought I heard someone singing in the pantry.

LADY ELIZABETH. Oh, I forgot. It's Gertrude's quiet hour.
I've been giving her lessons in recollection.
But she shouldn't be singing.

LUCASTA.   Well, what shall I do?

EGGERSON. Let me go down and explain to Mrs. Guzzard
And then bring her up.

SIR CLAUDE.   No, I want you here, Eggerson.
Will you show her up, Lucasta?

LUCASTA.   I'll make B. do it.

                                   [*Exit* LUCASTA]

SIR CLAUDE. I wish you could arrange the servants' time-table better.
This is a most unfortunate beginning.

LADY ELIZABETH. She's been making progress, under my direction;
But she shouldn't have been singing.

SIR CLAUDE.   Well, are we ready?

[*A quiet knock. Enter* KAGHAN, *escorting* MRS. GUZZARD. *Exit* KAGHAN]
Good morning, Mrs. Guzzard. I must apologise:
I'm afraid there has been some domestic incompetence.
You should have been announced.

MRS. GUZZARD.   I believe I was punctual.
But I didn't mind waiting in the least, Sir Claude.
I know that you are always much engaged.

SIR CLAUDE. First, let me introduce you to my wife.
Lady Elizabeth Mulhammer.

LADY ELIZABETH.   Good morning, Mrs. Guzzard.
You don't know me, but I know about you:
We have more in common than you are aware of.

MRS. GUZZARD. I suppose you mean Colby?

LADY ELIZABETH.   Yes. To do with Colby.

SIR CLAUDE. Elizabeth, you know we are to leave that to Eggerson.

This is Mr. Eggerson, Mrs. Guzzard:
My confidential clerk. That is to say,
Colby's predecessor, who recently retired.
Now he lives . . . in the country. But he knows the whole story:
He's been in my confidence — and I may say, my friend —
For very many years. So I asked him to be present.
I hope you don't mind?

MRS. GUZZARD.   Why should I mind?
I have heard about Mr. Eggerson from Colby.
I am very happy to make his acquaintance.

SIR CLAUDE. And I thought he might . . . conduct the proceedings:
He's the very soul of tact and discretion.

MRS. GUZZARD. Certainly, Sir Claude, if that is what you wish.
But is the subject of this meeting —
I suppose to do with Colby — so very confidential?

EGGERSON. Yes, that is what I should call it, Mrs. Guzzard.
I take it, Sir Claude, I should open the discussion?

SIR CLAUDE. If you please, Eggerson.

EGGERSON.   Then let's make a start.
The question has to do, as you surmised, with Mr. Simpkins.
It also concerns a problem of paternity.

LADY ELIZABETH. Or of maternity.

SIR CLAUDE.   Don't interrupt, Elizabeth.

MRS. GUZZARD. I don't understand you.

EGGERSON.   It's this way, Mrs. Guzzard.
It is only recently that Lady Elizabeth
Heard your name mentioned, by Mr. Simpkins.
She was struck by your name and your living in Teddington.
And now we must go back, many years:
Well, not so many years — when you get to my age
The past and the future both seem very brief —
But long enough ago for the question to be possible.
Lady Elizabeth, before her marriage
Had a child . . .

LADY ELIZABETH. A son.

EGGERSON.   Had a son
Whom she could not, in the circumstances, acknowledge.
That happens not infrequently, Mrs. Guzzard.

MRS. GUZZARD. So I am aware. I have known it to happen.

EGGERSON. — Who was taken charge of by the father.

That is to say, placed out to be cared for
Till further notice by a foster-mother.
Unfortunately, the father died suddenly . . .

LADY ELIZABETH. He was run over. By a rhinoceros
In Tanganyika.

SIR CLAUDE.   That's not relevant.
Leave it to Eggerson.

EGGERSON.   The father died abroad.
Lady Elizabeth did not know the name of the lady
Who had taken the child. Or rather, had forgotten it.
She was not, in any case, in a position
In which she could have instituted enquiries.
So, for many years, she has been without a clue
Until the other day. This son, Mrs. Guzzard,
If he is alive, must be a grown man.
I believe you have had no children of your own;
But I'm sure you can sympathise.

MRS. GUZZARD.   I can sympathise.
I had a child, and lost him. Not in the way
That Lady Elizabeth's child was lost.
Let us hope that her son may be restored to her.

EGGERSON. That is exactly what we are aiming at.
We have a clue — or what appears to be a clue.
That is why Sir Claude has asked you to be present.

MRS. GUZZARD. You think that I might be able to help you?

EGGERSON. It seems just possible. A few days ago,
As I said, Lady Elizabeth learned your name;
And the name struck her as being familiar.

MRS. GUZZARD. Indeed? It is not a very common name.

EGGERSON. That is what impressed her. Mrs. Guzzard
Of Teddington! Lady Elizabeth is convinced
That it was a Mrs. Guzzard of Teddington
To whom her new-born child was confided.
Of course she might be mistaken about Teddington . . .

LADY ELIZABETH. I am *not* mistaken about Teddington.

EGGERSON. I am only suggesting, Lady Elizabeth,
There are other places that sound like Teddington
But not so many names that sound like Guzzard —
Or if there are, they are equally uncommon.
But, Mrs. Guzzard, this is where you can help us —

Do you know of any other Mrs. Guzzard?

MRS. GUZZARD.   None.

EGGERSON. Whether, I mean, in Teddington or elsewhere?
Now I must ask a more delicate question:
Did you, at any time, take in a child —
A child, that is, of parents unknown to you —
Under such conditions?

MRS. GUZZARD.   Yes, I did take in a child.
My husband and I were childless . . . at the time,
And very poor. It offered two advantages.

EGGERSON. And did you know the name of the father
Or of the mother?

MRS. GUZZARD.   I was not told either.
I understood the child was very well connected:
Otherwise, I should not have taken him.
But he was brought to me by a third party,
Through whom the monthly payments were made.

EGGERSON. The terms were satisfactory?

MRS. GUZZARD.   Very satisfactory —
So long, that is to say, as the money was forthcoming.

EGGERSON. Did the payments come to an end?

MRS. GUZZARD.   Very suddenly.

LADY ELIZABETH. That must have been when Tony met with his
          accident.

MRS. GUZZARD. I was informed that the father had died
Without making a will.

LADY ELIZABETH.   He was very careless.

MRS. GUZZARD. And that the heirs acknowledged no responsibility.
The mother, I suppose, could have got an order
If she could have established the paternity;
But I didn't know who she was! What could I do?

LADY ELIZABETH. Oh, Claude, you see? You understand, Colby?

SIR CLAUDE. Don't be certain yet, Elizabeth.

LADY ELIZABETH.   There is no doubt about it.
Colby is my son.

MRS. GUZZARD.   Your son, Lady Elizabeth?
Are you suggesting that I kept a child of yours
And deceived Sir Claude by pretending it was his?

SIR CLAUDE. That is just the point. My wife has convinced herself
That Colby is her son. I know he is *my* son.

And I asked you here so that you might tell her so.

EGGERSON. Don't take this as a personal reflection,
Mrs. Guzzard. Far from it. You must make allowances
For a mother who has been hoping against hope
To find her son. Put yourself in her position.
If you had lost your son, in a similar way,
Wouldn't you grasp at any straw
That offered hope of finding him?

MRS. GUZZARD.   Perhaps I should.

LADY ELIZABETH. There isn't a shadow of doubt in my mind.
I'm surprised that you, Eggerson, with your legal training,
Should talk about straws! Colby is my son.

MRS. GUZZARD. In the circumstances, I ignore that remark.

EGGERSON. May I pour a drop of oil on these troubled waters?
Let us approach the question from another angle,
And ask Mrs. Guzzard what became of the child
She took in, which may have been Lady Elizabeth's.

SIR CLAUDE. That's a very sensible suggestion, Eggerson.
A breath of sanity. Thank you for that.

MRS. GUZZARD. We parted with it. A dear little boy.
I was happy to have him while the payments were made;
But we could not afford to adopt the child,
Or continue to keep him, when the payments ended.

EGGERSON. And how did you dispose of him?

MRS. GUZZARD.   We had neighbours
Who were childless, and eager to adopt a child.
They had taken a fancy to him. So they adopted him.
Then they left Teddington, and we lost sight of them.

EGGERSON. But you know their name?

MRS. GUZZARD.   Yes, I know their name:
Like mine, a somewhat unusual one.
Perhaps it might be possible to trace them.
The name was Kaghan.

SIR CLAUDE.   Their name was Kaghan!

MRS. GUZZARD. K-A-G-H-A-N. An odd name.
They were excellent people. Nonconformists.

EGGERSON. And the child, I suppose he had a Christian name?

MRS. GUZZARD. There was nothing to show that the child had been
baptised
When it came to us; but we could not be sure.

My husband was particular in such matters,
So we had it given conditional baptism.

EGGERSON. What name did you give him?

MRS. GUZZARD.   We named the child Barnabas.

LADY ELIZABETH. Barnabas? There's never been such a name
In my family. Or, I'm sure, in his father's.
But how did he come to be called Colby?

SIR CLAUDE. But, Elizabeth, it isn't Colby!
Don't you see who it is?

MRS. GUZZARD.   My husband chose the name.
We had been married in the church of St. Barnabas.

COLBY. Barnabas Kaghan. Is he the little cousin
Who died? Don't you remember, Aunt Sarah,
My finding a rattle and a jingle-bell,
And your telling me I had had a little cousin
Who had died?

MRS. GUZZARD.   Yes, Colby, that is what I told you.

LADY ELIZABETH. So my child is living. I was sure of that.
But I believe that Colby is Barnabas.

SIR CLAUDE. No, Elizabeth, Barnabas is Barnabas.
I must explain this, Mrs. Guzzard.
I have a very promising young colleague —
In fact, the young man who showed you upstairs —
Whose name is Barnabas Kaghan.

LADY ELIZABETH.   Barnabas?

SIR CLAUDE. Yes, Elizabeth. He sometimes has to sign his full name.
But he doesn't like the name, for some reason;
So we call him B.

MRS. GUZZARD.   A very good name.
He ought to be proud of it.

LADY ELIZABETH.   How old is this Barnabas?

SIR CLAUDE. About twenty-eight, I think.

MRS. GUZZARD.   He should be twenty-eight.

LADY ELIZABETH. Then I must be out in my calculations.

SIR CLAUDE. That wouldn't surprise me.

LADY ELIZABETH.   Yes, what year was it?
I'm getting so confused. What with Colby being Barnabas —
I mean, not Barnabas. And Mr. Kaghan
Being Barnabas. I suppose I'll get used to it.

COLBY. But he's waiting downstairs! Isn't this the moment

For me to bring him up? And Lucasta?
EGGERSON. An excellent suggestion, Mr. Simpkins.

[*Exit* COLBY]

EGGERSON. And now, if you agree, Lady Elizabeth,
    We can ask Mr. Kaghan about his parents;
    And if Mr. and Mrs. Kaghan are still living
    Mrs. Guzzard should be able to identify them.
LADY ELIZABETH. And will that prove that Mr. Kaghan —
    This Mr. Kaghan — is my son?
EGGERSON. It creates an inherent probability —
    If that's the right expression.
SIR CLAUDE.   I believe, Elizabeth,
    That you have found your son.
EGGERSON.   Subject to confirmation.
LADY ELIZABETH. And to my being able to adjust myself to it.
[*Re-enter* COLBY, *with* KAGHAN *and* LUCASTA]
COLBY. I have told them to be prepared for a surprise.
LADY ELIZABETH. Barnabas! Is your name Barnabas?
KAGHAN. Why, yes, it is. Did you tell her, Sir Claude?
SIR CLAUDE. No, B. It was Mrs. Guzzard who revealed it.
    This is Mr. Barnabas Kaghan —
    Mrs. Guzzard. And . . . my daughter Lucasta.
KAGHAN. But how did Mrs. Guzzard know my name?
MRS. GUZZARD. Were Mr. and Mrs. Alfred Kaghan your parents?
KAGHAN. Yes. They are. My adoptive parents.
MRS. GUZZARD. And did they at one time live in Teddington?
KAGHAN. I believe they did. But why are you interested?
MRS. GUZZARD. Lady Elizabeth, I believe that this is your son.
    If so, I am cleared from your unjust suspicion.
EGGERSON. Mr. Kaghan, are your adoptive parents living?
KAGHAN. In Kent. They wanted to retire to the country.
    So I found them a little place near Sevenoaks
    Where they keep bees. But why are you asking?
LADY ELIZABETH. Because, Barnabas, it seems you are my son.
EGGERSON. You will wish to obtain confirmation
    Of this interesting discovery, Mr. Kaghan,
    By putting your adoptive parents in touch
    With Mrs. Guzzard. It's for them to confirm
    That they took you, as a child, from Mrs. Guzzard,
    To whom, it seems, you had first been entrusted.

KAGHAN. I really don't know what emotion to register . . .

LUCASTA. You don't need to talk that language any longer:
Just say you're embarrassed.

KAGHAN.   Well, I am embarrassed.
If Lady Elizabeth is my mother . . .

LADY ELIZABETH. There is no doubt whatever about it, Barnabas.
I am your mother.

KAGHAN.   But who was my father?

LADY ELIZABETH. He died very suddenly. Of a fatal accident
When you were very young. That is why you were adopted.

KAGHAN. But what did he do? Was he a financier?

LADY ELIZABETH. He was not good at figures. Your business ability
Comes, I suppose, from my side of the family.
But he was in a very good regiment —
For a time, at least.

KAGHAN.   Well, I must get used to that.
But I should like to know how I ought to address you,
Lady Elizabeth. I've always been accustomed
To regard Mrs. Kaghan as my mother.

LADY ELIZABETH. Then in order to avoid any danger of confusion
You may address me as Aunt Elizabeth.

KAGHAN. That's easier, certainly.

LADY ELIZABETH.   And I shall wish to meet them.
Claude, we must invite the Kaghans to dinner.

SIR CLAUDE. By all means, Elizabeth.

KAGHAN.   But, Lady Elizabeth —
I mean, Aunt Elizabeth: if I call you Aunt Elizabeth
Would you mind very much calling me . . . just 'B'?

LADY ELIZABETH. Certainly, if you prefer that, Barnabas.

LUCASTA. Why is it that you don't like the name of Barnabas?

KAGHAN. I don't want people calling me 'Barney' —
Barney Kaghan! Kaghan's all right.
But Barney Kaghan — it sounds rather flashy:
It wouldn't make the right impression in the City.

LUCASTA. When you're an alderman, you'll be Sir Barney Kaghan!

LADY ELIZABETH. And I'm very glad you're announcing your
engagement.
Lucasta, I shall take charge of your wedding.

LUCASTA. We'd meant to be married very quietly
In a register office.

LADY ELIZABETH. You must have a church wedding.

MRS. GUZZARD. I am glad to hear you say so, Lady Elizabeth.
But are *you* satisfied?

LADY ELIZABETH. Satisfied? What about?

MRS. GUZZARD. That your suspicions of me were wholly unfounded.

LADY ELIZABETH. Oh, Mrs. Guzzard, I had no suspicions!
I thought there had been a confusion — that's all.

MRS. GUZZARD. I feared there might be a confusion in your mind
Between the meaning of *confusion* and *imposture*.

SIR CLAUDE. I don't think there is any confusion now:
I'm sure that my wife is perfectly convinced;
And Mr. Kaghan's . . . mother, I am sure, will confirm it.

MRS. GUZZARD. That is as much to my interest as anyone's.
But will your wife be satisfied,
When she has the evidence the Kaghans will supply,
To recognise Barnabas Kaghan as her son?
[*To* LADY ELIZABETH] Are you contented to have him as your son?

SIR CLAUDE. That seems a strange question, Mrs. Guzzard.

MRS. GUZZARD. I have been asked here to answer strange questions —
And now it is my turn to ask them.
I should like to gratify everyone's wishes.

LADY ELIZABETH. Oh, of course . . . Yes, I'm sure . . . I shall be very
happy.

MRS. GUZZARD. You wished for your son, and now you have your son.
We all of us have to adapt ourselves
To the wish that is granted. That can be a painful process,
As I know. And you, Barnabas Kaghan,
Are you satisfied to find yourself the son
Of Lady Elizabeth Mulhammer?

KAGHAN. It's very much better than being a foundling —
If I can live up to it. And . . . yes, of course,
If I can make it right with my parents.
I'm fond of them, you know.

LADY ELIZABETH. I shall see to that, Barnabas.

KAGHAN. B. — if you don't mind, Aunt Elizabeth.

LADY ELIZABETH. B. — and I'm sure we shall become great friends.

EGGERSON. I'm sure we all wish for nothing better.

MRS. GUZZARD. Wishes, when realised, sometimes turn
Against those who have made them.
[*To* LADY ELIZABETH *and* KAGHAN] Not, I think, with you.

[*To* LUCASTA] Nor, so far as I can judge, with you.
Perhaps you are the wisest wisher here:
I shall not ask you whether you are satisfied
To be the wife of Barnabas Kaghan,
The daughter-in-law of Lady Elizabeth,
And the daughter of Sir Claude Mulhammer.

SIR CLAUDE. That is *my* concern — that she shall be satisfied
To be my daughter.

MRS. GUZZARD.   Now, Colby,
I must ask *you* now, have you had your wish?

SIR CLAUDE. Colby only wanted to be sure of the truth.

COLBY. That is a very strange question, Aunt Sarah:
To which I can only give a strange answer.
Sir Claude is right: I wished to know the truth.
What it is, doesn't matter. All I wanted was relief
From the nagging annoyance of knowing there's a fact
That one doesn't know. But the fact itself
Is unimportant, once one knows it.

MRS. GUZZARD. You had no preference? Between a father and a
mother?

COLBY. I've never had a father or a mother —
It's different for B. He's had his foster-parents,
So he can afford another relationship.
Let my mother rest in peace. As for a father —
I have the idea of a father.
It's only just come to me. I should like a father
Whom I have never known and couldn't know now,
Because he would have died before I was born
Or before I could remember; whom I could get to know
Only by report, by documents —
The story of his life, of his success or failure . . .
Perhaps his failure more than his success —
By objects that belonged to him, and faded photographs
In which I should try to decipher a likeness;
Whose image I could create in my own mind,
To live with that image. An ordinary man
Whose life I could in some way perpetuate
By being the person he would have liked to be,
And by doing the things he had wanted to do.

MRS. GUZZARD. Whose son would you wish to be, Colby:

Sir Claude's — or the son of some other man
Obscure and silent? A dead man, Colby.
Be careful what you say.

COLBY.   A dead obscure man.

MRS. GUZZARD. You shall have your wish. And when you have your
    wish
You will have to come to terms with it. You shall have a father
Dead, and unknown to you.

SIR CLAUDE.   What do you mean?

MRS. GUZZARD. Colby is not your son, Sir Claude.

COLBY. Who was my father, then?

MRS. GUZZARD.   Herbert Guzzard.
You are the son of a disappointed musician.

COLBY. And who was my mother?

MRS. GUZZARD.   Let your mother rest in peace.
I *was* your mother; but I chose to be your aunt.
So you may have your wish, and have no mother.

SIR CLAUDE. Mrs. Guzzard, this is perfectly incredible!
You couldn't have carried out such a deception
Over all these years. And why *should* you have deceived me?

EGGERSON. Mrs. Guzzard, can you substantiate this statement?

MRS. GUZZARD. Registration of birth. To Herbert and Sarah Guzzard
A son.

EGGERSON. And what about your sister and her child?

MRS. GUZZARD. Registration of death. The child was never born.

SIR CLAUDE. I don't believe it. I simply can't believe it.
Mrs. Guzzard, you are inventing this fiction
In response to what Colby said he wanted.

EGGERSON. I'll examine the records myself, Sir Claude.
Not that we doubt your word, Mrs. Guzzard:
But in a matter of such extreme importance
You'll understand the need for exact confirmation.

MRS. GUZZARD. I understand that, Mr. Eggerson. Quite well.

SIR CLAUDE. I shall not believe it. I'll not believe those records.
You pretend to have carried out a deception
For twenty-five years? It's quite impossible.

MRS. GUZZARD. I had no intention of deceiving you, Sir Claude,
Till you deceived yourself. When you went to Canada
My sister found that she was to have a child:
That much is true. I also was expecting one.

That you did not know. It did not concern you.
As I have just said, my sister died
Before the child could be born. You were very far away;
I sent you a message, which never reached you.
On your return, you came at once to see me;
And I found that I had to break the news to you.
You saw the child. You assumed that it was yours;
And you were so pleased, I shrank, at the moment,
From undeceiving you. And then I thought — why not?
My husband also had died. I was left very poor.
If I let you continue to think the child was yours,
My son was assured of a proper start in life —
That I knew. And it would make you so happy!
If I said the child was mine, what future could he have?
And then I was frightened by what I had done.
Though I had never said 'this child is yours',
I feared you would ask for the birth certificate.
You never did. And so it went on.

SIR CLAUDE. This is horribly plausible. But it can't be true.

MRS. GUZZARD. Consider, Sir Claude. Would I tell you all this
Unless it was true? In telling you the truth
I am sacrificing my ambitions for Colby.
I am sacrificing also my previous sacrifice.
This is even greater than the sacrifice I made
When I let you claim him. Do you think it is a small thing
For me, to see my life's ambition come to nothing?
When I gave up my place as Colby's mother
I gave up something I could never have back.
Don't you understand that this revelation
Drives the knife deeper and twists it in the wound?
I had very much rather that the facts were otherwise.

COLBY. I believe you. I must believe you:
This gives me freedom.

SIR CLAUDE.   But, Colby —
If this should be true — of course it can't be true! —
But I see you believe it. You want to believe it.
Well, believe it, then. But don't let it make a difference
To our relations. Or, perhaps, for the better?
Perhaps we'll be happier together if you think
I am not your father. I'll accept that.

If you will stay with me. It shall make no difference
To my plans for your future.

COLBY.   Thank you, Sir Claude.

You're a very generous man. But now I know who was my father
I must follow my father — so that I may come to know him.

SIR CLAUDE. What do you mean?

COLBY.   I want to be an organist.

It doesn't matter about success —
I aimed too high before — beyond my capacity.
I thought I didn't want to be an organist
When I found I had no chance of getting to the top —
That is, to become the organist of a cathedral.
But my father was an unsuccessful organist.

MRS. GUZZARD. You should say, Colby, not very successful.

COLBY. And I wish to follow my father.

SIR CLAUDE.   But, Colby:

Don't you remember a talk we had —
So very long ago! — when we shared our ambitions
And shared our disappointment. And you described your feelings
On beginning to learn the ways of business;
The exhilaration of finding you could handle
Matters you would have thought so uncongenial;
And the way in which you felt that you were changing?
That conversation would have convinced me
With no other evidence, that you were my son,
Because you described my own experience, exactly.
Does that mean nothing to you, the experience we shared?
Heaven knows — and you know — I put no obstruction
In the way of your fulfilling your musical ambitions —
Had you been able to fulfil them.
Believe, if you like, that I am not your father:
I'll accept that. I put no claim upon you —
Except the claim of our likeness to each other.
We have undergone the same disillusionment:
I want us to make the best of it, together.

COLBY. No, Sir Claude. I hate to hurt you
As I am hurting you. But it is very different.
As long as I believed that you were my father
I was content to have had the same ambitions
And in the same way to accept their failure.

516

You had your father before you, as a model;
You knew your inheritance. Now I know mine.

SIR CLAUDE. I shall never ask you to think of me as a father;
All I ask you is — to regard me as a friend.

COLBY. But you would still think of me as your son.
There can be no relation of father and son
Unless it works both ways. For you to regard me —
As you would — as your son, when I could not think of you
As my father: if I accepted that
I should be guilty towards you. I like you too much.
You've become a man without illusions
About himself, and without ambitions.
Now that I've abandoned *my* illusions and ambitions
All that's left is love. But not on false pretences:
That's why I must leave you.

SIR CLAUDE.   Eggerson!
Can't you persuade him?

LADY ELIZABETH.   Yes. My poor Claude!
Do try to help him, Eggerson.

EGGERSON.   I wouldn't venture.
Mr. Simpkins is a man who knows his own mind.
Is it true, Mr. Simpkins, that what you desire
Is to become the organist of some parish church?

COLBY. That is what I want. If anyone will take me.

EGGERSON. If so, I happen to know of a vacancy
In my own parish, in Joshua Park —
If it should appeal to you. The organist we had
Died two months ago. We've been looking for another.

COLBY. Do you think that they would give me a trial?

EGGERSON. Give you a trial? I'm certain.
Good organists don't seem to want to come to Joshua Park.

COLBY. But I've told you, I'm not a very good organist!

EGGERSON. Don't say that, Mr. Simpkins, until you've tried our organ!

COLBY. Well, if you could induce them to try me . . .

EGGERSON. The Parochial Church Council will be only too pleased,
And I have some influence. *I* am the Vicar's Warden.

COLBY. I'd like to apply.

EGGERSON.   The stipend is small —
Very small, I'm afraid. Not enough to live on.
We'll have to think of other ways

Of making up an income. Piano lessons? —
As a temporary measure; because, Mr. Simpkins —
I hope you won't take this as an impertinence —
I don't see you spending a lifetime as an organist.
I think you'll come to find you've another vocation.
We worked together every day, you know,
For quite a little time, and I've watched you pretty closely.
Mr. Simpkins! You'll be thinking of reading for orders.
And you'll still have your music. Why, Mr. Simpkins,
Joshua Park may be only a stepping-stone
To a precentorship! And a canonry!

COLBY. We'll cross that bridge when we come to it, Eggers.
Oh, I'm sorry . . .

EGGERSON.   Don't be sorry: I'm delighted.
And by the way, a practical point:
If you took the position, you'd want to find your feet
In Joshua Park, before you settled on lodgings;
We have a spare room. We should be most happy
If you cared to stop with us, until you were settled.

COLBY. I'd be very glad indeed — if Mrs. Eggerson approved.

EGGERSON. There'll be no one so pleased as Mrs. E.;
Of that I can assure you.

MRS. GUZZARD.   Mr. Eggerson,
I cannot see eye to eye with you,
Having been, myself, the wife of an organist;
But you too, I think, have had a wish realised.
— I believe that this interview can now be terminated.
If you will excuse me, Sir Claude . . .

SIR CLAUDE.   Excuse you? Yes.

MRS. GUZZARD. I shall return to Teddington. Colby,
Will you get me a taxi to go to Waterloo?

COLBY. Get you a taxi? Yes, Aunt Sarah;
But I should see you home.

MRS. GUZZARD.   Home? Only to a taxi.
Do you mind if I take my leave, Sir Claude?
I'm no longer needed here.

                                    [*Exit* COLBY]

SIR CLAUDE.   Mind? What do I mind?

MRS. GUZZARD. Then I will say goodbye. You have all had your wish
In one form or another. You and I, Sir Claude,

Had *our* wishes twenty-five years ago;
But we failed to observe, when we had our wishes,
That there was a time-limit clause in the contract.

SIR CLAUDE. What's that? Oh. Good-bye, Mrs. Guzzard.

[*Exit* MRS. GUZZARD]

SIR CLAUDE. What's happened? Have they gone? Is Colby coming
back?

LADY ELIZABETH. My poor Claude!

[LUCASTA *crosses to* SIR CLAUDE *and kneels beside him*]

KAGHAN. You know, Claude, I think we all made the same mistake —
All except Eggers . . .

EGGERSON. Me, Mr. Kaghan?

KAGHAN. We wanted Colby to be something he wasn't.

LADY ELIZABETH. I suppose that's true of you and me, Claude.
Between not knowing what other people want of one,
And not knowing what one should ask of other people,
One does make mistakes! But I mean to do better.
Claude, we've got to try to understand our children.

KAGHAN. And we should like to understand *you* . . .
I mean, I'm including both of you,
Claude . . . and Aunt Elizabeth.
You know, Claude, both Lucasta and I
Would like to mean something to you . . . if you'd let us;
And we'd take the responsibility of meaning it.

[LUCASTA *puts her arms around* SIR CLAUDE]

SIR CLAUDE. Don't leave me, Lucasta.
Eggerson! Do *you* really believe her?

[EGGERSON *nods*]

CURTAIN

The Cast of the First Production
at the
Edinburgh Festival
August 25–September 5 1953

Sir Claude Mulhammer   PAUL ROGERS
Eggerson   ALAN WEBB
Colby Simpkins   DENHOLM ELLIOTT
B. Kaghan   PETER JONES
Lucasta Angel   MARGARET LEIGHTON
Lady Elizabeth Mulhammer   ISABEL JEANS
Mrs. Guzzard   ALISON LEGGATT

Presented by HENRY SHEREK
Directed by E. MARTIN BROWNE
Settings designed by HUTCHINSON SCOTT

THE ELDER STATESMAN

TO MY WIFE

To whom I owe the leaping delight
That quickens my senses in our wakingtime
And the rhythm that governs the repose of our sleepingtime,
    The breathing in unison

Of lovers . . .
Who think the same thoughts without need of speech
And babble the same speech without need of meaning:

To you I dedicate this book, to return as best I can
With words a little part of what you have given me.
The words mean what they say, but some have a further meaning
    For you and me only.

Characters

Monica Claverton-Ferry
Charles Hemington
Lambert
Lord Claverton
Federico Gomez
Mrs. Piggott
Mrs. Carghill
Michael Claverton-Ferry

ACT ONE

The drawing-room of Lord Claverton's London house. Four o'clock in the afternoon

ACT TWO

The Terrace at Badgley Court. Morning

ACT THREE

The Same. Late afternoon of the following day

Act One

The drawing-room of LORD CLAVERTON'S *London house. Four o'clock in the afternoon.*

[*Voices in the hall*]

CHARLES. Is your father at home to-day?

MONICA. You'll see him at tea.

CHARLES. But if I'm not going to have you to myself
There's really no point in my staying to tea.

[*Enter* MONICA *and* CHARLES *carrying parcels*]

MONICA. But you *must* stay to tea. That was understood
When you said you could give me the whole afternoon.

CHARLES. But I couldn't say what I wanted to say to you
Over luncheon . . .

MONICA. That's your own fault.
You should have taken me to some other restaurant
Instead of to one where the *maître d'hôtel*
And the waiters all seem to be your intimate friends.

CHARLES. It's the only place where I'm really well known
And get well served. And when *you're* with me
It must be a perfect lunch.

MONICA. It was a perfect lunch.
But I know what men are — they like to show off.
That's masculine vanity, to want to have the waiters
All buzzing round you: and it reminds the girl
That she's not the only one who's been there with him.

CHARLES. Well, tease me if you like. But a man does feel a fool
If he takes you to a place where he's utterly unknown
And the waiters all appear to be avoiding his eye.

MONICA. We're getting off the point . . .

CHARLES. You've got me off *my* point . . .
I was trying to explain . . .

MONICA. It's simply the question
Of your staying to tea. As you practically promised.

CHARLES. What you don't understand is that I have a grievance.

On Monday you're leaving London, with your father:
I arranged to be free for the whole afternoon
On the plain understanding . . .
MONICA.   That you should stop to tea.
CHARLES. When I said that I was free for the whole afternoon,
That meant you were to give *me* the whole afternoon.
I couldn't say what I wanted to, in a restaurant;
And then you took me on a shopping expedition . . .
MONICA. If you don't like shopping with me . . .
CHARLES.   Of course I like shopping with you.
But how can one *talk* on a shopping expedition —
Except to guess what you want to buy
And advise you to buy it.
MONICA.   But why not stop to tea?
CHARLES. Very well then, I will stop to tea,
But you know I won't get a chance to talk to you.
You know that. Now that your father's retired
He's at home every day. And you're leaving London.
And because your father simply can't bear it
That any man but he should have you to himself,
Before I've said two words he'll come ambling in . . .
MONICA. You've said a good deal more than two words already.
And besides, my father doesn't amble.
You're not at all respectful.
CHARLES.   I try to be respectful;
But you know that I shan't have a minute alone with you.
MONICA. You've already had several minutes alone with me
Which you've wasted in wrangling. But seriously, Charles,
Father's sure to be buried in the library
And he won't think of leaving it until he's called for tea.
So why not talk now? Though I know very well
What it is you want to say. I've heard it all before.
CHARLES. And you'll hear it again. You think I'm going to tell you
Once more, that I'm in love with you. Well, you're right.
But I've something else to say that I haven't said before,
That will give you a shock. I believe *you* love *me*.
MONICA. Oh, what a dominating man you are!
Really, you must imagine you're a hypnotist.
CHARLES. Is this a time to torment me? But I'm selfish
In saying that, because I think —

525

I think you're tormenting yourself as well.

MONICA. You're right. I am. Because *I am* in love with you.

CHARLES. So I was right! The moment I'd said it
      I was badly frightened. For I didn't *know* you loved me —
      I merely wanted to believe it. And I've made you say so!
      But now that you've said so, you must say it again,
      For I need so much assurance! Are you sure you're not mistaken?

MONICA. How did this come, Charles? It crept so softly
      On silent feet, and stood behind my back
      Quietly, a long time, a long long time
      Before I felt its presence.

CHARLES.   Your words seem to come
      From very far away. Yet very near. You are changing me
      And I am changing you.

MONICA.   Already
      How much of me is you?

CHARLES.   And how much of me is you?
      I'm not the same person as a moment ago.
      What do the words mean now — *I* and *you*?

MONICA. In our private world — now we have our private world —
      The meanings are different. Look! We're back in the room
      That we entered only a few minutes ago.
      Here's an armchair, there's the table;
      There's the door . . . and I hear someone coming:
      It's Lambert with the tea . . .
      [*Enter* LAMBERT *with trolley*]
                              and I shall say, 'Lambert,
      Please let his lordship know that tea is waiting'.

LAMBERT. Yes, Miss Monica.

MONICA.   I'm very glad, Charles,
      That you *can* stay to tea.

                                      [*Exit* LAMBERT]
                      — Now we're in the public world.

CHARLES. And your father will come. With his calm possessive air
      And his kindly welcome, which is always a reminder
      That I mustn't stay too long, for you belong to him.
      He seems so placidly to take it for granted
      That you don't really care for any company but his!

MONICA. You're not to assume that anything I've said to you
      Has given you the right to criticise my father.

In the first place, you don't understand him;
In the second place, we're not engaged yet.

CHARLES. Aren't we? We're agreed that we're in love with each other,
And, there being no legal impediment
Isn't that enough to constitute an engagement?
Aren't you sure that you want to marry me?

MONICA. Yes, Charles. I'm sure that I want to marry you
When I'm free to do so. But by that time
You may have changed your mind. Such things have happened.

CHARLES. That won't happen to me.

[*Knock. Enter* LAMBERT]

LAMBERT. Excuse me, Miss Monica. His Lordship said to tell you
Not to wait tea for him.

MONICA.   Thank you, Lambert.

LAMBERT. He's busy at the moment. But he won't be very long.

[*Exit*]

CHARLES. Don't you understand that you're torturing me?
How long will you be imprisoned, alone with your father
In that very expensive hotel for convalescents
To which you're taking him? And what after that?

MONICA. There are several good reasons why I should go with
him.

CHARLES. Better reasons than for marrying me?
What reasons?

MONICA.   First, his terror of being alone.
In the life he's led, he's never had to be alone.
And when he's been at home in the evening,
Even when he's reading, or busy with his papers
He needs to have someone else in the room with him,
Reading too — or just sitting — someone
Not occupied with anything that can't be interrupted.
Someone to make a remark to now and then.
And mostly it's been me.

CHARLES.   I know it's been you.
It's a pity that you haven't had brothers and sisters
To share the burden. Sisters, I should say,
For your brother's never been of any use to you.

MONICA. And never will be of any use to anybody,
I'm afraid. Poor Michael! Mother spoilt him
And Father was too severe — so they're always at loggerheads.

527

CHARLES. But you spoke of several reasons for your going with your
       father.

      Is there any better reason than his fear of solitude?

MONICA. The second reason is exactly the opposite:

      It's his fear of being exposed to strangers.

CHARLES. But he's most alive when he's among people

      Managing, manœuvring, cajoling or bullying —

      At all of which he's a master. Strangers!

MONICA. You don't understand. It's one thing meeting people

      When you're in authority, with authority's costume,

      When the man that people see when they meet you

      Is not the private man, but the public personage.

      In politics Father wore a public label.

      And later, as chairman of public companies,

      Always his privacy has been preserved.

CHARLES. His privacy has been so well preserved

      That I've sometimes wondered whether there was any . . .

      Private self to preserve.

MONICA.   There *is* a private self, Charles.

      I'm sure of that.

CHARLES.   You've given two reasons,

      One the contradiction of the other.

      Can there be a third?

MONICA.   The third reason is this:

      I've only just been given it by Dr. Selby —

      Father is much iller than he is aware of:

      It may be, he will never return from Badgley Court.

      But Selby wants him to have every encouragement —

      If he's hopeful, he's likely to live a little longer.

      That's why Selby chose the place. A *convalescent* home

      With the atmosphere of an hotel —

      Nothing about it to suggest the clinic —

      Everything about it to suggest recovery.

CHARLES. This is your best reason, and the most depressing;

      For this situation may persist for a long time,

      And you'll go on postponing and postponing our marriage.

MONICA. I'm afraid . . . not a very long time, Charles.

      It's almost certain that the winter in Jamaica

      Will never take place. 'Make the reservations'

      Selby said, 'as if you were going'.

But Badgley Court's so near your constituency!
You can come down at weekends, even when the House is sitting.
And you can take me out, if Father can spare me.
But he'll simply love having you to talk to!

CHARLES. I know he's used to seeing me about.

MONICA. I've seen him looking at you. He was thinking of himself
When he was your age — when he started like you,
With the same hopes, the same ambitions —
And of his disappointments.

CHARLES.   Is that wistfulness,
Compassion, or . . . envy?

MONICA.   Envy is everywhere.
Who is without envy? And most people
Are unaware or unashamed of being envious.
It's all we can ask if compassion and wistfulness . . .
And tenderness, Charles! are mixed with envy:
I do believe that he is fond of you.
So you must come often. And Oh, Charles dear —

[*Enter* LORD CLAVERTON]

MONICA. You've been very long in coming, Father. What have you been
doing?

LORD CLAVERTON. Good afternoon, Charles. You might have guessed,
Monica,
What I've been doing. Don't you recognise this book?

MONICA. It's your engagement book.

LORD CLAVERTON.   Yes, I've been brooding over it.

MONICA. But what a time for your engagement book!
You know what the doctors said: complete relaxation
And to think about nothing. Though I know that won't be easy.

LORD CLAVERTON. That is just what I was doing.

MONICA.   Thinking of nothing?

LORD CLAVERTON. Contemplating nothingness. Just remember:
Every day, year after year, over my breakfast,
I have looked at this book — or one just like it —
You know I keep the old ones on a shelf together;
I could look in the right book, and find out what I was doing
Twenty years ago, to-day, at this hour of the afternoon.
If I've been looking at this engagement book, to-day,
Not over breakfast, but before tea,
It's the empty pages that I've been fingering —

The first empty pages since I entered Parliament.
I used to jot down notes of what I had to say to people:
Now I've no more to say, and no one to say it to.
I've been wondering . . . how many more empty pages?

MONICA. You would soon fill them up if we allowed you to!
That's my business to prevent. You know I'm to protect you
From your own restless energy — the inexhaustible
Sources of the power that wears out the machine.

LORD CLAVERTON. They've dried up, Monica, and you know it.
They talk of rest, these doctors, Charles; they tell me to be cautious,
To take life easily. Take life easily!
It's like telling a man he mustn't run for trains
When the last thing he wants is to take a train for anywhere!
No, I've not the slightest longing for the life I've left —
Only fear of the emptiness before me.
If I had the energy to work myself to death
How gladly would I face death! But waiting, simply waiting,
With no desire to act, yet a loathing of inaction.
A fear of the vacuum, and no desire to fill it.
It's just like sitting in an empty waiting room
In a railway station on a branch line,
After the last train, after all the other passengers
Have left, and the booking office is closed
And the porters have gone. What am I waiting for
In a cold and empty room before an empty grate?
For no one. For nothing.

MONICA.   Yet you've been looking forward
To this very time! You know how you grumbled
At the farewell banquet, with the tributes from the staff,
The presentation, and the speech you had to make
And the speeches that you had to listen to!

LORD CLAVERTON [*pointing to a silver salver, still lying in its case*].
I don't know which impressed me more, the insincerity
Of what was said about me, or of my reply —
All to thank them for that.

                         Oh the grudging contributions
That bought this piece of silver! The inadequate levy
That made the Chairman's Price! And my fellow directors
Saying 'we must put our hands in our pockets
To double this collection — it must be something showy'.

530

This would do for visiting cards — if people still left cards
And if I was going to have any visitors.

MONICA. Father, you simply want to revel in gloom!
You know you've retired in a blaze of glory —
You've read every word about you in the papers.

CHARLES. And the leading articles saying 'we are confident
That his sagacious counsel will long continue
To be at the disposal of the Government in power'.
And the expectation that your voice will be heard
In debate in the Upper House . . .

LORD CLAVERTON.   The established liturgy
Of the Press on any conspicuous retirement.
My obituary, if I had died in harness,
Would have occupied a column and a half
With an inset, a portrait taken twenty years ago.
In five years' time, it will be the half of that;
In ten years' time, a paragraph.

CHARLES.   That's the reward
Of every public man.

LORD CLAVERTON.   Say rather, the exequies
Of the failed successes, the successful failures,
Who occupy positions that other men covet.
When we go, a good many folk are mildly grieved,
And our closest associates, the small minority
Of those who really understand the place we filled
Are inwardly delighted. They won't want my ghost
Walking in the City or sitting in the Lords.
And I, who recognise myself as a ghost
Shan't want to be seen there. It makes me smile
To think that men should be frightened of ghosts.
If they only knew how frightened a ghost can be of men!

[Knock. Enter LAMBERT]

LAMBERT. Excuse me, my Lord. There's a gentleman downstairs
Is very insistent that he must see you.
I told him you never saw anyone, my Lord,
But by previous appointment. He said he knew that,
So he had brought this note. He said that when you read it
You would want to see him. Said you'd be very angry
If you heard that he'd gone away without your seeing him.

LORD CLAVERTON. What sort of a person?

LAMBERT. A foreign person

By the looks of him. But talks good English.

A pleasant-spoken gentleman.

LORD CLAVERTON [*after reading the note*]. I'll see him in the library.

No, stop. I've left too many papers about there.

I'd better see him here.

LAMBERT. Very good, my Lord.

Shall I take the trolley, Miss Monica?

MONICA. Yes, thank you, Lambert.

[*Exit* LAMBERT]

CHARLES. I ought to be going.

MONICA. Let *us* go into the library. And then I'll see you off.

LORD CLAVERTON. I'm sorry to turn you out of the room like this,

But I'll have to see this man by myself, Monica.

I've never heard of this Señor Gomez

But he comes with a letter of introduction

From a man I used to know. I can't refuse to see him.

Though from what I remember of the man who introduces him

I expect he wants money. Or to sell me something worthless.

MONICA. You ought not to bother with such people now, Father.

If you haven't got rid of him in twenty minutes

I'll send Lambert to tell you that you have to take a trunk call.

Come, Charles. Will you bring my coat?

CHARLES. I'll say goodbye, sir.

And look forward to seeing you both at Badgley Court

In a week or two.

[*Enter* LAMBERT]

LAMBERT. Mr. Gomez, my Lord.

LORD CLAVERTON. Goodbye, Charles. And please remember

That we both want to see you, whenever you can come

If you're in the vicinity. Don't we, Monica?

MONICA. Yes, Father. (*To* CHARLES) We *both* want to see you.

[*Exeunt* MONICA *and* CHARLES]

[LAMBERT *shows in* GOMEZ]

LORD CLAVERTON. Good evening, Mr. . . . . Gomez. You're a friend of

Mr. Culverwell?

GOMEZ. We're as thick as thieves, you might almost say.

Don't you know me, Dick?

LORD CLAVERTON. Fred Culverwell!

Why do you come back with another name?

GOMEZ. You've changed your name too, since I knew you.
 When we were up at Oxford, you were plain Dick Ferry.
 Then, when you married, you took your wife's name
 And became Mr. Richard Claverton-Ferry;
 And finally, Lord Claverton. I've followed your example,
 And done the same, in a modest way.
 You know, where *I* live, people do change their names;
 And besides, my wife's name is a good deal more normal
 In my country, than Culverwell — and easier to pronounce.
LORD CLAVERTON. Have you lived out there ever since . . . you left
  England?
GOMEZ. Ever since I finished my sentence.
LORD CLAVERTON. What has brought you to England?
GOMEZ.   Call it homesickness,
 Curiosity, restlessness, whatever you like.
 But I've been a pretty hard worker all these years
 And I thought, now's the time to take a long holiday,
 Let's say a rest cure — that's what I've come for.
 You see, I'm a widower, like you, Dick.
 So I'm pretty footloose. Gomez, you see,
 Is now a highly respected citizen
 Of a central American republic: San Marco.
 It's as hard to become a respected citizen
 Out there, as it is here. With this qualification:
 Out there they respect you for rather different reasons.
LORD CLAVERTON. Do you mean that you've won respect out
  there
 By the sort of activity that lost you respect
 Here in England?
GOMEZ.   Not at all, not at all.
 I think that was rather an unkind suggestion.
 I've always kept on the right side of the law —
 And seen that the law turned its right side to *me*.
 Sometimes I've had to pay pretty heavily;
 But I learnt by experience whom to pay;
 And a little money laid out in the right manner
 In the right places, pays many times over.
 I assure you it does.
LORD CLAVERTON.   In other words
 You have been engaged in systematic corruption.

GOMEZ. No, Dick, there's a fault in your logic.
How can one corrupt those who are already corrupted?
I can swear that I've never corrupted anybody.
In fact, I've never come across an official
Innocent enough to be corruptible.

LORD CLAVERTON. It would seem then that most of your business
Has been of such a nature that, if carried on in England,
It might land you in gaol again?

GOMEZ.   That's true enough,
Except for a false inference. I wouldn't dream
Of carrying on such business if I lived in England.
I have the same standards of morality
As the society in which I find myself.
I do nothing in England that you would disapprove of.

LORD CLAVERTON. That's something, at least, to be thankful for.
I trust you've no need to engage in forgery.

GOMEZ. Forgery, Dick? An absurd suggestion!
Forgery, I can tell you, is a mug's game.
I say that — with conviction.
No, forgery, or washing cheques, or anything of that nature,
Is certain to be found out sooner or later.
And then what happens? You have to move on.
That wouldn't do for me. I'm too domestic.
And by the way, I've several children,
All grown up, doing well for themselves.
I wouldn't allow either of my sons
To go into politics. In my country, Dick,
Politicians can't afford mistakes. The prudent ones
Always have an aeroplane ready:
And keep an account in a bank in Switzerland.
The ones who don't get out in time
Find themselves in gaol and not very comfortable,
Or before a firing squad.
You don't know what serious politics is like!
I said to my boys: 'Never touch politics.
Stay out of politics, and play both parties:
What you don't get from one you may get from the other'.
Dick, don't tell me that there isn't any whisky in the house?

LORD CLAVERTON. I can provide whisky. [*Presses the bell*]
                          But why have you come?

GOMEZ. You've asked me that already!
　To see you, Dick. A natural desire!
　For you're the only old friend I can trust.
LORD CLAVERTON. You really trust me? I appreciate the compliment.
GOMEZ. Which you're sure you deserve. But when I say 'trust' . . .
[*Knock. Enter* LAMBERT]
LORD CLAVERTON. Lambert, will you bring in the whisky. And soda.
LAMBERT. Very good, my Lord.
GOMEZ. 　　　　　　　　　　And some ice.
LAMBERT. Ice? Yes, my Lord.

　　　　　　　　　　　　　　　　　　　　　　[*Exit*]

GOMEZ. I began to say: when I say 'trust'
　I use the term as experience has taught me.
　It's nonsense to talk of trusting people
　In general. What does that mean? One trusts a man
　Or a woman — in this respect or that.
　A won't let me down in this relationship,
　B won't let me down in some other connection.
　But, as I've always said to my boys:
　'When you come to the point where you need to trust someone
　You must make it worth his while to be trustworthy'.
　　　[*During this* LAMBERT *enters silently, deposits tray and exit*]
LORD CLAVERTON. Won't you help yourself?
　　　　　　　　[GOMEZ *does so, liberally*]
GOMEZ. 　　　　　　　　　　　　And what about you?
LORD CLAVERTON. I don't take it, thank you.
GOMEZ. 　　　　　　　　　　　　A reformed character!
LORD CLAVERTON. I should like to know why you need to trust *me*.
GOMEZ. That's perfectly simple. I come back to England
　After thirty-five years. Can you imagine
　What it would be like to have been away from home
　For thirty-five years? I was twenty-five —
　The same age as you — when I went away,
　Thousands of miles away, to another climate,
　To another language, other standards of behaviour,
　To fabricate for myself another personality
　And to take another name. Think what that means —
　To take another name.
　　　　　[*Gets up and helps himself to whisky*]
　　　　　　　　But of course you know!
　　　　　　　　　535

Just enough to think you know more than you do.
You've changed your name twice — by easy stages,
And each step was merely a step up the ladder,
So you weren't aware of becoming a different person:
But where *I* changed my name, there was no social ladder.
It was jumping a gap — and you can't jump back again.
I parted from myself by a sudden effort,
You, so slowly and sweetly, that you've never woken up
To the fact that Dick Ferry died long ago.
I married a girl who didn't know a word of English,
Didn't want to learn English, wasn't interested
In anything that happened four thousand miles away,
Only believed what the parish priest told her.
I made my children learn English — it's useful;
I always talk to them in English.
But do they think in English? No, they do not.
They think in Spanish, but their thoughts are Indian thoughts.
O God, Dick, *you* don't know what it's like
To be so cut off! Homesickness!
Homesickness is a sickly word.
You don't understand such isolation
As mine, you think you do . . .

LORD CLAVERTON.   I'm sure I do,
    I've always been alone.

GOMEZ.   Oh, loneliness —
    Everybody knows what that's like.
    Your loneliness — so cosy, warm and padded:
    You're not isolated — merely insulated.
    It's only when you come to see that you have lost *yourself*
    That you are quite alone.

LORD CLAVERTON.   I'm waiting to hear
    Why you should need to trust me.

GOMEZ.   Perfectly simple.
    My father's dead long since — that's a good thing.
    My mother — I dare say she's still alive,
    But she must be very old. And she must think I'm dead;
    And as for my married sisters — I don't suppose their husbands
    Were ever told the story. *They* wouldn't want to see me.
    No, I need one old friend, a friend whom I can trust —
    And one who will accept both Culverwell and Gomez —

See Culverwell as Gomez — Gomez as Culverwell.
I need you, Dick, to give me reality!

LORD CLAVERTON. But according to the description you have given
Of trusting people, how do you propose
To make it worth my while to be trustworthy?

GOMEZ. It's done already, Dick; done many years ago:
Adoption tried, and grappled to my soul
With hoops of steel, and all that sort of thing.
We'll come to that, very soon. Isn't it strange
That there should always have been this bond between us?

LORD CLAVERTON. It has never crossed my mind. Develop the point.

GOMEZ. Well, consider what we were when we went up to Oxford
And then what I became under your influence.

LORD CLAVERTON. You cannot attribute your . . . misfortune to *my*
influence.

GOMEZ. I was just about as different as anyone could be
From the sort of men you'd been at school with —
I didn't fit into your set, and I knew it.
When you started to take me up at Oxford
I've no doubt your friends wondered what you found in me —
A scholarship boy from an unknown grammar school.
I didn't know either, but I was flattered.
Later, I came to understand: you made friends with me
Because it flattered *you* — tickled your love of power
To see that I was flattered, and that I admired you.
Everyone expected that I should get a First.
I suppose your tutor thought you'd be sent down.
It went the other way. You stayed the course, at least.
I had plenty of time to think things over, later.

LORD CLAVERTON. And what is the conclusion that you came to?

GOMEZ. This is how it worked out, Dick. You liked to play the rake,
But you never went too far. There's a prudent devil
Inside you, Dick. He never came to *my* help.

LORD CLAVERTON. I certainly admit no responsibility,
None whatever, for what happened to you later.

GOMEZ. You led me on at Oxford, and left me to it.
And so it came about that I was sent down
With the consequences which you remember:
A miserable clerkship — which your father found for me,
And expensive tastes — which you had fostered in me,

And, equally unfortunate, a talent for penmanship.
Hence, as you have just reminded me
Defalcation and forgery. And then my stretch
Which gave me time to think it all out.

LORD CLAVERTON. That's the second time you have mentioned your
reflections.
But there's just one thing you seem to have forgotten:
I came to your assistance when you were released.

GOMEZ. Yes, and paid my passage out. I know the reason:
You wanted to get rid of me. I shall tell you why presently.
Now let's look for a moment at *your* life history.
You had plenty of money, and you made a good marriage —
Or so it seemed — and with your father's money
And your wife's family influence, you got on in politics.
Shall we say that you did very well by yourself?
Though not, I suspect, as well as you had hoped.

LORD CLAVERTON. I was never accused of making a mistake.

GOMEZ. No, in England mistakes are anonymous
Because the man who accepts responsibility
Isn't the man who made the mistake.
That's your convention. Or if it's known you made it
You simply get moved to another post
Where at least you can't make quite the same mistake.
At the worst, you go into opposition
And let the other people make mistakes
Until your own have been more or less forgotten.
I dare say you did make some mistake, Dick . . .
That would account for your leaving politics
And taking a conspicuous job in the City
Where the Government could always consult you
But of course didn't have to take your advice . . .
I've made a point, you see, of following your career.

LORD CLAVERTON. I am touched by your interest.

GOMEZ.   I have a gift for friendship.
I rejoiced in your success. But one thing has puzzled me.
You were given a ministry before you were fifty:
That should have led you to the very top!
And yet you withdrew from the world of politics
And went into the City. Director of a bank
And chairman of companies. You looked the part —

    Cut out to be an impressive figurehead.
    But again, you've retired at sixty. Why at sixty?
LORD CLAVERTON. Knowing as much about me as you do
    You must have read that I retired at the insistence of my doctors.
GOMEZ. Oh yes, the usual euphemism.
    And yet I wonder. It *is* surprising:
    You should have been good for another five years
    At least. Why did they let you retire?
LORD CLAVERTON. If you want to know, I had had a stroke.
    And I might have another.
GOMEZ.   Yes. You might have another.
    But I wonder what brought about this . . . stroke;
    And I wonder whether you're the great economist
    And financial wizard that you're supposed to be.
    And I've learned something of other vicissitudes.
    Dick, I was very very sorry when I heard
    That your marriage had not been altogether happy.
    And as for your son — from what I've heard about *him*,
    He's followed your undergraduate career
    Without the protection of that prudent devil
    Of yours, to tell him not to go too far.
    Well, now, I'm beginning to be thirsty again.
               [*Pours himself whisky*]
LORD CLAVERTON. An interesting historical epitome.
    Though I cannot accept it as altogether accurate.
    The only thing I find surprising
    In the respected citizen of San Marco
    Is that in the midst of the engrossing business
    Of the nature of which dark hints have been given,
    He's informed himself so carefully about my career.
GOMEZ. I don't propose to give you a detailed account
    Of my own career. I've been very successful.
    What would have happened to me, I wonder,
    If I had never met you? I should have got my First,
    And I might have become the history master
    In a school like that from which I went to Oxford.
    As it is, I'm somebody — a more important man
    In San Marco than I should ever have been in England.
LORD CLAVERTON. So, as you consider yourself a success . . .
GOMEZ. A worldly success, Dick. In another sense

539

We're both of us failures. But even so,

I'd rather be my kind of failure than yours.

LORD CLAVERTON. And what do you call failure?

GOMEZ.   What do I call failure?

The worst kind of failure, in my opinion,

Is the man who has to keep on pretending to himself

That he's a success — the man who in the morning

Has to make up his face before he looks in the mirror.

LORD CLAVERTON. Isn't that the kind of pretence that you're

        maintaining

In trying to persuade me of your . . . worldly success?

GOMEZ. No, because I know the value of the coinage

I pay myself in.

LORD CLAVERTON. Indeed! How interesting!

I still don't know why you've come to see me

Or what you mean by saying you can trust me.

GOMEZ. Dick, do you remember the moonlight night

We drove back to Oxford? *You* were driving.

LORD CLAVERTON. That happened several times.

GOMEZ.   One time in particular.

You know quite well to which occasion I'm referring —

A summer night of moonlight and shadows —

The night you ran over the old man in the road.

LORD CLAVERTON. You *said* I ran over an old man in the road.

GOMEZ. You knew it too. If you had been surprised

When I said 'Dick, you've run over somebody'

Wouldn't you have shown it, if only for a second?

You never lifted your foot from the accelerator.

LORD CLAVERTON. We were in a hurry.

GOMEZ.   More than in a hurry.

You didn't want it to be known where we'd been.

The girls who were with us (what were their names?

I've completely forgotten them) you didn't want *them*

To be called to give evidence. You just couldn't face it.

Do you see now, Dick, why I say I can trust you?

LORD CLAVERTON. If you think that this story would interest the

        public

Why not sell your version to a Sunday newspaper?

GOMEZ. My dear Dick, what a preposterous suggestion!

Who's going to accept the unsupported statement

Of Federico Gomez of San Marco
About something that happened so many years ago?
What damages you'd get! The Press wouldn't look at it.
Besides, you can't think I've any desire
To appear in public as Frederick Culverwell?
No, Dick, your secret's safe with me.
Of course, I might give it to a few friends, in confidence.
It might even reach the ears of some of your acquaintance —
But you'd never know to whom I'd told it,
Or who knew the story and who didn't. I promise you.
Rely upon me as the soul of discretion.

LORD CLAVERTON. What do you want then? Do you need money?

GOMEZ. My dear chap, you are obtuse!
I said: 'Your secret is safe with me',
And then you . . . well, I'd never have believed
That you would accuse an old friend of . . . blackmail!
On the contrary, I dare say I could buy you out
Several times over. San Marco's a good place
To make money in — though not to *keep* it in.
My investments — not all in my own name either —
Are pretty well spread. For the matter of that,
My current account in Stockholm or Zürich
Would keep me in comfort for the rest of my life.
Really, Dick, you owe me an apology.
Blackmail! On the contrary
Any time you're in a tight corner
My entire resources are at your disposal.
You were a generous friend to me once
As you pointedly reminded me a moment ago.
Now it's my turn, perhaps, to do you a kindness.

[*Enter* LAMBERT]

LAMBERT. Excuse me, my Lord, but Miss Monica asked me
To remind you there's a trunk call coming through for you
In five minutes' time.

LORD CLAVERTON.   I'll be ready to take it.

[*Exit* LAMBERT]

GOMEZ. Ah, the pre-arranged interruption
To terminate the unwelcome intrusion
Of the visitor in financial distress.
Well, I shan't keep you long, though I dare say your caller

    Could hang on for another quarter of an hour.

LORD CLAVERTON. Before you go — what is it that you want?

GOMEZ. I've been trying to make clear that I only want your friendship!
    Just as it used to be in the old days
    When you taught me expensive tastes. Now it's my turn.
    I can have cigars sent direct to you from Cuba
    If your doctors allow you a smoke now and then.
    I'm a lonely man, Dick, with a craving for affection.
    All I want is as much of your company,
    So long as I stay here, as I can get.
    And the more I get, the longer I may stay.

LORD CLAVERTON.   This is preposterous!
    Do you call it friendship to impose your company
    On a man by threats? Why keep up the pretence?

GOMEZ. Threats, Dick! How can you speak of threats?
    It's most unkind of you. My only aim
    Is to renew our friendship. Don't you understand?

LORD CLAVERTON. I see that when I gave you my friendship
    So many years ago, I only gained in return
    Your envy, spite and hatred. That is why you attribute
    Your downfall to me. But how was I responsible?
    We were the same age. You were a free moral agent.
    You pretend that I taught you expensive tastes:
    If you had not had those tastes already
    You would hardly have welcomed my companionship.

GOMEZ. Neatly argued, and almost convincing:
    Don't you wish you could believe it?

LORD CLAVERTON.   And what if I decline
    To give you the pleasure of my company?

GOMEZ. Oh, I can wait, Dick. You'll relent at last.
    You'll come to feel easier when I'm with you
    Than when I'm out of sight. You'll be afraid of whispers,
    The reflection in the mirror of the face behind you,
    The ambiguous smile, the distant salutation,
    The sudden silence when you enter the smoking room.
                         Don't forget, Dick:
    You *didn't stop*! Well, I'd better be going.
    I hope I haven't outstayed my welcome?
    Your telephone pal may be getting impatient.
    I'll see you soon again.

LORD CLAVERTON.   Not very soon, I think.
    I am going away.
GOMEZ.   So I've been informed.
    I have friends in the press — if not in the peerage.
    Goodbye for the present. It's been an elixir
    To see you again, and assure myself
    That we can begin just where we left off.

[*Exit* GOMEZ]

[LORD CLAVERTON *sits for a few minutes brooding. A knock. Enter*
                MONICA.]

MONICA. Who was it, Father?
LORD CLAVERTON.   A man I used to know.
MONICA. Oh, so you knew him?
LORD CLAVERTON.   Yes. He'd changed his name.
MONICA. Then I suppose he wanted money?
LORD CLAVERTON.   No, he didn't want money.
MONICA. Father, this interview has worn you out.
    You must go and rest now, before dinner.
LORD CLAVERTON. Yes, I'll go and rest now. I wish Charles was
        dining with us.
    I wish we were having a dinner party.
MONICA. Father, can't you bear to be alone with me?
    If you can't bear to dine alone with me tonight,
    What will it be like at Badgley Court?

CURTAIN

Act Two

The terrace of Badgley Court. A bright sunny morning, several days later.
Enter LORD CLAVERTON *and* MONICA.

MONICA. Well, so far, it's better than you expected,
  Isn't it, Father? They've let us alone;
  The people in the dining-room show no curiosity;
  The beds are comfortable, the hot water is hot,
  They give us a very tolerable breakfast;
  And the chambermaid really *is* a chambermaid:
  For when I asked about morning coffee
  She said 'I'm not the one for elevens's,
  That's Nurse's business'.
LORD CLAVERTON.   So far, so good.
  I'll feel more confidence after a fortnight —
  After fourteen days of people not staring
  Or offering picture papers, or wanting a fourth at bridge;
  Still, I'll admit to a feeling of contentment
  Already. I only hope that it will last —
  The sense of wellbeing! It's often with us
  When we are young, but then it's not noticed;
  And by the time one has grown to consciousness
  It comes less often.
                I hope this benignant sunshine
  And warmth will last for a few days more.
  But this early summer, that's hardly seasonable,
  Is so often a harbinger of frost on the fruit trees.
MONICA. Oh, let's make the most of this weather while it lasts.
  I never remember you as other than occupied
  With anxieties from which you were longing to escape;
  Now I want to see you learning to enjoy yourself!
LORD CLAVERTON. Perhaps I've never really enjoyed living
  As much as most people. At least, as they seem to do
  Without knowing that they enjoy it. Whereas I've often known

544

That I didn't enjoy it. Some dissatisfaction
With myself, I suspect, very deep within myself
Has impelled me all my life to find justification
Not so much to the world — first of all to myself.
What is this self inside us, this silent observer,
Severe and speechless critic, who can terrorise us
And urge us on to futile activity,
And in the end, judge us still more severely
For the errors into which his own reproaches drove us?

MONICA. You admit that at the moment you find life pleasant,
That it really does seem quiet here and restful.
Even the matron, though she looks rather dominating,
Has left us alone.

LORD CLAVERTON. Yes, but remember
What she said. She said: 'I'm going to leave you alone!
You want perfect peace: that's what Badgley Court is for.'
I thought that very ominous. When people talk like that
It indicates a latent desire to interfere
With the privacy of others, which is certain to explode.

MONICA. Hush, Father. I see her coming from the house.
Take your newspaper and start reading to me.

[*Enter* MRS. PIGGOTT]

MRS. PIGGOTT. Good morning, Lord Claverton! Good morning, Miss
Claverton!
Isn't this a glorious morning!
I'm afraid you'll think I've been neglecting you;
So I've come to apologise and explain.
I've been in such a rush, these last few days,
And I thought, 'Lord Claverton will understand
My not coming in directly after breakfast:
He's led a busy life, too.' But I hope you're happy?
Is there anything you need that hasn't been provided?
All you have to do is to make your wants known.
Just ring through to my office. If I'm not there
My secretary will be — Miss Timmins.
She'd be overjoyed to have the privilege of helping you!

MONICA. You're very kind . . . Oh, I'm sorry,
We don't know how we ought to address you.
Do we call you 'Matron'?

MRS. PIGGOTT. Oh no, not 'Matron'!

Of course, I *am* a matron in a sense —
No, I don't simply mean that I'm a married woman —
A widow in fact. But I was a Trained Nurse,
And of course I've always lived in what you might call
A medical milieu. My father was a specialist
In pharmacology. And my husband
Was a distinguished surgeon. Do you know, I fell in love with him
During an appendicitis operation!
I was a theatre nurse. But you mustn't call me 'Matron'
At Badgley Court. You see, we've studied to avoid
Anything like a nursing-home atmosphere.
We don't want our guests to think of themselves as ill,
Though we never have guests who are perfectly well —
Except when they come like you, Miss Claverton.

MONICA. Claverton-Ferry. Or Ferry: it's shorter.

MRS. PIGGOTT. So sorry. Miss Claverton-Ferry. I'm Mrs. Piggott.
Just call me Mrs. Piggott. It's a short and simple name
And easy to remember. But, as I was saying,
Guests in perfect health are exceptional
Though we never accept any guest who's incurable.
You know, we've been deluged with applications
From people who want to come here to die!
We never accept them. Nor do we accept
Any guest who *looks* incurable —
We make that stipulation to all the doctors
Who send people here. When you go in to lunch
Just take a glance around the dining-room:
Nobody looks ill! They're all convalescents,
Or resting, like you. So you'll remember
Always to call me Mrs. Piggott, won't you?

MONICA. Yes, Mrs. Piggott, but please tell me one thing.
We haven't seen her yet, but the chambermaid
Referred to a nurse. When we see her
Do we address her as 'Nurse'?

MRS. PIGGOTT. Oh yes, that's different.
She is a real nurse, you know, fully qualified.
Our system is very delicately balanced:
For me to be simply 'Mrs. Piggott'
Reassures the guests in one respect;
And calling our nurses 'Nurse' reassures them

In another respect.

LORD CLAVERTON.   I follow you perfectly.

MRS. PIGGOTT. And now I must fly. I've so much on my hands!
But before I go, just let me tuck you up . . .
You must be very careful at this time of year;
This early warm weather can be very treacherous.
There, now you look more comfy. Don't let him stay out late
In the afternoon, Miss Claverton-Ferry.
And remember, when you want to be *very* quiet
There's the Silence Room. With a television set.
It's popular in the evenings. But not *too* crowded.

[*Exit*]

LORD CLAVERTON. Much as I had feared. But I'm not going to say
Nothing could be worse. Where there's a Mrs. Piggott
There may be, among the guests, something worse than Mrs.
Piggott.

MONICA. Let's hope this was merely the concoction
Which she decants for every newcomer.
Perhaps after what she considers proper courtesies,
She will leave us alone.

[*Re-enter* MRS. PIGGOTT]

MRS. PIGGOTT.   I really *am* neglectful!
Miss Claverton-Ferry, I ought to tell you more
About the amenities which Badgley Court
Can offer to guests of the younger generation.
When there are enough young people among us
We dance in the evening. At the moment there's no dancing,
And it's still too early for the bathing pool.
But several of our guests are keen on tennis,
And of course there's always croquet. But I don't advise croquet
Until you know enough about the other guests
To know whom *not* to play with. I'll mention no names,
But there are one or two who don't like being beaten,
And that spoils any sport, in my opinion.

MONICA. Thank you, Mrs. Piggott. But I'm very fond of walking
And I'm told there are very good walks in this neighbourhood.

MRS. PIGGOTT. There are indeed. I can lend you a map.
There are lovely walks, on the shore or in the hills,
Quite away from the motor roads. You must learn the best walks.
I won't apologise for the lack of excitement:

547

THE ELDER STATESMAN

After all, peace and quiet is our *raison d'être*.
Now I'll leave you to enjoy it.

[*Exit*]

MONICA. I hope she won't remember anything else.
LORD CLAVERTON. She'll come back to tell us more about the peace
    and quiet.
MONICA. I don't believe she'll be bothering us again:
    I could see from her expression when she left
    That she thought she'd done her duty by us for to-day.
    I'm going to prowl about the grounds. Don't look so alarmed!
    If you spy any guest who seems to be stalking you
    Put your newspaper over your face
    And pretend you're pretending to be asleep.
    If they think you *are* asleep they'll do something to wake you,
    But if they see you're shamming they'll have to take the hint.

[*Exit*]

A moment later, LORD CLAVERTON *spreads his newspaper over his face.
Enter* MRS. CARGHILL. *She sits in a deckchair nearby, composes
herself and takes out her knitting.*

MRS. CARGHILL [*after a pause*]. I hope I'm not disturbing you. I
    always sit here.
    It's the sunniest and most sheltered corner,
    And none of the other guests have discovered it.
    It was clever of you to find it so quickly.
    What made you choose it?
LORD CLAVERTON [*throwing down newspaper*]. My daughter chose it.
    She noticed that it seemed to offer the advantages
    Which you have just mentioned. I am glad you can confirm them.
MRS. CARGHILL. Oh, so that *is* your daughter — that very charming
    girl?
    And obviously devoted to her father.
    I was watching you both in the dining-room last night.
    You are the great Lord Claverton, aren't you?
    Somebody said you were coming here —
    It's been the topic of conversation.
    But I couldn't believe that it would really happen!
    And now I'm sitting here talking to you.
    Dear me, it's astonishing, after all these years;
    And you don't even recognise me! I'd know you anywhere.
    But then, we've all seen your portrait in the papers

So often. And everybody knows *you*. But still,
I wish you could have paid *me* that compliment, Richard.

LORD CLAVERTON. What!

MRS. CARGHILL. Don't you know me yet?

LORD CLAVERTON. I'm afraid not.

MRS. CARGHILL. There were the three of us — Effie, Maudie and me.
That day we spent on the river — I've never forgotten it —
The turning point of all my life!
Now whatever were the names of those friends of yours
And which one was it invited us to lunch?
I declare, I've utterly forgotten their names.
And you gave us lunch — I've forgotten what hotel —
But such a good lunch — and we all went in a punt
On the river — and we had a tea basket
With some lovely little cakes — I've forgotten what you called them,
And you made me try to punt, and I got soaking wet
And nearly dropped the punt pole, and you all laughed at me.
Don't you remember?

LORD CLAVERTON. Pray continue.
The more you remind me of, the better I'll remember.

MRS. CARGHILL. And the three of us talked you over afterwards —
Effie and Maud and I. What a time ago it seems!
It's surprising I remember it all so clearly.
You attracted me, you know, at the very first meeting —
I can't think why, but it's the way things happen.
I said 'there's a man I could follow round the world!'
But Effie it was — you know, Effie was very shrewd —
Effie it was said 'you'd be throwing yourself away.
Mark my words' Effie said, 'if you chose to follow *that* man
He'd give you the slip: he's not to be trusted.
That man is hollow'. That's what she said.
Or did she say 'yellow'? I'm not quite sure.
You do remember now, don't you, Richard?

LORD CLAVERTON. Not the conversation you have just repeated.
That is new to me. But I do remember you.

MRS. CARGHILL. Time has wrought sad changes in me, Richard.
I was very lovely once. So *you* thought,
And others thought so too. But as you remember,
Please, Richard, just repeat my name — just once:
The name by which you knew me. It would give me such a thrill

To hear you speak my name once more.

LORD CLAVERTON. Your name was Maisie Batterson.

MRS. CARGHILL. Oh, Richard, you're only saying that to tease me.
You know I meant my stage name. The name by which you knew
me.

LORD CLAVERTON. Well, then, Maisie Montjoy.

MRS. CARGHILL. Yes. Maisie Montjoy.
I was Maisie Montjoy once. And you didn't recognise me.

LORD CLAVERTON. You've changed your name, no doubt. And I've
changed mine.
Your name now and here . . .

MRS. CARGHILL. Is Mrs. John Carghill.

LORD CLAVERTON. You married, I suppose, many years ago?

MRS. CARGHILL. Many years ago, the first time. That didn't last long.
People sometimes say: 'Make one mistake in love,
You're more than likely to make another'.
How true that is! Algy was a weakling,
But simple he was — not sly and slippery.
Then I married Mr. Carghill. Twenty years older
Than me, he was. Just what I needed.

LORD CLAVERTON. Is he still living?

MRS. CARGHILL. He had a weak heart.
And he worked too hard. Have you never heard
Of Carghill Equipments? They make office furniture.

LORD CLAVERTON. I've never had to deal with questions of equipment.
I trust that the business was very successful . . .
I mean, that he left you comfortably provided for?

MRS. CARGHILL. Well, Richard, my doctor could hardly have sent me
here
If I wasn't well off. Yes, I'm provided for.
But isn't it strange that you and I
Should meet here at last? Here, of all places!

LORD CLAVERTON. Why not, of all places? What I don't understand
Is why you should take the first opportunity,
Finding me here, to revive old memories
Which I should have thought we both preferred to leave buried.

MRS. CARGHILL. There you're wrong, Richard. Effie always said —
What a clever girl she was! — 'he doesn't understand women.
Any woman who trusted *him* would soon find that out'.
A man may prefer to forget all the women

He has loved. But a woman doesn't want to forget
A single one of her admirers. Why, even a faithless lover
Is still, in her memory, a kind of testimonial.
Men live by forgetting — women live on memories.
Besides a woman has nothing to be ashamed of:
A man is always trying to forget
His own shabby behaviour.

LORD CLAVERTON.   But we'd settled our account.
What harm was done? I learned my lesson
And you learned yours, if you needed the lesson.

MRS. CARGHILL. You refuse to believe that I was really in love with
you!
Well, it's natural that you shouldn't want to believe it.
But you think, or try to think, that if I'd really suffered
I shouldn't want to let you know who I am,
I shouldn't want to come and talk about the past.
You're wrong, you know. It's both pain and pleasure
To talk about the past — about you and me.
These memories are painful — but I cherish them.

LORD CLAVERTON. If you had really been broken-hearted
I can't see how you could have acted as you did.

MRS. CARGHILL. Who can say whether a heart's been broken
Once it's been repaired? But I know what you mean.
You mean that I would never have started an action
For breach of promise, if I'd really cared for you.
What sentimental nonsense! One starts an action
Simply because one must do *something*.
Well, perhaps I shouldn't have settled out of court.
My lawyer said: 'I advise you to accept',
'Because Mr. Ferry will be standing for Parliament:
His father has political ambitions for him.
If he's lost a breach of promise suit
Some people won't want to appear as his supporters.'
He said: 'What his lawyers are offering in settlement
Is twice as much as I think you'd be awarded.'
Effie was against it — she wanted you exposed.
But I gave way. I didn't want to ruin you.
If I'd carried on, it might have ended your career,
And then you wouldn't have become Lord Claverton.
So perhaps I laid the foundation of your fortunes!

LORD CLAVERTON. And perhaps at the same time of your own?
    I seem to remember, it was only a year or so
    Before your name appeared in very large letters
    In Shaftesbury Avenue.
MRS. CARGHILL.   Yes, I had my art.
    Don't you remember what a hit I made
    With a number called *It's Not Too Late For You To Love
        Me?*
    I couldn't have put the feeling into it I did
    But for what I'd gone through. Did you hear me sing it?
LORD CLAVERTON. Yes, I heard you sing it.
MRS. CARGHILL.   And what did you feel?
LORD CLAVERTON. Nothing at all. I remember my surprise
    At finding that I felt nothing at all.
    I thought, perhaps, what a lucky escape
    It had been, for both of us.
MRS. CARGHILL.   That 'both of us'
    Was an afterthought, Richard. A lucky escape
    You thought, for you. You felt no embarrassment?
LORD CLAVERTON. Why should I feel embarrassment? My conscience
        was clear.
    A brief infatuation, ended in the only way possible
    To our mutual satisfaction.
MRS. CARGHILL.   Your conscience was clear.
    I've very seldom heard people mention their consciences
    Except to observe that their consciences were clear.
    You got out of a tangle for a large cash payment
    And no publicity. So your conscience was clear.
    At bottom, I believe you're still the same silly Richard
    You always were. You wanted to pose
    As a man of the world. And now you're posing
    As what? I presume, as an elder statesman;
    And the difference between being an elder statesman
    And posing successfully as an elder statesman
    Is practically negligible. And you look the part.
    Whatever part you've played, I must say you've always looked it.
LORD CLAVERTON. I've no longer any part to play, Maisie.
MRS. CARGHILL. There'll always be some sort of part for you
    Right to the end. You'll still be playing a part
    In your obituary, whoever writes it.

LORD CLAVERTON. Considering how long ago it was when you knew
 me
 And considering the brevity of our acquaintance,
 You're surprisingly confident, I must say,
 About your understanding of my character.
MRS. CARGHILL. I've followed your progress year by year, Richard.
 And although it's true that our acquaintance was brief,
 Our relations were intense enough, I think,
 To have given me one or two insights into you.
 No, Richard, don't imagine that I'm still in love with you;
 And you needn't think I idolise your memory.
 It's simply that I feel that we belong together . . .
 Now, don't get alarmed. But you touched my soul —
 Pawed it, perhaps, and the touch still lingers.
 And I've touched yours.
 It's frightening to think that we're still together
 And more frightening to think that we may *always* be together.
 There's a phrase I seem to remember reading somewhere:
 Where their fires are not quenched. Do you know what I do?
 I read your letters every night.
LORD CLAVERTON.   My letters!
MRS. CARGHILL. Have you forgotten that you wrote me letters?
 Oh, not very many. Only a few worth keeping.
 Only a few. But very beautiful!
 It was Effie said, when the break came,
 'They'll be worth a fortune to you, Maisie.'
 They would have figured at the trial, I suppose,
 If there had been a trial. Don't you remember them?
LORD CLAVERTON. Vaguely. Were they very passionate?
MRS. CARGHILL. They were very loving. Would you like to read them?
 I'm afraid I can't show you the originals;
 They're in my lawyer's safe. But I have photostats
 Which are quite as good, I'm told. And I like to read them
 In your own handwriting.
LORD CLAVERTON.   And have you shown these letters
 To many people?
MRS. CARGHILL.   Only a few friends.
 Effie said: 'If he becomes a famous man
 And you should be in want, you could have these letters
  auctioned.'

Yes, I'll bring the photostats tomorrow morning,
And read them to you.
                    — Oh, there's Mrs. Piggott!
She's bearing down on us. Isn't she frightful!
She never stops talking. Can you bear it?
If I go at once, perhaps she'll take the hint
And leave us alone tomorrow.
                              Good morning, Mrs. Piggott!
Isn't it a glorious morning!

[*Enter* MRS. PIGGOTT]

MRS. PIGGOTT. Good morning, Mrs. Carghill!

MRS. CARGHILL.   Dear Mrs. Piggott!
    It seems to me that you never sit still:
    You simply sacrifice yourself for us.

MRS. PIGGOTT. It's the breath of life to me, Mrs. Carghill,
    Attending to my guests. I like to feel they *need* me!

MRS. CARGHILL. You do look after us well, Mrs. Piggott:
    You're so considerate — and so understanding.

MRS. PIGGOTT. But I ought to introduce you. You've been talking to
        Lord Claverton,
    The famous Lord Claverton. This is Mrs. Carghill.
    Two of our very nicest guests!
    I just came to see that Lord Claverton was comfortable:
    We can't allow him to tire himself with talking.
    What he needs is *rest*! You're not going, Mrs. Carghill?

MRS. CARGHILL. Oh, I knew that Lord Claverton had come for a rest
        cure,
    And it struck me that he might find it a strain
    To have to cope with both of us at once.
    Besides, I ought to do my breathing exercises.

                                                    [*Exit*]

MRS. PIGGOTT. As a matter of fact, I flew to your rescue
    (That's why I've brought your morning tipple myself
    Instead of leaving it, as usual, to Nurse)
    When I saw that Mrs. Carghill had caught you.
    You wouldn't know that name, but you might remember her
    As Maisie Montjoy in revue.
    She was well-known at one time. I'm afraid her name
    Means nothing at all to the younger generation,
    But you and I should remember her, Lord Claverton.

That tune she was humming, *It's Not Too Late For You To Love Me,*
Everybody was singing it once. A charming person,
I dare say, but not quite your sort or mine.
I suspected that she wanted to meet you, so I thought
That I'd take the first opportunity of hinting —
Tactfully, of course — that you should not be disturbed.
Well, she's gone now. If she bothers you again
Just let me know. I'm afraid it's the penalty
Of being famous.
[*Enter* MONICA]
                    Oh, Miss Claverton-Ferry!
I didn't see you coming. Now I must fly.

                                                    [*Exit*]

MONICA. I saw Mrs. Piggott bothering you again
    So I hurried to your rescue. You look tired, Father.
    She ought to know better. But I'm all the more distressed
    Because I have some . . . not very good news for you.
LORD CLAVERTON. Oh, indeed. What's the matter?
MONICA.   I didn't get far.
    I met Michael in the drive. He says he must see you.
    I'm afraid that something unpleasant has happened.
LORD CLAVERTON. Was he driving his car?
MONICA.   No, he was walking.
LORD CLAVERTON. I hope he's not had another accident.
    You know, after that last escapade of his,
    I've lived in terror of his running over somebody.
MONICA. Why, Father, should you be afraid of that?
    This shows how bad your nerves have been.
    He only ran into a tree.
LORD CLAVERTON.   Yes, a tree.
    It might have been a man. But it can't be that,
    Or he wouldn't be at large. Perhaps he's in trouble
    With some woman or other. I'm sure he has friends
    Whom he wouldn't care for you or me to know about.
MONICA. It's probably money.
LORD CLAVERTON.   If it's only debts
    Once more, I expect I can put up with it.
    But where is he?
MONICA.   I told him he must wait in the garden

555

Until I had prepared you. I've made him understand
That the doctors want you to be free from worry.
He won't make a scene. But I can see he's frightened.
And you know what Michael is like when he's frightened.
He's apt to be sullen and quick to take offence.
So I hope you'll be patient.

LORD CLAVERTON.   Well then, fetch him.

Let's get this over.

MONICA.   [calls] Michael!

[Enter MICHAEL]

LORD CLAVERTON.   Good morning, Michael.

MICHAEL. Good morning, Father.

[A pause]

What a lovely day!

I'm glad you're here, to enjoy such weather.

LORD CLAVERTON. You're glad I'm here? Did you drive down from
London?

MICHAEL. I drove down last night. I'm staying at a pub
About two miles from here. Not a bad little place.

LORD CLAVERTON. Why are you staying there? I shouldn't have thought
It would be the sort of place that you'd choose for a holiday.

MICHAEL. Well, this isn't a holiday exactly.
But this hotel was very well recommended.
Good cooking, for a country inn. And not at all expensive.

LORD CLAVERTON. You don't normally consider that a
recommendation.
Are you staying there long? For the whole of this holiday?

MICHAEL. Well, this isn't a holiday, exactly.
Oh. I said that before, didn't I?

MONICA. I wish you'd stop being so polite to each other.
Michael, you know what you've come to ask of Father
And Father knows that you want something from him.
Perhaps you'll get to the point if I leave you together.

[Exit]

MICHAEL. You know, it's awfully hard to explain things to you.
You've always made up your mind that I was to blame
Before you knew the facts. The first thing I remember
Is being blamed for something I hadn't done.
I never got over that. If you always blame a person
It's natural he should end by getting into trouble.

LORD CLAVERTON. You started pretty early getting into trouble,
    When you were expelled from your prep school for stealing.
    But come to the point. You're in trouble again.
    We'll ignore, if you please, the question of blame:
    Which will spare you the necessity of blaming someone else.
    Just tell me what's happened.

MICHAEL.   Well, I've lost my job.

LORD CLAVERTON. The position that Sir Alfred Walter made for you.

MICHAEL. I'd stuck it for two years. And deadly dull it was.

LORD CLAVERTON. Every job is dull, nine-tenths of the time . . .

MICHAEL. I need something much more stimulating.

LORD CLAVERTON.   Well?

MICHAEL. I want to find some more speculative business.

LORD CLAVERTON. I dare say you've tried a little private speculation.

MICHAEL. Several of my friends gave me excellent tips.
    They always came off — the tips I didn't take.

LORD CLAVERTON. And the ones you did take?

MICHAEL.   Not so well, for some reason.
    The fact is, I needed a good deal more capital
    To make anything of it. If I could have borrowed more
    I might have pulled it off.

LORD CLAVERTON.   Borrowed? From whom?
    Not . . . from the firm?

MICHAEL.   I went to a lender,
    A man whom a friend of mine recommended.
    He gave me good terms, on the strength of my name:
    The only good the name has ever done me.

LORD CLAVERTON. On the strength of your name. And what do you
        call good terms?

MICHAEL. I'd nothing at all to pay for two years:
    The interest was just added on to the capital.

LORD CLAVERTON. And how long ago was that?

MICHAEL.   Nearly two years.
    Time passes pretty quickly, when you're in debt.

LORD CLAVERTON. And have you other debts?

MICHAEL.   Oh, ordinary debts:
    My tailor's bill, for instance.

LORD CLAVERTON.   I expected that.
    It was just the same at Oxford.

MICHAEL.   It's their own fault.

They won't send in their bills, and then I forget them.

It's being your son that gets me into debt.

Just because of your name they insist on giving credit.

LORD CLAVERTON. And your debts: are they the cause of your being
    discharged?

MICHAEL. Well, partly. Sir Alfred did come to hear about it,

And so he pretended to be very shocked.

Said he couldn't retain any man on his staff

Who'd taken to gambling. Called me a gambler!

Said he'd communicate with you about it.

LORD CLAVERTON. That accounts for your coming down here so
    precipitately —

In order to let me have your version first.

I dare say Sir Alfred's will be rather different.

And what else did he say?

MICHAEL.   He took the usual line,

Just like the headmaster. And my tutor at Oxford.

'Not what we expected from the son of your father'

And that sort of thing. It's for your sake, he says,

That he wants to keep things quiet. I can tell you, it's no joke

Being the son of a famous public man.

You don't know what I suffered, working in that office.

In the first place, they all knew the job had been made for me

Because I was your son. They considered me superfluous;

They knew I couldn't be living on my pay;

They had a lot of fun with me — sometimes they'd pretend

That I was overworked, when I'd nothing to do.

Even the office boys began to sneer at me.

I wonder I stood it as long as I did.

LORD CLAVERTON. And does this bring us to the end of the list of your
    shortcomings?

Or did Sir Alfred make other unflattering criticisms?

MICHAEL. Well, there was one thing he brought up against me,

That I'd been too familiar with one of the girls.

He assumed it had gone a good deal further than it had.

LORD CLAVERTON. Perhaps it had gone further than you're willing to
    admit.

MICHAEL. Well, after all, she was the only one

Who was at all nice to me. She wasn't exciting,

But it served to pass the time. It would never have happened

If only I'd been given some interesting work!

LORD CLAVERTON. And what do you now propose to do with yourself?

MICHAEL. I want to go abroad.

LORD CLAVERTON.   You want to go abroad?
 Well, that's not a bad idea. A few years out of England
 In one of the Dominions, might set you on your feet.
 I have connections, or at least correspondents
 Almost everywhere. Australia — no.
 The men I know there are all in the cities:
 An outdoor life would suit you better.
 How would you like to go to Western Canada?
 Or what about sheep farming in New Zealand?

MICHAEL. Sheep farming? Good Lord, no.
 That's not my idea. I want to make money.
 I want to be somebody on my own account.

LORD CLAVERTON. But what do you want to do? Where do you want
  to go?
 What kind of a life do you think you want?

MICHAEL. I simply want to lead a life of my own,
 According to my own ideas of good and bad,
 Of right and wrong. I want to go far away
 To some country where no one has heard the name of Claverton;
 Or where, if I took a different name — and I might choose to —
 No one would know or care what my name had been.

LORD CLAVERTON. So you are ready to repudiate your family,
 To throw away the whole of your inheritance?

MICHAEL. What is my inheritance? As for your title,
 I know why you took it. And Mother knew.
 First, because it gave you the opportunity
 Of retiring from politics, not without dignity,
 Being no longer wanted. And you wished to be Lord Claverton
 Also, to hold your own with Mother's family —
 To lord it over them, in fact. Oh, I've no doubt
 That the thought of passing on your name and title
 To a son, was gratifying. But it wasn't for *my* sake!
 I was just your son — that is to say,
 A kind of prolongation of your existence,
 A representative carrying on business in your absence.
 Why should I thank you for imposing this upon me?
 And what satisfaction, I wonder, will it give you

In the grave? If you're still conscious after death,
I bet it will be a surprised state of consciousness.
Poor ghost! reckoning up its profit and loss
And wondering why it bothered about such trifles.

LORD CLAVERTON. So you want me to help you to escape from your
        father!

MICHAEL. And to help my father to be rid of *me*.
You simply don't know how very much pleasanter
You will find life become, once I'm out of the country.
What I'd like is a chance to go abroad
As a partner in some interesting business.
But I might be expected to put up some capital.

LORD CLAVERTON. What sort of business have you in mind?

MICHAEL. Oh, I don't know. Import and export,
With an opportunity of profits both ways.

LORD CLAVERTON. This is what I will do for you, Michael.
I will help you to make a start in any business
You may find for yourself — if, on investigation,
I am satisfied about the nature of the business.

MICHAEL. Anyway, I'm determined to get out of England.

LORD CLAVERTON. Michael! Are there reasons for your wanting to go
Beyond what you've told me? It isn't . . . manslaughter?

MICHAEL. Manslaughter? Why manslaughter? Oh, you mean on the
        road.
Certainly not. I'm far too good a driver.

LORD CLAVERTON. What then? That young woman?

MICHAEL.   I'm not such a fool
As to get myself involved in a breach of promise suit
Or somebody's divorce. No, you needn't worry
About that girl — or any other.
But I want to get out. I'm fed up with England.

LORD CLAVERTON. I'm sure you don't mean that. But it's natural
        enough
To want a few years abroad. It might be very good for you
To find your feet. But I shouldn't like to think
That what inspired you was no positive ambition
But only the desire to escape.

MICHAEL.   I'm not a fugitive.

LORD CLAVERTON. No, not a fugitive from justice —
Only a fugitive from reality.

Oh Michael! If you had some aim of high achievement,
Some dream of excellence, how gladly would I help you!
Even though it carried you away from me forever
To suffer the monotonous sun of the tropics
Or shiver in the northern night. Believe me, Michael:
Those who flee from their past will always lose the race.
I know this from experience. When you reach your goal,
Your imagined paradise of success and grandeur,
You will find your past failures waiting there to greet you.
You're all I have to live for, Michael —
You and Monica. If I lived for twenty years
Knowing that my son had played the coward —
I should merely be another twenty years in dying.

MICHAEL. Very well: if you like, call me a coward.
I wonder whether you would play the hero
If you were in my place. I don't believe you would.
You didn't suffer from the handicap that I've had.
Your father was rich, but was no one in particular,
So you'd nothing to live up to. Those standards of conduct
You've always made so much of, for my benefit:
I wonder whether *you* have always lived up to them.

                   [MONICA *has entered unobserved*]

MONICA. Michael! How can you speak to Father like that?
Father! What has happened? Why do you look so angry?
I know that Michael must be in great trouble,
So can't you help him?

LORD CLAVERTON.   I am trying to help him,
And to meet him half way. I have made him an offer
Which he must think over. But if he goes abroad
I want him to go in a very different spirit
From that which he has just been exhibiting.

MONICA. Michael! Say something.

MICHAEL.   What is there to say?
I want to leave England, and make my own career:
And Father simply calls me a coward.

MONICA. Father! You know that I would give my life for you.
Oh, how silly that phrase sounds! But there's no vocabulary
For love within a family, love that's lived in
But not looked at, love within the light of which
All else is seen, the love within which

All other love finds speech.
This love is silent.
                    What can I say to you?
However Michael has behaved, Father,
Whatever Father has said, Michael,
You must forgive each other, you must love each other.

MICHAEL. I could have loved Father, if he'd wanted love,
But he never did, Monica, not from me.
You know I've always been very fond of you —
I've a very affectionate nature, really,
But . . .

[*Enter* MRS. CARGHILL *with despatch-case*]

MRS. CARGHILL. Richard! I didn't think you'd still be here.
I came back to have a quiet read of your letters;
But how nice to find a little family party!
I know who you are! You're Monica, of course:
And this must be your brother, Michael.
I'm right, aren't I?

MICHAEL.   Yes, you're right.
But . . .

MRS. CARGHILL. How did I know? Because you're so like your father
When he was your age. He's the picture of you, Richard,
As you were once. You're not to introduce us,
I'll introduce myself. I'm Maisie Montjoy!
That means nothing to you, my dears.
It's a very long time since the name of Maisie Montjoy
Topped the bill in revue. Now I'm Mrs. John Carghill.
Richard! It's astonishing about your children:
Monica hardly resembles you at all,
But Michael — your father has changed a good deal
Since I knew him ever so many years ago,
Yet you're the image of what he was then.
Your father was a very dear friend of mine once.

MICHAEL. Did he really look like me?

MRS. CARGHILL. You've his voice! and his way of moving! It's
marvellous.
And the charm! He's inherited all of your charm, Richard.
There's no denying it. But who's this coming?
It's another new guest here. He's waving to us.
Do you know him, Richard?

LORD CLAVERTON.   It's a man I used to know.

MRS. CARGHILL. How interesting! He's a very good figure
    And he's rather exotic-looking. Is he a foreigner?

LORD CLAVERTON. He comes from some place in Central
            America.

MRS. CARGHILL. How romantic! I'd love to meet him.
    He's coming to speak to us. You must introduce him.

[*Enter* GOMEZ]

GOMEZ. Good morning, Dick.

LORD CLAVERTON.   Good morning, Fred.

GOMEZ. You weren't expecting me to join you here, were you?
    You're here for a rest cure. I persuaded my doctor
    That I was in need of a rest cure too.
    And when I heard you'd chosen to come to Badgley Court
    I said to my doctor, 'Well, what about it?
    What better recommendation could I have?'
    So he sent me here.

MRS. CARGHILL.   Oh, you've seen each other lately?
    Richard, I think that you might introduce us.

LORD CLAVERTON. Oh. This is . . .

GOMEZ.   Your old friend Federico Gomez,
    The prominent citizen of San Marco.
    That's my name.

LORD CLAVERTON. So let me introduce you — by that name —
    To Mrs. . . . Mrs. . . . .

MRS. CARGHILL.   Mrs. John Carghill.

GOMEZ. We seem a bit weak on the surnames, Dick!

MRS. CARGHILL. Well, you see, Señor Gomez, when we first became
            friends —
    Lord Claverton and I — I was known by my stage name.
    There was a time, once, when everyone in London
    Knew the name of Maisie Montjoy in revue.

GOMEZ. If Maisie Montjoy was as beautiful to look at
    As Mrs. Carghill, I can well understand
    Her success on the stage.

MRS. CARGHILL.   Oh, did you never see me?
    That's a pity, Señor Gomez.

GOMEZ.   I lost touch with things in England.
    Had I been in London, and in Dick's position
    I should have been your most devoted admirer.

MRS. CARGHILL. *It's Not Too Late For You To Love Me!* That's the song

That made my reputation, Señor Gomez.

GOMEZ. It will never be too late. Don't you agree, Dick?

— This young lady I take to be your daughter?

And this is your son?

LORD CLAVERTON.   This is my son Michael,

And my daughter Monica.

MONICA.   How do you do.

Michael!

MICHAEL.   How do you do.

MRS. CARGHILL. I don't believe you've known Lord Claverton

As long as I have, Señor Gomez.

GOMEZ. My dear lady, you're not old enough

To have known Dick Ferry as long as I have.

We were friends at Oxford.

MRS. CARGHILL.   Oh, so you were at Oxford!

Is that how you come to speak such perfect English?

Of course, I could tell from your looks that you were Spanish.

I do like Spaniards. They're so aristocratic.

But it's very strange that we never met before.

You were a friend of Richard's at Oxford

And Richard and I became great friends

Not long afterwards, didn't we, Richard?

GOMEZ. I expect that was after I had left England.

MRS. CARGHILL. Of course, that explains it. After Oxford

I suppose you went back to . . . where is your home?

GOMEZ. The republic of San Marco.

MRS. CARGHILL.   Went back to San Marco.

Señor Gomez, if it's true you're staying at Badgley Court,

I warn you — I'm going to cross-examine you

And make you tell me all about Richard

In his Oxford days.

GOMEZ.   On one condition:

That you tell me all about Dick when you knew him.

MRS. CARGHILL [*pats her despatch-case*]. Secret for secret, Señor Gomez!

You've got to be the first to put your cards on the table!

MONICA. Father, I think you should take your rest now.

— I must explain that the doctors were very insistent

That my father should rest and have absolute quiet
Before every meal.

LORD CLAVERTON.   But Michael and I
Must continue our discussion. This afternoon, Michael.

MONICA. No, I think you've had enough talk for to-day.
Michael, as you're staying so close at hand
Will you come back in the morning? After breakfast?

LORD CLAVERTON. Yes, come tomorrow morning.

MICHAEL.   Well, I'll come tomorrow morning.

MRS. CARGHILL. Are you staying in the neighbourhood, Michael?
Your father is such an old friend of mine
That it seems most natural to call you Michael.
You don't mind, do you?

MICHAEL.   No, I don't mind.
I'm staying at the George — it's not far away.

MRS. CARGHILL. Then I'd like to walk a little way with you.

MICHAEL. Delighted, I'm sure.

GOMEZ.   Taking a holiday?
You're in business in London, aren't you?

MICHAEL. Not a holiday, no. I've been in business in London,
But I think of cutting loose, and going abroad.

MRS. CARGHILL. You must tell me all about it. Perhaps I could advise
    you.
We'll leave you now, Richard. Au revoir, Monica.
And Señor Gomez, I shall hold you to your promise!

                    [*Exeunt* MRS. CARGHILL *and* MICHAEL]

GOMEZ. Well, Dick, we've got to obey our doctors' orders.
But while we're here, we must have some good talks
About old times. Bye bye for the present.

                                        [*Exit*]

MONICA. Father, those awful people. We mustn't stay here.
I want you to escape from them.

LORD CLAVERTON.   What I want to escape from
Is myself, is the past. But what a coward I am,
To talk of escaping! And what a hypocrite!
A few minutes ago I was pleading with Michael
Not to try to escape from his own past failures:
I said I knew from experience. Do I understand the meaning
Of the lesson I would teach? Come, I'll start to learn again.
Michael and I shall go to school together.

THE ELDER STATESMAN

We'll sit side by side, at little desks
And suffer the same humiliations
At the hands of the same master. But have I still time?
There is time for Michael. Is it too late for me, Monica?

CURTAIN

Act Three

Same as Act Two. Late afternoon of the following day. MONICA *seated alone. Enter* CHARLES.

CHARLES. Well, Monica, here I am. I hope you got my message.
MONICA. Oh Charles, Charles, Charles, I'm so glad you've come!
    I've been so worried, and rather frightened.
    It was exasperating that they couldn't find me
    When you telephoned this morning. That Mrs. Piggott
    Should have heard my beloved's voice
    And I couldn't, just when I had been yearning
    For the sound of it, for the caress that is in it!
    Oh Charles, how I've wanted you! And now I *need* you.
CHARLES. My darling, what I want is to know that you need me.
    On that last day in London, you admitted that you loved me,
    But I wondered . . . I'm sorry, I couldn't help wondering
    How much your words meant. You didn't seem to need me then.
    And you said we weren't engaged yet . . .
MONICA.   We're engaged now.
    At least *I'm* engaged. I'm engaged to you for ever.
CHARLES. There's another shopping expedition we must make!
    But my darling, since I got your letter this morning
    About your father and Michael, and those people from his past,
    I've been trying to think what I could do to help him.
    If it's blackmail, and that's very much what it looks like,
    Do you think I could persuade him to confide in me?
MONICA. Oh Charles! How could anyone blackmail Father?
    Father, of all people the most scrupulous,
    The most austere. It's quite impossible.
    Father with a guilty secret in his past!
    I just can't imagine it.
               [CLAVERTON *has entered unobserved*]
MONICA. I never expected you from *that* direction, Father!
    I thought you were indoors. Where have you been?

LORD CLAVERTON. Not far away. Standing under the great beech tree.

MONICA. Why under the beech tree?

LORD CLAVERTON.   I feel drawn to that spot.
    No matter. I heard what you said about guilty secrets.
    There are many things not crimes, Monica,
    Beyond anything of which the law takes cognisance:
    Temporary failures, irreflective aberrations,
    Reckless surrenders, unexplainable impulses,
    Moments we regret in the very next moment,
    Episodes we try to conceal from the world.
    Has there been nothing in your life, Charles Hemington,
    Which you wish to forget? Which you wish to keep unknown?

CHARLES. There are certainly things I would gladly forget, Sir,
    Or rather, which I wish had never happened.
    I can think of things you don't yet know about me, Monica,
    But there's nothing I would ever wish to conceal from you.

LORD CLAVERTON. If there's nothing, truly nothing, that you couldn't
        tell Monica
    Then all is well with you. You're in love with each other —
    I don't need to be told what I've seen for myself!
    And if there is nothing that you conceal from *her*
    However important you may consider it
    To conceal from the rest of the world — your soul is safe.
    If a man has one person, just one in his life,
    To whom he is willing to confess everything —
    And that includes, mind you, not only things criminal,
    Not only turpitude, meanness and cowardice,
    But also situations which are simply ridiculous,
    When he has played the fool (as who has not?) —
    Then he loves that person, and his love will save him.
    I'm afraid that I've never loved anyone, really.
    No, I do love my Monica — but there's the impediment:
    It's impossible to be quite honest with your child
    If you've never been honest with anyone older,
    On terms of equality. To one's child one can't reveal oneself
    While she is a child. And by the time she's grown
    You've woven such a web of fiction about you!
    I've spent my life in trying to forget myself,
    In trying to identify myself with the part
    I had chosen to play. And the longer we pretend

The harder it becomes to drop the pretence,
Walk off the stage, change into our own clothes
And speak as ourselves. So I'd become an idol
To Monica. She worshipped the part I played:
How could I be sure that she would love the actor
If she saw him, off the stage, without his costume and makeup
And without his stage words. Monica!
I've had your love under false pretences.
Now, I'm tired of keeping up those pretences,
But I hope that you'll find a little love in your heart
Still, for your father, when you know him
For what he is, the broken-down actor.

MONICA. I think I should only love you the better, Father,
 The more I knew about you. I should understand you better.
 There's nothing I'm afraid of learning about Charles,
 There's nothing I'm afraid of learning about you.

CHARLES. I was thinking, Sir — forgive the suspicion —
 From what Monica has told me about your fellow guests,
 Two persons who, she says, claim a very long acquaintance —
 I was thinking that if there's any question of blackmail,
 I've seen something of it in my practice at the bar.
 I'm sure I could help.

MONICA.   Oh Father, do let him.

CHARLES. At least, I think I know the best man to advise you.

LORD CLAVERTON. Blackmail? Yes, I've heard that word before,
 Not so very long ago. When I asked him what he wanted.
 Oh no, he said, I want nothing from you
 Except your friendship and your company.
 He's a very rich man. And she's a rich woman.
 If people merely blackmail you to get your company
 I'm afraid the law can't touch them.

CHARLES.   Then why should you submit?
 Why not leave Badgley and escape from them?

LORD CLAVERTON. Because they are not real, Charles. They are merely
  ghosts:
 Spectres from my past. They've always been with me
 Though it was not till lately that I found the living persons
 Whose ghosts tormented me, to be only human beings,
 Malicious, petty, and I see myself emerging
 From my spectral existence into something like reality.

MONICA. But what did the ghosts mean? All these years
    You've kept them to yourself. Did Mother know of them?
LORD CLAVERTON. Your mother knew nothing about them. And I
    know
    That I never knew your mother, as she never knew me.
    I thought that she would never understand
    Or that she would be jealous of the ghosts who haunted me.
    And I'm still of that opinion. How open one's heart
    When one is sure of the wrong response?
    How make a confession with no hope of absolution?
    It was not her fault. We never understood each other.
    And so we lived, with a deep silence between us,
    And she died silently. She had nothing to say to me.
    I think of your mother, when she lay dying:
    Completely without interest in the life that lay behind her
    And completely indifferent to whatever lay ahead of her.
MONICA. It is time to break the silence! Let us share your ghosts!
CHARLES. But these are only human beings, who can be dealt with.
MONICA. Or only ghosts, who can be exorcised!
    Who are they, and what do they stand for in your life?
LORD CLAVERTON. . . . And yet they've both done better for
    themselves
    In consequence of it all. He admitted as much,
    Fred Culverwell . . .
MONICA.   Fred Culverwell?
    Who is Fred Culverwell?
LORD CLAVERTON.   He no longer exists.
    He's Federico Gomez, the Central American,
    A man who's made a fortune by his own peculiar methods,
    A man of great importance and the highest standing
    In his adopted country. He even has sons
    Following in their father's footsteps
    Who are also successful. What would *he* have been
    If he hadn't known me? Only a schoolmaster
    In an obscure grammar school somewhere in the Midlands.
    As for Maisie Batterson . . .
MONICA.   Maisie Batterson?
    Who is Maisie Batterson?
LORD CLAVERTON.   She no longer exists.
    Nor the musical comedy star, Maisie Montjoy.

There is Mrs. John Carghill, the wealthy widow.
But Freddy Culverwell and Maisie Batterson,
And Dick Ferry too, and Richard Ferry —
These are my ghosts. They were people with good in them,
People who might all have been very different
From Gomez, Mrs. Carghill and Lord Claverton.
Freddy admired me, when we were at Oxford;
What did I make of his admiration?
I led him to acquire tastes beyond his means:
So he became a forger. And so he served his term.
Was I responsible for that weakness in him?
Yes, I was.
How easily we ignore the fact that those who admire us
Will imitate our vices as well as our virtues —
Or whatever the qualities for which they did admire us!
And that again may nourish the faults that they were born with.
And Maisie loved me, with whatever capacity
For loving she had — self-centred and foolish —
But we should respect love always when we meet it;
Even when it's vain and selfish, we must not abuse it.
That is where I failed. And the memory frets me.

CHARLES. But all the same, these two people mustn't persecute you.
We can't allow that. What hold have they upon you?

LORD CLAVERTON. Only the hold of those who know
Something discreditable, dishonourable . . .

MONICA. Then, Father, you should tell *us* what they already know.
Why should you wish to conceal from those who love you
What is known so well to those who hate you?

LORD CLAVERTON.   I will tell you very briefly
And simply. As for Frederick Culverwell,
He re-enters my life to make himself a reminder
Of one occasion the memory of which
He knows very well, has always haunted me.
I was driving back to Oxford. We had two girls with us.
It was late at night. A secondary road.
I ran over an old man lying in the road
And I did not stop. Then another man ran over him.
A lorry driver. He stopped and was arrested,
But was later discharged. It was definitely shown
That the old man had died a natural death

And had been run over after he was dead.
It was only a corpse that we had run over
So neither of us killed him. But *I* didn't stop.
And all my life I have heard, from time to time,
When I least expected, between waking and sleeping,
A voice that whispered, 'you didn't stop!'
I knew the voice: it was Fred Culverwell's.

MONICA. Poor Father! All your life! And no one to share it with;
    I never knew how lonely you were
    Or why you were lonely.

CHARLES.   And Mrs. Carghill:
    What has she against you?

LORD CLAVERTON.   I was her first lover.
    I would have married her — but my father prevented that:
    Made it worth while for her not to marry me —
    That was his way of putting it — and of course
    Made it worth while for me not to marry her.
    In fact, we were wholly unsuited to each other,
    Yet she had a peculiar physical attraction
    Which no other woman has had. And she knows it.
    And she knows that the ghost of the man I was
    Still clings to the ghost of the woman who was Maisie.
    We should have been poor, we should certainly have quarrelled,
    We should have been unhappy, might have come to divorce;
    But she hasn't forgotten or forgiven me.

CHARLES. This man, and this woman, who are so vindictive:
    Don't you see that they were as much at fault as you
    And that they know it? That's why they are inspired
    With revenge — it's their means of self-justification.
    Let them tell their versions of their miserable stories,
    Confide them in whispers. They cannot harm you.

LORD CLAVERTON. Your reasoning's sound enough. But it's
        irrelevant.
    Each of them remembers an occasion
    On which I ran away. Very well.
    I shan't run away now — run away from *them*.
    It is through this meeting that I shall at last escape them.
    — I've made my confession to you, Monica:
    That is the first step taken towards my freedom,
    And perhaps the most important. I know what you think.

You think that I suffer from a morbid conscience,
From brooding over faults I might well have forgotten.
You think that I'm sickening, when I'm just recovering!
It's hard to make other people realise
The magnitude of things that appear to them petty;
It's harder to confess the sin that no one believes in
Than the crime that everyone can appreciate.
For the crime is in relation to the law
And the sin is in relation to the sinner.
What has made the difference in the last five minutes
Is not the heinousness of my misdeeds
But the fact of my confession. And to you, Monica,
To you, of all people.

CHARLES.   I grant you all that.
But what do you propose? How long, Lord Claverton,
Will you stay here and endure this persecution?

LORD CLAVERTON. To the end. The place and time of liberation
Are, I think, determined. Let us say no more about it.
Meanwhile, I feel sure they are conspiring against me.
I see Mrs. Carghill coming.

MONICA.   Let us go.

LORD CLAVERTON. We will stay here. Let her join us.

[*Enter* MRS. CARGHILL]

MRS. CARGHILL. I've been hunting high and low for you, Richard!
I've some very exciting news for you!
But I suspect . . . Dare I? Yes, I'm sure of it, Monica!
I can tell by the change in your expression to-day;
This must be your fiancé. Do introduce him.

MONICA. Mr. Charles Hemington. Mrs. Carghill.

CHARLES. How do you do.

MRS. CARGHILL.   What a charming name!

CHARLES. I'm glad my name meets with your approval, Mrs. Carghill.

MRS. CARGHILL. And let me congratulate *you*, Mr. Hemington.
You're a very lucky man, to get a girl like Monica.
I take a great interest in her future.
Fancy! I've only known her two days!
But I feel like a mother to her already.
You may say that I just missed being her mother!
I've known her father for a very long time,
And there was a moment when I almost married him,

    Oh so long ago. So you see, Mr. Hemington,
    I've come to regard her as my adopted daughter.
    So much so, that it seems odd to call you Mr. Hemington:
    I'm going to call you Charles!

CHARLES.   As you please, Mrs. Carghill.

LORD CLAVERTON. You said you had some exciting news for us.
    Would you care to impart it?

MRS. CARGHILL.   It's about dear Michael.

LORD CLAVERTON. Oh? What about Michael?

MRS. CARGHILL.   He's told me all his story.
    You've cruelly misunderstood him, Richard.
    How he must have suffered! So I put on my thinking cap.
    I know you've always thought me utterly brainless,
    But I have an idea or two, now and then.
    And in the end I discovered what Michael really wanted
    For making a new start. He wants to go abroad!
    And find his own way in the world. That's very natural.
    So I thought, why not appeal to Señor Gomez?
    He's a wealthy man, and very important
    In his own country. And a friend of Michael's father!
    And I found him only too ready to help.

LORD CLAVERTON. And what was Señor Gomez able to suggest?

MRS. CARGHILL. Ah! That's the surprise for which I've come to
        prepare you.
    Dear Michael is so happy — all his problems are solved;
    And he was so perplexed, poor lamb. Let's all rejoice together.

[*Enter* GOMEZ *and* MICHAEL]

LORD CLAVERTON. Well, Michael, you know I expected you this
        morning,
    But you never came.

MICHAEL.   No, Father. I'll explain why.

LORD CLAVERTON. And I learn that you have discussed your problems
    With Mrs. Carghill and then with Señor Gomez.

MICHAEL. When I spoke, Father, of my wish to get abroad,
    You couldn't see my point of view. What's the use of chasing
    Half round the world, for the same sort of job
    You got me here in London? With another Sir Alfred
    Who'd constitute himself custodian of my morals
    And send you back reports. Some sort of place
    Where everyone would sneer at the fellow from London,

The limey remittance man for whom a job was made.
No! I want to go where I can make my own way,
Not merely be your son. That's what Señor Gomez sees.
He understands my point of view, if *you* don't.
And he's offered me a job which is just what I wanted.

LORD CLAVERTON. Yes, I see the advantage of a job created for you
By Señor Gomez . . .

MICHAEL.   It's not created for me.
Señor Gomez came to London to find a man to fill it,
And he thinks I'm just the man.

GOMEZ.   Yes, wasn't it extraordinary.

LORD CLAVERTON. Of course you're just the man that Señor Gomez
wants,
But in a different sense, and for different reasons
From what you think. Let me tell you about Gomez.
He's unlikely to try to be custodian of your morals;
His real name is Culverwell . . .

GOMEZ.   My dear Dick,
You're wasting your time, rehearsing ancient history.
Michael knows it already. I've told him myself.
I thought he'd better learn the facts from me
Before he heard your distorted version.
But, Dick, I was nettled by that insinuation
About my not being custodian of Michael's morals.
That is just what I should be! And most appropriate,
Isn't it, Dick, when we recall
That you were once custodian of *my* morals:
Though of course you went a little *faster* than I did.

LORD CLAVERTON. On that point, Fred, you're wasting *your* time:
My daughter and my future son-in-law
Understand that allusion. I have told them the story
In explanation of our . . . intimacy
Which they found puzzling.

MRS. CARGHILL.   Oh, Richard!
Have you explained to them our intimacy too?

LORD CLAVERTON. I have indeed.

MRS. CARGHILL.   The romance of my life.
Your father was simply *irresistible*
In those days. I melted the first time he looked at me!
Some day, Monica, I'll tell you all about it.

MONICA. I am satisfied with what I know already, Mrs. Carghill,
About you.

MRS. CARGHILL. But I was very lovely then.

GOMEZ. We are sure of that! You're so lovely now
That we can well imagine you at . . . what age were you?

MRS. CARGHILL. Just eighteen.

LORD CLAVERTON. Now, Michael,
Señor Gomez says he has told you his story.
Did he include the fact that he served a term in prison?

MICHAEL. He told me everything. It was his experience
With you, that made him so understanding
Of my predicament.

LORD CLAVERTON. And made him invent
The position which he'd come to find the man for.

MICHAEL. I don't care about that. He's offered me the job
With a jolly good screw, and some pickings in commissions.
He's made a fortune there. San Marco for me!

LORD CLAVERTON. And what are your duties to be? Do you know?

MICHAEL. We didn't go into details. There's time for that later.

GOMEZ. Much better to wait until we get there.
The nature of business in San Marco
Is easier explained in San Marco than in England.

LORD CLAVERTON. Perhaps you intend to change your name to
Gomez?

GOMEZ. Oh no, Dick, there are plenty of other good names.

MONICA. Michael ,Michael, you can't abandon your family
And your very self — it's a kind of suicide.

CHARLES. Michael, you think Señor Gomez is inspired by
benevolence —

MICHAEL. I told you he'd come to London looking for a man
For an important post on his staff —

CHARLES. A post the nature of which is left very vague

MICHAEL. It's confidential, I tell you.

CHARLES. So I can imagine:
Highly confidential . . .

GOMEZ. Be careful, Mr. Barrister.
You ought to know something about the law of slander.
Here's Mrs. Carghill, a reliable witness.

CHARLES. I know enough about the law of libel and slander
To know that you are hardly likely to invoke it.

And, Michael, here's another point to think of:
Señor Gomez has offered you a post in San Marco,
Señor Gomez pays your passage . . .

MICHAEL.   And an advance of salary.

CHARLES. Señor Gomez pays your passage . . .

GOMEZ.   Just as many years ago
His father paid mine.

CHARLES.   This return of past kindness
No doubt gives you pleasure?

GOMEZ.   Yes, it's always pleasant
To repay an old debt. And better late than never.

CHARLES. I see your point of view. Can you really feel confidence,
Michael, in a man who aims to gratify, through you,
His lifelong grievance against your father?
Remember, you put yourself completely in the power
Of a man you don't know, of the nature of whose business
You know nothing. All you can be sure of
Is that he served a prison sentence for forgery.

GOMEZ. Well, Michael, what do you say to all this?

MICHAEL. I'll say that Hemington has plenty of cheek.
Señor Gomez and I have talked things over, Hemington . . .

GOMEZ. As two men of the world, we discussed things very frankly;
And I can tell you, Michael's head is well screwed on.
He's got brains, he's got flair. When he does come back
He'll be able to buy you out many times over.

MRS. CARGHILL. Richard, I think it's time *I* joined the conversation.
My late husband, Mr. Carghill, was a business man —
I wish you could have known him, Señor Gomez!
You're very much alike in some ways —
So I understand business. Mr. Carghill told me so.
Now, Michael has great abilities for business.
I saw that, and so does Señor Gomez.
He's simply been suffering, poor boy, from frustration.
He's been waiting all this time for opportunity
To make use of his gifts; and now, opportunity —
Opportunity has come knocking at the door.
Richard, you must not bar his way. That would be shameful.

LORD CLAVERTON. I cannot bar his way, as you know very well.
Michael's a free agent. So if he chooses
To place himself in your power, Fred Culverwell,

577

THE ELDER STATESMAN

Of his own volition to contract his enslavement,
I cannot prevent him. I have something to say to you,
Michael, before you go. I shall never repudiate you
Though you repudiate me. I see now clearly
The many many mistakes I have made
My whole life through, mistake upon mistake,
The mistaken attempts to correct mistakes
By methods which proved to be equally mistaken.
I see that your mother and I, in our failure
To understand each other, both misunderstood you
In our divergent ways. When I think of your childhood,
When I think of the happy little boy who was Michael,
When I think of your boyhood and adolescence,
And see how all the efforts aimed at your good
Only succeeded in defeating each other,
How can I feel anything but sorrow and compunction?

MONICA. Oh Michael, remember, you're my only brother
And I'm your only sister. You never took much notice of me.
When we were growing up we seldom had the same friends.
I took all that for granted. So I didn't know till now
How much it means to me to have a brother.

MICHAEL. Why of course, Monica. You know I'm very fond of you
Though we never really seemed to have much in common.
I remember, when I came home for the holidays
How it used to get on my nerves, when I saw you
Always sitting there with your nose in a book.
And once, Mother snatched a book away from you
And tossed it into the fire. How I laughed!
You never seemed even to want a flirtation,
And my friends used to chaff me about my highbrow sister.
But all the same, I was fond of you, and always shall be.
We don't meet often, but if we're fond of each other,
That needn't interfere with your life or mine.

MONICA. Oh Michael, you haven't understood a single word
Of what I said. You must make your own life
Of course, just as I must make mine.
It's not a question of your going abroad
But a question of the spirit which inspired your decision:
If you wish to renounce your father and your family
What is left between you and me?

MICHAEL. That makes no difference.
You'll be seeing me again.

MONICA. But who will you be
When I see you again? Whoever you are then
I shall always pretend that it is the same Michael.

CHARLES. And when do you leave England?

MICHAEL. When we can get a passage.
And I must buy my kit. We're just going up to London.
Señor Gomez will attend to my needs for that climate.
And you see, he has friends in the shipping line
Who he thinks can be helpful in getting reservations.

MRS. CARGHILL. It's wonderful, Señor Gomez, how you manage
everything!
— No sooner had I put my proposal before him
Than he had it all planned out! It really was an inspiration —
On my part, I mean. Are you listening to me, Richard?
You look very *distrait*. You ought to be excited!

LORD CLAVERTON. Is this good-bye then, Michael?

MICHAEL. Well, that just depends.
I could look in again. If there's any point in it.
Personally, I think that when one's come to a decision,
It's as well to say good-bye at once and be done with it.

LORD CLAVERTON. Yes, if you're going, and I see no way to stop you,
Then I agree with you, the sooner the better.
We may never meet again, Michael.

MICHAEL. I don't see why not.

GOMEZ. At the end of five years he will get his first leave.

MICHAEL. Well . . . there's nothing more to say, is there?

LORD CLAVERTON. Nothing at all.

MICHAEL. Then we might as well be going.

GOMEZ. Yes, we might as well be going.
You'll be grateful to me in the end, Dick.

MRS. CARGHILL. A parent isn't always the right person, Richard,
To solve a son's problems. Sometimes an outsider,
A friend of the family, can see more clearly.

GOMEZ. Not that I deserve any credit for it.
We can only regard it as a stroke of good fortune
That I came to England at the very moment
When I could be helpful.

MRS. CARGHILL. It's truly providential!

MONICA. Good-bye Michael. Will you let me write to you?

GOMEZ. Oh, I'm glad you reminded me. Here's my business card
With the full address. You can always reach him there.
But it takes some days, you know, even by air mail.

MONICA. Take the card, Charles. If I write to you, Michael,
Will you ever answer?

MICHAEL.   Oh of course, Monica.
You know I'm not much of a correspondent;
But I'll send you a card, now and again,
Just to let you know I'm flourishing.

LORD CLAVERTON.   Yes, write to Monica.

GOMEZ. Well, good-bye Dick. And good-bye Monica.
Good-bye, Mr. . . . Hemington.

MONICA.   Good-bye Michael.

[*Exeunt* MICHAEL *and* GOMEZ]

MRS. CARGHILL. I'm afraid this seems awfully sudden to you,
Richard;
It isn't so sudden. We talked it all over.
But I've got a little piece of news of my own:
Next autumn, I'm going out to Australia,
On my doctor's advice. And on my way back
Señor Gomez has invited me to visit San Marco.
I'm so excited! But what pleases me most
Is that I shall be able to bring you news of Michael.
And now that we've found each other again,
We must always keep in touch. But you'd better rest now.
You're looking rather tired. I'll run and see them off.

[*Exit* MRS. CARGHILL]

MONICA. Oh Father, Father, I'm so sorry!
But perhaps, perhaps, Michael may learn his lesson.
I believe he'll come back. If it's all a failure
Homesickness, I'm sure, will bring him back to us;
If he prospers, that will give him confidence —
It's only self-confidence that Michael is lacking.
Oh Father, it's not you and me he rejects,
But himself, the unhappy self that he's ashamed of.
I'm sure he loves us.

LORD CLAVERTON.   Monica my dear,
What you say comes home to me. I fear for Michael;
Nevertheless, you are right to hope for something better.

And when he comes back, if he does come back,
I know that you and Charles will do what you can
To make him feel that he is not estranged from you.

CHARLES. We will indeed. We shall be ready to welcome him
And give all the aid we can. But it's both of you together
Make the force to attract him: you and Monica combined.

LORD CLAVERTON. I shall not be here. You heard me say to him
That this might be a final good-bye.
I am sure of it now. Perhaps it is as well.

MONICA. What do you mean, Father? You'll be here to greet him.
But one thing I'm convinced of: you must leave Badgley Court.

CHARLES. Monica is right. You should leave.

LORD CLAVERTON. This may surprise you: I feel at peace now.
It is the peace that ensues upon contrition
When contrition ensues upon knowledge of the truth.
Why did I always want to dominate my children?
Why did I mark out a narrow path for Michael?
Because I wanted to perpetuate myself in him.
Why did I want to keep you to myself, Monica?
Because I wanted you to give your life to adoring
The man that I pretended to myself that I was,
So that I could believe in my own pretences.
I've only just now had the illumination
Of knowing what love is. We all think we know,
But how few of us do! And now I feel happy —
In spite of everything, in defiance of reason,
I have been brushed by the wing of happiness.
And I am happy, Monica, that you have found a man
Whom you can love for the man he really is.

MONICA. Oh Father, I've always loved you,
But I love you more since I have come to know you
Here, at Badgley Court. And I love you the more
Because I love Charles.

LORD CLAVERTON.   Yes, my dear.
Your love is for the real Charles, not a make-believe,
As was your love for me.

MONICA.   But not now, Father!
It's the real you I love — the man you are,
Not the man I thought you were.

LORD CLAVERTON.   And Michael —

I love him, even for rejecting me,
For the *me* he rejected, I reject also.
I've been freed from the self that pretends to be someone;
And in becoming no one, I begin to live.
It is worth while dying, to find out what life is.
And I love you, my daughter, the more truly for knowing
That there is someone you love more than your father —
That you love and are loved. And now that I love Michael,
I think, for the first time — remember, my dear,
I am only a beginner in the practice of loving —
Well, that is something.
                      I shall leave you for a while.
This is your first visit to us at Badgley Court,
Charles, and not at all what you were expecting.
I am sorry you have had to see so much of persons
And situations not very agreeable.
You two ought to have a little time together.
I leave Monica to you. Look after her, Charles,
Now and always. I shall take a stroll.

MONICA. At this time of day? You'll not go far, will you?
    You know you're not allowed to stop out late
    At this season. It's chilly at dusk.

LORD CLAVERTON. Yes, it's chilly at dusk. But I'll be warm enough.
    I shall not go far.

                           [*Exit* CLAVERTON]

CHARLES. He's a very different man from the man he used to be.
    It's as if he had passed through some door unseen by us
    And had turned and was looking back at us
    With a glance of farewell.

MONICA. I can't understand his going for a walk.

CHARLES. He wanted to leave us alone together!

MONICA. Yes, he wanted to leave us alone together.
    And yet, Charles, though we've been alone to-day
    Only a few minutes, I've felt all the time . . .

CHARLES. I know what you're going to say!
    We *were* alone together, in some mysterious fashion,
    Even with Michael, and despite those people,
    Because somehow we'd begun to belong together,
    And that awareness . . .

MONICA. Was a shield protecting both of us . . .

CHARLES. So that now we are conscious of a new person
     Who is you and me together.
                              Oh my dear,
     I love you to the limits of speech, and beyond.
     It's strange that words are so inadequate.
     Yet, like the asthmatic struggling for breath,
     So the lover must struggle for words.
MONICA. I've loved you from the beginning of the world.
     Before you and I were born, the love was always there
     That brought us together.
                              Oh Father, Father!
     I could speak to you now.
CHARLES.   Let me go and find him.
MONICA. We will go to him together. He is close at hand,
     Though he has gone too far to return to us.
     He is under the beech tree. It is quiet and cold there.
     In becoming no one, he has become himself.
     He is only my father now, and Michael's.
     And I am happy. Isn't it strange, Charles,
     To be happy at this moment?
CHARLES.   It is not at all strange.
     The dead has poured out a blessing on the living.
MONICA. Age and decrepitude can have no terrors for me,
     Loss and vicissitude cannot appal me,
     Not even death can dismay or amaze me
     Fixed in the certainty of love unchanging.
                                    I feel utterly secure
     In you; I am a part of you. Now take me to my father.

CURTAIN

The Cast of the First Production
at the
Edinburgh Festival
August 25–August 30 1958

Monica Claverton-Ferry	ANNA MASSEY
Charles Hemington	RICHARD GALE
Lambert	GEOFFREY KERR
Lord Claverton	PAUL ROGERS
Federico Gomez	WILLIAM SQUIRE
Mrs. Piggott	DOROTHEA PHILLIPS
Mrs. Carghill	EILEEN PEEL
Michael Claverton-Ferry	ALEC McCOWEN

Presented by HENRY SHEREK
Directed by E. MARTIN BROWNE
Settings designed by HUTCHINSON SCOTT

POEMS WRITTEN IN EARLY YOUTH

A Fable for Feasters

In England, long before that royal Mormon
　King Henry VIII found out that monks were quacks,
And took their lands and money from the poor men,
　And brought their abbeys tumbling at their backs,
There was a village founded by some Norman
　Who levied on all travelers his tax;
　　Nearby this hamlet was a monastery
　　Inhabited by a band of friars merry.

They were possessors of rich lands and wide,
　An orchard, and a vineyard, and a dairy;
Whenever some old villainous baron died,
　He added to their hoards — a deed which ne'er he
Had done before — their fortune multiplied,
　As if they had been kept by a kind fairy.
　　Alas! no fairy visited their host,
　　Oh, no; much worse than that, they had a ghost.

Some wicked and heretical old sinner
　Perhaps, who had been walled up for his crimes;
At any rate, he sometimes came to dinner,
　Whene'er the monks were having merry times.
He stole the fatter cows and left the thinner
　To furnish all the milk — upset the chimes,
　　And once he sat the prior on the steeple,
　　To the astonishment of all the people.

When Christmas time was near the Abbot vowed
　They'd eat their meal from ghosts and phantoms free,
The fiend must stay at home — no ghosts allowed
　At this exclusive feast. From over sea
He purchased at his own expense a crowd
　Of relics from a Spanish saint — said he:

587

'If ghosts come uninvited, then, of course,
    I'll be compelled to keep them off by force.'

He drencht the gown he wore with holy water,
    The turkeys, capons, boars, they were to eat,
He even soakt the uncomplaining porter
    Who stood outside the door from head to feet.
To make a rather lengthy story shorter,
    He left no wise precaution incomplete;
        He doused the room in which they were to dine,
        And watered everything except the wine.

So when all preparations had been made,
    The jovial epicures sat down to table.
The menus of that time I am afraid
    I don't know much about — as well's I'm able
I'll go through the account: They made a raid
    On every bird and beast in Æsop's fable
        To fill out their repast, and pies and puddings,
        And jellies, pasties, cakes among the good things.

A mighty peacock standing on both legs
    With difficulty kept from toppling over,
Next came a viand made of turtle eggs,
    And after that a great pie made of plover,
And flagons which perhaps held several kegs
    Of ale, and cheese which they kept under cover.
        Last, a boar's head, which to bring in took four pages,
        His mouth an apple held, his skull held sausages.

Over their Christmas wassail the monks dozed,
    A fine old drink, though now gone out of use —
His feet upon the table superposed
    Each wisht he had not eaten so much goose.
The Abbot with proposing every toast
    Had drank more than he ought t' have of grape juice.
        The lights began to burn distinctly blue,
        As in ghost stories lights most always do.

The doors, though barred and bolted most securely,
  Gave way — my statement nobody can doubt,
Who knows the well known fact, as you do surely —
  That ghosts are fellows whom you *can't* keep out;
It is a thing to be lamented sorely
  Such slippery folk should be allowed about,
    For often they drop in at awkward moments,
    As everybody'll know who reads this romance.

The Abbot sat as pasted to his chair,
  His eye became the size of any dollar,
The ghost then took him roughly by the hair
  And bade him come with him, in accents hollow.
The friars could do nought but gape and stare,
  The spirit pulled him rudely by the collar,
    And before any one could say 'O jiminy!'
    The pair had vanisht swiftly up the chimney.

Naturally every one searcht everywhere,
  But not a shred of Bishop could be found,
The monks, when anyone questioned, would declare
  St. Peter'd snatcht to heaven their lord renowned,
Though the wicked said (such rascals are not rare)
  That the Abbot's course lay nearer underground;
    But the church straightway put to his name the handle
    Of Saint, thereby rebuking all such scandal.

But after this the monks grew most devout,
  And lived on milk and breakfast food entirely;
Each morn from four to five one took a knout
  And flogged his mates 'till they grew good and friarly.
Spirits from that time forth they did without,
  And lived the admiration of the shire. We
    Got the veracious record of these doings
    From an old manuscript found in the ruins.

[A Lyric]

If Time and Space, as Sages say,
   Are things which cannot be,
The sun which does not feel decay
   No greater is than we.
So why, Love, should we ever pray
   To live a century?
The butterfly that lives a day
   Has lived eternity.

The flowers I gave thee when the dew
   Was trembling on the vine,
Were withered ere the wild bee flew
   To suck the eglantine.
So let us haste to pluck anew
   Nor mourn to see them pine,
And though our days of love be few
   Yet let them be divine.

Song

If space and time, as sages say,
　　Are things that cannot be,
The fly that lives a single day
　　Has lived as long as we.
But let us live while yet we may,
　　While love and life are free,
For time is time, and runs away,
　　Though sages disagree.

The flowers I sent thee when the dew
　　Was trembling on the vine
Were withered ere the wild bee flew
　　To suck the eglantine.
But let us haste to pluck anew
　　Nor mourn to see them pine,
And though the flowers of life be few
　　Yet let them be divine.

[At Graduation 1905]

I

Standing upon the shore of all we know
We linger for a moment doubtfully,
Then with a song upon our lips, sail we
Across the harbor bar — no chart to show
No light to warn of rocks which lie below,
But let us yet put forth courageously.

II

As colonists embarking from the strand
To seek their fortunes on some foreign shore
Well know they lose what time shall not restore,
And when they leave they fully understand
That though again they see their fatherland
They there shall be as citizens no more.

III

We go; as lightning-winged clouds that fly
After a summer tempest, when some haste
North, South, and Eastward o'er the water's waste,
Some to the western limits of the sky
Which the sun stains with many a splendid dye,
Until their passing may no more be traced.

IV

Although the path be tortuous and slow,
Although it bristle with a thousand fears,
To hopeful eye of youth it still appears
A lane by which the rose and hawthorn grow.
We hope it may be; would that we might know!
Would we might look into the future years.

V

Great duties call — the twentieth century
More grandly dowered than those which came before,
Summons — who knows what time may hold in store,
Or what great deeds the distant years may see,
What conquest over pain and misery,
What heroes greater than were e'er of yore!

VI

But if this century is to be more great
Than those before, her sons must make her so,
And we are of her sons, and we must go
With eager hearts to help mold well her fate,
And see that she shall gain such proud estate
As shall on future centuries bestow

VII

A legacy of benefits — may we
In future years be found with those who try
To labor for the good until they die,
And ask no other guerdon than to know
That they have helpt the cause to victory,
That with their aid the flag is raised on high.

VIII

Sometime in distant years when we are grown
Gray-haired and old, whatever be our lot,
We shall desire to see again the spot
Which, whatsoever we have been or done
Or to what distant lands we may have gone,
Through all the years will ne'er have been forgot.

IX

For in the sanctuaries of the soul
Incense of altar-smoke shall rise to thee
From spotless fanes of lucid purity,
O school of ours! The passing years that roll
Between, as we press onward to the goal,
Shall not have power to quench the memory.

X

We shall return; and it will be to find
A different school from that which now we know;
But only in appearance t'will be so.
That which has made it great, not left behind,
The same school in the future shall we find
As this from which as pupils now we go.

XI

We go; like flitting faces in a dream;
Out of thy care and tutelage we pass
Into the unknown world — class after class,
O queen of schools — a momentary gleam,
A bubble on the surface of the stream,
A drop of dew upon the morning grass;

XII

Thou dost not die — for each succeeding year
Thy honor and thy fame shall but increase
Forever, and may stronger words than these
Proclaim the glory so that all may hear;
May worthier sons be thine, from far and near
To spread thy name o'er distant lands and seas!

XIII

As thou to thy departing sons hast been
To those that follow may'st thou be no less;
A guide to warn them, and a friend to bless

Before they leave thy care for lands unseen;
And let thy motto be, proud and serene,
Still as the years pass by, the word 'Progress!'

XIV

So we are done; we may no more delay;
Thus is the end of every tale: 'Farewell',
A word that echoes like a funeral bell
And one that we are ever loth to say.
But 'tis a call we cannot disobey,
Exeunt omnes, with a last 'farewell'.

Song

When we came home across the hill
  No leaves were fallen from the trees;
  The gentle fingers of the breeze
Had torn no quivering cobweb down.

The hedgerow bloomed with flowers still,
  No withered petals lay beneath;
  But the wild roses in your wreath
Were faded, and the leaves were brown.

Before Morning

While all the East was weaving red with gray,
The flowers at the window turned toward dawn,
Petal on petal, waiting for the day,
Fresh flowers, withered flowers, flowers of dawn.

This morning's flowers and flowers of yesterday
Their fragrance drifts across the room at dawn,
Fragrance of bloom and fragrance of decay,
Fresh flowers, withered flowers, flowers of dawn.

Circe's Palace

Around her fountain which flows
With the voice of men in pain,
Are flowers that no man knows.
Their petals are fanged and red
With hideous streak and stain;
They sprang from the limbs of the dead. —
We shall not come here again.

Panthers rise from their lairs
In the forest which thickens below,
Along the garden stairs
The sluggish python lies;
The peacocks walk, stately and slow,
And they look at us with the eyes
Of men whom we knew long ago.

On a Portrait

Among a crowd of tenuous dreams, unknown
To us of restless brain and weary feet,
Forever hurrying, up and down the street,
She stands at evening in the room alone.

Not like a tranquil goddess carved of stone
But evanescent, as if one should meet
A pensive lamia in some wood-retreat,
An immaterial fancy of one's own.

No meditations glad or ominous
Disturb her lips, or move the slender hands;
Her dark eyes keep their secrets hid from us,
Beyond the circle of our thought she stands.

The parrot on his bar, a silent spy,
Regards her with a patient curious eye.

Song

The moonflower opens to the moth,
    The mist crawls in from sea;
A great white bird, a snowy owl,
    Slips from the alder tree.

Whiter the flowers, Love, you hold,
    Than the white mist on the sea;
Have you no brighter tropic flowers
    With scarlet life, for me?

Nocturne

Romeo, *grand sérieux*, to importune
Guitar and hat in hand, beside the gate
With Juliet, in the usual debate
Of love, beneath a bored but courteous moon;
The conversation failing, strikes some tune
Banal, and out of pity for their fate
Behind the wall I have some servant wait,
Stab, and the lady sinks into a swoon.

Blood looks effective on the moonlit ground —
The hero smiles; in my best mode oblique
Rolls toward the moon a frenzied eye profound,
(No need of 'Love forever?' — 'Love next week?')
While female readers all in tears are drowned: —
'The perfect climax all true lovers seek!'

Humouresque

(AFTER J. LAFORGUE)

One of my marionettes is dead,
Though not yet tired of the game —
But weak in body as in head,
(A jumping-jack has such a frame).

But this deceasèd marionette
I rather liked: a common face,
(The kind of face that we forget)
Pinched in a comic, dull grimace;

Half bullying, half imploring air,
Mouth twisted to the latest tune;
His who-the-devil-are-you stare;
Translated, maybe, to the moon.

With Limbo's other useless things
Haranguing spectres, set him there;
'The snappiest fashion since last spring's,
'The newest style, on Earth, I swear.

'Why don't you people get some class?
(Feebly contemptuous of nose),
'Your damned thin moonlight, worse than gas —
'Now in New York' — and so it goes.

Logic a marionette's, all wrong
Of premises; yet in some star
A hero! — Where would he belong?
But, even at that, what mask *bizarre!*

Spleen

Sunday: this satisfied procession
Of definite Sunday faces;
Bonnets, silk hats, and conscious graces
In repetition that displaces
Your mental self-possession
By this unwarranted digression.

Evening, lights, and tea!
Children and cats in the alley;
Dejection unable to rally
Against this dull conspiracy.

And Life, a little bald and gray,
Languid, fastidious, and bland,
Waits, hat and gloves in hand,
Punctilious of tie and suit
(Somewhat impatient of delay)
    On the doorstep of the Absolute.

Ode

THOMAS STEARNS ELIOT

For the hour that is left us, Fair Harvard, with thee,
   Ere we face the importunate years,
In thy shadow we wait, while thy presence dispels
   Our vain hesitations and fears.
And we turn as thy sons ever turn, in the strength
   Of the hopes that thy blessings bestow,
From the hopes and ambitions that sprang at thy feet
   To the thoughts of the past as we go.

Yet for all of these years that to-morrow has lost
   We are still the less able to grieve,
With so much that of Harvard we carry away
   In the place of the life that we leave.
And only the years that efface and destroy
   Give us also the vision to see
What we owe for the future, the present, and past,
   Fair Harvard, to thine and to thee.

The Death of Saint Narcissus

Come under the shadow of this gray rock —
Come in under the shadow of this gray rock,
And I will show you something different from either
Your shadow sprawling over the sand at daybreak, or
Your shadow leaping behind the fire against the red rock:
I will show you his bloody cloth and limbs
And the gray shadow on his lips.

He walked once between the sea and the high cliffs
When the wind made him aware of his limbs smoothly passing each other
And of his arms crossed over his breast.
When he walked over the meadows
He was stifled and soothed by his own rhythm.
By the river
His eyes were aware of the pointed corners of his eyes
And his hands aware of the pointed tips of his fingers.

Struck down by such knowledge
He could not live men's ways, but became a dancer before God
If he walked in city streets
He seemed to tread on faces, convulsive thighs and knees.
So he came out under the rock.

First he was sure that he had been a tree,
Twisting its branches among each other
And tangling its roots among each other.

Then he knew that he had been a fish
With slippery white belly held tight in his own fingers,
Writhing in his own clutch, his ancient beauty
Caught fast in the pink tips of his new beauty.

Then he had been a young girl
Caught in the woods by a drunken old man

605

Knowing at the end the taste of his own whiteness
The horror of his own smoothness,
And he felt drunken and old.

   So he became a dancer to God.
Because his flesh was in love with the burning arrows
He danced on the hot sand
Until the arrows came.
. As he embraced them his white skin surrendered itself to the redness of
     blood, and satisfied him.
Now he is green, dry and stained
With the shadow in his mouth.

INDEX OF FIRST LINES OF POEMS

INDEX OF FIRST LINES OF POEMS